Handbook of Research on Deep Learning Innovations and Trends

Aboul Ella Hassanien
Cairo University, Egypt

Ashraf Darwish
Helwan University, Egypt

Chiranji Lal Chowdhary
VIT University, India

A volume in the Advances in Computational
Intelligence and Robotics (ACIR) Book Series

Published in the United States of America by
IGI Global
Engineering Science Reference (an imprint of IGI Global)
701 E. Chocolate Avenue
Hershey PA, USA 17033
Tel: 717-533-8845
Fax: 717-533-8661
E-mail: cust@igi-global.com
Web site: http://www.igi-global.com

Library of Congress Cataloging-in-Publication Data

Names: Hassanien, Aboul Ella, editor. | Darwish, Ashraf, editor. | Chowdhary,
    Chiranji Lal, 1975- editor.
Title: Handbook of research on deep learning innovations and trends / Aboul
    Ella Hassanien, Ashraf Darwish, and Chiranji Lal Chowdhary, editors.
Other titles: Research on deep learning innovations and trends
Description: Hershey, PA : Engineering Science Reference, [2019] | Includes
    bibliographical references.
Identifiers: LCCN 2018036340| ISBN 9781522578628 (h/c) | ISBN 9781522578635
    (eISBN)
Subjects: LCSH: Artificial intelligence--Handbooks, manuals, etc. | Machine
    learning--Handbooks, manuals, etc. | Neural networks (Computer
    science)--Handbooks, manuals, etc.
Classification: LCC TA347.A78 .H357 2019 | DDC 621.36/78--dc23 LC record available at https://lccn.loc.gov/2018036340

This book is published in the IGI Global book series Advances in Computational Intelligence and Robotics (ACIR) (ISSN: 2327-0411; eISSN: 2327-042X)

British Cataloguing in Publication Data
A Cataloguing in Publication record for this book is available from the British Library.

All work contributed to this book is new, previously-unpublished material. The views expressed in this book are those of the authors, but not necessarily of the publisher.

For electronic access to this publication, please contact: eresources@igi-global.com.

Advances in Computational Intelligence and Robotics (ACIR) Book Series

Ivan Giannoccaro
University of Salento, Italy

ISSN:2327-0411
EISSN:2327-042X

MISSION

While intelligence is traditionally a term applied to humans and human cognition, technology has progressed in such a way to allow for the development of intelligent systems able to simulate many human traits. With this new era of simulated and artificial intelligence, much research is needed in order to continue to advance the field and also to evaluate the ethical and societal concerns of the existence of artificial life and machine learning.

The **Advances in Computational Intelligence and Robotics (ACIR) Book Series** encourages scholarly discourse on all topics pertaining to evolutionary computing, artificial life, computational intelligence, machine learning, and robotics. ACIR presents the latest research being conducted on diverse topics in intelligence technologies with the goal of advancing knowledge and applications in this rapidly evolving field.

COVERAGE

- Machine Learning
- Adaptive and Complex Systems
- Intelligent control
- Pattern Recognition
- Artificial Intelligence
- Brain Simulation
- Cognitive Informatics
- Agent technologies
- Computer Vision
- Automated Reasoning

IGI Global is currently accepting manuscripts for publication within this series. To submit a proposal for a volume in this series, please contact our Acquisition Editors at Acquisitions@igi-global.com or visit: http://www.igi-global.com/publish/.

Titles in this Series

For a list of additional titles in this series, please visit: www.igi-global.com/book-series

Artificial Intelligence and Security Challenges in Emerging Networks
Ryma Abassi (University of Carthage, Tunisia)
Engineering Science Reference • copyright 2019 • 293pp • H/C (ISBN: 9781522573531) • US $195.00 (our price)

Emerging Trends and Applications in Cognitive Computing
Pradeep Kumar Mallick (Vignana Bharathi Institute of Technology, India) and Samarjeet Borah (Sikkim Manipal University, India)
Engineering Science Reference • copyright 2019 • 300pp • H/C (ISBN: 9781522557937) • US $215.00 (our price)

Predictive Intelligence Using Big Data and the Internet of Things
P.K. Gupta (Jaypee University of Information Technology, India) Tuncer Ören (University of Ottawa, Canada) and Mayank Singh (University of KwaZulu-Natal, South Africa)
Engineering Science Reference • copyright 2019 • 300pp • H/C (ISBN: 9781522562108) • US $245.00 (our price)

Advanced Metaheuristic Methods in Big Data Retrieval and Analytics
Hadj Ahmed Bouarara (Dr. Moulay Tahar University of Saïda, Algeria) Reda Mohamed Hamou (Dr. Moulay Tahar University of Saïda, Algeria) and Amine Rahmani (Dr. Moulay Tahar University of Saïda, Algeria)
Engineering Science Reference • copyright 2019 • 320pp • H/C (ISBN: 9781522573388) • US $205.00 (our price)

Nature-Inspired Algorithms for Big Data Frameworks
Hema Banati (Dyal Singh College, India) Shikha Mehta (Jaypee Institute of Information Technology, India) and Parmeet Kaur (Jaypee Institute of Information Technology, India)
Engineering Science Reference • copyright 2019 • 412pp • H/C (ISBN: 9781522558521) • US $225.00 (our price)

Novel Design and Applications of Robotics Technologies
Dan Zhang (York University, Canada) and Bin Wei (York University, Canada)
Engineering Science Reference • copyright 2019 • 341pp • H/C (ISBN: 9781522552765) • US $205.00 (our price)

Optoelectronics in Machine Vision-Based Theories and Applications
Moises Rivas-Lopez (Universidad Autónoma de Baja California, Mexico) Oleg Sergiyenko (Universidad Autónoma de Baja California, Mexico) Wendy Flores-Fuentes (Universidad Autónoma de Baja California, Mexico) and Julio Cesar Rodríguez-Quiñonez (Universidad Autónoma de Baja California, Mexico)
Engineering Science Reference • copyright 2019 • 433pp • H/C (ISBN: 9781522557517) • US $225.00 (our price)

IGI Global
DISSEMINATOR OF KNOWLEDGE

701 East Chocolate Avenue, Hershey, PA 17033, USA
Tel: 717-533-8845 x100 • Fax: 717-533-8661
E-Mail: cust@igi-global.com • www.igi-global.com

Editorial Advisory Board

List of Contributors

Table of Contents

Section 1
Deep Learning Applications

Section 2
Advanced Deep Learning Techniques

Section 3
Security in Deep Learning

Detailed Table of Contents

Section 1
Deep Learning Applications

Rajithkumar B. K., R. V. College of Engineering, India
Shilpa D. R., R. V. College of Engineering, India
Uma B. V., R. V. College of Engineering, India

Image processing offers medical diagnosis and it overcomes the shortcomings faced by traditional laboratory methods with the help of intelligent algorithms. It is also useful for remote quality control and consultations. As machine learning is stepping into biomedical engineering, there is a huge demand for devices which are intelligent and accurate enough to target the diseases. The platelet count in a blood sample can be done by extrapolating the number of platelets counted in the blood smear. Deep neural nets use multiple layers of filtering and automated feature extraction and detection and can overcome the hurdle of devising complex algorithms to extract features for each type of disease. So, this chapter deals with the usage of deep neural networks for the image classification and platelets count. The method of using deep neural nets has increased the accuracy of detecting the disease and greater efficiency compared to traditional image processing techniques. The method can be further expanded to other forms of diseases which can be detected through blood samples.

Sergei Savin, Southwest State University, Russia
Aleksei Ivakhnenko, Applied Parallel Computing LLC, Russia

In this chapter, the problem of finding a suitable foothold for a bipedal walking robot is studied. There are a number of gait generation algorithms that rely on having a set of obstacle-free regions where the robot can step to and there are a number of algorithms for generating these regions. This study breaches the gap between these algorithms, providing a way to quickly check if a given obstacle free region is accessible for foot placement. The proposed approach is based on the use of a classifier, constructed as a convolutional neural network. The study discusses the training dataset generation, including datasets with uncertainty related to the shapes of the obstacle-free regions. Training results for a number of different datasets and different hyperparameter choices are presented and showed robustness of the proposed network design both to different hyperparameter choices as well as to the changes in the training dataset.

Chapter 3

Chantana Chantrapornchai, Kasetsart University, Thailand
Samrid Duangkaew, Kasetsart University, Thailand

Several kinds of pretrained convolutional neural networks (CNN) exist nowadays. Utilizing these networks with the new classification task requires the retraining with new data sets. With the small embeded device, large network cannot be implemented. The authors study the use of pretrained models and customizing them towards accuracy and size against face recognition tasks. The results show 1) the performance of existing pretrained networks (e.g., AlexNet, GoogLeNet, CaffeNet, SqueezeNet), as well as size, and 2) demonstrate the layers customization towards the model size and accuracy. The studied results show that among the various networks with different data sets, SqueezeNet can achieve the same accuracy (0.99) as others with small size (up to 25 times smaller). Secondly, the two customizations with layer skipping are presented. The experiments show the example of SqueezeNet layer customizing, reducing the network size while keeping the accuracy (i.e., reducing the size by 7% with the slower convergence time). The experiments are measured based on Caffe 0.15.14.

Chapter 4

Rekh Ram Janghel, NIT Raipur, India
Satya Prakash Sahu, NIT Raipur, India
Yogesh Kumar Rathore, NIT Raipur, India
Shraddha Singh, NIT Raipur, India
Urja Pawar, NIT Raipur, India

Speech is the vocalized form of communication used by humans and some animals. It is based upon the syntactic combination of items drawn from the lexicon. Each spoken word is created out of the phonetic combination of a limited set of vowel and consonant speech sound units (phonemes). Here, the authors propose a deep learning model used on tensor flow speech recognition dataset, which consist of 30 words. Here, 2D convolutional neural network (CNN) model is used for understanding simple spoken commands using the speech commands dataset by tensor flow. Dataset is divided into 70% training and 30% testing data. While running the algorithm for three epochs average accuracy of 92.7% is achieved.

Chapter 5

Ramgopal Kashyap, Amity University Chhattisgarh, India

This chapter will address challenges with IoT and machine learning including how a portion of the difficulties of deep learning executions while planning the arrangement and choice of right calculation. Existing research in deep learning and IoT was focused to find how garbage in will deliver waste out, which is exceptionally appropriate for the scope of the informational index for machine learning. The quality, sum, readiness, and choice of information are essential to the achievement of a machine learning arrangement. Consequently, this chapter aims to provide an overview of how the system can use technologies along with deep learning and challenges to realize the security challenges IoT can support. Even though calculations can work in any nonexclusive conditions, there are particular rules to determine which calculation would work best under which circumstances. How reinforcement learning deep learning is useful for IoT will also be covered in the chapter.

Chapter 6

Sahil Sharma, Thapar Institute of Engineering and Technology, India
Vijay Kumar, Thapar Institute of Engineering and Technology, India

Face depth image has been used for occlusion presence and gender prediction by transfer learning. This chapter discusses about the overfitting problem and how augmentation helps overcoming it. Pre-processing of the dataset includes converting a 3D object image into depth image for further processing. Five state-of-the-art 2D deep learning models (e.g., AlexNet, VGG16, DenseNet121, ResNet18, and SqueezeNet) have been discussed along with their architecture. The effect of increasing the number of epochs on the top-1 error rate has been presented in the experimental section. The result section consists of error rates in comparison of with and without augmentation on the datasets.

Chapter 7

Kamaljit I. Lakhtaria, Gujarat University, India
Darshankumar Modi, Shantilal Shah Engineering College, India

Deep learning is a subset of machine learning. As the name suggests, deep learning means more and more layers. Deep leaning basically works on the principle of neurons. With the increase in big data or large quantities of data, deep learning methods and techniques have been widely used to extract the useful information. Deep learning can be applied to computer vision, bioinformatics, and speech recognition or on natural language processing. This chapter covers the basics of deep learning, different architectures of deep learning like artificial neural network, feed forward neural network, CNN, recurrent neural network, deep Boltzmann machine, and their comparison. This chapter also summarizes the applications of deep learning in different areas.

Chapter 8

Vanyashree Mardi, Alva's Institute of Engineering and Technology, India
Naresh E., Jain University, India & Ramaiah Institute of Technology, India
Vijaya Kumar B. P., Ramaiah Institute of Technology, India

In the current era, software development and software quality has become extensively important for implementing the real-world software application, and it will enhance the software functionality. Moreover, early prediction of expected error and fault level in the quality process is critical to the software development process. Deep learning techniques are the most appropriate methods for this problem, and this chapter carries out an extensive systematic survey on a variety of deep learning. These techniques are used in the software quality process along with a hypothesis justification for each of the proposed solutions. The deep learning and machine learning techniques are considered to be the most suitable systems for software quality prediction. Deep learning is a computational model made up of various hidden layers of investigation used to portray of information with the goal that researchers can better understand complex information issues.

    Anitha S. Pillai, Hindustan Institute of Technology and Science, India
    Bindu Menon, Apollo Hospitals, India

Advancement in technology has paved the way for the growth of big data. We are able to exploit this data to a great extent as the costs of collecting, storing, and analyzing a large volume of data have plummeted considerably. There is an exponential increase in the amount of health-related data being generated by smart devices. Requisite for proper mining of the data for knowledge discovery and therapeutic product development is very essential. The expanding field of big data analytics is playing a vital role in healthcare practices and research. A large number of people are being affected by Alzheimer's Disease (AD), and as a result, it becomes very challenging for the family members to handle these individuals. The objective of this chapter is to highlight how deep learning can be used for the early diagnosis of AD and present the outcomes of research studies of both neurologists and computer scientists. The chapter gives introduction to big data, deep learning, AD, biomarkers, and brain images and concludes by suggesting blood biomarker as an ideal solution for early detection of AD.

Section 2
Advanced Deep Learning Techniques

    M. Parimala Boobalan, VIT University, India

Clustering is an unsupervised technique used in various application, namely machine learning, image segmentation, social network analysis, health analytics, and financial analysis. It is a task of grouping similar objects together and dissimilar objects in different group. The quality of the cluster relies on two factors: distance metrics and data representation. Deep learning is a new field of machine learning research that has been introduced to move machine learning closer to artificial intelligence. Learning using deep network provides multiple layers of representation that helps to understand images, sound, and text. In this chapter, the need for deep network in clustering, various architecture, and algorithms for unsupervised learning is discussed.

    Md Mahmudul Hasan, Anglia Ruskin University, UK
    Md Shahinur Rahman, Daffodil International University, Bangladesh
    Adrian Bell, Anglia Ruskin University, UK

Deep reinforcement learning (DRL) has transformed the field of artificial intelligence (AI) especially after the success of Google DeepMind. This branch of machine learning epitomizes a step toward building autonomous systems by understanding of the visual world. Deep reinforcement learning (RL) is currently applied to different sorts of problems that were previously obstinate. In this chapter, at first, the authors started with an introduction of the general field of RL and Markov decision process (MDP). Then, they clarified the common DRL framework and the necessary components RL settings. Moreover, they analyzed the stochastic gradient descent (SGD)-based optimizers such as ADAM and a non-specific multi-policy selection mechanism in a multi-objective Markov decision process. In this chapter, the authors also included the comparison for different Deep Q networks. In conclusion, they describe several challenges and trends in research within the deep reinforcement learning field.

Parvathi R., VIT University Chennai, India
Pattabiraman V., VIT University Chennai, India

This chapter proposes a hybrid method for classification of the objects based on deep neural network and a similarity-based search algorithm. The objects are pre-processed with external conditions. After pre-processing and training different deep learning networks with the object dataset, the authors compare the results to find the best model to improve the accuracy of the results based on the features of object images extracted from the feature vector layer of a neural network. RPFOREST (random projection forest) model is used to predict the approximate nearest images. ResNet50, InceptionV3, InceptionV4, and DenseNet169 models are trained with this dataset. A proposal for adaptive finetuning of the deep learning models by determining the number of layers required for finetuning with the help of the RPForest model is given, and this experiment is conducted using the Xception model.

Chiranji Lal Chowdhary, VIT University, India
Ashraf Darwish, Helwan University, Egypt
Aboul Ella Hassanien, Scientific Research Group in Egypt, Egypt

Deep learning states the scientific algorithms that are accustomed to come through a particular assignment. Such tidy issues could also be meteorology or brain diagnosing wherever records are obtainable as text. In such a state of affairs, cognitive computing can help medical practitioners to diagnose patterns that they might not observe, and they will extend the flexibility to diagnose the brain with efficiency. Deep learning is additionally able to introduce new APIs.

Section 3
Security in Deep Learning

Yassine Maleh, Hassan 1st University, Morocco

Over the past decade, malware has grown exponentially. Traditional signature-based approaches to detecting malware have proven their limitations against new malware, and categorizing malware samples has become essential to understanding the basics of malware behavior. Recently, antivirus solutions have increasingly started to adopt machine learning approaches. Unfortunately, there are few open source data sets available for the academic community. One of the largest data sets available was published last year in a competition on Kaggle with data provided by Microsoft for the big data innovators gathering. This chapter explores the problem of malware classification. In particular, this chapter proposes an innovative and scalable approach using convolutional neural networks (CNN) and long short-term memory (LSTM) to assign malware to the corresponding family. The proposed method achieved a classification accuracy of 98.73% and an average log loss of 0.0698 on the validation data.

Chapter 15

Manu C., Ramaiah Institute of Technology, India
Vijaya Kumar B. P., Ramaiah Institute of Technology, India
Naresh E., Ramaiah Institute of Technology, India

In daily realistic activities, security is one of the main criteria among the different machines like IOT devices, networks. In these systems, anomaly detection is one of the issues. Anomaly detection based on user behavior is very essential to secure the machines from the unauthorized activities by anomaly user. Techniques used for an anomaly detection is to learn the daily realistic activities of the user, and later it proactively detects the anomalous situation and unusual activities. In the IOT-related systems, the detection of such anomalous situations can be fine-tuned with minor and major erroneous conditions to the machine learning algorithms that learn the activities of a user. In this chapter, neural networks, with multiple hidden layers to detect the different situation by creating an environment with random anomalous activities to the machine, are proposed. Using deep learning for anomaly detection would help in enhancing the accuracy and speed.

Preface

Deep learning has become an extremely active area of research that is paving the way for modern machine learning. Deep Learning is being ubiquitous with machine learning applications. Leading technology firms, like Apple, Google, Facebook, Microsoft etc., and research institutions are involved in research on this hot technique for artificial intelligence, data analytics, and machine learning applications. Artificial Intelligence is being rebranded by machine learning. With the deep learning approach, researchers and engineers are writing new success stories on innovative specific tasks.

The history of Deep Learning dates to the 1940s. However, traditional gradient-based training methods for multilayer neural networks are susceptible to local optima issues. Therefore, the training of multilayer neural networks with several hidden layers has not received extensive interest for use in different applications until recently, with the advent of various adaptive stochastic versions of the gradient descent strategy. Currently, Deep Learning has been widely applied due to improvements in computing hardware and the discovery of fast optimization algorithms. This new technique can learn many representations at various abstraction levels for sound, text, and image data. Moreover, Deep Learning can be used to analyse big data and obtain relevant solutions. Different Deep Learning architectures and methods, such as convolutional neural networks, deep belief networks, deep Boltzmann machines, restricted Boltzmann machines, and recursive auto-encoders have been used in the literature.

Deep Learning does not have to figure out the features ahead of time. That is using same neural net approach for many different problems. With deep learning approach, there is the possibility of developing an artificial neural network system which is more fault tolerant and they scale well. This technology applies quite strongly to computer vision, image processing, biometrics, pattern recognition and medical imaging. The application is extended to other real-life applications and it is making many tasks easier for people.

The main objective of this book is to present the current trends, original and latest research on different selected research topic on Deep Learning in order to deal with new applications on this topic. In addition, to solicit the latest research findings on major and emerging topics related to distributed platforms, techniques and applications for deep learning and machine learning. The target audience includes researchers, practitioners and students. Moreover, this book provides a platform for researchers to open new opportunities to other researchers and new scholars to explore their work. This book is divided into three sections:

Section 1: Deep Learning Applications
Section 2: Advanced Deep Learning Techniques
Section 3: Security in Deep Learning

Finally, warm thanks and greeting to all editors for their efforts in editing this book.

Aboul Ella Hassanien
Cairo University, Egypt

Ashraf Darwish
Helwan University, Egypt

Chiranji Lal Chowdhary
VIT University, India

Section 1
Deep Learning Applications

Chapter 1
Detection of Blood–Related Diseases Using Deep Neural Nets

Rajithkumar B. K.
R. V. College of Engineering, India

Shilpa D. R.
R. V. College of Engineering, India

Uma B. V.
R. V. College of Engineering, India

ABSTRACT

Image processing offers medical diagnosis and it overcomes the shortcomings faced by traditional laboratory methods with the help of intelligent algorithms. It is also useful for remote quality control and consultations. As machine learning is stepping into biomedical engineering, there is a huge demand for devices which are intelligent and accurate enough to target the diseases. The platelet count in a blood sample can be done by extrapolating the number of platelets counted in the blood smear. Deep neural nets use multiple layers of filtering and automated feature extraction and detection and can overcome the hurdle of devising complex algorithms to extract features for each type of disease. So, this chapter deals with the usage of deep neural networks for the image classification and platelets count. The method of using deep neural nets has increased the accuracy of detecting the disease and greater efficiency compared to traditional image processing techniques. The method can be further expanded to other forms of diseases which can be detected through blood samples.

DOI: 10.4018/978-1-5225-7862-8.ch001

INTRODUCTION

Dengue is the most prevalent and widespread diseases in the countries like India (Poornima & Krishnaveni, 2006), with an increasing population and massive stress on land and water, new boulevard open for mosquitoes to breed and spread the virus. While mosquito control is the most effective method for prevention of dengue. An equal amount of awareness should pay to the diagnosis of dengue diseases to avert further spread. The conventional lab methods for the detections of dengue in human's anatomy involve the extracting of blood and subjecting it for various tests to count and detect the numbers of platelets (Maitra, Gupta & Mukherjee, 2012; Schoentag & Pedersen, 1979). The low platelets count would indicate the presence of dengue virus in the body (Sharif et al., 2012). The standard method undertake by labs across the world is use of the conventional chemicals procedure which takes few hours to get the results. The advent of technologies and AI (artificial intelligence), it is likely to reduce the Computational time to a mere few seconds. Image processing is one of the highly useful tools to combat this shortcoming. Through the image processing, few portion of the blood smear can be analysed and examined using digital microscope and obtained platelets count can be projected to map the whole smear (Venkatalakshmi & Thilagavathi, 2013). It provides an efficient method to overcome any drawback of conventional laboratory methods and conventional machine learning techniques are generally used for extensively in the simple tasks (Vijayalaxmi et al., 2014). But these conventional techniques are generally more difficult to implement, and some stray cases of data may cause to erroneous results. Hence with the help of deep neural network, such anomalies will be removed. Thus, with help of image processing and deep neural nets, the smear images will be classified based on required purpose. This chapter mainly deals with use of image processing and deep neural network for image classifications and the results were compared with traditional techniques and the deep learning method is found to be superior, in terms of robustness, adaptability and accuracy (Vala & Baxi, 2013). Initially the image was collected using A-deltavision microscope of 100x, using image processing process, the images are first subjected to pre-processing using Otsu Thresholding techniques and then the platelets are counted using the connected-component images labelling technique. In deep learning technique, the pre-processed images were sent to deep learning tool for classification and here Convolutional Neural Networks (CNNs) was used to check the status of dengue in a sample.

RELATED WORKS

The review of the literature pertaining to the present topic is presented to the readers. The automatic detection of platelets and diagnosis of Dengue Haemorrhagic Fever was proposed, and the Segmentation techniques was used to investigate the number of platelets to diagnose dengue using the microscopic image of a sample blood smear (Poornima & Krishnaveni, 2016). Flood fill Morphological operation was utilized to detect platelet using the platelet size. The image processing technique (Bhatt & Prabha, 2015) for detecting the abnormalities of blood cells was developed and blood cells were segregated into different categories based on the developed form factor.

An automatic platelet counting system was developed to support diagnosis labs (Lazuardia et al., 2013) for primary health care services. The developed system consists of a conventional microscope equipped and digital camera linked to a personal computer. Authors have compared the accuracy of the developed system with traditional laboratory approach. The method was proven to have great potential as a tool to help primary health centres and other facilities with limited resources to deal with the burden of dengue.

The advanced face detection techniques were developed (Dussart et al., 2013) and module was developed using openCV library. The automatic counting and segmentation of RBC(Red blood cells) in captured blood cell images using Hough Transform (Ceelie, Dinkelaar & van Gelder, 2007) and few sample images were captured using automated microscope and compared the results with manual counting method.

Motivation

All over the world, especially in impoverished nations of Africa and Asia, there is a severe problem of epidemics. Every year, thousands of lives are lost to diseases which cannot be detected easily due to shortage of laboratory equipment, medicines, medical professionals (Hemangi & Nikhita, 2016). An effective way of solving this problem is to solve a widespread dearth of laboratory equipment; a solution which reduces the need for sophisticated laboratory equipment and can be used anywhere with minimal infrastructure. Thus, through this work, aim to strike at this problem through the detection of dengue by extrapolating the platelet count through deep learning techniques.

Problem Statement

The conventional method to detect any blood related disorders is time consuming and it needs expertise in the related field to detect or narrow it down to any one disease and that kind of expertise might not be available in every part of the country. The other drawback is that it tends to be more expensive compared to the proposed method. Thus, the need for a highly sophisticated and inexpensive method for detection of platelets arises.

PROPOSED WORK

The proposed method consists of the steps as shown in the Figure 1.

Figure 1. Block diagram of proposed method

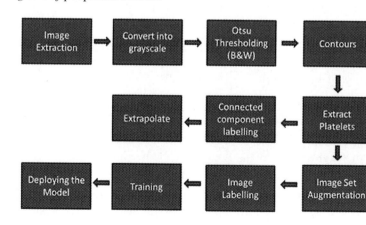

Objectives

The aim of this proposed work is to:

1. To study the characteristics of dengue diseases through blood samples
2. To design and develop a system to capture the blood smear image automatically through microscope.
3. Extract the morphological features of blood components and using image processing techniques.
4. To detect the illness based on deep neural networks by identifying the typical characteristic of a disease in blood by training the algorithm using data set.

Methodology

Input Image

The Blood samples Images were captured from A-deltavision microscope available in Government of Karnataka certified laboratories. Initially the image of blood samples were obtained using blood smear using giemsa stain. The giemsa stain allowed the blood cells to deferentially stained with respect to plasma and other blood constituents.

The 100x resolution A-deltavision microscope was used and the extracted image was converted to grayscale for Pre- processing.

Otsu Thresholding

Otsu Thresholding was used for convert the gray scale image into binary image. The black and white image provides the ideal stage to process images further. Otsu Thresholding provides the correct level of the threshold to meet requirements as shown in Equation 1

$$\sigma^2_w(t) = \omega_0(t)\, \sigma^2_0(t) + \omega_1(t)\, \sigma^2_1(t) \tag{1}$$

ω_0, ω_1 = probabilities of two classes and σ_0^2, σ_1^2 = variance of those two classes.

The Otsu Thresholding algorithm performs:

*   It computes the histogram and probabilities of each intensity level
*   It set up initial of $\omega_i(0)$ and step all possible thresholds t=1 to maximum intensity
*   It update ω_i and compute $\sigma_b^2(t)$ and preferred threshold corresponds to the maximum ($\sigma_b^2(t)$).

Connected Component Labelling

Connected-component labelling is an algorithmic application of graph theory, where subsets of connected components are uniquely labelled based on a given heuristic. Connected-component labelling is not to be confused with segmentation.

Connected-component labelling is used in computer vision to detect connected regions in binary digital images, although color images and data with higher dimensionality can also be processed. When integrated into an image recognition system or human-computer interaction interface, connected component labelling can operate on a variety of information. Blob extraction is generally performed on the resulting binary image from a thresholding step. Blobs may be counted, filtered, and tracked.

Image Set Augmentation

Data preparation is required when working with neural network and deep learning models. Increasingly data augmentation is also required on more complex object recognition tasks. It is common knowledge that the more data an ML algorithm has access to, the more effective it can be. Even when the data is of lower quality, algorithms can actually perform better, as long as useful data can be extracted by the model from the original data set. Rather than starting with an extremely large corpus of unstructured and unlabelled data, can instead take a small, curated corpus of structured data and augment in a way that increases the performance of models trained on it. Specialized image and video classification tasks often have insufficient data. This is particularly true in the medical industry, where access to data is heavily protected due to privacy concerns. At the end of the day, realized a large limiting factor for most projects is access to reliable data, and as such, explore the effectiveness of distinct data augmentation techniques in image classification tasks. This section provides a brief review of past work that has augmented data to improve image classifier performance. The problem with small datasets is that models trained with them do not generalize well data from the validation and test set. Hence, these models suffer from the problem of overfitting. Data augmentation is another way can reduce overfitting on models, where increase the amount of training data using information only in our training data. The field of data augmentation is not new, and in fact, various data augmentation techniques have been applied to specific problems. The main techniques fall under the category of data warping, which is an approach which seeks to directly augment the input data to the model in data space. A very generic and accepted current practice for augmenting image data is to perform geometric and colour augmentations, such as reflecting the image, cropping and translating the image, and changing the colour palette of the image. Data augmentation has been shown to produce promising ways to increase the accuracy of classification tasks.

Platelets Isolation and Contours

The contour is found in the corresponding binary image and it is outline representing or bounding for the shape or form of something. The contour range was sets in the range of 20 and 80 pixels and any platelets found in the images were treated as holes and covered with a white background. The platelets were extracted from original image and mask to yield black platelets on white background

Platelets Count and Extrapolations

The platelets were counted with the help of clustering labeling algorithms shown in Figure 2 and Figure 3. The number of zeros clusters in the image was found using connected components labeling technique (Pore & Kalshetty, 2014). The Platelets were counted and extrapolated as shown in the Figure 4 and Figure 5.

Figure 2. Original image

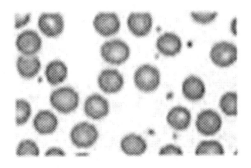

Figure 3. Binary image after Otsu Thresholding

Figure 4. Platelets covered

Figure 5. Platelets shown on white background

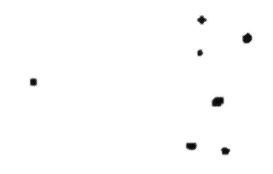

Convolutional Neural Network (CNN)

The convolution neural network is a class of AI networks (artificial neural networks) and it uses a variation of multilayer perceptrons, designed for a minimal pre-processing shown in Figure 6.

Convolutional Layer

The Convolutional layers was applied to the input and passing the extracted result to the next layer. In each convolutional neuron processes the data only taken from receptive field.

Pooling Layer

The Convolutional networks includes local or global pooling layers whichis used for combine the outputs of each neuron clusters layer into a single neuron in the next layer for proceedings stages. The maximum pooling uses the maximum value from each of a clusters of neuron at the prior layer

Weights

The CNNs shares the weights in each convolutional layers and weights bank filters is used for each receptive fields in the layer and also it reduces memory footprints and improves the performance as shown in Figure 7.

The AlexNet is the tool of a CNN, the programmed in Compute Unified device Architecture (CUDA) to run on a GPU in a system. The network achieved top-5 error of 15.3% and more than 10.8 percentage points ahead of runner up. The Alexnet is a deep Convolutional Neural Network for images classification. It has 8 layers and the first 5 are convolutional and last 3 are fully connected layers. In between some 'layers' are located called pooling and activation layers.

The different layers of Alexnet are shown Figure 8 and Figure 9.

The Figure 9 is the sequence of layers of Alexnet and the problem set is divided into 2 parts, half executing on GPU 1 and another half is on GPU 2. The communication overheads are kept low and this helps to get better performance overall.

Figure 6. Overview of CNN with various layers involved in the architecture

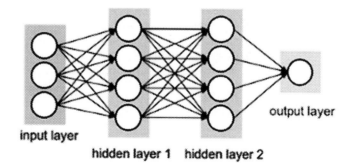

Figure 7. Convolution method

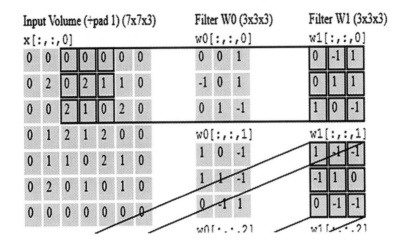

Figure 8. AlexNet Layers

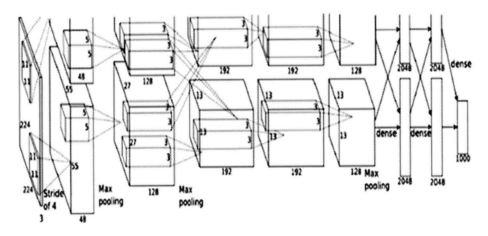

Figure 9. Layer1 of AlexNet

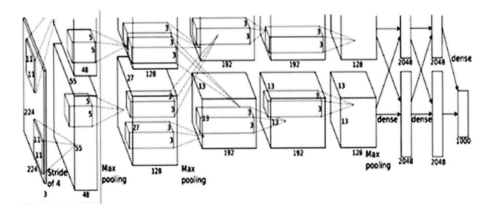

The Rectified Linear Unit activation is function used for activate Alexnet, the function is more than max(x, 0). The other activation functions are include the sigmoid and tanh functions shown in Figure 10 and Figure 11.

The description subsequent layers is as follows:

- The Layer 2 is a max Pooling Followed by Convolutions and the Input – 55 x 55 x 96
- The Max pooling – 55/2 x 55/2 x 96 = 27 x 27 x 96, Number of filters – 256
- The Filter size – 5 x 5 x 48 and Layer 2 Output: 27 x 27 x 256

The Split across 2 GPUs as 27 x 27 x 128 for each GPU and Pooling is a sub-sampling of 2×2 window(usually). Max pooling is max for 4 values in a 2×2 window. The intuitions behind pooling is, it reduces computation and controls overfitting. The Layer 6 is fully connected and input is 13 x 13 x 128 is transformed into a vector and multiplied with a matrix of the following dim – (13 x 13 x 128) x 2048 and GEMV (General Matrix Vector Multiply) is used here: Vector X = 1 x (13x13x128) and Matrix A = (13x13x128) x 2048. This is an external input to the network Output is 1 x 2048. The Layers 7 & 8 follow on the similar line

Tensorflow

The TensorFlow is an open-source software and it is a symbolic math library and specially used for machine learning application such as networks. The TensorFlow can run on a multiple CPUs and GP-GPUs using CUDA extensions

Deep Learning Technique

A convolution neural network is a class of deep, feed-forward artificial neural networks that has been applied to analysing visual imagery. CNNs use a variation of multilayer perceptrons designed to require minimal pre-processing. Convolutional networks were inspired by biological processes in which the connectivity pattern between neurons is inspired by the organization of the animal visual cortex. Individual

Figure 10. Layer 2 of AlexNet

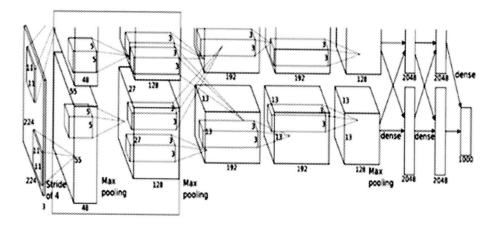

Figure 11. Layer 6 of AlexNet

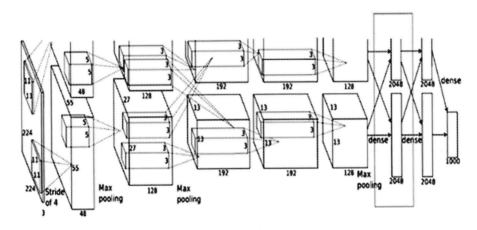

cortical neurons respond to stimuli only in a restricted region of the visual field known as the receptive field. The receptive fields of different neurons partially overlap such that they cover the entire visual field.

Data Set

The data set was contained 400 images and it collected from well-known diagnostic laboratory to train the neural networks. The pre-processed image are fed into the tool and erroneous data were prevented by variations in color, pixel density etc.

The structure used for training CNN was AlexNet. The target classes were two: dengue negative and dengue positive. The Pre-processed images were fed into the CNN to make the training quickly. An alternate technique would be to used for color images and but it would requires more time for training the image along with more powerful GPU. The main advantage of using binary images is it saves the developer from synthesize codes for pre-processing images. The deep Neural learning method involved the use of Tensorflow and it involved feeding the labeled images into the tool. The Data set of 400 images were trained and set of 50 images were used for testing. The training is carried out till average loss approached 1 and the training was stopped at that point. The deployed model onto a set of random images were selected from the images (not used for testing or training).

To increase dataset used for training, the data set augmentation was carried out which yielded a considerably large amounts of training data for CNN a shown in Figure 12 and Figure 13. Thus, images dataset augmentations provide a useful and necessary extrapolation of scarce dataset for training of a deep neural networks.

RESULTS AND DISCUSSION

Step 1: The blood smear images are captured from microscope as shown in Figure 14 and input images was applied to Otsu's Thresholding method as shown Figure 15 was obtained. The RBC (red blood cells) were extracted from the binary image and common components were taken out as shown in Figure 16, Figure 17 and Figure 18 shows the extracted platelets in blood samples.

Figure 12. Augmented image 1

Figure 13. Augmented image 2

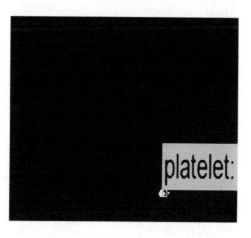

Figure 14. Platelet image 1 four detected platelets in the image

Step 2: The platelet were counted in the sample images of images 1-5 and the projected platelet count was found to be 1.56 Lakh, 1.95 Lakh, 1.95 Lakh, 0.64Lakh, and 1.56Lakh respectively on sample blood smear images.

Step 3: Two classes were declared namely Dengue Negative and Dengue Positive as shown in Table 1. When it compared to the actual classes, the last one found to be incorrect. and this is due to inaccuracy attribution of the presence of stray pixels in the images. it will lead to be incorrect count in the connected components labeling technique.

Figure 15. Platelet image 2 five detected platelets in the image

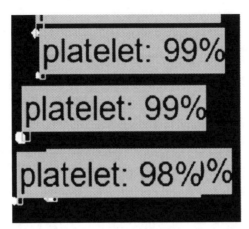

Figure 16. Platelet image 3 five detected platelets in the image

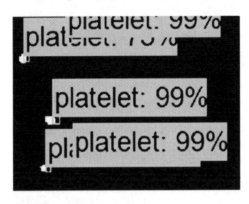

Figure 17. Platelet image 4 one detected platelets

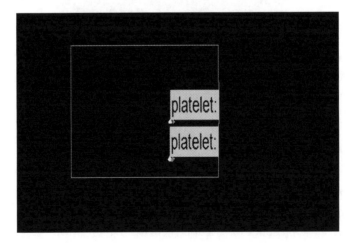

Figure 18. Platelet image 5 three detected platelets

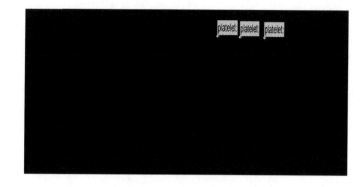

Table 1. Results of image traditional processing technique

SI No.	Obtained Platelets Count	Projected Platelets Count	Obtained Report	Laboratory Report
1	1.59L	1.56L	Dengue Negative,	Dengue Negative,
2	1.82L	1.95L	Dengue Negative,	Dengue Negative
3	1.80L	1.95L	Dengue Negative,	Dengue Negative,
4	0.60L	0.64L	Dengue Positive,	Dengue Positive,
5	1.12L	1.56L	Dengue Negative,	Dengue Positive,

Deep Learning Method Results

The deep learning method to detected dengue and there were two classes obtained namely dengue positive and dengue negative. From the experimental results its shown that the accuracy was found to be very high.

The images used for testing yielded the following results:

- The extrapolated counts was found to be 1.56 Lakh, 1.95 Lakh, 1.95 Lakh, 0.37 Lakh and 1.17 Lakh
- When it compared with original classes, the accuracy of five images were found to be a 99%

From Table 2 it is shown that the proposed method is 99% accuracy and faster compared to traditional image processing techniques (Poornima & Krishnaveni, 2006).

CONCLUSION

The proposed method was successfully detected and counted the platelets with satisfactory results. It was not only reduced the time needed for detection but it also minimize the amount of work required. The sampled are tested using a microscope. This method also ruled out the need of any domain skilled person for handle the tasks and laboratory tests involved in the traditional methods of detecting platelets.

Table 2. Results of deep learning technique

Sl No	Obtained Count	Projected Count	Obtained Result	Actual Result
1	1.56L	1.56L	Dengue Negative	Dengue Negative
2	1.96L	1.95L	Dengue Negative	Dengue Negative
3	1.96L	1.95L	Dengue Negative	Dengue Negative
4	0.36L	0.37L	Dengue Positive	Dengue Positive
5	1.16L	1.17L	Dengue Positive	Dengue Positive
Accuracy Obtained				100%

The method also extremely reduces the costs involved for setting up a laboratory and hiring experts for the purpose of testing.

The system explored the applications of deep neural nets in the fields of blood images. While in the most of the fields, deep neural nets are used for detection of macroscopic images that are visible to naked eye, the application of deep neural nets is also not explored in the field of the microscopic images. This application proved to be an effective in the microscopic scale as well as macroscopic scale. In general consensus of application of deep neural nets is that the images do not require pre-processing. However, through this proposed application, it has been observed that through a pre-processing, a high level of accuracy can be obtained through a small number of iterations and also it reduces the time for training deep neural net. The proposed method obtained an accuracy of 99% using odeep neural nets compared to traditional image processing techniques (accuracy obtained 80%) and it was much lower when compared to the latter used method.

Future Scope

The limitation of traditional image processing techniques are enhanced using deep learning nets. However, in the deep learning technique, there were numerous shortcomings which slowed down the accuracy levels. The usage of more sophisticated deep neural learning tools identified the platelets individually, and it isolate them in a higher rate of success. Due to over-generalization of CNN (convolutional neural nets), there is a possibility of getting single one, leading to incorrect classification and This can be overcome with more training data and the network for large number of iterations or steps.

The developed model took large space on the disk for training so this model would need to be deployed on mobile devices, due to the large amount of space. The unknown factor from internet connectivity can also provide a hindrance to the deployed model in certain rural areas. Thus, these shortcomings would be overcome and the method of deep neural nets could be deployed on large scale with high penetration in rural areas in future

REFERENCES

Bhatt, M., & Prabha, S. (2015). Detection of Abnormal Blood Cells Using Image Processing Technique. *International Journal of Electrical and Electronics Engineers, 07*, 1–6.

Ceelie, H., Dinkelaar, R. B., & van Gelder, W. (2007). Examination of peripheral blood films using automated microscopy; evaluation of Diffmaster Octavia and Cellavision DM96. *Journal of Clinical Pathology*, *60*(1), 72–79. doi:10.1136/jcp.2005.035402 PMID:16698955

Dussart, P., Petit, L., Labeau, B., Bremand, L., Leduc, A., Moua, D., ... Baril, L. (2008). Evaluation of Two New Commercial Tests for the Diagnosis of Acute Dengue Virus Infection Using NS1 Antigen Detection in Human Serum. *PLoS Neglected Tropical Diseases*, *2*(8), e280. doi:10.1371/journal.pntd.0000280 PMID:18714359

Hemangi, B., & Nikhita, K. (2016). People counting system using raspberry pi with openCV. *International Journal for Research in Engineering Application & Management*, *2*(1).

Lazuardia, L., Sanjaya, G. Y., Candradewi, I., & Holmner, A. (2013). Automatic Platelets Counter for Supporting Dengue Case Detection in Primary Health Care. *Studies in Health Technology and Informatics*, *192*. PMID:23920623

Maitra, M., Gupta, R. K., & Mukherjee, M. (2012). Detection and Counting of Red Blood Cells in Blood Cell Images using Hough Transform. *International Journal of Computers and Applications*, *53*(16).

Poornima, J., & Krishnaveni, K. (2016). Detection of Dengue Fever with Platelets Count using Image Processing Technique. *Indian Journal of Science and Technology*, *9*(19), 1–7. doi:10.17485/ijst/2016/v9i19/93852

Pore, Y.N., & Kalshetty, Y.R. (2014). Review on Blood Cell Image Segmentation and Counting. *International Journal of Application or Innovation in Engineering & Management*, *3*(11).

Schoentag, R. A., & Pedersen, J. T. (1979). Evaluation of an Automated Blood Smear Analyzer. *American Society of Clinical Pathologists*, *71*(6), 685–694. doi:10.1093/ajcp/71.6.685 PMID:453085

Sharif, J. M., Miswan, M. F., Ngadi, M. A., Salam, M. S. H., & Jamil, M. M. B. A. (2012) Red Blood Cell Segmentation Using Masking and Watershed Algorithm: A Preliminary Study. *International Conference on Biomedical Engineering (ICoBE)*, *7*, 27-28. 10.1109/ICoBE.2012.6179016

Vala, H.J., & Baxi, A. (2013). A review on Otsu image segmentation algorithm. *International Journal of Advanced Research in Computer Engineering & Technology*, *2*(2).

Venkatalakshmi, B., & Thilagavathi, K. (2013 May) Automatic Red Blood Cell Counting Using Hough Transform. *Proceedings of IEEE Conference on Information and Communication Technologies (ICT)*, *5*. 10.1109/CICT.2013.6558103

Vijayalaxmi, A. K., Srujana, B., & Kumar, P.R. (2014). Object detection and tracking using image processing. *Global Journal of Advanced Engineering Technologies*.

Chapter 2

Enhanced Footsteps Generation Method for Walking Robots Based on Convolutional Neural Networks

Sergei Savin

https://orcid.org/0000-0001-7954-3144
Southwest State University, Russia

Aleksei Ivakhnenko
Applied Parallel Computing LLC, Russia

ABSTRACT

In this chapter, the problem of finding a suitable foothold for a bipedal walking robot is studied. There are a number of gait generation algorithms that rely on having a set of obstacle-free regions where the robot can step to and there are a number of algorithms for generating these regions. This study breaches the gap between these algorithms, providing a way to quickly check if a given obstacle free region is accessible for foot placement. The proposed approach is based on the use of a classifier, constructed as a convolutional neural network. The study discusses the training dataset generation, including datasets with uncertainty related to the shapes of the obstacle-free regions. Training results for a number of different datasets and different hyperparameter choices are presented and showed robustness of the proposed network design both to different hyperparameter choices as well as to the changes in the training dataset.

DOI: 10.4018/978-1-5225-7862-8.ch002

INTRODUCTION

Gait generation is one of the central problems in walking robotics, as it encapsulates a number of challenges associated with this type of robots. Unlike the robots with wheels or tracks, the motion of walking robots of all types is characterized by acquiring and breaking contacts with the supporting surface, which makes the motion planning fundamentally difficult. As discussed in (Bouyarmane et al., 2017), the task of planning the motion trajectory that includes periodic contacts requires placing the contact points at a zero-measure subset of the configuration space of the robot. The difficulty of this problem is increased further by the requirements associated with the robot's dynamics, limiting possible motions and placing restrictions associated with vertical balance of the robot (Vukobratovic & Borovac, 2004), the limitations associated with friction cones, finite torques available for the robot motors and others (Kuindersma et al., 2016).

As a result, many of the successful approaches to motion planning for walking robots rely on decomposition of the original problem into a number of more tractable sub-problems. A particularly popular approach is to first plan the sequence of steps for the robot (Kanoulas et al., 2018), then plan the trajectories for some of its key points, usually its feet and its center of mass (Kajita et al., 2001, 2002), then solve the inverse kinematics problem (Suleiman et al., 2018) and finally use its solution as a control input to the feedback controller that is designed to stabilize the obtained trajectory of the robot (Galloway et al., 2015). Some of these sub-problems had been solved by designing highly efficient algorithms. For example, paper (Kuindersma et al., 2014) suggested reformulation of the stable trajectory generation problem for the center of mass of the robot as a linear quadratic regulator (LQR) problem, which allows solving it using the robot's on-board computers. In (Panovko et al., 2016; Jatsun et al., 2016b) the center of mass trajectory for a bipedal exoskeleton was obtained by directly solving the dynamic ZMP equation. The trajectory generation problem can be more challenging when there are additional contacts between the robot and the environment. In (Jatsun et al., 2017a) the problem of standing up from a chair is considered. This requires breaking the contact between the chair and the robot while retaining the contact between the robot and the supporting surface. In the paper, the problem of trajectory generation was decomposed into states, allowing treating the two different contact scenarios separately.

However, the problem of planning footstep sequences for bipedal walking robots has not yet been solved completely. It can be said that the challenges of the original task of motion planning for the walking robots had been embedded into this sub-problem. In particular, planning footstep sequences requires finding feasible paths over terrain with obstacles, such that the free space is non-convex. This type of motion planning problems can be solved via methods such as rapidly exploring random trees (RRT) or probabilistic roadmaps (PRM), which rely on random sampling to generate a feasible path (LaValle, 1998; LaValle & Kuffner, 2000). Alternative approaches are based on decomposition of the free space into convex obstacle-free regions, and then using mixed integer convex programming to find the optimal step sequence. The disadvantage of the later approach is that it requires the use of additional decomposition algorithm to create a set of the convex obstacle-free regions. There are a number of algorithms proposed, including IRIS based on semidefinite programming (Deits & Tedrake, 2015) and a stereographic projection-based method (Savin, 2017).

The use of mixed integer convex programming methods for motion planning is associated with a significant computational cost. The computational complexity of the problem rises with the number of obstacle-free regions. This motivates filtering out the regions that cannot be used as footholds (due to their size or shape) before initiating the optimization procedure. This is a classification problem which is one of the problem types that can be efficiently solved using machine learning methods. In particular, this problem features spatially connected input data represented as a two-dimensional grid, which suggests that convolutional neural networks can be used to effectively solve this problem.

In this chapter, the methods for improving the efficiency of the footstep planners using convolutional neural networks for the obstacle-free regions classification is studied. The next section provides the background for this procedure, discusses the existing methods, their advantages and disadvantages.

The structure of the rest of the chapter is as follows. The next section describes the research background for the problem of footstep sequence generation, including the problem of obstacle-free scape decomposition, walking robot classifications and the neural networks as applied in Robotics and Computer Vision. Next, the footstep placement problem is discussed, following by a presentation of training dataset generation method, based on this description. After that, neural network architecture and training is discussed, followed by analysis of the effects of the uncertainties, the training length and the dataset size on the training results. The approach to using the proposed solution to for step size optimization is given in the last section before the conclusion and future research direction sections.

BACKGROUND

Obstacle-Free Space Decomposition

As mentioned in the previous sections, the difficulty of path planning is largely associated with the non-convex nature of the free space. This is true in general, however there are some important distinctions in the types of free spaces that occur in practice. We can distinguish the following types: free spaces with individual convex obstacles, free spaces with non-convex obstacles and mazes. Figure 1 illustrates this classification.

The distinction of the first category is related to the fact that when the obstacles are convex it is easy to check if a point lies inside the obstacle, which is not true in the general case. This is especially true in the case of convex polygonal obstacles. These obstacles can be represented as a system of linear inequalities, providing a natural way of checking if the point lies inside the obstacle. The linear inequalities that describe the shape of the obstacle provide a natural way to separate the free space into regions. General convex obstacles with smooth edges can be closely approximated by convex polygons. The ac-

Figure 1. Different types of obstacle-free spaces

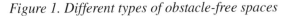

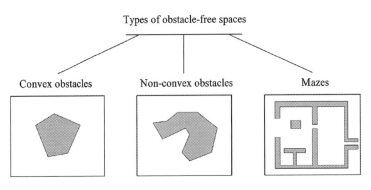

curacy of this approximation can be assessed and controlled, and the approximation error can be taken into account in the safety margins in algorithms that use the information about obstacles. Figure 2 (a) shows a convex polygonal obstacle and Figure 2 (b) shows a convex obstacle with smooth edges and its approximation by a polygonal obstacle.

In the case when the obstacles are not convex, it is generally difficult to check if a point lies inside one. However, when the obstacle is a non-convex polygon, the obstacle can be decomposed into a set of convex polygons. In practice, it is not necessary to decompose an obstacle exactly, as a conservative approximation might suffice. Figure 2 (c) shows a non-convex polygon and its exact decomposition into a set of convex polygons. Figure 2 (d) shows a non-convex polygon and its conservative approximation by set of convex polygons.

The two types of free spaces discussed above can represent a number of practical scenarios. This includes rooms with individual pieces of furniture, open space with individual mobile or immobile objects and others. Mazes, on the other hand, represent the case when the robot moves inside buildings, traversing rooms and corridors.

Unlike the cases of single obstacles, mazes present the case when the form of obstacles in general is too complex to analyze. Moreover, when a robot moves along a maze, it might not have enough information about the shape of the obstacles. It is still possible to approximate this type of obstacles as a set of convex polygons, updating this approximation as new information becomes available. On the other hand, the shape of the visible obstacle-free space might be simpler and easier to approximate than the obstacles. This is related to the fact the information about the obstacles and the obstacle-free spaces comes from sensors which obtain the information about the objects that lie in the line of sight. An example of this setup is a mobile robot equipped with laser range finder and a stereo vision system (Sabe et al., 2004; Kuindersma et al., 2016, Fallon et al., 2015). Such setup was used in ATLAS, a bipedal robot developed by Boston Dynamics and other walking robots.

It should also be noted that some types of terrains with sharp height variations naturally lead to a decomposition of the obstacle-free space to separate regions. Such terrain types include stairs (Jatsun et al., 2017c) and individual supports as illustrated in (Deits & Tedrake, 2014; Kajita et al., 2003).

Walking Robots Classification

There are a number of different walking robot designs, and different designs require different approaches to walking gait generation. This section briefly discusses these differences and highlights the place of the algorithms presented in this work.

Figure 2. Obstacles and their approximations

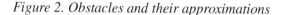

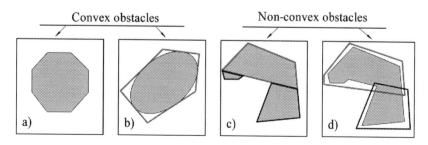

One of the fundamental differences between walking robot designs is associated with the environment where they are meant to function. In particular, it is related to the type of supporting surface which the robot is walking on. Most of the walking robots are designed to walk "on the ground", where the ground refers to surfaces such as building floors, roads, natural landscape, etc. There are alternative types of robots, such as walking robots designed to climb or function inside pipelines (Balaguer et al., 2005; Savin et al., 2017b). The gait generation problem for this type of robots is linked with the geometry of the supporting surface. In (Savin & Vorochaeva, 2017a) it was shown that exploiting the properties of this geometry can yield efficient algorithms for step sequence generation in the case of motion inside spatially curved pipelines with circular cross-section.

The robots walking on the ground can be further categorized by the number of legs they have. The main categories of interest are bipeds, quadrupeds and multi-legged robots. The importance of this categorization is related to the fact that for bipedal robots the gait generation problem needs to be considered together with the vertical balance problem (Vukobratovic & Borovac, 2004). It is possible to use the same approaches to step sequence generation for both bipeds and quadrupeds, as was shown by (Kuindersma et al., 2016; Focchi et al., 2017). However, with the increasing number of extremities the complexity of the gait generation problem rises and it might be beneficial to use simpler algorithms to avoid significant computation costs.

Bipedal walking robots could have anthropomorphic and non-anthropomorphic designs. The anthropomorphic walking robots (humanoids) can be classified according to their function, distinguishing disaster response robots, office robots, exoskeletons and other categories (Atkeson et al., 2015; Jatsun et al., 2016a, 2016c, 2016d). Another approach is to classify them according to their mobility, distinguishing robots that can and cannot turn without sliding, robots that can and cannot change the relative orientation of their feet and others. An ability to orient their feet and perform turns is especially important for the cases when the motion takes place over rough terrain (Kuindersma et al., 2016; Jatsun et al., 2017b). If the robot is unable to perform some of the listed motions, it places an important constraint on the step sequence generation.

Another classification criteria, important from the perspective of step sequence generation, is the feet shape. The feet can be completely identical or symmetrical, they can contact the supporting surface at a number of points or have a continuous contact, they can have a constant shape or be deformable. An example of the later can be found in (Jatsun et al., 2016e). In this chapter, symmetrical feet with constant shape contacting the supporting surface at their vertices are considered.

The algorithms discussed here are valid for walking robot with any number of legs; however, they could be especially beneficial to bipedal robots. This is related to the fact that quadrupeds are often designed with smaller feet, allowing them more freedom in the foot placement. On the other hand, the bipedal robots with rigid feet require more accurate foot placement procedures.

Deep Neural Networks and Computer Vision in Robotics

Neural networks represent a scientific field with a rich history and a vast amount of diverse results (Funahashi, 1989; Schmidhuber, 2015). There are a number of ways to view neural networks: as function approximators or as a way to generate algorithms from data or as a convenient data processing tool. The common ground in these views lies in the fact that neural networks are useful in a number of practical applications where some particular information needs to be extracted from data.

A prolific example of an application for neural networks is image processing. It was shown that neural network could be used to efficiently solve image classification problems, perform object recognition, image segmentation, image enhancement and others. In many cases, it was possible to replace carefully constructed and tuned algorithms for solving a particular image-processing problem with a neural network, trained on a sufficient amount of data. There are multiple advantages to this change. One advantage is that small changes in the original task could be responded to by retraining the network, given the appropriate training data. This allows converting a highly complex task of writing new algorithm into a simpler task of collecting and processing additional training data. Other advantages of using neural nets as a part of the software design include stable running times, the ability to control the computational load generated by the algorithm by choosing the appropriate structure of the network and the natural way of controlling the accuracy of the resulting algorithm.

One of the breakthroughs in the field of neural networks is associated with the proliferation of deep learning (Schmidhuber, 2015). Using neural networks with multiple hidden layers allowed to improve learning results, combat overfitting and other issues associated with practical implementations of neural nets. New neural network architectures allowed solving a number of challenging computer vision problems, such as classifying images from Imagenet database (Krizhevsky et al., 2012). In a number of image categorization tests the deep neural networks perform better than the alternative approaches.

Convolutional neural networks (CNN) are one of the successfully implemented designs for neural nets. It is distinguished by the use of small tunable filters, allowing building networks capable of processing large inputs with relatively small number of tunable parameters (weights and biases). This network architecture had been successfully used in robotics applications, such as scene segmentation, generating bounding boxes for grasping objects and other (Liao et al., 2016; Redmon & Angelova, 2015). These works report better results compared with traditional approaches based on task-specific algorithms, while demonstrating acceptable computational speeds. Cited above papers used standard architecture with convolutional layers followed by fully connected layers. In (Redmon & Angelova, 2015) a sequential architecture was used, where as in (Liao et al., 2016) a branching architecture was employed in order to solve a segmentation problem.

The use of neural networks in robotics is not limited to CNN architectures. In (Savin, 2018a) a fully connected network with three hidden layers was used to solve a problem of predicting normal reactions for a walking robot. Such predictor can be used as a part of the feedback controller design, simplifying the model-based feedback controller for systems with explicit mechanical constraints. In can be viewed as an alternative to a constrained LQR controller (Mason et al., 2014; Savin et al., 2017a) or quadratic programming-based controllers for explicitly constrained systems (Galloway et al., 2015; Mason et al., 2017; Savin & Vorochaeva, 2017b).

One of the most promising examples of using neural network in robotics is associated with reinforcement learning algorithms. These techniques allow training models without pre-labelled data and can be used to solve a number of problems in mobile robot control (Kober et al., 2013). Even though the discussion of these methods is beyond the scope of this chapter, it is important to note that many of the reinforcement learning algorithms rely on CNN architectures for image processing.

This chapter is focused on the use of CNN-based neural network for classification of obstacle-free regions. The purpose of the classification is to determine if the region is suitable for stepping to; in other words, the neural network needs to be able to answer the question of whether or not a particular obstacle-free region has a shape that would potentially allow the robot to fit its foot into it. The choice of CNN architecture is motivated by the fact that the input data is spatially connected and features a large number of elements.

The Footstep Placement Problem

Foot placement is a complex problem with a number of different aspects. From the geometric perspective, it can be seen as a problem of finding the desired position and orientation of the robot's foot, such that the foot comes in contact with the supporting surface in a specified way. For example, in the case when the foot is a polyhedron, it might be desirable that the foot only contacts the surface via particular set of faces. Another example is a requirement that the foot only contacts the patches of the supporting surface with particular geometric properties (such as flat or planar patches).

To make it more concrete, the following simplifications are introduced. The feet are considered to be convex polygons, able to contact the surface at their vertices v_i. The surface is modelled as a two-dimensional space with a map $M: \mathbb{R}^2 \rightarrow \{0, 1\}$ that maps each point on the surface to one of the two categories: accessible for contact (numbered as 1) or not accessible for contact (numbered as 0). The position of the foot is determined by vector r and the orientation of the foot is given by a rotation matrix T. The position of the vertices v_i in absolute coordinates are then given as follows:

$$v_i^{abs} = Tv_i + r,$$
(1)

where v_i are constants that determine the shape of the foot. Then the foot placement problem can be viewed as a problem of finding suitable values of r and T, such that the convex hull of v_i^{abs} lies in an obstacle-free region, as determined by the map M:

$$find: \quad T, r$$
$$subject\ to: \quad \begin{cases} M(x) = 1 \\ \forall x \in convhull(Tv_i + r) \end{cases},$$
(2)

This problem is generally non-convex and can be problematic to solve either analytically or numerically. These difficulties and the ways to mitigate them have been discussed in the previous sections. The focus of this work is to generate a categorization tool that can recognize obstacle-free regions for which the solution of (2) is possible. In particular, the type of obstacle-free regions considered here are limited to convex polygons (as motivated by the discussion in the previous sections). This allows to replace a general notion of map M with a concrete definition:

$$M(x) = \begin{cases} 1 & if \quad Ax \le b \\ 0 & otherwise \end{cases},$$
(3)

where A and b are a matrix and a vector in a linear inequality representation of a convex obstacle-free region. Then, using the properties of convex combination, the problem (2) can be rewritten as follows:

$$find: \quad T, r$$
$$subject \ to: \quad A(Tv_i + r) \leq b \ \cdot$$
(4)

Figure 3 illustrates the geometry of this problem.

The problem (4) is still not convex because the matrix T is rotation matrix, which is a non-convex subset of all matrices. In (Deits & Tedrake, 2014) a non-convex problem equivalent to (4) is discussed, and it is proposed to use a specific approximate parameterization of T with integer parameters, turning the original non-convex problem into a mixed-integer convex optimization. The approach proposed in that paper relies on a piecewise linear approximation of harmonic functions. It is also possible to instead of finding T in a continuous set of rotation matrices, to find it in its discrete subset $R = \{T_j\}$. Then the problem can be treated either as a mixed integer optimization or as a set of convex optimization, one for each example of $T \in R$. In this study, the later approach is used.

Therefore, in order to find if a convex obstacle-free region is accessible to step to, the following set of quadratic programs is solved:

$$\min imize: \quad r^{\mathrm{T}}r$$
$$subject \ to: \quad A(T_j v_i + r) \leq b \ \cdot$$
(5)

where $T_j \in R$. The problem (5) is solved for every element of the set of rotation matrices R, and then if at least one of them has a solution, then the obstacle-free region is categorized as accessible (numbered as 1). If not, then it is categorized as not accessible (numbered as 0). This can be viewed as a map that provides a correspondence between obstacle-free regions and their categories:

$$C: \quad (A, \quad b) \rightarrow \{1, \quad 0\}.$$
(6)

The map $C(A,b)$ provides an instrument for the dataset generation.

Figure 3. The geometry of fitting the robot's foot in an obstacle-free region; 1 – obstacle-free region, 2 – obstacles; 3 – robot's foot

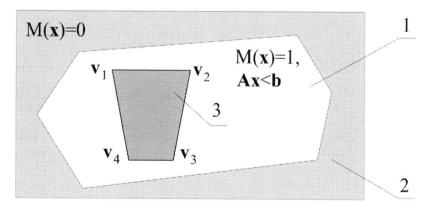

TRAINING DATASET GENERATION

The training dataset needs to include a sufficient variety of obstacle-free regions in order to generalize well. Since we consider only convex polygonal regions, the differences between them are encapsulated by the number and position of their vertices. As a result of choosing different vertices for these regions, they might differ in area, shape, position of the center of the region and other parameters.

In order to generate a diverse dataset, the following rules for generating obstacle free regions are proposed. For each region, a random integer n_k is generated, determining the number of vertices in that region. The value of n_k is restricted to the interval $3 \leq n_k \leq n_{max}$. Then, the pseudo vertices of the obstacle-free regions p_i^* (where $i = 1, ..., n_k$) are generated as a random number from a normal distribution with mean μ_k and standard deviation σ_k. The obstacle-free region P_k is then given as a convex hull of points p_i^*:

$$P_k = convhull(p_i^*). \tag{7}$$

The vertices of the region P_k correspond to particular points p_i^*; however some of the points p_i^* may lie inside P_k, which is why the number of vertices in the region P_k is less than or equal to n_k.

Then, for each region P_k an $m \times m$ array of points is generated, where all points that lie inside P_k are labeled with 1, and all points that lie outside P_k are labeled with 0. The region itself is labeled as accessible or not using the map (6).

In total, N regions are generated. The resulting dataset has a shape of an $m \times m \times N$ array. In the experiments presented in the sections below, the following values of training dataset parameters were used: $n_{max} = 20$, $\mu_k = 0.5$, $\sigma_k = 0.1$, $m = 100$; the number of regions N was varying between experiments. In most of the experiments N was chosen to be $2 \cdot 10^4$, which means that the dataset consists of $2 \cdot 10^8$ numbers.

Figure 4 shows examples of the regions generated for the dataset.

Figure 4. Obstacle-free regions generated for the dataset. The green regions (a) and (c) are classified as accessible, while the red regions (b) and (d) are classified as not accessible. The accessible regions show the foot placement

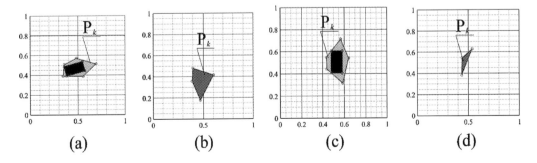

As shown in Figure 4, the ambient space where the obstacle-free regions are located is given as a rectangle spanning the range between 0 and 1 along both axes. This choice is made to improve the network training. If the training data needs to include regions that do not fit into this range or regions that are too small to be well represented for the given resolution of the grid mesh on this range, different ranges could be used, but then the data should be normalized.

NEURAL NETWORK ARCHITECTURE AND TRAINING

In this section, a neural network-based classifier is proposed. The classifier is based on a standard convolutional neural network (CNN) architecture. The network includes five convolutional modules. Each module consists of a convolutional layer and a max pooling layer. The convolutional layers use rectified linear unit (ReLU) activation function. The modules use batch normalization (Ioffe & Szegedy, 2015). The convolutional modules are followed by fully connected layers which also use ReLU activations. The last layer uses a categorical cross-entropy activation. Each of the convolutional layers uses 3 by 3 filters, each max pooling layer uses pool size of 2 by 2. Figure 5 shows the structure of the proposed network.

The network shown in the Figure 5 was built using Tensorflow machine learning library (Abadi et al., 2016) and a high level neural network programming system Keras. The network was trained using the dataset discussed in the previous section with Adam optimization algorithm (Kingma & Ba, 2014; Reddi et al., 2018). The categorical cross entropy loss function is used in the training.

The properties of the proposed architecture depend on the choice of parameters, such as stride length for the convolutional and max pooling layers, the number of filters in the convolutional layers and the number of neurons in the fully connected (dense) layers. Let us consider the case when each convolutional layer has 32 filters, the fully connected layers have 32 elements each and first three max pooling layer use strides equal to 2 and the remaining max pooling layer use strides equal to 1. These numbers present a set of hyperparameters that can be tuned to change the behavior of the neural network during training.

Figure 6 show the loss function dynamics observed during training with the listed above parameters. The learning rate of the algorithm was decreasing after each 40 epochs, starting with $2 \cdot 10^{-3}$ and ending at $2 \cdot 10^{-4}$. The dataset was split into a training set (90% of the data points) and a validation set (10% of the data points).

Figure 5. The architecture of the proposed neural network

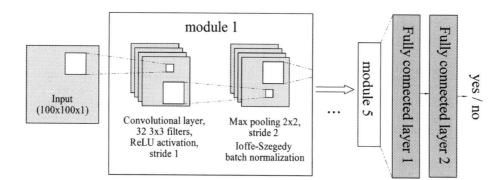

Figure 6. Loss function dynamics for the neural network training; the vertical axis uses logarithmic scale

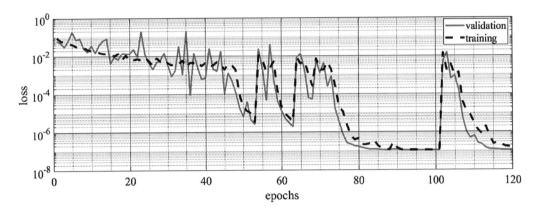

Figure 6 shows that the loss function declines on both the training and the validation datasets. However, this decline is not monotonic and features rapid changes and peaks. This indicates that this training setup is not optimal. However, the quality of the resulting classifier is acceptable, as can be illustrated by observing the accuracy metric (see Figure 7).

It can be seen that the network training converges towards 100% accuracy, which is the desired outcome. However, the presence of peaks in the graphs shown in Figures 6 and 7 suggests that the training is not robust and requires supervision. This motivates studying possible alternative setups with different sets of hyperparameters. Table 1 shows six different types of the proposed network with varied hyperparameters.

The Table 1 uses the following notation: "Conv. strides" refers to the number of strides used in the convolutional layers, "Number of neurons in the FC layer" refers to the number of elements (neurons) in the fully connected layers and "The first FC layer's input size" refers to the number of inputs the first fully connected layer has. This last property is emerging, as it depends on the other parameters of the network. Its significance is related to the fact that the number of inputs to that layer affects the size of its weight matrix, which can be large enough to noticeably influence the training time of the entire network. For example, the first fully connected layer of the network with the type 1 hyperparameter set

Figure 7. Accuracy function dynamics for the neural network training

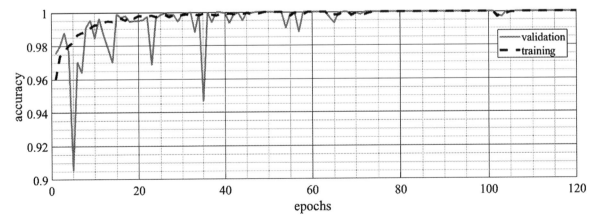

Table 1. The parameters of the proposed types of the neural network

	Type 1	**Type 2**	**Type 3**	**Type 4**	**Type 5**	**Type 6**
Number of filters	all 32	all 16	all 16	all 64	all 64	32, 32, 16
Conv. strides	all 1	all 1	2, 1, 1, 1	2, 1, 1, 1	all 1	all 2
Max pooling strides	2, 2, 2, 1, 1	2, 2, 2, 1, 1	all 2	all 2	all 2	all 2
Number of conv. modules	5	5	4	4	5	3
Number of neurons in the FC layer	32, 32	32, 32	32, 32	32, 32	64, 256	16, 32
The first FC layer's input size	3200	1600	144	576	576	16

has a weight matrix of the dimensions 3200 by 32, resulting in 102400 tunable parameters in that matrix alone. For the type 6 hyperparameter set, the number of elements in this matrix is only 256. The type 1 hyperparameter set corresponds to the network discussed above, which training results are shown in Figures 6 and 7.

Figure 8 shows the loss function dynamics observed when training the neural network with each of the shown hyperparameter sets.

Analyzing the graphs shown in Figure 8 we can observe that all proposed hyperparameter sets behave similar in terms of the overall loss function dynamics. Type 2 performs better than the others, while type 6 performs worse than the others. This can be related to the number of inputs in the first fully connected layer. However, the Figure 8 shows that it is possible to use the network with significantly smaller number of tunable parameters without significantly compromising the training quality.

It can be shown that the instability effects observed during longer training sessions in the type 1 hyperparameter set (Figures 6 and 7) could be mitigated with a type 6 design. Figure 9 shows the loss function dynamics for this case.

Figure 8. Loss function dynamics on the training dataset for different sets of hyperparameters; the type in the figure legend corresponds to the type in the Table 1; the vertical axes use logarithmic scale

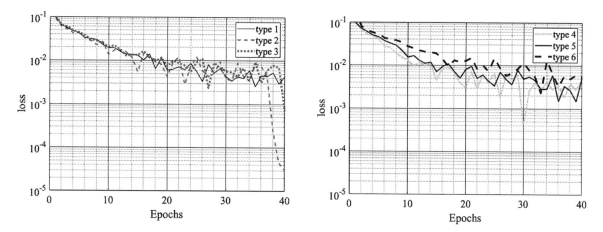

Figure 9. Loss function dynamics for the type 6 hyperparameter set; the vertical axis uses logarithmic scale

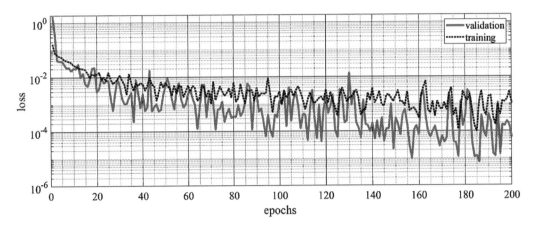

Comparing the results shown in Figure 6 and Figure 9 we observe that the loss function tends to zero slower in the case type 6 hyperparameter set, but it does not exhibit the instability patterns shown by the type 1 hyperparameter set. The difference between the two sets lies in the much simpler design used for the type 6 set, with less convolutional modules and a smaller number of tunable parameters.

OBSTACLE-FREE REGIONS WITH UNCERTAINTY

As described in the previous sections, the training dataset used in this study contains the data about the shapes of the obstacle-free regions in a form of square arrays with binary elements. This reflect the fact that the system is certain about the shape of the obstacle-free region. In some practical applications it might only be possible to obtain a probability of a point being inside an obstacle-free region. In this section, this case is studied.

The case when there is an uncertainty regarding the shape of the obstacle-free regions can be modelled using the following modification of the map (3):

$$M(x) = \begin{cases} 1 - \eta & if \quad Ax \le b \\ \eta & otherwise \end{cases}, \tag{8}$$

where $\eta \in [0 \quad \eta_{\max}]$ is a random number sampled from a uniform distribution, A and b are a matrix and a vector in the linear inequality representation of the obstacle-free region and x is a point in space. Calculating the values of the map $M(x)$ on a uniform grid we obtain an array with real values in the range $[0 \quad 1]$.

Unlike the previously discussed dataset generated for the case when the map $M(\mathbf{x})$ assumes binary values, here every element in dataset is a real number. This requires considerations regarding computer memory use during training. The efficient use of graphic processor units for neural network training, facilitated by Tensorflow library, can be hindered by the significant data transfers during the training process. In this study the dataset was limited by 10^4 points.

Three different datasets with uncertainty had been generated: one for $\eta_{\max} = 0.2$, one for $\eta_{\max} = 0.5$ and one where $\eta_{\max}$ was sampled from a random uniform distribution in the range $\begin{bmatrix} 0 & 1 \end{bmatrix}$ for each obstacle-free region. These datasets with uncertainty were used to train the network with type 6 hyperparameter set. The training was done with a constant learning rate 10^{-3}. As previously, Adam optimization algorithm was used. The training results for these three datasets are shown in Figure 10.

As is shown in Figure 10, all three datasets allowed the network to converge. The convergence rate is comparable with the cases when the deterministic dataset was used. The levels of uncertainty in the datasets did not appear to affect the observed convergence rates.

Another way to analyze the training results is by studying the so-called confusion matrix, which shows the difference between the actual and the predicted categories for the given data and the given predictor. Table 2 shows confusion matrices for the networks trained on the three datasets discussed above (illustrated with Figure 10). It also shows a confusion matrix for a network trained on the dataset without uncertainty discussed in the previous section. The two categories here are "accessible" and "not accessible", as discussed previously.

The content of the Table 2 can be interpreted as follows. For each dataset, the table provides a 2 by 2 matrix, which elements give percentages related to the actual categorization and the one obtained by using a trained network. For a completely accurate network, these matrices would be diagonal. The off-diagonal elements represent prediction (categorization) errors made by the network.

The Table 2 shows that the networks trained on the datasets with uncertainty perform worse than the one trained on the dataset without uncertainty. The error rates are close to 1% for all networks trained on the datasets with uncertainty.

The confusion matrices shown here had been generated using both the training and the verification data, which might affect the results. However, the networks used in this section were trained for only 40 epochs as to prevent overfitting and the quality of the results on both the training and the verification datasets had been comparable during the training.

Thus, the main impact of introducing the uncertainty in the training data had been seen in a significant increase in the dataset size for the same number of data points. This needs to be taken into account when choosing the number of points in the dataset. The quality of the resulting network and the training dynamics did not appear to be affected.

Figure 10. Loss function dynamics for the datasets with uncertainty; the vertical axis uses logarithmic scale

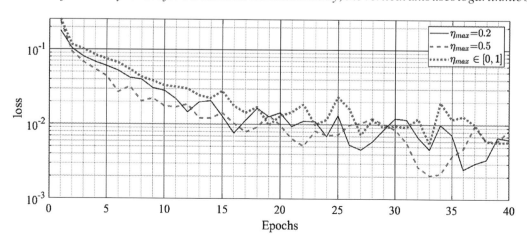

Table 2. Confusion matrices for the neural networks

	Actual Category "Accessible"	Actual Category "Not Accessible"
Dataset With $\eta_{max} = 0.2$		
Predicted category "accessible"	63.56%	0.09%
Predicted category "not accessible"	1.08%	35.27%
Dataset With $\eta_{max} = 0.5$		
Predicted category "accessible"	64.06%	0.07%
Predicted category "not accessible"	0.81%	35.06%
Dataset With $\eta_{max} \in \begin{bmatrix} 0 & 1 \end{bmatrix}$		
Predicted category "accessible"	64.15%	0.46%
Predicted category "not accessible"	0.23%	35.16%
Dataset With $\eta_{max} = 0$ (No Uncertainty)		
Predicted category "accessible"	63.39%	0.1%
Predicted category "not accessible"	0%	36.51%

THE EFFECTS OF THE TRAINING LENGTH AND THE DATASET SIZE ON THE TRAINING RESULTS

The previous sections showed that the proposed neural network design is robust to the changes in structure and to the changes in the data quality. This allows certain freedom in the choice of hyperparameters for the network. It also indicates that the network could be successfully retrained on different datasets, taking into account specific properties of the sensor system and the control system of the robot that is going to use it. However, there is still a question of how long should the training sessions be and what is the optimal size of the training dataset. This section addresses these questions.

Segmented Training Datasets

The goal of having longer training sessions is to improve the quality of the trained network. One of the problems associated with longer training sessions is overfitting, the effect when the network learns to precisely predict the categorization on the training dataset, while failing to generalize, resulting in a poor performance on the verification dataset. The overfitting can be delayed by training on larger datasets, by using dropout and other methods. The structure of the network also influences its behavior during training, in terms of achievable quality and overfitting.

Let us consider the case when three datasets D_j with $2 \cdot 10^4$ elements each are being used for training. A separate dataset of $5 \cdot 10^3$ elements is used for verification. The training procedure is structured as follows. First, a dataset D_j is chosen, and the network is trained on it for n epochs. Then, a different dataset D_{j+1} is chosen and the procedure is repeated. When the network had been trained on each of the three datasets, the training iteration is finished. The training is performed for m iterations. This training method potentially allows using more training data then what fits into memory. We refer to this method as a segmented dataset method.

However, we can show that this segmented dataset approach does not lead to a better generalization on long training sessions. The overfitting can be assessed using the mean ratio σ_{mean} between the accuracy on the validation set and the accuracy on the training set. For a trained network this parameter is expected to be slightly less than 1 (although it can assume any positive values).

Training a neural network with the type 6 set of hyperparameters using the described above procedure yields $\sigma_{mean} = 0.977$. For comparison, the mean ratio σ_{mean} for the training session shown in Figure 9 is $\sigma_{mean} = 0.997$. That training session was performed using a single dataset with $2 \cdot 10^4$ elements, and both training sessions lasted 200 epochs. This demonstrates that the increase in the dataset as proposed here does not improve the overfitting and poor generalization problems.

To show that a longer training session does not improve this performance metric, we train this network using the proposed procedure for 520 epochs. The resulting value of mean ratio is $\sigma_{mean} = 0.974$, which is less than the one obtained for the session with 200 epochs. It shows that the overfitting is getting worse with longer sessions, which is a typical behavior for neural networks.

Small Training Datasets

In this study, the training data was generated and the generation procedure was fast enough to make it feasible to construct a training dataset of the desired size. However, there might be cases when the generation of the dataset of sufficient size is difficult. In this section, we study how using smaller training datasets affects the training results.

The next experiments had been conducted as follows. First, a new training dataset was constructed using M elements of the original dataset. Then each of the neural network types discussed above (with hyperparameters shown in Table 1) was trained using this new dataset. The values of M were chosen to be 10^3, $2.5 \cdot 10^3$, $5 \cdot 10^3$, 10^4 and $2 \cdot 10^4$. These datasets were used for training only, the verification was performed on a separate dataset with 5000 elements. The training session included 40 epochs, with learning rate 10^{-3}. The results of the training are shown in the Table 3. The columns on the Table 3 correspond to the hyperparameter types shown in the Table 1.

The results shown in the Table 3 demonstrate that the increase in the number of samples in the dataset correlates with the increase in the obtained accuracy. The dataset with 1000 elements shows

Table 3. Accuracy on the verification dataset obtained for different types of the neural network

Number of Samples, M	Type 1	Type 2	Type 3	Type 4	Type 5	Type 6
1000	0.956	0.951	0.962	0.978	0.947	0.957
2500	0.982	0.969	0.978	0.979	0.973	0.956
5000	0.985	0.985	0.982	0.985	0.984	0.973
10000	0.987	0.978	0.935	0.986	0.971	0.977
20000	0.9995	1	1	1	1	0.9995

accuracy of 94-95%, where as the dataset with 5000 elements demonstrates accuracy of 97-98% for all hyperparameter types.

There are outliers, such as the result shown by the type 3 network on the dataset with $M = 10^4$. This reflects the stochastic nature of the neural network training procedure. This illustrates that the particular values shown in this table should only be taken as performance indicators, useful for the comparative analysis. It usually possible to improve them by performing multiple training sessions and choosing the results of the best one in terms of the chosen metric.

In order to study the overfitting effects associated with using small datasets, we can calculate the values of the mean ratio σ_{mean} between the accuracy on the validation set and the accuracy on the training set for all training sessions presented in Table 3. These values are shown in Table 4.

The results shown in the Table 4 demonstrate a strong correlation between the mean ratio σ_{mean} and the number of samples M in the dataset. We can observe that the mean ratio σ_{mean} for a fixed dataset size is similar across all hyperparameter sets. For larger datasets the type 1 and type 2 hyperparameter sets performed significantly better, while for the smaller datasets type 5 and type 6 performed slightly better than the others.

STEP SIZE OPTIMIZATION

The network trained in the previous sections can be used to pick obstacle-free regions P_k accessible for foot placement. This can be used a part of step size optimization procedure.

The obtained neural network can be seen as an approximate map $\tilde{C}(\cdot)$ that maps an obstacle-free regions P_k to one of the two categories: accessible or not accessible. Let us consider all accessible regions $P_{k,a}$. For each of these regions it is possible to find position and orientation of the robot's foot that allows it to fit inside that region. Let r_d and T_d be the desired position and orientation of the robot's foot after the step. Then, let the closest to r_d and T_d position and orientation which allows the foot to fit inside the i-th region be denoted as r_i and T_i. Then we can introduce the position and orientation error as follows:

Table 4. The mean ratio σ_{mean} obtained for different types of the neural network

Number of Samples, M	Type 1	Type 2	Type 3	Type 4	Type 5	Type 6
1000	0.577	0.549	0.602	0.615	0.606	0.595
2500	0.843	0.849	0.801	0.795	0.850	0.840
5000	0.913	0.915	0.897	0.901	0.911	0.908
10000	0.958	0.964	0.951	0.943	0.962	0.954
20000	0.994	0.994	0.982	0.976	0.976	0.984

$$\begin{cases} \Delta r = r_d - r_i \\ \Delta T = T_d^{-1} T_i \end{cases},$$
(9)

where Δr is a position error and ΔT is an orientation error. By construction, the orientation error ΔT is a rotation matrix, which means it can be represented as an axis and an angle. Let $g(T): \quad SO(3) \rightarrow \mathbb{R}$ be a map that maps a rotation matrix to the corresponding angle in an axis-angle representation. Then we can define an angle error $\Delta \varphi$ as follows:

$$\Delta \varphi = g(T_d^{-1} T_i).$$
(10)

This allows us to introduce the following quadratic cost function with respect to Δr and $\Delta \varphi$:

$$J = \Delta r^{\mathrm{T}} \begin{bmatrix} w_1 & 0 \\ 0 & w_2 \end{bmatrix} \Delta r + w_3 \Delta \varphi^2,$$
(11)

where w_1, w_2 and w_3 are positive scalar weights. Finding the value of cost J for every accessible obstacle free region $\mathrm{P}_{k,a}$ we generate a set $\{J_i\}$, which can be used to solve the step size optimization problem:

$$\begin{cases} I = \arg\min_i \{J_i\} \\ r = r_I \\ T = T_I \end{cases},$$
(12)

where I is the index of the optimal obstacle-free region on terms of the metric (11), and r and T are the optimal position and orientation of the robot's foot. This is a very simple method for computing the optimal step size which relies on the assumption that there is sufficiently small number of accessible obstacle free regions. More involved approaches can be found in (Kuindersma et al., 2016).

FUTURE RESEARCH DIRECTIONS

The results presented in this chapter indicate that the use of neural networks (and convolutional neural networks in particular) in gait generation for bipedal robots is a viable option. The advantages of using neural networks as a part of the gait generation pipeline include stable computational costs, ease of changing the properties of the algorithm and the ability to control the accuracy. In this study, it was shown that there are a number of ways to control the accuracy of the trained network. It is not clear if there exists an upper bound for the accuracy of the proposed network.

The further studies might be focused on the use of neural networks to directly predict the optimal foot placement for the robot. Same as with the obstacle-free regions classification, this problem allows to generate training data, using the existing gait generation algorithms. The existing algorithms that use the information about the available obstacle-free regions often rely on mixed-integer programming (Deits & Tedrake, 2016) which is computationally expensive and exhibits varying run times, which hinders the analysis of the control system and poses a practical engineering problem. Using neural networks to directly predict the next optimal step might significantly improve the performance of walking robots and lower the requirements to the on-board computer.

Another possible research direction in this field is to use the neural networks to reconstruct the obstacle-free regions from the camera images. This would allow to skip the use of obstacle-detection algorithms and to skip the obstacle-free region generation algorithms, which are also computationally expensive. The main problem for this task might be the training dataset generation, as it is not easy to map a camera image to a suitable representation of an obstacle-free region. This problem might be easier solved with LIDAR images, which are compatible with the stereographic projection algorithms (Savin, 2017) and could also be used with a IRIS algorithm after a proper preprocessing (Deits & Tedrake, 2015).

Another future research direction is associated with optimization of the walking gait parameters using the information about the supporting surface. This can also be formulated as a machine learning problem, using nonlinear numerical optimization for the training dataset generation. An example of using the nonlinear optimization to find optimal gait parameters for a walking robot moving over a supporting surface with a complex geometry can be found in (Savin, 2018b).

CONCLUSION

In this chapter, the problem of walking gait generation for a bipedal walking robot was considered. In particular, the task of finding a suitable foot placements was discussed. Modern approaches to solving this problem include dividing the supporting surface into obstacle-free regions. Depending on the method used to generate these regions, there might be a significant number of them, which poses a problem for the gait generation pipelines relying on optimization-based approaches to find the optimal foot place-ment. In the chapter, this problem is approached with the use of neural networks.

The fact that the obstacle-free regions could be classified into two relevant categories (accessible and not accessible) by solving an optimization problem allows to generate a training dataset, which in turn allows the use of machine learning techniques to train a classifier. Here, a convolutional neural network was proposed and trained. The structure of the network and the different choices of hyperparameters were discussed and the training results for different choices had been shown.

In this work, it was demonstrated that the proposed network design is robust to significant structural changes (such as changing the number of tunable parameters in some layers by as much as 400 times and changing the number of layers in the network). The behavior of the network was shown to depend on the amount of available training data. The quality degradation and the overfitting effects for small datasets had been observed for all studied network types.

It was also shown that the introduction of uncertainty into the dataset does negatively effect the quality of the training result; however, these negative effects were relatively small and could be acceptable in practical applications.

ACKNOWLEDGMENT

The reported study was funded by Russian Foundation of Basic Research (RFBR) according to the research project N°18-38-00140\18.

REFERENCES

Abadi, M., Barham, P., Chen, J., Chen, Z., Davis, A., Dean, J., . . . Kudlur, M. (2016, November). Tensorflow: a system for large-scale machine learning. In OSDI (Vol. 16, pp. 265-283). Academic Press.

Atkeson, C. G., Babu, B. P. W., Banerjee, N., Berenson, D., Bove, C. P., Cui, X., . . . Gennert, M. (2015, November). No falls, no resets: Reliable humanoid behavior in the DARPA robotics challenge. In *Humanoid Robots (Humanoids), 2015 IEEE-RAS 15th International Conference on* (pp. 623-630). IEEE.

Balaguer, C., Gimenez, A., & Jardón, A. (2005). Climbing robots' mobility for inspection and maintenance of 3D complex environments. *Autonomous Robots, 18*(2), 157–169. doi:10.100710514-005-0723-0

Bouyarmane, K., Caron, S., Escande, A., & Kheddar, A. (2017). *Multi-Contact Planning and Control.* Academic Press.

Deits, R., & Tedrake, R. (2014, November). Footstep planning on uneven terrain with mixed-integer convex optimization. In *Humanoid Robots (Humanoids), 2014 14th IEEE-RAS International Conference on* (pp. 279-286). IEEE. 10.21236/ADA609276

Deits, R., & Tedrake, R. (2015). Computing large convex regions of obstacle-free space through semidefinite programming. In *Algorithmic foundations of robotics XI* (pp. 109–124). Cham: Springer. doi:10.1007/978-3-319-16595-0_7

Fallon, M. F., Marion, P., Deits, R., Whelan, T., Antone, M., McDonald, J., & Tedrake, R. (2015, November). Continuous humanoid locomotion over uneven terrain using stereo fusion. In *Humanoid Robots (Humanoids), 2015 IEEE-RAS 15th International Conference on* (pp. 881-888). IEEE. 10.1109/HUMANOIDS.2015.7363465

Focchi, M., Del Prete, A., Havoutis, I., Featherstone, R., Caldwell, D. G., & Semini, C. (2017). High-slope terrain locomotion for torque-controlled quadruped robots. *Autonomous Robots, 41*(1), 259–272. doi:10.100710514-016-9573-1

Funahashi, K. I. (1989). On the approximate realization of continuous mappings by neural networks. *Neural Networks, 2*(3), 183–192. doi:10.1016/0893-6080(89)90003-8

Galloway, K., Sreenath, K., Ames, A. D., & Grizzle, J. W. (2015). Torque saturation in bipedal robotic walking through control Lyapunov function-based quadratic programs. *IEEE Access: Practical Innovations, Open Solutions, 3*, 323–332. doi:10.1109/ACCESS.2015.2419630

Ioffe, S., & Szegedy, C. (2015). *Batch normalization: Accelerating deep network training by reducing internal covariate shift.* arXiv preprint arXiv:1502.03167

Jatsun, S., Savin, S., Lushnikov, B., & Yatsun, A. (2016). Algorithm for motion control of an exoskeleton during verticalization. In *ITM Web of Conferences* (Vol. 6). EDP Sciences. 10.1051/itmconf/20160601001

Jatsun, S., Savin, S., & Yatsun, A. (2016, July). Motion control algorithm for a lower limb exoskeleton based on iterative LQR and ZMP method for trajectory generation. In *International Workshop on Medical and Service Robots* (pp. 305-317). Springer.

Jatsun, S., Savin, S., & Yatsun, A. (2016, June). Improvement of energy consumption for a lower limb exoskeleton through verticalization time optimization. In *Control and Automation (MED), 2016 24th Mediterranean Conference on* (pp. 322-326). IEEE. 10.1109/MED.2016.7535882

Jatsun, S., Savin, S., & Yatsun, A. (2016). Parameter optimization for exoskeleton control system using sobol sequences. In *ROMANSY 21-Robot Design, Dynamics and Control* (pp. 361–368). Cham: Springer. doi:10.1007/978-3-319-33714-2_40

Jatsun, S., Savin, S., & Yatsun, A. (2016, August). A Control Strategy for a Lower Limb Exoskeleton with a Toe Joint. In *International Conference on Interactive Collaborative Robotics* (pp. 1-8). Springer. 10.1007/978-3-319-43955-6_1

Jatsun, S., Savin, S., & Yatsun, A. (2017, August). Walking pattern generation method for an exoskeleton moving on uneven terrain. *Proceedings of the 20th International Conference on Climbing and Walking Robots and Support Technologies for Mobile Machines (CLAWAR 2017)*. 10.1142/9789813231047_0005

Jatsun, S., Savin, S., & Yatsun, A. (2017, September). Footstep Planner Algorithm for a Lower Limb Exoskeleton Climbing Stairs. In *International Conference on Interactive Collaborative Robotics* (pp. 75-82). Springer. 10.1007/978-3-319-66471-2_9

Jatsun, S., Savin, S., Yatsun, A., & Gaponov, I. (2017). Study on a two-staged control of a lower-limb exoskeleton performing standing-up motion from a chair. In *Robot Intelligence Technology and Applications 4* (pp. 113–122). Cham: Springer. doi:10.1007/978-3-319-31293-4_10

Kajita, S., Kanehiro, F., Kaneko, K., Fujiwara, K., Harada, K., Yokoi, K., & Hirukawa, H. (2003, September). *Biped walking pattern generation by using preview control of zero-moment point* (Vol. 3, pp. 1620–1626). ICRA. doi:10.1109/ROBOT.2003.1241826

Kajita, S., Kanehiro, F., Kaneko, K., Fujiwara, K., Yokoi, K., & Hirukawa, H. (2002). A realtime pattern generator for biped walking. In *Robotics and Automation, 2002. Proceedings. ICRA'02. IEEE International Conference on* (Vol. 1, pp. 31-37). IEEE. 10.1109/ROBOT.2002.1013335

Kajita, S., Kanehiro, F., Kaneko, K., Yokoi, K., & Hirukawa, H. (2001). The 3D Linear Inverted Pendulum Mode: A simple modeling for a biped walking pattern generation. In *Intelligent Robots and Systems, 2001. Proceedings. 2001 IEEE/RSJ International Conference on* (Vol. 1, pp. 239-246). IEEE.

Kanoulas, D., Stumpf, A., Raghavan, V. S., Zhou, C., Toumpa, A., von Stryk, O., . . . Tsagarakis, N. G. (2018, February). Footstep Planning in Rough Terrain for Bipedal Robots using Curved Contact Patches. In *Robotics and Automation (ICRA), 2018 IEEE International Conference on* (pp. 108-113). IEEE.

Kingma, D. P., & Ba, J. (2014). *Adam: A method for stochastic optimization.* arXiv preprint arXiv:1412.6980

Kober, J., Bagnell, J. A., & Peters, J. (2013). Reinforcement learning in robotics: A survey. *The International Journal of Robotics Research, 32*(11), 1238–1274. doi:10.1177/0278364913495721

Krizhevsky, A., Sutskever, I., & Hinton, G. E. (2012). Imagenet classification with deep convolutional neural networks. In Advances in neural information processing systems (pp. 1097-1105). Academic Press.

Kuindersma, S., Deits, R., Fallon, M., Valenzuela, A., Dai, H., Permenter, F., ... Tedrake, R. (2016). Optimization-based locomotion planning, estimation, and control design for the Atlas humanoid robot. *Autonomous Robots, 40*(3), 429–455. doi:10.100710514-015-9479-3

Kuindersma, S., Permenter, F., & Tedrake, R. (2014, May). An efficiently solvable quadratic program for stabilizing dynamic locomotion. In *Robotics and Automation (ICRA), 2014 IEEE International Conference on* (pp. 2589-2594). IEEE. 10.1109/ICRA.2014.6907230

LaValle, S. M. (1998). *Rapidly-exploring random trees: A new tool for path planning.* Academic Press.

LaValle, S. M., & Kuffner Jr, J. J. (2000). *Rapidly-exploring random trees: Progress and prospects.* Academic Press.

Liao, Y., Kodagoda, S., Wang, Y., Shi, L., & Liu, Y. (2016, May). Understand scene categories by objects: A semantic regularized scene classifier using convolutional neural networks. In *Robotics and Automation (ICRA), 2016 IEEE International Conference on* (pp. 2318-2325). IEEE.

Mason, S., Righetti, L., & Schaal, S. (2014, November). Full dynamics LQR control of a humanoid robot: An experimental study on balancing and squatting. In *Humanoid Robots (Humanoids), 2014 14th IEEE-RAS International Conference on* (pp. 374-379). IEEE.

Mason, S., Rotella, N., Schaal, S., & Righetti, L. (2017). *A MPC Walking Framework With External Contact Forces.* arXiv preprint arXiv:1712.09308

Panovko, G. Y., Savin, S. I., Yatsun, S. F., & Yatsun, A. S. (2016). Simulation of exoskeleton sit-to-stand movement. *Journal of Machinery Manufacture and Reliability, 45*(3), 206–210. doi:10.3103/S1052618816030110

Reddi, S. J., Kale, S., & Kumar, S. (2018). *On the convergence of adam and beyond.* Academic Press.

Redmon, J., & Angelova, A. (2015, May). Real-time grasp detection using convolutional neural networks. In *Robotics and Automation (ICRA), 2015 IEEE International Conference on* (pp. 1316-1322). IEEE. 10.1109/ICRA.2015.7139361

Sabe, K., Fukuchi, M., Gutmann, J. S., Ohashi, T., Kawamoto, K., & Yoshigahara, T. (2004, April). Obstacle avoidance and path planning for humanoid robots using stereo vision. In *Robotics and Automation, 2004. Proceedings. ICRA'04. 2004 IEEE International Conference on* (Vol. 1, pp. 592-597). IEEE. 10.1109/ROBOT.2004.1307213

Savin, S. (2017, June). An algorithm for generating convex obstacle-free regions based on stereographic projection. In *Control and Communications (SIBCON), 2017 International Siberian Conference on* (pp. 1-6). IEEE. 10.1109/SIBCON.2017.7998590

Savin, S. (2018). *Neural Network-based Reaction Estimator for Walking Robots.* Academic Press.

Savin, S. (2018). *Parameter Optimization for Walking Patterns and the Geometry of In-Pipe Robots*. Academic Press.

Savin, S., Jatsun, S., & Vorochaeva, L. (2017). Trajectory generation for a walking in-pipe robot moving through spatially curved pipes. In *MATEC Web of Conferences* (Vol. 113, p. 02016). EDP Sciences. 10.1051/matecconf/201711302016

Savin, S., Jatsun, S., & Vorochaeva, L. (2017, November). Modification of Constrained LQR for Control of Walking in-pipe Robots. In Dynamics of Systems, Mechanisms and Machines (Dynamics), 2017 (pp. 1-6). IEEE. doi:10.1109/Dynamics.2017.8239502

Savin, S., & Vorochaeva, L. (2017, June). Footstep planning for a six-legged in-pipe robot moving in spatially curved pipes. In *Control and Communications (SIBCON), 2017 International Siberian Conference on* (pp. 1-6). IEEE. 10.1109/SIBCON.2017.7998581

Savin, S., & Vorochaeva, L. Y. (2017). Nested Quadratic Programming-based Controller for In-pipe Robots. *Proceedings of the International Conference On Industrial Engineering 2017*.

Schmidhuber, J. (2015). Deep learning in neural networks: An overview. *Neural Networks*, *61*, 85–117. doi:10.1016/j.neunet.2014.09.003 PMID:25462637

Suleiman, W., Ayusawa, K., Kanehiro, F., & Yoshida, E. (2018, March). On prioritized inverse kinematics tasks: Time-space decoupling. In *Advanced Motion Control (AMC), 2018 IEEE 15th International Workshop on* (pp. 108-113). IEEE.

Vukobratovic, M., & Borovac, B. (2004). Zero-moment point—thirty five years of its life. *International Journal of Humanoid Robotics, 1*(1), 157-173.

ADDITIONAL READING

Cruz, N., Lobos-Tsunekawa, K., & Ruiz-del-Solar, J. (2017). Using Convolutional Neural Networks in Robots with Limited Computational Resources: Detecting NAO Robots while Playing Soccer. *arXiv preprint arXiv:1706.06702*.

Gonzalez, R., & Iagnemma, K. (2018). DeepTerramechanics: Terrain Classification and Slip Estimation for Ground Robots via Deep Learning. *arXiv preprint arXiv:1806.07379*.

Harper, M., Pace, J., Gupta, N., Ordonez, C., & Collins, E. G. (2017, May). Kinematic modeling of a RHex-type robot using a neural network. In *Unmanned Systems Technology XIX* (Vol. 10195, p. 1019507). International Society for Optics and Photonics. doi:10.1117/12.2262894

Nguyen, A., Kanoulas, D., Caldwell, D. G., & Tsagarakis, N. G. (2017, September). Object-based affordances detection with convolutional neural networks and dense conditional random fields. In *Intelligent Robots and Systems (IROS), 2017 IEEE/RSJ International Conference on* (pp. 5908-5915). IEEE. 10.1109/IROS.2017.8206484

Ran, L., Zhang, Y., Zhang, Q., & Yang, T. (2017). Convolutional neural network-based robot navigation using uncalibrated spherical images. *Sensors (Basel), 17*(6), 1341. doi:10.339017061341 PMID:28604624

Such, F. P., Madhavan, V., Conti, E., Lehman, J., Stanley, K. O., & Clune, J. (2017). Deep neuroevolution: genetic algorithms are a competitive alternative for training deep neural networks for reinforcement learning. *arXiv preprint arXiv:1712.06567.*

Tan, J., Zhang, T., Coumans, E., Iscen, A., Bai, Y., Hafner, D., . . . Vanhoucke, V. (2018). Sim-to-Real: Learning Agile Locomotion For Quadruped Robots. *arXiv preprint arXiv:1804.10332.*

Wang, Z., Wang, B., Liu, H., & Kong, Z. (2017, October). Recurrent convolutional networks based intention recognition for human-robot collaboration tasks. In *Systems, Man, and Cybernetics (SMC), 2017 IEEE International Conference on*(pp. 1675-1680). IEEE. 10.1109/SMC.2017.8122856

KEY TERMS AND DEFINITIONS

Bipedal Walking Robot: A mobile robot with two legs, which primary mode of operation requires these legs to periodically acquire and break contact with the supporting surface.

Confusion Matrix: A matrix which shows the distribution of categorizations performed by the network on a labeled dataset, where the correct categorizations lie on the main diagonal.

Convolutional Neural Network: A type of artificial neural networks, which uses a set of filters with tunable (learnable) parameters to extract local features from the input data.

Fully Connected Layer: A layer of an artificial neural networks where each element of the layer is connected to each element of the following layer.

Obstacle-Free Region: A region in space (on the supporting surface), which points are suitable for making contact.

Training: A process of tuning parameters of an artificial neural networks, based on comparing the current output of the network with the desired output; the process is often performed with gradient decent-like methods.

Chapter 3
CNN Customizations With Transfer Learning for Face Recognition Task

Chantana Chantrapornchai
Kasetsart University, Thailand

Samrid Duangkaew
Kasetsart University, Thailand

ABSTRACT

Several kinds of pretrained convolutional neural networks (CNN) exist nowadays. Utilizing these networks with the new classification task requires the retraining with new data sets. With the small embedded device, large network cannot be implemented. The authors study the use of pretrained models and customizing them towards accuracy and size against face recognition tasks. The results show 1) the performance of existing pretrained networks (e.g., AlexNet, GoogLeNet, CaffeNet, SqueezeNet), as well as size, and 2) demonstrate the layers customization towards the model size and accuracy. The studied results show that among the various networks with different data sets, SqueezeNet can achieve the same accuracy (0.99) as others with small size (up to 25 times smaller). Secondly, the two customizations with layer skipping are presented. The experiments show the example of SqueezeNet layer customizing, reducing the network size while keeping the accuracy (i.e., reducing the size by 7% with the slower convergence time). The experiments are measured based on Caffe 0.15.14.

INTRODUCTION

Face recognition is one of the recognition task that has various applications in many areas such as surveillance, access control, video retrieval, interactive gaming etc. (Huang, Xiong, & Zhang, 2011) The techniques for face recognition start from face identification, face feature extraction, and matching feature template. Face identification is a process which identifies the face bounding box of images. Feature extraction is an important phase for creating a recognition model. Several methods have been used such as local feature extraction, template creation, eigenface, etc. Recently, deep learning has been popularly

DOI: 10.4018/978-1-5225-7862-8.ch003

used for image classification. With a deep network, it can also be used to perform image feature extraction (Yosinski, Clune, Bengio, & Lipson, 2014).

Currently, there are many popular pretrained deep neural net models for recognition tasks. However, choosing a proper one requires a lot of training experiments. Also, the model is adopted in the embedded device, the large model may not be deployed.

While most of the literatures are focused on the model accuracy, in this work, we study the two aspects of the available pretrained models: the accuracy and model size. The models studied are AlexNet, GoogLeNet, SqueezeNet. The face recognition task is used as a classification benchmark since it has various applications on embedded platform. The experiment methodology demonstrated to serve the following goals.

1.   To find the performance of all these nets, towards face recognition tasks and compare with the consumed resources and times.
2.   To selectively transfer the pretrained weights to help accelerate the accuracy convergence.
3.   To reduce the model size via the layer customization.

Without pretrained models, constructing a face recognition model requires many hundred thousand iterations and million images for training. Adopting these networks via transfer learning can speed up the number of training iterations. Meanwhile, it may be possible to customize the architecture and weight adopting, which can lead to the smaller network with the similar performance.

Public face data sets contains many thousand to million subjects. The large ones are such as MegaFace (Kemelmacher-Shlizerman, Seitz, Miller, & Brossard, 2016) containing around 600,000 subjects, containing 10 million images. Another example is the data set from Institute of Automation, Chinese Academy of Sciences (CASIA) which contains 400,000 images (Yi, Lei, Liao, & Li, 2014). To find a proper network, one needs to train against these large data sets which is very time consuming. In this paper, our study contains extensive experiments to explore a variety of existing networks with pretrained weights, fine tuning and customizing them.

BACKGROUND

Currently, there are many existing works that apply deep learning in face recognition. Most works deploy a deep network for the face detection task. Some of the work requires a special loss function while some required special training labels.

One of the popular works that uses neural nets to perform face recognition is OpenFace (Amos, Ludwiczuk, & Satyanarayanan, 2016), which uses the dlib library to detect faces. The pose estimation and affine transformation to align eyes and noses at the same positions are performed afterwards. Next, the embedding of each face is generated by the deep neural net. The embedding is then used for classification by a conventional approach such as Support Vector Machine (SVM). The generated model can be very large depending the number of subjects. Wen et.al. used deep neural net where the approach is based on the center loss (Wen, Zhang, Li, & Qiao, 2016). The center loss approach tries to find a center for deep features of each class and to minimize the distances between the deep features and their corresponding class centers. The authors combined center loss with softmax loss to enhance the recognition accuracy. Parkhi et.al. presented a deep face network that utilizes the triplet loss to learn face embedding (Parkhi,

Vedaldi, & Zisserman, 2015). Their approach constructs a face classifier by a scoring vector and tuning it using the triplet loss. These approaches require the special loss layer to be computed in the network which requires effort in changing code the existing model.

Faster Regions-based Convolutional Neural Network (Faster RCNN) can also be used for face detection and recognition (Sun, Wu, & Hoi, 2017). There are two steps in faster RCNN: 1) detecting the bounding box and 2) object classification. It is an improved version from fast RCNN and RCNN which makes the computation to detect objects faster (Girshick, 2015; Shaoqing, Kaiming, Ross, & Jian, 2015). Using this approach requires the training data be also labeled by both classes and bounding boxes which are not commonly found in public face data sets.

Sun et.al. followed the training approach from faster RCNN (Sun, Wu, & Hoi, 2017). They started with the pretrained model with 16 layers from Visual Geometry Group, called VGG16. The model was pretrained from ImageNet data set and then tune on Face Detection Data set and Benchmark (FDDB) for the higher-level and lower-level features. Zhang et.al. designed Multi-task Cascaded Convolutional Networks (MTCNN) to detect and aligned faces (Zhang, Zhang, Li, & Qiao, 2016) which gives a very high accuracy on the large data set, namely WIDER Face (Yang, Luo, Loy, & Tang, 2016). They focused on face detection model.

Training deep and specific network is known to be difficult, time consuming, and require much memory resources. Some data sets are known to be even harder to train to achieve high accuracy. Some network required more work for the data labeling. For example, training using faster-RCNN requires data labeling with bounding boxes and preprocessing in a certain form. These nets such as (Parkhi et al., 2015; Shaoqing et al., 2015) implement their own loss layers because they compute loss functions differently. In some framework, such as Caffe (Jia et al., 2014), the source code needs to be compiled to accommodate the new loss function, written in C or using a python layer. Thus, the existing off-the-shelve training framework may not be directly applied.

Model compression technique is a common solution used to reduce the model size. In this approach, the given model is compacted by several approaches (Chen, et.al., 2017). The typical approaches are parameter pruning and sharing, low-rank factorization, transferred/compact convolutional filters. Some can apply to only convolutional layers while some can apply to both convolutional layers and fully connected layers. The low rank factorization is a design technique to obtain the small number of weights such as the model Network in a Network (NIN) (Simonyan, K., & Zisserman, 2014) SqueezeNet (Iandola et al., 2016), MobileNet (Howard, et.al., 2017). Residual Net (ResNet) utilizes the parameter pruning and sharing (Masi, Tran, Hassner, Leksut, & Medioni, 2016). ResNet also utilizes the compact filter approach to transform the weight matrix. These models are designed to be deep to contain many the small weight matrices. Parameter pruning and weight sharing is to reduce the weight redundancy and use encoding (quantization) to shorten the weight representation,.e.,g Huffman coding (Han et.al., 2016). Such approach encodes the weights obtained after the training; thus, the deployment phase requires decoding.

Lapuschkin et.al. utilized several networks against age and gender classification (Lapuschkin, Binder, Mller, & Samek, 2017), towards four types of networks: AdienceNet, CaffeNet, Googlenet and VGG-16, they concluded that preprocessing such as alignment can increase the accuracy but may increase noises in data sets. Also, using pretrained weight can lead to faster convergence. In contrast to ours, we do not focus on the preprocessing variation.

In this paper, we would like to compare the utilization of off-the-shelve deep learning models towards the face recognition task since nowadays, there are lots of pretrained models around. Adopting common simple pretrained model can be speedup the training process. (Lapuschkin et al., 2017). We propose to optimize the size of the network via layer reductions due to the resource requirement in a target embedded device while keeping the accuracy at an acceptable level. The difference between the above previous works and this work is that we study the use of pretrained models and their variation rather than designing a new model, or loss function. The resulting model size is also investigated. The speed of recognition in the deployment platform will be also considered in the near future.

METHODOLOGY

The face recognition task implicitly contains two major steps. First is the face detection and second is the recognition. We describe each step as it is required in our experiments.

Face Detection

The original images may contain several objects. It is needed to specify only the face bounding box as shown in where it is obvious to find one frontal face while in there are many faces which may not be well-pose. Many face data sets contain well-pose images, while this may not applicable in most situations like in a surveillance system. With frontal-face image, basic face detection as in can be done by various tools such as OpenCV (OPENCV, n.d.; Dlib, n.d.) while for the ill-pose image, the more complicated approach is needed as mentioned in the previous work section. There are also many other approaches which extract important face landmark as main features. The landmarks can be 3, 5 or 68 points. If these landmarks are found in the image, the face is detected. This approach requires the frontal face as in (Amos et al., 2016) while MTCNN does not.

Face Recognition Preprocessing

After the face detection returns the bounding box, the face is cropped. Next, the model to represent a face for each class must be constructed. This model is used for recognition. The method to create the representation can utilize combined several local features. Before creating the representation, preprocessing is needed. First is the resizing to scale all training images. Pose adjustment, and face alignment may be required for the face landmark-style approach. The image augmentation may be required to increase the diversity of the training set. The typical augmentation is cropping, translate, noise inserting, brightening or adding contrast. Also, it is required to compute a mean image before training. If augmented images are created during the training time, the training iteration time is increased.

Face Recognition Model Construction

The training images are used to create a model. Various approaches can be done for model construction. A typical approach to extract a representation for each class such as Support Vector Machine, Baysian etc. are commonly used. The representation can be an average of the class features. Or as in (Parkhi et al., 2015) the features of the classes are extracted after iterations of learning with a given model. They may be used next by a typical machine learning classification approach.

Face Data Sets

There exist public face data sets for many purposes. WIDER face is a face detection data set which contains 32,203 images with a variability in scale, pose and occlusion (Yang et al., 2016).

For a traditional face recognition task, the popular data set is LFW (Labeled Faces in a Wild) containing 5,749 subjects and 13,233 face images (Celebi & Smolka, 2016). Most pictures are from Yahoo news. The images are pictures of celebrities with different light conditions, pose, expression. The number of images per subject is varied. Some subject has only one image while some has a few more. The smaller set, FDDB, contains 5,171 faces in a set of 2,845 images taken from LFW (Labeled Faces in a Wild) (Jain & Learned-Miller, 2010).

The larger sets are such as FaceScrub which includes 100,000 pictures of celebrities, containing 265 males (55,742 pictures) and 265 females (52,076 pictures). It is a deep data set where each celebrity has around hundreds to thousands of pictures (Ng & Winkler, 2014). CASIA-WebFace (Yi et al., 2014) contains 10,575 subjects with 494,414 images. Each subject contains varying number of images, from ten to hundred images.

MegaFace (Kemelmacher-Shlizerman et al., 2016) data set was developed for a face recognition challenge at a large scale. It was aimed to provide as the largest training set and it embeds several distractors such as ages, pose to check the performance of recognition. The data set contains a million of faces, where each face consists of around 10 or more images. The image quality is more than 40 pixels interocular distance. The images were derived from Yahoo 100 Million Flickr creative common sets (Thomee et al., 2015).

MS-Celeb-1M contains 1 million celebrities, containing 10 million images which is one of the largest one currently. Figure 1(a) shows the example of CASIA data set where each image contains one celebrity while Figure 1(b) is an example of FaceScrub data set in which only faces are given. Also, in MegaFace data set (Figure 1(d)), there can bc more than one face in a picture. LFW in Figure 1(c) is similar to CASIA where the cropping is needed.

Available Pretrained Model

One of the popular well-known pretrained models are such as AlexNet Krizhevsky, Sutskever, & Hinton, 2012) was developed by Krizhevsky et.al. It was trained by ImageNet data set in ILSVRC-2010 and ILSVRC-2012, with 1.2 million images in 1,000 categories.

The architecture contains eight learned layers five convolutional and three fully-connected layers, called *fc6,fc7,fc8*. The reference CaffeNet (Jia et al., 2014) is a variation of AlexNet, except that max pooling precedes the local response normalization (LRN) to reduce the memory usage. GoogLeNet (Szegedy et al., 2014) is a deep convolutional neural network structure. It was used as a classification and detection tool in ILSVRC14 with the goal to work with small data sets and use small computing power and memory. It employs an inception module that simultaneously computes 1x1, 3x3, and 5x5 convolutions, enabling selecting proper filter sizes automatically. It was trained in ILSVRC 2014 challenge to classify the image into one of 1,000 leaf-node categories for ImageNet, which uses about 1.2 million images for training, 50,000 for validation and 100,000 images for testing.

Figure 1. Face data set (a) CASIA (b) FaceScrub (c) LFW (d) MegaFace

(a)   (b)

(c)   (d)

SqueezeNet (Iandola et al., 2016) aims to improve AlexNet efficiency while keeping the same level of accuracy. The squeezing idea was partly from Network-In-Network (NIN) (Lin, Chen, & Yan, 2013) which stacks small networks and utilizes convolutions instead of the fully connected one at the last layer. The minimized convolutional neural network has advantages: saving communication time between the server and the clients for over-the-air update, and feasibility for embedded deployment. SqueezeNet utilizes the methods such as reducing filter sizes, reducing input channels, delaying downsampling. SqueezeNet was trained on ILSVRC2012 ImageNet. The design was to focus on the smaller model size while keeping the same accuracy level as AlexNet's.

VGG net improved the accuracy by adding more convolutional layers and removes LRN layers. It was trained on ImageNet ILSVRC-2014 (Simonyan & Zisserman, 2014). The model has variations from 11, 13, 16 and 19 layers, where the model parameters vary from 133 - 144 million. It was trained against ILSVRC2012 ImageNet (1.3 million images, with 50,000 validation images, and 100,000 testing images).

ResNet101 is a very deep model for a face recognition task. The model was fine-tuned based on (Masi, Tran, Hassner, Leksut, & Medioni, 2016) using CASIA data set (Yi et al., 2014). The data set originally has 400,000 training images with 10,575 subjects. In (Masi et al., 2016), the data augmentation method was to synthesize new faces based on the given data set with variations: poses, shapes, and expression. Finally, when including augmented images, there are 2 million images. ResNet101 was constructed based on all augmented data.

To utilize these pretrained models, transfer learning is a common approach that transfers the knowledge from the source model to the target model (Torrey & Shavlik, 2009). For image applications, image features such as edges, shapes are learned in the early fully connected layers. They are used in the later fully connected layers which are supposed to be fine-tuned for specific tasks. It is useful when the new data set is smaller than the original ones and when the nature of target images are closed to the source images. The closer they are, the fewer tuned layers there should be. The small learning rate should be used for pretrained models so as not to skipping unlearned features.

EXPERIMENTS

Our objectives of the study is to explore 1) accuracy of various pretrained models against different data sets 2) effect of fine tuning weights of various layers towards the accuracy convergence and 3) minimizing or changing the number of layers in a network against the accuracy.

Figure 2 shows the methodology for exploring the accuracy. The face data sets are varied as well as the models. The preprocessing for the data sets is the downloading the image data sets from original sources, and crop only faces using a face detection approach. Then, we gather images into one folder and labeling the image IDs and image numbers. Only faces in the images are cropped and are resized into 256 × 256 and are put in Lightning Memory-Mapped Database (LMDB) format in a form of (image,label). Then, the preprocessed images are used for training using Caffe 0.15.14 on Intel i5-4460, 3.2GHz with 32G memory and two NVIDIA GTX 1080. The data sets are divided into 50% training and testing. The images are shuffle and randomly selected as training / testing sets. The accuracy is measured by the number of images that are identified correctly. The pretrained weights are downloaded from the original site: AlexNet, CaffeNet, GoogLeNet (https://github.com/BVLC/caffe/wiki/Model-Zoo), SqueezeNet (https://github.com/DeepScale/SqueezeNet).

We use the default solver files that comes with the pretrained models in the model zoo. We set $\gamma=0.1$, momentum=0.9, learning rate = [0.0001,0.01] depending on the network types. The small learning rate converges to good accuracy slowly and does not give significant accuracy improvement when compared to bigger learning rate. If the divergence occurs, reducing learning rate may make the divergence happen slower and we may reach the optimal loss. The number of maximum iterations is set to 200,000. We may stop earlier if the loss does not seem to decrease further.

The following subsection reports the numerical results in the aspect of accuracy, fine tuning options, data size, and training time.

Various Network Comparison

First, the studied nets with pretrained weights on Caffe Model Zoo that are easy to train are such as: AlexNet, CaffeNet, GoogLeNet, SqueezeNet.

Figure 2. Methodology for measurement

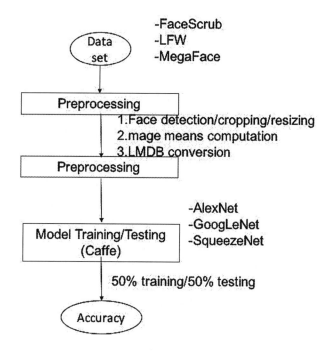

Table 1 compares these net layers. GoogLeNet is the most complex which contains more number of convolutions including inception layers. AlexNet and CaffeNet have fewer convolution layers. SqueezeNet has 26 convolution layers and ReLU (Rectified Linear Unit) and the last layer is also a convolution layer.

Accuracy, Size, Time

Table 2 shows the training accuracy for FaceScrub, CASIA, MegaFace on AlexNet, SqueezeNet, CaffeNet, and GoogLeNet (all with pretrained weights). All images in the data set are used for training except for CASIA where we limit the number of training classes to 5,000 and MegaFace where we limit the number of training classes to 10,000 to save the training time. The testing set is selected randomly from 50% of the total images used for training. The pretrained weights are used in the training. These four nets can yield the accuracy reaching 1 while the other nets cannot give the good accuracy over 300,000

Table 1. Layers of different networks

Type	AlexNet	GoogLeNet	CaffeNet	SqueezeNet
Conv	5	59	5	26
InnerProd	3	5	3	-
Pooling	3	16	3	3
ReLU	7	61	7	2
LRN	2	2	2	-
Dropout	2	3	2	1

iterations. Both SqueezeNet and CaffeNet perform very well. They can reach accuracy of 0.99 within 1,000 and 2,000 iterations respectively for some data set while AlexNet and GoogLeNet can reach 0.99 and 0.98 in 10,000 and 20,000 iterations respectively.

Table 2 summarizes the highest training accuracy value achieved within 300,000 iterations and the iteration number in thousands to achieve such accuracy. AlexNet and SqueezeNet can give a high accuracy very fast while GoogLeNet can also perform well but with a slow rate for some data set.

Figure 3 shows the model size of the above networks (in caffemodel file) in Table 2. The model size is estimated by the number of parameters in the networks multiplied by the size of float. The size is measured by the model size given by Caffe snapshot. From the figure, SqueezeNet has the smallest size among all. Next, is GoogLeNet, and AlexNet/Caffe. GoogLeNet also utilizes the technique of factorization which results in many small matrices rather than few number of large matrices. Compared to the traditional model like Openface (Amos et al., 2016) using SVM or KNN classifiers, the model sizes of data set FaceScrub is over 20G which depend directly on the size of training subjects. AlexNet/CaffeNet has about the same size since the structure is the same except swapping order of layers.

In Table 3, Column ``mem'' presents the maximum memory estimated in Gigabyte for training and Column``Time(s)'' shows the training time (not including testing) per iteration each data set training. Each net consistently takes the memory about the same size for all data sets since mostly the memory usages depends on weight parameters. However, GoogLeNet consumes more memory than others. AlexNet, and CaffeNet consumes about the same memory. SqueezeNet has fewer number of parameters but takes more time per iteration due to the sequential nature of the models. Compared to the GoogLeNet, which has the training time per epoch is fast since its design is wider which can utilize the parallelism better.

Figure 3. Comparison of model sizes

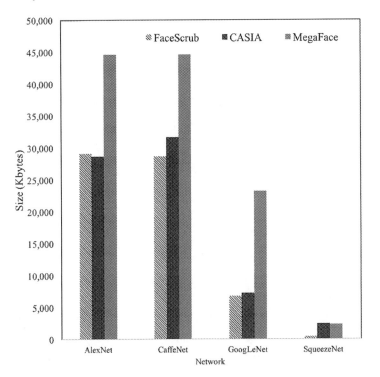

Table 2. Accuracy values of various nets

Net	LFW		CASIA		FaceScrub		MegaFace	
	Acc	Iter (K)	Acc	Iter (K)	Acc	Iter (K)	Acc	Iter (K)
AlexNet	0.99	9	0.99	9	0.99	2	0.99	8
CaffeNet	0.99	2	0.99	8	0.99	2	0.99	7
GoogLeNet	0.97	8	0.97	270	0.96	16	0.84	21
SqueezeNet	1.00	1	0.98	10	0.98	4	0.99	6

Table 3. Net memory and time per iteration

Net	LFW		CASIA		FaceScrub		MegaFace	
	Mem	Time(s)	Mem	Time(s)	Mem	Time(s)	Mem	Time(s)
AlexNet	0.53	0.25	0.53	0.26	0.55	0.25	0.54	0.29
CaffeNet	0.33	0.26	0.45	0.24	0.43	0.60	0.45	1.89
GoogLeNet	3.60	0.12	3.01	0.10	3.63	0.09	3.67	0.13
SqueezeNet	1.21	0.10	0.91	0.79	1.41	2.76	1.40	2.68

Fine Tuning Different Layers

Consider the default pretrained weights from CaffeModel zoo. We attempt to fine-tune AlexNet for MegaFace data set in the previous experiment for 20,000 iterations. The fine tune approach starts from the output layer. The output layers are fine tune to be the number of classes. We consider to omit the pretrained weight backwardly. In theory, the last layers correspond to the classification task and the previous last layers represent higher abstraction of the tasks.

For AlexNet, there are the last three fully connected layers, *fc6,fc7,fc8* as in Figure 4. We selectively tune from the last fully connected layers. The input image size we use is 256×256. First, we omit weights only *fc6,fc8*, called Alex-1. That is we do not use pretrained weights for them. Then in Alex-2, we also do not use the existing weight for *fc7*. In Alex-3, Alex-4, Alex-5, we do not use the pretrained weights for *conv5, conv4, conv3* respectively. The accuracy results are shown in the left side of Figure 6. It is shows that Alex-2 reaches the best accuracy fastest while Alex-1 does not improve an accuracy at all. Other cases improve the accuracy slower. Training from scratch (AlexNet) takes more time per training iteration (1.24 second/iteration) while using pretrained weights (5 cases), consumes 0.47 second/iteration.

Consider SqueezeNet. Fine tuning SqueezeNet has lots of design choices. SqueezeNet uses the convolution layer in place of the fully connected layer. It has 8 fire modules (*fire2,...fire9*) as in Figure 5. The fire module first squeezes the input using 1x1 filter and expand it. The expand step expands using two filter sizes, 1x1 and 3x3 (called expand1x1, expand3x3) in parallel and then concatenates both results. Each squeeze and expand layers are connected to ReLU.

Similarly, we start with using pretrained weights and omit the pretrained weight from the last layer, namely. We backwardly omit the pretrained weights for the next convolution layers, fire9/expand3x3, *fire9/expand1x1*[1] and obtain accuracy results as shown in the right graph of Figure 6. In the figure,

Figure 4. AlexNet structure: Fine tuning at FC6,FC7, FC8

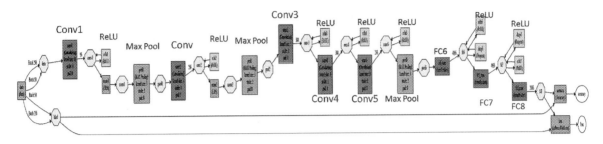

Figure 5. SqueezeNet structure: Fine tuning at Fire9

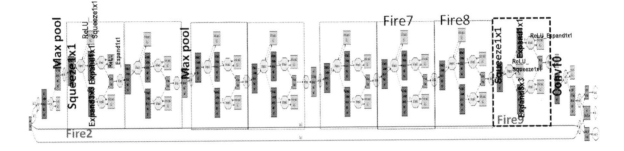

Figure 6. Fine tuning AlexNet and SqueezeNet towards MegaFace

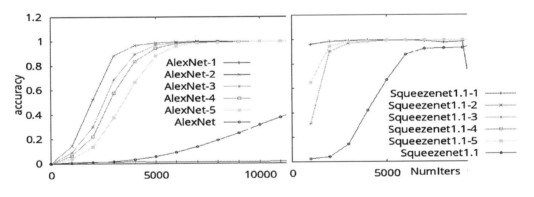

Squeeze1.1-1 is where we omit the pretrained weights for only *conv10*. Squeeze1.1-2 is where we also omit the pretrained weights: *fire9/expand3x3* and *conv10*. Squeeze1.1-4 is where we omit the pretrained weights: *fire9/expand1x1, fire9/expand3x3* and *conv10*. Squeeze1.1-3 is where we omit the pretrained weights: *fire9/relu_expand1x1, fire9/expand1x1, fire9/expand3x3* and conv*10*. Squeeze1.1-5 is where we omit these pretrained weights: *fire9/squeeze1x1_tune, fire9/relu_squeeze1x1, fire9/relu_expand1x1, fire9/expand1x1, fire9/expand3x3* and *conv_10*, and Squeeze1.1 is where the pretrained weight is not applied respectively. When the fewer pretrained weights of layers are used, the more time it takes to train and the slower it converges to the better accuracy. When we do not use pretrained weights, more GPU memory is needed. We need to reduce batch size to 1/3 in order to fit the data in GPU memory.

Customizing Layers

We present the customization of SqueezeNet1.1 which intends to explore the possible layers and fire modules skipping to shorten the network and the resulting accuracy. The new network may give the equivalent accuracy and has a small size. The original SqueezeNet model downloaded from https://github.com/DeepScale/SqueezeNet contains 8 fire modules connected as shown in Figure 7 (original). The simple tuning is imitated from bypassing where we rather select to skip some firing modules instead (Figure 4). On the right hand side of the figure, like complex bypassing, we replace some fire modules with simple 1x1 convolution (Iandola et al., 2016).

Table 4 shows the inclusion of modules for each net, where `x' refers to include the fire module in the net. Fire modules that were not mentioned are kept for all cases. Figure 8 presents the example of skipping: SqueezeNet1.1-bp1, SqueezeNet1.1-bp2 in Table 4.

Figure 7. SqueezeNet modules and different skipping and replacing fire modules (Iandola et al., 2016)

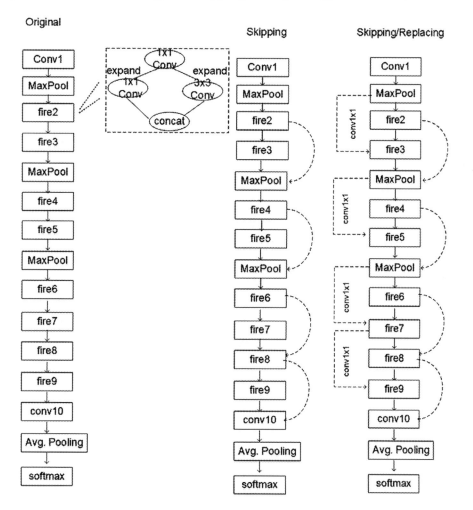

Figure 8. SqueezeNet1.1 with simple skipping examples

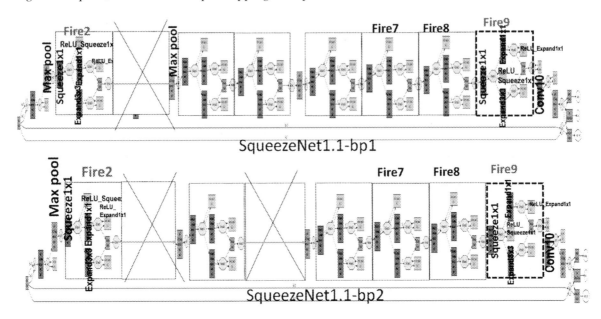

Table 4. SqueezeNet1.1 with simple skipping fire modules. (x: denote inclusion)

Net Types	Fire3	Fire5	Fire7	Fire9
SqueezeNet1.1	x	x	x	x
SqueezeNet1.1-bp1		x	x	x
SqueezeNet1.1-bp2			x	x
SqueezeNet1.1-bp3				x
SqueezeNet1.1-bp4			x	
SqueezeNet1.1-bp5				
SqueezeNet1.1-bp6	x	x	x	
SqueezeNet1.1-bp7	x	x		
SqueezeNet1.1-bp8	x			
SqueezeNet1.1-bp9		x		x
SqueezeNet1.1-bp10	x			x
SqueezeNet1.1-bp11		x	x	
SqueezeNet1.1-bp12		x		x
SqueezeNet1.1-bp13	x		x	x
SqueezeNet1.1-bp14	x		x	
SqueezeNet1.1-bp15	x	x		x

Table 5. SqueezeNet1.1 with skipping and replacing fire modules

Net Types	Replace with conv1x1			
	Fire2	Fire4	Fire6	Fire8
SqueezeNet1.1-bp16	x			
SqueezeNet1.1-bp17	x	x		
SqueezeNet1.1-bp18	x	x	x	
SqueezeNet1.1-bp19	x	x	x	x

Figure 9. SqueezeNet1.1-bp5 and replacing with conv1x1 becomes SqueezeNet1.1-bp16

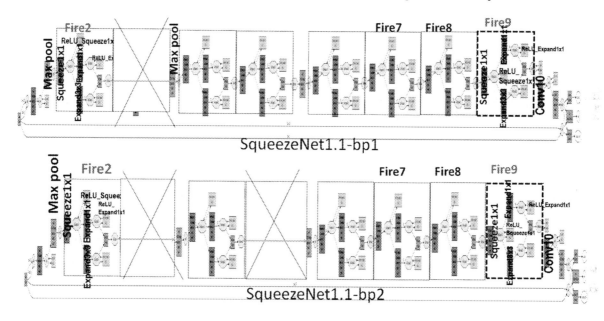

From Figure 8, consider ``SqueezeNet1.1-bp5'' which should have the smallest number of parameters in the group of simple skipping. Then we perform replacing the fire modules as in Column ``Replace with *conv1x1*'' with *conv1x1* one by one as in Table 5. When considering the possibility of replacing the Fire module with *conv1x1*, ``SqueezeNet1.1-bp19'' should have the least number of parameters. Figure 10 shows the number of parameters on different combination of skipping and replacing. The number of parameters is calculated by the number of weights used in each model using Caffe. This supports our guess on the model sizes.

Figure 11 presents the accuracy of these customized nets. We tested against MegaFace data set used in the previous section. ``SqueezeNet1.1-bp6'' converges the fastest. When sorted from smallest to largest number of parameters, it has the least 12th number of parameters. Actually, these nets perform about the same except that the shorter ones give a slower convergence. Thus, using this approach, we can find that ``SqueezeNet1.1-bp5'' and its variations are also good choices.

Figure 10. Various SqueezeNet1.1 parameters for simple skipping and skipping/replacing

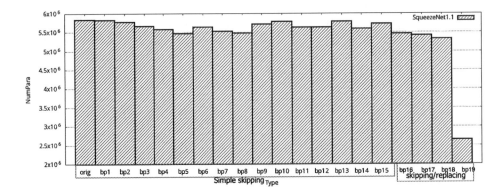

Figure 11. Accuracy of different customization

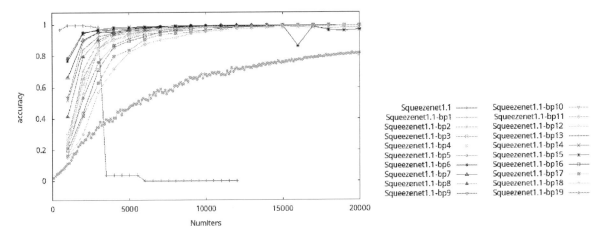

CONCLUSION AND FUTURE WORK

In this chapter, we consider the performance of various CNNs and their customization approaches towards the model size, against face recognition tasks. The experiment methodology is demonstrated in order to compare the model size and accuracy of various off-the-shelf CNN for this task. The focused pretrained models are SqueezeNet, AlexNet, and GoogLeNet. Caffe framework is used to perform the experiments and the training/testing accuracy are measured. The model size is measured from the size of the snapshot saved.

From the study, SqueezeNet is a smaller net compared to AlexNet and GoogLeNet which gives comparable performances. The size is only around 5%-25% of these nets. Depending on the network design, the deep network with smaller number of parameters may result in a slow training iteration. The deep network such as SqueezeNet has smaller parameters but takes more time per iteration for training compared to GoogLeNet and AlexNet. The results of the customizing the number of layers of SqueezeNet shows that we can obtain the smaller size with similar accuracy. However, there is a tradeoff with the convergence time. It is possible to replace with fire modules with the convolution layer (1x1) makes the network smaller but takes longer time to train due to the fewer reuse of pretrain weights.

In the future work, the customizing with various loss functions improve the accuracy and training convergence will be studied.

ACKNOWLEDGMENT

The work was supported in part by Office of Higher Education Commission and Royal Thai Army Research and Development.

REFERENCES

Amos, B., Ludwiczuk, B., & Satyanarayanan, M. (2016). *OpenFace: A general- purpose face recognition library with mobile applications (Tech. Rep.). CMU-CS-16-118.* CMU School of Computer Science.

Celebi, M. E., & Smolka, B. (2016). Labeled faces in the wild: A survey. In M. Kawulok (Ed.), *Advances in face detection and facial image analysis* (pp. 189–248). Springer.

Cheng, Y., Wang, D., Zhou, D., & Zhang, T. (2017). A Survey of Model Compression and Acceleration for Deep Neural Networks. *IEEE Signal Processing Magazine.* Retrieved from https://arxiv.org/pdf/1710.09282.pdf

Dlib. (n.d.). *Dlib C++ library.* Retrieved from http://dlib.net/

Girshick, R. B. (2015). *Fast R-CNN.* CoRR, abs/1504.08083. Retrieved from http://arxiv.org/abs/1504.08083

Guo, Y., Zhang, L., Hu, Y., He, X., & Gao, J. (n.d.). *MS-Celeb-1M: a dataset and benchmark for large-scale face recognition.* Retrieved from https://arxiv.org/abs/1607.08221

Han, S., Mao, S., & Dally, W. J. (2016). Deep compression: Compressing deep neural networks with pruning, trained quantization and Huffman coding. *International Conference on Learning Representations (ICLR).*

Howard, A. (2017). MobileNets: Efficient Convolutional Neural Networks for Mobile Vision Applications. *CVPR.* Retrieved from https://arxiv.org/abs/1704.04861

Huang, T., Xiong, Z., & Zhang, Z. (2011). Face recognition applications. In *Handbook of face recognition* (pp. 617–638). London: Springer London. doi:10.1007/978-0-85729-932-1_24

Iandola, F. N., Moskewicz, M. W., Ashraf, K., Han, S., Dally, W. J., & Keutzer, K. (2016). *SqueezeNet: AlexNet-level accuracy with 50x fewer parameters and <1MB model size.* CoRR, abs/1602.07360. Retrieved from http:// arxiv.org/abs/1602.07360

Jain, V., & Learned-Miller, E. (2010). *Fddb: A benchmark for face detection in unconstrained settings* (Tech. Rep. No. UM-CS-2010-009). University of Massachusetts, Amherst.

Jia, Y., Evan, S., Donahue, J., Karayev, S., Long, J., Girshick, R., & Darrell, T. (2014). *Caffe: Convolutional architecture for fast feature embedding.* arXiv preprint arXiv:1408.5093

Kemelmacher-Shlizerman, I., Seitz, S. M., Miller, D., & Brossard, E. (2016). The Megaface benchmark: 1 million faces for recognition at scale. In *Proceedings of the IEEE conference on computer vision and pattern recognition* (pp. 4873–4882). IEEE. 10.1109/CVPR.2016.527

Krizhevsky, A., Sutskever, I., & Hinton, G. E. (2012). ImageNet classification with deep convolutional neural networks. In F. Pereira, C. J. C. Burges, L. Bottou, & K. Q. Weinberger (Eds.), *Advances in neural information processing systems 25* (pp. 1097–1105). Curran Associates, Inc. Retrieved from http://papers.nips.cc/paper/4824-imagenet-classification -with-deep-convolutional-neural-networks.pdf

Lapuschkin, S., Binder, A., Mller, K.-R., & Samek, W. (2017). *Understanding and comparing deep neural networks for age and gender classification.* Retrieved from https://arxiv.org/abs/1708.07689

Lin, M., Chen, Q., & Yan, S. (2013). *Network in network.* CoRR, abs/1312.4400. Retrieved from http://arxiv.org/abs/1312.4400

Masi, I., Tran, A., Hassner, T., Leksut, J. T., & Medioni, G. (2016). Do We Really Need to Collect Millions of Faces for Effective Face Recognition? *European conference on computer vision.* 10.1007/978-3-319-46454-1_35

Ng, H. W., & Winkler, S. (2014, Oct). A data-driven approach to cleaning large face datasets. In *2014 IEEE international conference on image processing (ICIP)* (pp. 343-347). IEEE.

OPENCV. (n.d.). *Face detection using HAAR cascades.* Retrieved from https:// docs.opencv.org/3.4.1/d7/d8b/tutorial_py_face detection.html

Parkhi, O. M., Vedaldi, A., & Zisserman, A. (2015). *Deep face recognition.* Retrieved from https://www.robots.ox.ac.uk/~vgg/publications/2015/Parkhi15/parkhi15.pdf

Shaoqing, R., Kaiming, H., Ross, G., & Jian, S. (2015). Faster R-CNN: Towards real-time object detection with region proposal networks. In *Proceedings of the 28th international conference on neural information processing systems* (pp. 91–99). Cambridge, MA: MIT Press.

Simonyan, K., & Zisserman, A. (2014). *Very deep convolutional networks for large-scale image recognition.* CoRR, abs/1409.1556

Sun, X., Wu, P., & Hoi, S. C. H. (2017). *Face detection using deep learning: An improved faster RCNN approach.* CoRR, abs/1701.08289. Retrieved from http://arxiv.org/abs/1701.08289

Szegedy, C., Liu, W., Jia, Y., Sermanet, P., Reed, S. E., Anguelov, D., . . . Rabinovich, A. (2014). *Going deeper with convolutions.* CoRR, abs/1409.4842. Retrieved from http://arxiv.org/abs/1409.4842

Thomee, B., Shamma, D. A., Friedland, G., Elizalde, B., Ni, K., Poland, D., . . . Li, L. (2015). *The new data and new challenges in multimedia research.* CoRR, abs/1503.01817. Retrieved from http://arxiv.org/abs/1503.01817

Torrey, L., & Shavlik, J. (2009). Transfer learning. In E. Soria, J. Martin, R. Magdalena, M. Martinez, & A. Serrano (Eds.), *Handbook of research on machine learning applications.* IGI Global. Retrieved from ftp://ftp.cs.wisc.edu/machine-learning/shavlik -group/torrey.handbook09.pdf

Wen, Y., Zhang, K., Li, Z., & Qiao, Y. (2016). A discriminative feature learning approach for deep face recognition. In *European conference on computer vision* (pp. 499–515). Academic Press. 10.1007/978-3-319-46478-7_31

Yang, S., Luo, P., Loy, C. C., & Tang, X. (2016). Wider face: A face detection benchmark. In *IEEE conference on computer vision and pattern recognition.* CVPR. doi:10.1109/CVPR.2016.596

Yi, D., Lei, Z., Liao, S., & Li, S. Z. (2014). *Learning face representation from scratch.* CoRR, abs/1411.7923. Retrieved from http://arxiv.org/abs/1411.7923

Yosinski, J., Clune, J., Bengio, Y., & Lipson, H. (2014). *How transferable are features in deep neural networks?* CoRR, abs/1411.1792. Retrieved from http://arxiv.org/abs/1411.1792

Zhang, K., Zhang, Z., Li, Z., & Qiao, Y. (2016). *Joint face detection and alignment using multi-task cascaded convolutional networks.* CoRR, abs/1604.02878. Retrieved from http://arxiv.org/abs/1604.02878

ADDITIONAL READING

Amos, B. (2016). OpenFace. https://cmusatyalab.github.io/openface/

An, G., Kazuko, O., Satoru, T., ... (2018). Comparison of Machine-Learning Classification Models for Glaucoma Management. Journal of Healthcare Engineering. Vol. 2018. Article ID. 6874765, 8 pages. doi:10.1155/2018/6874765

Goodfellow, I., Bengio, Y., & Courville, A. (2016). Deep learning. MIT Press. Retrieved from https://arxiv.org/abs/1512.03385. (Accessed: 25 August 2018)

He, K., Zhang, X., Ren, S., & Sun, J. (2015). Deep Residual Learning for Image Recognition. CoRR, abs/ 1512.03385. Retrieved from http://arxiv.org/abs/1512.03385 (Accessed: 25 June 2018)

Szeliski, R. (2010). *Computer Vision: Algorithms and Applications.* Springer.

Zhang, K., Zhang, Z., Li, Z., & Qiao, Y. (2016). Joint face detection and alignment using multi-task cascaded convolutional networks. CoRR, abs/1604.02878. Retrieved from http://arxiv.org/abs/1604.02878. https://github.com/kpzhang93/MTCNN_face_detection_alignment (Accessed: 25 June 2018)

KEY TERMS AND DEFINITIONS

Eigenface: A principal components of a distribution of faces (eigenvectors). It is a covariance of matrix of the set of face images.

Fire Module: The sequence of layers that perform 1) squeezing by using conv1x1, 2) expanding into conv1x1 and conv3x3, and 3) concatenating them.

Keypoints: Points in an image that are interesting. They do not change when they are applied affine transformation.

SIFT Transform: Scale-invariant feature transform. It is a kind of transformation which is used to find local features such as keypoints which tolerate to operations such as rotate and scale operations.

ENDNOTE

[1]   Expand3x3 and expand1x1 layers of fire9 module.

Chapter 4
Application of Deep Learning in Speech Recognition

Rekh Ram Janghel
NIT Raipur, India

Satya Prakash Sahu
NIT Raipur, India

Yogesh Kumar Rathore
NIT Raipur, India

Shraddha Singh
NIT Raipur, India

Urja Pawar
NIT Raipur, India

ABSTRACT

Speech is the vocalized form of communication used by humans and some animals. It is based upon the syntactic combination of items drawn from the lexicon. Each spoken word is created out of the phonetic combination of a limited set of vowel and consonant speech sound units (phonemes). Here, the authors propose a deep learning model used on tensor flow speech recognition dataset, which consist of 30 words. Here, 2D convolutional neural network (CNN) model is used for understanding simple spoken commands using the speech commands dataset by tensor flow. Dataset is divided into 70% training and 30% testing data. While running the algorithm for three epochs average accuracy of 92.7% is achieved.

DOI: 10.4018/978-1-5225-7862-8.ch004

INTRODUCTION

Speech is "the vocalized form of communication used by humans and some animals, which is based upon the syntactic combination of items drawn from the lexicon. Each spoken word is created out" of the phonetic combination of a limited set of vowel and consonant speech sound units (phonemes). The 30 words included in the database differ from person-to-person such that their accent, their speaking frequency differentiates one person from the other. Speech recognition is the inter-disciplinary sub-field of computational linguistics. It develops methodologies and technologies that enable the recognition and translation of spoken language into text by computers shown in Figure 1.

It is also known as "automatic speech recognition" (ASR), "computer speech recognition", or just "speech to text" (STT). It incorporates knowledge and research in the linguistics, computer science, and electrical engineering fields."

The "spectrogram is a basic tool in audio spectral analysis and other fields. It has been applied extensively in speech analysis (Deller, Proakis & Hansen, 1993; Schafer & Markel, 1979). The spectrogram can be defined as an intensity plot (usually on a log scale, such as dB) of the Short-Time Fourier Transform (STFT) magnitude. The STFT is simply a sequence of FFTs of windowed data segments, where the windows are usually allowed to overlap in time, typically by 25-50% (Allen & Rabiner, 1977). It is an important representation of audio data because human hearing is based on a kind of real-time spectrogram encoded by the cochlea of the inner ear (O'Shaughnessy, 1987). The spectrogram has been used extensively in the field of computer music as a guide during the development of sound synthesis algorithms. When working with an appropriate synthesis model, matching the spectrogram often corresponds to" matching the sound extremely well. In fact, spectral modeling synthesis (SMS) is based on synthesizing the short-time spectrum directly by some means (Zölzer, 2002).

Fast "Fourier Transform (FFT)-based computations are more accurate than the other slow transforms as the functions applied are different in FFT. Discrete Fourier transforms computed through the FFT are more accurate than slow transforms and the convolutions computed with the help of FFT are more accurate than the directly acquired results." Nonetheless, these results are critically dependent on the employed FFT software's accuracy, which should generally be considered suspect. Due to inherent instability, some popular recursions for fast computation of trigonometric table (or twiddle factors) are inaccurate. FFT is highly stable even in the higher dimensions (Schatzman, 1996).

Mel frequency cepstral coefficient (MFCC) has become a standard speech recognition system and is most popular due to the high efficiency of computation schemes available for it and due to its robustness in the presence of different types of noises. In the computation process of MFCC, we pass the voice signal through various triangular filters. These triangular filters are placed in a perceptual Mel scale linearly

Figure 1. Voice recognition

Analog voice   Analog to Digital Conversion   Pattern Recognisation

(Sahidullah & Saha, 2012). In speech recognition, the mel-frequency cepstrum is very effective and also helps to model the subjective pitch and frequency components of the audio signals (Xu et al., 2004).

There are so many applications of speech recognition like in-car systems, healthcare, Therapeutic use, Military- High-performance fighter aircraft, helicopters, Telephony and other domains and education systems as shown in Figure 2.

LITERATURE REVIEW

For speech recognition using deep learning may perform better by using combined features of recurrent neural network and convolution neural network (Saon & Picheny, 2017). Some of the researcher suggested to use convolution neural network of 5 layer to normalize variations in voice, to increase the recognition capability (Guiming et al., 2016). Some researcher suggested convolution neural network and weight sharing technique for better feature extraction from speech (Abdel-Hamid et al., 2014). Some other methodologies used by different authors are shown in Table 1

Table 1 shows the basic methodology and limitation of existing methods

METHODS AND MATERIALS

Tensor Flow Library

Tensor Flow is "an open-source software library for dataflow programming across a range of tasks. It is a symbolic math library, and also used for machine learning applications such as neural networks. It is" used for both research and production at Google,replacing its closed-source predecessor, Dist Belief.

ALGORITHM

Dataset Investigation

See Figure 3.

Figure 2. Speech recognition model

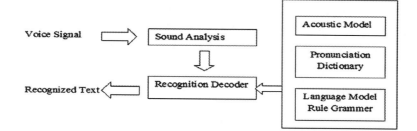

Table 1. Review of literatures

S.No.	Reference	Methodology	Description
1.	Castro Martinez et al., 2017	DNN-HMM	Auditory-based Gabor features for deep learning in robust speech recognition
2.	Fayek et al., 2017	UAR, LSTM-RNN	Deep learning architectures evaluation for Speech Emotion Recognition
3.	Xiao et al., 2016	RNN	"Speech dereverberation for enhancement and recognition using dynamic features constrained deep neural networks and feature adaptation"
4.	Mimura et al., 2015	DNN-HMM, DAE	"Reverberant speech recognition combining deep neural networks and deep autoencoders augmented with a phone-class feature."
5.	Yin et al., 2015	DNN	Noisy training for deep neural networks in speech recognition
6.	Pironkov et al., 2015	MTL	Investigating the Impact of the Training Data Volume for Robust Speech Recognition using Multi-Task Learning
7.	Hinton et al., 2015	DBN-DNN	Deep Neural Network for acoustic modelling in Speech Recognition
8.	Deng et al., 2013	RNN	Recent advances in deep learning for apeech research at Microsoft
9.	Dahl, et al., 2012	DNN-HMM	Context-Dependent Pre-Trained Deep Neural Networks for Large-Vocabulary Speech Recognition
10.	Deng et al., 2013	DNN	New types of deep neural network learning for speech recognition and related applications: an Overview

Figure 3. Flow diagram of dataset investigation

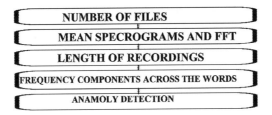

Visualization of the Recordings

There are two theories of a human hearing - place (frequency-based) and temporal. In speech recognition, there are two main tendencies - to input spectrogram (frequencies), and more sophisticated features MFCC - Mel-Frequency Cepstral Coefficients, PLP. You rarely work with raw, temporal data. We calculated the spectrogram and took logarithm of spectrogram values. It makes our plot much clearer, moreover, it is strictly connected to the way people hear. We need to assure that there should be no 0(zero) values as input to logarithm. Frequencies are in range (0, 8000) according to Nyquist theorem. If you use spectrogram as an input features for NN, you have to remember to normalize features shown in Figure 4. (you need to normalize over all the dataset).

Figure 4. Conversion of audio file to spectrogram of the sample "yes"

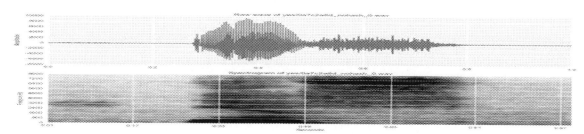

We have ~160 features for each frame, frequencies are between 0 and 8000. It means, that one feature corresponds to 50 Hz. However, frequency resolution of the ear is 3.6 Hz within the octave of 1000 – 2000 Hz It means, that people are far more precise and can hear much smaller details than those represented by spectrograms like above.

We calculated *Mel power spectrogram* and *MFCC* using for example *librosa* python package. In classical, but still state-of-the-art systems, *MFCC* or similar features are taken as the input to the system instead of spectrograms as shown in Figure 5. However, in end-to-end (often neural-network based) systems, the most common input features are probably raw spectrograms, or mel power spectrograms. For example, *MFCC* decorrelates features, but NNs deal with correlated features well. Then the spectrogram was plotted in 3D.

We consider that some *VAD* (Voice Activity Detection) will be really useful here. Although the words are short, there is a lot of silence in them. A decent *VAD* can reduce training size a lot, accelerating training speed significantly. We cut a bit of the file from the beginning and from the end.

Another way to reduce the dimensionality of our data is to resample recordings. The recording don't sound very natural, because they are sampled with 16k frequency, and we usually hear much more. However, the most speech related frequencies are presented in smaller band. That's why you can still understand another person talking to the telephone, where GSM signal is sampled to 8000 Hz. Summarizing, we could resample our dataset to 8k. We discarded some information that shouldn't be important and reduced the size of the data. Then we calculated FFT (Fast Fourier Transform) shown in Figure 6.

FFT looks different for every word. We could model each FFT with a mixture of Gaussian distributions. Some of them, however, look almost identical on FFT, like *stop* and *up*... But wait, they are still distinguishable when we look at spectrograms! High frequencies are earlier than low at the beginning of *stop* (probably *s*). That's why temporal component is also necessary. There is a Kaldi library, that can

Figure 5. Mel power spectrogram

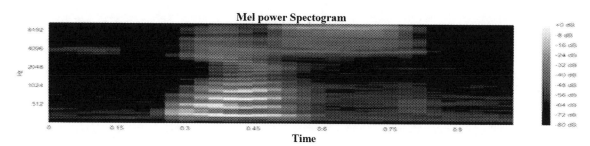

Figure 6. FFT of recording sampled with 8000 Hz

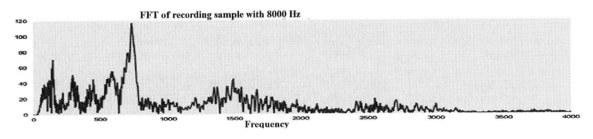

model words (or smaller parts of words) with GMMs and model temporal dependencies with Hidden Markov Models. Then we used PCA for dimensionality reduction as shown in Figure 7.

Convolutional Neural Network

Different phases of convolutional neural network are shown in Figure 8

Pseudo Code

```
input_shape: = (99, 81, 1)
nclass:= 30
BatchNormalization()
```

Figure 7. Flow diagram of data visualization process

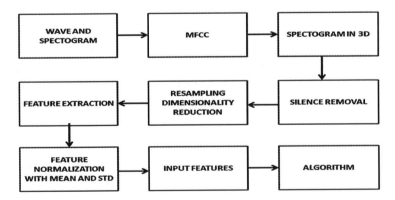

Figure 8. Convolutional neural network flow diagram

Convolution Layers

```
Convolution2D (filters:=8, kernel_size:=2, activation:=Relu)
Convolution2D (filters:=8, kernel_size:=2, activation:=Relu)
MaxPooling2D (pool_size:=(2, 2))
Dropout (rate=0.2)
Convolution2D (filters:=16, kernel_size:=3, activation:=Relu)
Convolution2D (filters:=16, kernel_size:=3, activation:=Relu)
MaxPooling2D (pool_size:=(2, 2))
Dropout (rate:=0.2)
Convolution2D (filters:=32, kernel_size:=3, activation:=Relu)
MaxPooling2D(pool_size:=(2, 2))
Dropout (rate:=0.2)
Flatten ()
```

Dense Layers

```
BatchNormalization() of Dense(128, activation:=Relu)
BatchNormalization() of (Dense(128, activation:=Relu)
Dense(activation:=Softmax)
Optimizers:=Adam()
Loss:=losses.binary_crossentropy
```

In CNN, we use multiple layers of convolution and max pooling layers. A convolution layer applies multiple filters which are processed on small local parts along whole input space. The maximum filter activation is taken by the max-pooling layer from various positions within a specific window and generates a lesser resolution version of convolution layer activations. This results in addition of translation invariance. It also adds tolerance to small differences of positions of the objects parts. Higher levels use broader filters working on lower resolution inputs to process more complex parts of input. Top fully connected layers then combine inputs from all positions to classify the whole set of inputs. CNN introduces three extra concepts over the simple fully connected feed-forward NN: local filters, max-pooling and weight sharing.

Max Pooling

The speech spectrum has many local structures which are distributed over a range of frequency axis where each local structure centers around one particular frequency varying within a limited range. The central frequencies of formants for the same characters may vary within a limited range, they differ between different speakers or different utterances from the same speaker. CNN removes the variability between speakers by the transformation of the speech features of each speaker into a canonical speaker space by using max-pooling where a max-pooling layer is added on top of each convolution layer (Abdel-Hamid et al., 2012)

These kinds of layers perform local temporal max operations over an input sequence. More formally, the transformation at frame t is written as (Palaz, Magimai-Doss & Collobert, 2015):

$$\max t - \frac{(kW-1)}{2} * s * t + \frac{(kW-1)}{2} * X^d * s \text{ for all d}$$

with x being the input, kW the kernel width and d the dimension.

Fully Connected Layers

Fully connected means each neuron in one layer is connected to every neuron in another layer of the model.

Weight Sharing

In CNN, weight sharing helps to reduce the number of trainable parameters. It may also lead to more efficient and effective training model when resembling local structures appear in multiple places in the input space. In speech signals, the local structures at different frequency bands might behave quite differently. So it's better to limit weight sharing to those local filters which are close to each other and that are pooled together in the max-pooling layer. Weight sharing can be applied only on the topmost pooling layer because the filters outputs in different pooling bands are unrelated.

Model Structure

CNN has one or more than one convolution pairs and max-pooling layers. The lowest layers process less number of input frequency bands to generate higher level representation with lower frequency resolution independently. In higher levels, the number of bands is less. The input given to each convolution layer is padded to make sure that both the first and the last input bands are processed by a suitable number of filters in the convolution layer. Generally, in CNN the top layers are fully connected like that in a normal feed-forward neural network and these top layers finally combine the different local structures extracted in the lower layers (Abdel-Hamid et al., 2012)

EXPERIMENTAL RESULTS

Dataset Description

Many voice recognition datasets require preprocessing before a neural network model can be built on them. Tensor Flow recently released the Speech Commands Datasets. It includes 65,000 one-second long utterances of 30 short words, by thousands of different people.

This is a set of one-second .wav audio files, each containing a single spoken English word. These words are from a small set of commands and are spoken by a variety of different speakers. The audio files are organized into folders based on the word they contain, and this data set is designed to help train simple machine learning models.

The audio files were collected using crowd sourcing. The goal was to gather examples of people speaking single-word commands, rather than conversational sentences, so they were prompted for individual words over the course of a five minute session. Twenty core command words were recorded, with most speakers saying each of them five times. The core words are "Yes", "No", "Up", "Down", "Left", "Right", "On", "Off", "Stop", "Go", "Zero", "One", "Two", "Three", "Four", "Five", "Six", "Seven", "Eight", and "Nine". To help distinguish unrecognized words, there are also ten auxiliary words, which most speakers only said once. These include "Bed", "Bird", "Cat", "Dog", "Happy", "House", "Marvin", "Sheila", "Tree", and "Wow".

- **Organizing:** The files are organized into folders, with each directory name labelling the word that is spoken in all the contained audio files.
- **Partitioning:** The audio clips haven't been separated into training, test, and validation sets explicitly, but by convention a hashing function is used to stably assign each file to a set.
- **Processing:** The data was captured in a variety of formats, for example Ogg Vorbis encoding for the web app, and then converted to a 16-bit little-endian PCM-encoded .wav file at a 16000 sample rate. The audio was then trimmed to a one second length to align most utterances, using the extract_loudest_section tool. The audio files were then screened for silence or incorrect words and arranged into folders by label as shown in Table 2.

Table 2. Tensorflow speech recognition dataset, number of files of each word

Words	No. of Files	Words	No. of Files
Zero	2376	Bed	1713
Bird	1731	Cat	1733
Dog	1746	Down	2359
Eight	2352	Five	2357
Four	2372	Go	2372
Happy	1742	House	1750
Left	2353	Marvin	1746
Nine	2364	No	2375
Off	2357	On	2367
One	2370	Right	2367
Sheila	1734	Seven	2377
Six	2369	Stop	2380
Three	2356	Tree	1733
Two	2373	Up	2375
Wow	1745	Yes	2377

Performance Measure

Train on 45304 Samples

Training details shown in Table 3 shows that where after each epoch loss and accuracy is recorded

Testing on 19417 Samples

Testing details shown in Table 4 shows that where after each epoch loss and accuracy is recorded

Comparison With Other Work

In all the works listed, Speech Commands Datasets released by Tensorflow is used. It includes 65,000 one-second long utterances of 30 short words, by thousands of different people.

Comparison with other existing method is shown in Table 4. The accuracy obtained is 92.79% on applying Convolutional Neural Network with all 30 words present in the Tensorflow dataset shown in Table5. The accuracy is obtained by applying pre-processing to the dataset such that the spectrogram and the length of recordings can be determined and can be accurately recognized. This result has been obtained by applying 5 covolution layer and 3 max pooling layer in particular combination. first 2 convolution layer contains 8 filters for feature extraction and next 2 convolution layer contains 16 filters for feature extraction and last convolution layer contains 32 filters. Whereas, max pooling layer has been applied after 2nd, 4th and 5th convolution layer.

The work helps us to recognize short words when spoken or written in text. This can help us to move further in the field of speech recognition where starting from short words paragraph can be generated such that this can be used in various applications now-a-days.

Table 3. Training details

Epoch	Loss(%)	Accuracy(%)
1	6.25	97.85
2	5.44	98.13
3	4.82	98.33

Table 4. Testing data details

Epoch	Loss(%)	Accuracy(%)
1	4.57	91.44
2	4.02	91.61
3	3.56	92.79

Table 5. Comparison with previous work

Literature	Model	Classes	Accuracy
M. Alzantot et al., 2018	GAN	10	89%
D. Harrison et al.,	CNN(16)	10	92%
Proposed work	CNN(5)	30	92.79%

CONCLUSION AND FURTHER WORK

In this work, we have used 2D Convolutional neural network (CNN) model for understanding simple spoken commands using the Speech Commands dataset by Tensor flow. We divided the dataset into 70% training and 30% testing data. We have taken all the 30 classes into consideration. The setup of CNN network contains total 5 convolution layer for feature extraction, 3 max pooling and dropout layers for feature reduction followed by one output layer. When we run the algorithm for 3 epochs, the accuracy of 92.79% has been obtained. For future work, we suggest the use of hybrid models like CNN and RNN together for better performance in recognition accuracy and to reduce the time complexity of this model, some different filters or different combination of convolution and max pooling layers may be applied in proposed CNN models.

REFERENCES

Abdel-Hamid, O., Mohamed, A., Jiang, H., Deng, L., Penn, G., & Yu, D. (2014). Convolutional Neural Networks for Speech Recognition. *IEEE/ACM Transactions on Audio, Speech, and Language Processing*, *22*(10), 1533–1545.

Abdel-Hamid, O., Mohamed, A. R., Jiang, H., & Penn, G. (2012). Applying convolutional neural networks concepts to hybrid NN-HMM model for speech recognition. *ICASSP, IEEE Int. Conf. Acoust. Speech Signal Process. - Proc.*, 4277–4280.

Allen, J. B., & Rabiner, L. R. (1977). A unified approach to short-time Fourier analysis and synthesis. *Proceedings of the IEEE*, *65*(11), 1558–1564. doi:10.1109/PROC.1977.10770

Alzantot, M., Balaji, B., & Srivastava, M. (2018). *Did you hear that? Adversarial Examples Against Automatic Speech Recognition*. Nips.

Castro Martinez, A. M., Mallidi, S. H., & Meyer, B. T. (2017). On the relevance of auditory-based Gabor features for deep learning in robust speech recognition. *Computer Speech & Language*, *45*, 21–38. doi:10.1016/j.csl.2017.02.006

Dahl, G. E., Yu, D., Deng, L., & Acero, A. (2012). Context-dependent pre-trained deep neural networks for large-vocabulary speech recognition. *IEEE Transactions on Audio, Speech, and Language Processing*, *20*(1), 30–42. doi:10.1109/TASL.2011.2134090

Deller, J. R. Jr, Proakis, J. G., & Hansen, J. H. (1993). *Discrete-time processing of speech signals*. New York: Macmillan.

Deng, L., Hinton, G. E., & Kingsbury, B. (2013) New types of deep neural network learning for speech recognition and related applications: An overview. *2013 IEEE Int. Conf. Acoust. Speech Signal Process*, 8599–8603. 10.1109/ICASSP.2013.6639344

Fayek, H. M., Lech, M., & Cavedon, L. (2017). Evaluating deep learning architectures for Speech Emotion Recognition. *Neural Networks*, *92*, 60–68. doi:10.1016/j.neunet.2017.02.013 PMID:28396068

Guiming, D., Xia, W., Guangyan, W., Yan, Z., & Dan, L. (2016). Speech recognition based on convolutional neural networks. *IEEE International Conference on Signal and Image Processing (ICSIP)*, 708-711. 10.1109/SIPROCESS.2016.7888355

Harrison, Spaeth, & Braun. (2007). *Speech Recognition: Key Word Spotting through Image Recognition*. Retrieved from http://ccrma.stanford.edu/~jos/mdft/

He, Y., Zhang, Z., Yu, F. R., Zhao, N., Yin, H., Leung, V. C. M., & Zhang, Y. (2017). Deep-reinforcement-learning-based optimization for cache-enabled opportunistic interference alignment wireless networks. *IEEE Transactions on Vehicular Technology*, *66*(11), 10433–10445. doi:10.1109/TVT.2017.2751641

Hinton, G., Deng, L., Yu, D., Dahl, G., Mohamed, A., Jaitly, N., ... Kingsbury, B. (2012). Deep neural networks for acoustic modeling in speech recognition: The shared views of four research groups. *Signal Processing*, *29*(6), 82–97. doi:10.1109/MSP.2012.2205597

Microsoft Corporation, . (2013). *Recent Advances in Deep Learning for Speech Research At Microsoft*. Author.

Mimura, M., Sakai, S., & Kawahara, T. (2015). Deep autoencoders augmented with phone-class feature for reverberant speech recognition. *ICASSP, IEEE Int. Conf. Acoust. Speech Signal Process. - Proc.*, 4365–4369.

O'Shaughnessy, D. (1987). *Speech Communication*. Reading, MA: Addison-Wesley.

Palaz, D., Magimai-Doss, M., & Collobert, R. (2015). *Analysis of CNN-based speech recognition system using raw speech as input*. Retrieved from: https://ronan.collobert.com/pub/matos/2015_cnnspeech_interspeech.pdf

Pironkov, G., Dupont, S., & Dutoit, T. (2017). Investigating the impact of the training data volume for robust speech recognition using multi-task learning. *2017 IEEE International Symposium on Signal Processing and Information Technology (ISSPIT)*. 10.1109/ISSPIT.2017.8388673

Sahidullah, M., & Saha, G. (2012). Design, analysis and experimental evaluation of block based transformation in MFCC computation for speaker recognition. *Speech Communication*, *54*(4), 543–565. doi:10.1016/j.specom.2011.11.004

Saon, G., & Picheny, M. (2017). Recent advances in conversational speech recognition using convolutional and recurrent neural networks. *IBM Journal of Research and Development*, *61*(4/5), 1:1–1:10. doi:10.1147/JRD.2017.2701178

Schafer, R. W., & Markel, J. D. (Eds.). (1979). Speech Analysis. New York: IEEE Press.

Xiao, X., Zhao, S., Nguyen, D.H.H., Zhong, X., Jones, D.L., Chng, E.S., & Li, H. (2016). Speech dereverberation for enhancement and recognition using dynamic features constrained deep neural networks and feature adaptation. *EURASIP J. Adv. Signal Process.*, *2016*(1), 1–18.

Xu, M., Duan, L., Cai, J., Chia, L., Xu, C., & Tian, Q. (2004) HMM-based audio keyword generation. *5th Pacific Rim Conf. Multimed,* 566–574.

Yin, S., Liu, C., Zhang, Z., Lin, Y., Wang, D., Tejedor, J., Zheng, T.F., & Li, Y. (2015). Noisy training for deep neural networks in speech recognition. *Eurasip J. Audio, Speech, Music Process.*, *2015*(1), 1–14.

Zölzer, U. (Ed.). (2002). DAFX--Digital Audio Effects. West Sussex, UK: John Wiley and Sons, LTD. Retrieved from http://www.dafx.de/

Chapter 5
Sensation of Deep Learning in Image Processing Applications

Ramgopal Kashyap
https://orcid.org/0000-0002-5352-1286
Amity University Chhattisgarh, India

ABSTRACT

This chapter will address challenges with IoT and machine learning including how a portion of the difficulties of deep learning executions while planning the arrangement and choice of right calculation. Existing research in deep learning and IoT was focused to find how garbage in will deliver waste out, which is exceptionally appropriate for the scope of the informational index for machine learning. The quality, sum, readiness, and choice of information are essential to the achievement of a machine learning arrangement. Consequently, this chapter aims to provide an overview of how the system can use technologies along with deep learning and challenges to realize the security challenges IoT can support. Even though calculations can work in any nonexclusive conditions, there are particular rules to determine which calculation would work best under which circumstances. How reinforcement learning deep learning is useful for IoT will also be covered in the chapter.

INTRODUCTION

In the previous years, profound fake neural systems have turned out to be particularly great for different machine learning assignments. Deep learning (DL) systems are as of now the best in class for different machine learning errands, for example, picture and discourse acknowledgment or normal dialect handling. While to a great degree skilled, they are additionally asset requesting, both to prepare and to assess. The majority of the examination on profound learning centers on preparing these profound models. Progressively, profound and complex systems are built to be more exact on different benchmark datasets. Urgent for preparing these enormous models are graphical handling units. Top of the line graphical processing units (GPUs) were once saved for 3-dimensional displaying and gaming however their parallel engineering makes them likewise amazingly appropriate for profound learning. Web of-Things have grown quick late years, which can associate distinctive gadgets to one another. These gadgets are typically inserted

DOI: 10.4018/978-1-5225-7862-8.ch005

with programming, sensors, hardware and some connective capacities. The vast majority of them are vitality controlled, which implies they have restricted execution and requires minimal effort and less vitality devouring. The IoT gadgets are utilized to gather and exchange information to fabricate the data organizes with the end goal to comprehend this crude information and get some important data from it to utilize the machine learning calculation. These days, machine adapting particularly the profound learning has turned into a well known field which can assist us with recognizing diverse examples in a more advantageous and quick way. In machine learning and subjective science, profound taking in calculation has created from the fundamental counterfeit neural systems and demonstrates to us an all the more incredible capacity on highlight extraction and picture acknowledgment and additionally a more smart mindfulness towards various self-governing frameworks. The time expected to prepare a profound neural system is by and large not extremely basic (Hong & Lee, 2013). The assessment of a prepared model, be that as it may, can be amazingly time touchy. At the point when the system is utilized to manage a robot or to decipher voice orders from a client, it ought to have the capacity to work progressively. Any deferral will bring about poor client encounter or perhaps in unsafe circumstances when a robot or automaton is included. While preparing the system is regularly done on an elite framework, once prepared, the system must be utilized as a part of a certifiable condition the assets accessible to frameworks in these situations are much more restricted.

In this chapter, main focus is in the center on picture order issues utilizing profound neural systems, the methods introduced here are, be that as it may, not restrict to this area but rather can be reached out to all profound learning grouping undertakings. Conceivable applications incorporate home computerization and security frameworks, savvy apparatuses, and family unit robots. The need to utilize profound neural systems on obliged gadgets that can't assess the whole system because of confinements in accessible memory, preparing force or battery limit. Current remote advancements are quick and sufficiently moderate to consider off-stacking every one of the calculations to a cloud back end as an answer. This obviously presents an additional dormancy (10– 500 ms) and makes the gadgets subject to the system association; this reliance might be unsuitable now and again.

In this chapter this strikes a center ground a neural system comprises of consecutive layers where each layer changes the yield from the past layer to a portrayal appropriate for the following layer. Each layer extricates more intricate highlights from its info the last layer utilizes the abnormal state highlights to arrange the info and misuse the characteristic consecutive plan of a neural system to empower an early-halting instrument to utilize the layers of a pre-trained arrange as stages in a course. Each layer can catch extra multifaceted nature yet additionally requires extra assets, for example, processing time and memory to store the parameters. Each stage groups the info and returns certainty esteem and stops the assessment of more profound layers once a specific required certainty edge is come to. The decision of this limit esteem enables us to exchange off precision and speed.

The idea of a falling system and the developing enthusiasm for the Internet of Things (IoT) and its subsidiary huge information require partners to plainly get it their definition, building squares, possibilities and difficulties. IoT what's more, enormous information have a two way relationship. On one hand, IoT is a primary maker of enormous information, and then again, it is a vital focus for huge information examination to enhance the procedures also, administrations of IoT (Sezer, Dogdu & Ozbayoglu, 2018). Additionally, IoT huge information examination has demonstrated to convey an incentive to the general public. For instance, it is revealed that, by recognizing harmed pipes and settling them, the Division of Park Management in Miami has spared about one million USD on their water bills. IoT information is unique in relation to the general enormous information (Gomes & Mayes, 2014). To better comprehend the necessities for IoT information examination, to investigate the properties of IoT information and how they are extraordinary from those of general enormous information. IoT information displays the accompanying qualities:

- **Large-Scale Streaming Data:** A heap of information catching gadgets are dispersed and conveyed for IoT applications, what's more, produce floods of information consistently. This prompts a tremendous volume of persistent information.
- **Heterogeneity**: Various IoT information securing gadgets assemble diverse data bringing about information heterogeneity.
- **Time and Space Relationship**: In the vast majority of IoT applications, sensor gadgets are appended to a particular area, and hence have an area and time-stamp for every one of the information things.
- **High Clamor Information:** Due to minor bits of information in IoT applications, a significant number of such information might be liable to blunders what's more, commotion amid securing and transmission. Despite the fact that getting concealed learning and data out of huge information is promising to improve the nature of our lives, it isn't a simple and direct assignment. For such a complex also, difficult assignment that goes past the abilities of the conventional derivation and learning approaches, new innovations, calculations, and foundations are required (Kashyap & Piersson, 2018). Fortunately, the ongoing advances in both quick processing and progressed machine learning strategies are opening the entryways for huge information investigation and learning extraction that is appropriate for IoT applications.

Past the huge information investigation, IoT information requires another new class of examination, to be specific quick and spilling information investigation, to bolster applications with rapid information streams and requiring time-touchy i.e., ongoing or close constant activities without a doubt, applications, for example, self-ruling driving, fire forecast, driver/elderly stance and in this manner awareness as well as wellbeing condition acknowledgment requests for quick handling of approaching information and speedy activities to accomplish their objective. A few scientists have proposed methodologies and systems for quick gushing information examination that use the capacities of cloud foundations and administrations that as it may, for the previously mentioned IoT applications among others, require quick examination in littler scale stages i.e., at the framework edge or even on the IoT gadgets themselves (Chae & Quick, 2014). For instance, self-ruling autos need to settle on quick choices on driving activities, for example, path or speed change. In reality, this sort of choices ought to be bolstered by quick investigation of potentially multi-modular information spilling from a few sources, including the various vehicle sensors e.g., cameras, radars, LIDARs, speedometer, left/right flags, and so on, correspondences from different vehicles, and movement substances (e.g., activity light, activity signs) for this situation, exchanging information to a cloud server for investigation and returning back the reaction is liable to inactivity that could cause petty criminal offenses or mishaps. A more basic situation would distinguish walkers by such vehicles. Exact acknowledgment ought to be performed in strict ongoing to forestall lethal mishaps. These situations suggest that quick information investigation for IoT must be near or at the wellspring of information to evacuate pointless and restrictive correspondence delays.

Better utilization of profound learning for distinguishing steering assaults that objective to IoT. Before giving data about DL, Machine learning (ML) ought to be disclosing to all the more likely get it DL. Since, ML can be viewed as the progenitor of DL.

MACHINE LEARNING

Machine learning is one of the pathways in driving Artificial Intelligence (AI) inquiring about. Fame of ML originates from two reasons or two undertaking must be finished by ML. First the undertaking that should be possible by machines, second the errand that can't be performed by people. Learning movement becomes a force to be reckoned with to be savvy what eludes a framework has capacity staying aware of changes of its condition. On the off chance that a framework can accord to the changes, this capacity can assist it with surviving. ML examines are put at the intersection territory of insights, computer science and engineering, it can likewise give answers for different controls. Since use of ML relies upon utilizing information that can be from back, geosciences or prehistoric studies. ML additionally delivers data from the information with the end goal that PCs utilize information while taking a shot at a procedure yet the information, typically, is useless from human point of view (Campbell & Ying, 2011) to take care of deterministic issues effortlessly for instance, a product to control lighting framework in a brilliant home can complete a decent work constantly, utilizing the action and sunshine. Yet, there are loads of non-deterministic issues that don't have enough data about or power and time to tackle to require measurements for taking care of these sorts of issues for example; demonstrating the dread of people against unforeseen circumstance is so difficult without measurements. Essentially, measurement manufactures numerical models and ML trains them. Starting here of view, ML has fundamentally the same as importance with traditional programming (Li, Ota & Dong, 2018). This depiction have less demanding to see the effect between traditional programming and ML; a established program is sustained by information and manage as an info which change the appropriate response as an yield after the procedure, in the complexity, a ML calculation is nourished by information and reply, which is relied upon to comprehend the connection between them. This relationship can be utilized as a part of various types of information to assess their yields.

In ML, there isn't any express programming, it ought to be called 'preparing' as a result of the learning process. ML framework does not do anything with the exception of investigating the factual structure of given information. For instance, which is significant with the following assignment, the genuine information? For instance, somebody, who suppose is our questioning Thomas, needs to know the reason for a specific movement that occurs in the evening around his home (Ksiezopolski, 2012). He puts reconnaissance cameras to specific purposes of his home and one of the vital highlights of the cameras is taking photographs and sparing them on the PC when they distinguish any movement with their sensors that as it may, the security arrangement of the house is extremely monotonous and exhausting, in light of the fact that the proprietor of the home needs to check all the photographs, of the previous evening, each day to be fulfilled about his home's security. On the off chance that wishes to set up a superior framework, it needs to caution Thomas when a genuine danger happens. The framework shouldn't give an alert when the night action happens on account of a feline or squirrel. Along these lines can give loads of cases of pictures to ML calculation, that are as of now labeled previously, called target variable, previously.

These objective factors incorporate the highlights, case pictures, called preparing set, incorporate objects of people, felines, leaf and so forth. At that point, the ML calculation learns measurable guidelines for corresponding clear picture to distinct labels and the yield is a ML show that points to recognize night action. At last, the framework breaks down throughout the night movement for every day over taken pictures and if there is a suspicious movement of intrigue, it gives a notice or an alarm, as our questioning Thomas needed from the earliest starting point. A few specialists think about on ML process in two sections; the adapting part and the inducing part. As specified previously, the adapting part is bolstering the ML calculation with the preparation set and the gathering part is making expectations about the reason for action by the framework (Ksiezopolski, 2012). Managed learning and unsupervised learning are fundamental kinds of ML, first of them are exist by utilizing completely named dataset while other one are exist completely unlabelled dataset. In managed taking in, the model gets datasets which incorporates a few highlights vectors and names that are the relating yields of highlight vectors. Consequently the model figures out how to deliver adjust yields because of given new information. Order and relapse are most famous result of regulated learning. In unsupervised taking in, the other path round, there is no chief who supplies the marks that incorporate right consequence of comparing contribution, to prepare the models (Li, Ota & Dong, 2018). So the display has just information esteems, watches the consequences of its activity. In the other alluding, unsupervised learning is an undertaking to depict concealed examples from input information. Grouping and dimensionality diminishment are two basic unsupervised learning illustrations.

Deep Learning

Profound learning is a sort of Neural Networks (NN) preparing and has NN design contrast between 'old fashioned' NN and profound learning is that DL has many concealed layers. DL additionally takes in the highlights itself, which empowers the learning procedure to be more precise and furthermore it is appeared to be more productive and exact than shallow learning. DL has achieved accomplishment in the PC vision, design acknowledgment, picture and sound handling. It additionally empowered noteworthy change for arrangement and forecast issues. Complex profound neural calculations are prepared with the utilization of ground-breaking GPUs. For AI, DL speaks to the best in class, additionally to deal with big data particularly in regards to versatility and speculation. In directed learning, there are three kinds of datasets. In the first place, preparing set is one of the key terms of learning process. It is an empowering influence for learning calculation to be managed furthermore; it contains the normal outcomes under the name highlight (Vu et al., 2018). The weights of the interior layers of NN are re-solved in light of the information and their normal outcomes. What's more, ideal weights are acquired. Another term is approval set that helps the learning procedure for tuning the parameters of capacities to get ideal weights. At long last, the test set is utilized for assessing the execution of preparing process. Before beginning the learning procedure, the dataset is isolated into the preparation set and the testing set, that approval dataset is part from the preparation set. While setting up the neural system calculation, ages are utilized as learning time. One age implies the preparation set is gone through the system totally; NN preparing calculations plan to decide the 'best' conceivable arrangement of weight values for the issue under thought. Of course, deciding the ideal arrangement of weight is regularly an exchange off between limiting the system mistake, calculation time and keeping up the system's capacity to sum up.

Deep Learning Model

Two imperative upgrades over the customary machine learning approaches in the two periods of preparing and expectation to begin with, they diminish the need for hand created and designed capabilities to be utilized for the preparation. Subsequently, a few highlights that may not be evident to a human view can be removed effectively by DL models. Furthermore, DL models enhance the accuracy. In this chapter, audit an extensive variety of profound neural system models and investigate the IoT applications that have profited from DL calculations (Koakutsu, 2018). This chapter recognizes five principle central IoT administrations that can be utilized as a part of various vertical areas past the particular administrations in every space. It will likewise talk about the qualities of IoT applications and the manual for coordinating them with the most fitting DL demonstrate. The study does not cover conventional machine learning calculations for IoT information investigation as there are some different endeavors that have secured such methodologies. Besides, this overview too does not delve into the subtle elements of the IoT framework from an interchanges and systems administration point of view.

One preferred standpoint of DL models, contrasted with the ordinary ANNs, is that DL success plans can learn hid highlights from the rough information (LeCun, Bengio & Hinton, 2015). Each layer prepares on an arrangement of highlights in view of the past layer's yields. The inward generally layers can perceive more confusing highlights, since they total and recombine highlights from the past layers. This is called the pecking order of highlights. For instance, if there should be an event of a face recognition show, rude picture information of representations as vector of pixels are helped to a model in its info layer. Each hidden layer would then be able to take in more related to ideas about how things work highlights from the past layer's yields, e.g., the principal covered layer recognizes the lines and edges, the second layer recognizes angrily stand up to parts, for example, nose, eyes, and so forth., and the third layer groups together all the past highlights to produce a face.

The described upgrades of DL models are because of take assessments, and there is still no solid disease identifying establishment to answer why DL methods beat their shallow partners. Also, there is no absolutely clear limit among very deep and shallow systems dependent on the number of covered layers. Mostly, nerve-related systems with two or then again more hidden layers that join the (happening now) went forward preparing calculations are carefully thought about as very deep/extreme models. More than that, on-and-off nerve-related systems with one hid layer are carefully thought about as very deep/extreme since they have a cycle on the units of the covered layer, which can be unrolled to an identical very deep system. Very interested carefully readers can suggest other writing that reviewed the models and designs of DL in more points of interest, for example (Deng, 2014). Table 1 shortens these models, their qualities, attributes, and some example computer programs.

The enemy qualities of IoT gadgets and DL methods make this heading all the more difficult since IoT gadgets can once in a while have DL models even to just perform forecasts because of their asset limitations. To handle these challenges, a few strategies were presented in the ongoing writing including:

- DNN pressure
- Approximate registering for DL
- Accelerators
- Tinymotes with DL.

These methodologies center on the induction usefulness of accessible or pre-prepared DL models. Along these lines, preparing DL models on asset obliged and implanted gadgets are as yet an open challenge. Moving the preparation procedure to IoT gadgets is wanted for versatile and conveyed arrangement of IoT gadgets. For instance, having many shrewd surveillance cameras conveyed in a network for face-based confirmation, the preparing process for every camera should be possible on location. System pressure includes recognizing insignificant associations and neurons in a DNN through a few rounds of preparing. While this is a promising methodology for drawing near to continuous examination on IoT gadgets, more examinations should be performed to deal with a few difficulties, for example, • It isn't evident whether arrange pressure approaches are appropriate for information spilling, particularly

Table 1. Outline of deep learning models

S.N.	Model	Attributes	Sample IoT Applications
1.	Auto-encoder	• Appropriate for highlight extraction, dimensionality decrease • Same number of information and yield units • The yield reproduces input information • Works with unlabeled information	Machinery blame conclusion and emotion acknowledgment
2.	Recurrent Neural Network (RNN)	• Processes groupings of information through inner memory • Useful in IoT applications with time-subordinate information	Identify development design and behavior recognition
3.	Deep Belief Network (DBN)	• Suitable for progressive highlights disclosure • Greedy preparing of the arrange layer by layer	• Fault recognition grouping • Security danger recognizable proof
4.	Convolutional Neural Network (CNN)	• Convolution layers take greatest piece of calculations • Less association looked at to DNNs • Needs an extensive preparing dataset for visual assignments.	Plant sickness location and traffic sign recognition
5.	Ladder Net	• Suitable for loud information • Composed of three systems two encoders and one decoder	Face acknowledgment and authentication

when the DL show is dynamic and may advance after some time. • The pressure techniques for time-arrangement designs (Li, Ota & Dong, 2018), for example, RNN and DBN, have not been all around researched; what's more, there is a hole to check whether the current pressure techniques are relevant to these DL structures. • There is a need to determine the exchange off between the rate of pressure and precision of a DNN, as additional pressure prompts debased precision. All the more as of late, inexact processing approaches have likewise been used in making DL models less difficult and the sky is the limit from there vitality productive, with the end goal to work them on asset compelled gadgets. Like system pressure methods, these strategies likewise exploit irrelevant neurons. Be that as it may, rather than controlling the system structure, they safeguard the structure yet change the calculation portrayals through piece length decrease. Consequently, they appear pertinent to an assortment of DL designs and can even cover the dynamic development of system models amid run-time. Keeping a harmony among exactness and vitality use is their shared objective. In any case, more works are expected to discover the prevalence of one of these methodologies for installing DL models in IoT gadgets (Bendre & Thool, 2016).

Image Processing, IOT, and Deep Learning

There are few works exhibiting normal information mining and machine learning techniques that have been utilized as a part of IoT conditions. It tended to diverse arrangement, bunching, and visit design mining calculations for the IoT framework and administrations. Be that as it may, that work did not consider DL approaches, which is the core interest of our overview. Additionally, their attention is basically on disconnected information mining, while additionally think about learning and digging for both constant (i.e., quickly) and enormous information investigation. Machine learning approaches administered and unsupervised, rules, fluffy rationale, and so on in the thinking period of a context aware registering framework, and have talked about the possibilities of applying those strategies in IoT frameworks. Regardless, they too did not think about the part of DL on the setting thinking. The work gives a study of machine learning strategies for remote sensor systems (Li, Ota & Dong, 2018). In that work, the creators examined machine learning strategies in the useful parts of Wireless sensor networks (WSNs), for example, steering, limitation, furthermore, grouping, and also non-practical prerequisites, such as security and nature of administration. They investigated a few calculations in managed, unsupervised, and support learning approaches. This work centers around the framework of WSN which is one potential foundation for executing IoT applications, while our work isn't reliant on the wellsprings of information i.e., IoT foundations and spreads a wide scope of IoT applications and administrations. Besides, the core interest was on conventional machine learning techniques, while this article centers on cutting edge and DL strategies. At long last DL approaches in arrange movement control frameworks. While this work basically centers on the framework of system, it varies from our work that spotlights on the utilization of DL in IoT applications. In particular, they featured the association of diverse machine learning strategies with flag preparing advancements to process and dissect opportune huge information applications.

Also, discussed about the development of unique and little shape factor equipment that is intended to effectively run DL models on installed and asset compelled gadgets (Li, Ota & Dong, 2018). These structures can be used in wearable, portable, and IoT gadgets, because of their decreased asset requests and their relevance to time-delicate IoT applications. Notwithstanding, their consensus to help any sort of DNN and additionally their interoperability and similarity with existing equipment stages stay as clear difficulties.

Table 2 abridges the techniques and advances used in the ongoing writing to have DL investigation on IoT gadgets alongside their advantages and disadvantages likewise assessed a few applications that have actualized DL on asset compelled gadgets. Due to the previously mentioned difficulties, there are very few all around created applications in this classification. Notwithstanding, by settling these difficulties what's more, hindrances, we will see the ascent of numerous IoT applications.

Commitments

IoT scientists and engineers who need to manufacture examination, AI frameworks, and learning arrangements over their IoT framework, utilizing the developing DL machine learning approaches. The commitments of this chapter can be outlined as takes after:

Table 2. Strategies and technologies to bring DL on IoT devices

S.N.	Strategy/Technology	Advantages	Disadvantages
1	System Compression	Reduce stockpiling and calculation	• Not general for all DL models • Need particular equipment • The pruning procedure bring over-burden to preparing
2	Inexact Computing	Makes quick DL models and Save vitality	Not appropriate for exact frameworks
3	Quickening agents	Integrates DL show with the equipment	Efficient calculations and does not work with the conventional equipment stages
4	Tinymote with DL	• Good for time-basic IoT applications • Energy-productive • Provides greater security and protection for information	Special-reason systems

- Keeping in mind the end goal to embrace DL approaches in the IoT environments it recognize the key attributes and issues of IoT information.
- Compared to some related work in the writing that have tended to machine learning for IoT, audit the state of-the-craftsmanship DL strategies and their pertinence in the IoT area both for enormous information and spilling information investigation (Yao et al., 2018).
- Audit an extensive variety of IoT applications that have utilized DL in their unique circumstance likewise gives an examination furthermore, a rule for utilizing diverse kinds of DNN in the different IoT areas and applications.
- Audit the ongoing methodologies and innovations for conveying DL on all levels of IoT chain of importance from asset obliged gadgets to the mist and the cloud.
- Feature the difficulties and future research headings for the effective and productive converging of DL and IoT applications. It additionally incorporates a concise depiction of headways toward continuous and quick DL models (Yao et al., 2018) and state-of the-craftsmanship calculations that are joint with DL. A brief audit of a few structures and devices with various capacities what's more, calculations that help DL and NNs is likewise exhibited. IoT applications in various areas e.g., medicinal services, agribusiness and so on.

IOT DATA CHARACTERISTICS AND REQUIREMENTS FOR ANALYTICS

IoT information can be spilled consistently or collected as a wellspring of enormous information. Spilling information alludes to the information created or caught inside small interims of time and need to be expeditiously broke down to remove quick bits of knowledge as well as settle on quick choices. Enormous information alludes to colossal datasets that the ordinarily utilized equipment and programming stages are not capable to store, oversee, process, and break down. These two methodologies ought to be dealt with distinctively since their prerequisites for explanatory reaction are not the same (Kim, Jeong & Kim, 2017). Understanding from enormous information investigation can be conveyed following a few long periods of information age, be that as it may, understanding from spilling information investigation ought to be prepared in a scope of couple of several milliseconds to few moments. Information combination and sharing assume a basic part in creating pervasive conditions in light of IoT information. This part is more basic for time-delicate IoT applications where an auspicious combination of information is expected to bring all bits of information together for investigation and thusly giving dependable and exact significant bits of knowledge, Figure 1 has shown the applications of the deepl learning models and Iot along with the image processing.

IOT Quick and Spilling Information

Many research endeavors recommended gushing information examination that can be chiefly conveyed on superior figuring frameworks or cloud stages. The gushing information investigation on such systems depends on information parallelism and incremental preparing by information parallelism, a substantial dataset is apportioned into a few littler datasets, on which parallel investigation are performed all the while. Incremental preparing alludes to getting a little clump of information to be prepared rapidly in a pipeline of calculation undertakings. In spite of the fact that these systems decrease time dormancy to restore a reaction from the spilling information diagnostic structure, they are not the most ideal ar-

Figure 1. Application of IoT, image processing with deep learning models

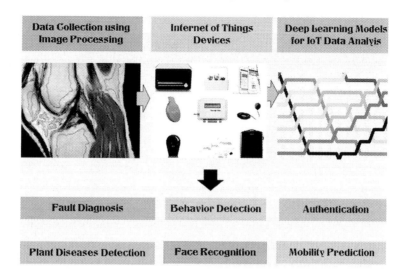

rangement for time-stringent IoT applications by bringing spilling information examination closer to the wellspring of information i.e., IoT gadgets or edge gadgets the requirement for information parallelism and incremental handling is less sensible as the extent of the information in the source enables it to be handled quickly (Mazzei, Baldi, Montelisciani & Fantoni, 2018). It may, bringing quick examination on IoT gadgets presents its own particular difficulties for example, confinement of figuring, stockpiling, and power assets at the wellspring of information.

IOT Big Information

IoT is notable to be one of the real wellsprings of huge information, as it depends on interfacing countless gadgets to the Internet to report their habitually caught status of their surroundings. Perceiving and extricating significant designs from gigantic crude information is the center utility of enormous information investigation as it brings about larger amounts of experiences for basic leadership and pattern expectation (Jang, 2015). Along these lines, separating these experiences and learning from the enormous information is of outrageous significance to numerous organizations, since it empowers them to increase upper hands. In sociologies thinks about the effect of enormous information examination to that of the development of the telescope and magnifying lens for cosmology and science, individually.

Profound Learning

DL comprises of managed or unsupervised learning systems in view of numerous layers of Artificial Neural Networks (ANNs) that can learn progressive portrayals in profound models. DL structures comprise of numerous handling layers. Each layer can deliver non-direct reactions in light of the information from its info layer. The usefulness of DL is imitated from the instruments of human cerebrum and neurons for preparing of signs. DL structures have increased more consideration as of late contrasted with the other customary machine learning approaches. Such methodologies are considered as being shallow-organized learning structures variants i.e., a constrained subset of DL (Rayner, 2011). In spite of the fact that ANNs have been presented in the previous decades, the developing pattern for DNNs began in 2006 the idea of profound conviction systems from that point, the state of-the-workmanship execution of this innovation has been watched in various fields of AI including picture acknowledgment, picture recovery, web crawlers and data recovery, and regular dialect preparing, Figure 2 is showing the data collection, pre processing using image processing techniques and integration of this with the deep learning model after that how IoT sensors and devices are connected to the deep learning models.

DL procedures (Yao et al., 2018) have been produced over customary ANNs, Feed-forward Neural Networks (FNNs), Multilayer Perceptions (MLPs) have been utilized as a part of the past decades to prepare frameworks, however when the quantity of layers is expanded, they end up hard to prepare. The little size of preparing information was another calculates that outcomes over fitted models. In addition, the restriction in computational abilities in those days denied the usage of productive more profound FNNs (Despotovic & Tanikic, 2017). These computational impediments have been settled of late because of equipment progresses as a rule and the advancement of Graphics Processing Units (GPUs) and equipment quickening agents particularly. Past the auxiliary perspectives and centrality of profundity of DL models, and in addition equipment propels, DL strategies have profited from progressions in viable preparing calculations of profound systems including:

- Using Rectified Linear Units (ReLUs) as enactment work,
- Introducing dropout strategies,
- Random introduction for the weights of the system,
- Addressing the debasement of preparing precision by remaining learning systems,
- Solving vanishing angle issue and in addition detonating inclination issue by presenting and upgrading

One favorable position of DL designs, contrasted with the conventional ANNs, is that DL methods can learn concealed highlights from the crude information. Each layer prepares on an arrangement of highlights in view of the past layer's yields. The internal generally layers can perceive more mind boggling highlights, since they total and recombine highlights from the past layers. This is called the pecking order

Figure 2. IoT sensors integration with deep learning models for the processed data

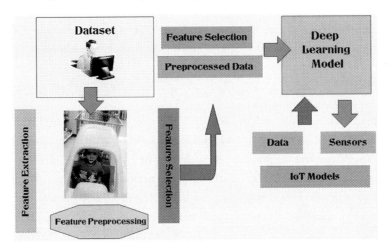

of highlights for instance, if there should arise an occurrence of a face acknowledgment demonstrate, crude picture information of representations as vector of pixels are encouraged to a model in its info layer (Carta, Cabrera, Matías & Castellano, 2015). Each concealed layer would then be able to take in more unique highlights from the past layer's yields, e.g., the primary shrouded layer distinguishes the lines and edges, the second layer recognizes confront parts, for example, nose, eyes, and so forth., and the third layer consolidates all the past highlights to produce a face. Nonetheless, the detailed upgrades of DL models are in view of experimental assessments, and there is still no solid expository establishment to answer why DL procedures beat their shallow partners. Additionally, there is no unmistakable limit amongst profound and shallow systems in light of the number of shrouded layers. For the most part, neural systems with two or on the other hand more shrouded layers that fuse the ongoing progressed preparing calculations are considered as profound models. Too, intermittent neural systems with one shrouded layer are considered as profound since they have a cycle on the units of the concealed layer, which can be unrolled to a proportionate profound system.

Deep Learning Models

In this area, introduce a concise review of a few normal DL models and additionally the most bleeding edge structures that have been presented as of late. Intrigued per users can allude to other writing that overviewed the models and designs of DL in more subtle elements. A DL and NN comprises of an information layer, a few shrouded layers, also, a yield layer. Each layer incorporates a few units called neurons; a neuron gets a few sources of info, plays out a weighted Figure 3. Internet of things attacks like DDoS attack, routing attack and social engineering attack is shown. Summation over its sources of info, at that point the subsequent whole experiences an actuation capacity to deliver a yield (Addo, Guegan & Hassani, 2018). Every neuron has a vector of weights related to its info measure and in addition a predisposition that ought to be upgraded amid the preparation procedure.

In the preparation procedure, the information layer allots more often than not haphazardly weights to the information preparing information and passes it to the following layer. Each ensuing layer additionally relegates weights to their info and produces their yield, which fills in as the contribution for

Figure 3. Internets of Things attacks

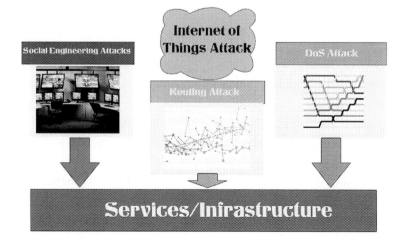

the accompanying layer. At the last layer, the last yield speaking to the model expectation is created a misfortune work decides the rightness of this forecast by registering the blunder rate between the anticipated and genuine qualities. An advancement calculation, for example, Stochastic Gradient Descent (SGD) is utilized to change the heaviness of neurons by figuring the slope of the misfortune work (Senov, 2015). The mistake rate is spread back over the system to the information layer known as back propagation calculation. The system at that point rehashes this preparation cycle, in the wake of adjusting the weights on each neuron in each cycle, until the point that the blunder rate falls beneath a coveted edge. Now, the DNN is prepared and is prepared for surmising. In a general arrangement, DL models fall into three classifications, to be specific generative, discriminative, and half and half models. Despite the fact that not being a firm limit, discriminative models more often than not give administered learning approaches, while generative models are utilized for unsupervised learning. Half breed models consolidate the advantages of both discriminative and generative models.

In this investigation, Keras is used as DL system since it guarantees numerous points of interest like its seclusion, and since it empowers us to construct and test complex neural systems rapidly. To start with, Keras is an open source DL library that incorporated into the Python biological community. Second, Keras additionally has wide range network and a nitty gritty client manual. From that point forward, Keras empowers to assemble complex neural system effectively (B Arnold, 2017); Tensorflow is a system that is produced by Google for DL. It is reasonable for working with CPUs and GPUs. Tensorflow likewise contains a few usages to fabricate complex DL models. It is runnable on Mac, Windows and linux, as a python bundle. It is likewise utilities with Keras. Initially the rearranged the dataset to enhance the profound model execution and abstain from over fitting and fabricated Neural Network as 7 layers first layer is input layer that has 10 neuron, number of information layer ought to be equivalent to the quantity of highlights sections in the dataset. The last layer is the yield layer that has only 1 neuron. This is known as a regression display. Our neural system has 5 concealed layers. First and fifth layers have 50 neuron and second and fourth layers have 100 neuron. Third layer has 300 neuron. The neural arrange layers are delineated in Figure 4. Prior to the preparation begins, dataset is part again at the rate of 0.3 as approval dataset to tune the preparation execution of the model the neural system demonstrates is appeared in Figure 4.

Convolution Neural Networks

For vision-based errands, DNNs with a thick association between layers are difficult to prepare and don't scale well. One imperative reason is the interpretation invariance property of such models. They along these lines don't take in the highlights that may change in the picture e.g., pivot of submit posture recognition. CNNs have tackled this issue by supporting translation equivariance calculations. A CNN gets a 2-D input e.g., a picture or discourse flag and concentrates abnormal state highlights through a progression of shrouded layers (Fu, Li, Gao & Wang, 2018). Everyone are living in information driven age, information has been finding or will find each purpose of our life. A great many people imagine that this impact is an outcome of industry 4.0 that makes our life speedier than before as all other modern upsets. Industry 4.0 empowered the collaboration between PCs or digital area and physical frameworks.

This collaboration is called digital physical frameworks that point made the IoT by implanting sensors, controllers, and actuators. Another outcome of the upset the tremendous information that is produced and should be overseen, called big data. To build up effective correspondence of IoT is troublesome point to accomplish and keep up, while number of created information has been expanding, condition-

Figure 4. Deep learning model

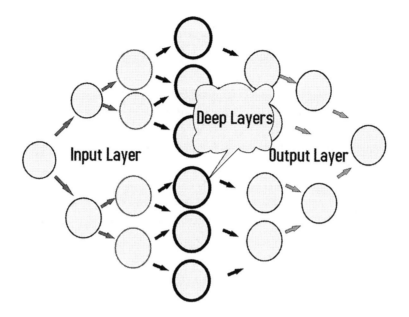

ally, the term information security has turned into a significant term particularly in regards to security of touchy information in arrangement with the three standards of data security classification, integrity and availability. There are numerous assaults auto hacking, DDoS or physical assaults to IoT in view of, especially, an absence of strong steering conventions. The measurements guarantee that DDoS assaults expanded 91% of every 2017 because of the misuse of IoT gadgets (Vlajic & Zhou, 2018). IoT, which is in all branches of life, is powerless against a few sorts of assaults that as it may, there is likewise no successful answer for shielding our life from being influenced by these assaults. These days, machine learning is the most well known examination theme for recognizing digital assaults for IoT security. Since, ML based arrangements can offer a vigorous framework to inconspicuous assaults. In actuality, the most concerning issue of research on IoT security is the absence of open datasets. Subsequently there must be far reaching thinks about to discover arrangements in these issues.

RESEARCH WORK

The picture division errand, CNN extricated two sorts of highlights for every locale: full district highlight and forefront highlight, and found that it could prompt better execution while linking them together as the area include. CNN accomplished noteworthy execution enhancements because of utilizing the exceptionally discriminative CNN highlights. In any case, it likewise experiences three fundamental disadvantages for the division assignment, which roused huge research: The element isn't good with the division undertaking. In spite of the fact that the CNN include has been over and again appeared to give higher execution when contrasted with ordinary hand-made, it isn't particularly intended for the picture division errand, CNN used was in reality adjusted to characterize jumping boxes i.e., to separate full area highlights, making it imperfect to remove closer view highlights. To address this issue, they presented one extra system which was particularly tweaked on the area closer view and proposed to mutually prepare the two systems (Guo, Liu, Georgiou & Lew, 2017). It acquainted a differentiable locale with pixel layer which could delineate districts to picture pixels, making the entire system particularly calibrated for the picture division undertaking. On the off chance that can perform programmed picture explanation, at that point this can have both handy and hypothetical advantages. In exemplary protest acknowledgment outline a calculation which can investigate a sub-window inside the picture to distinguish a specific question. For instance, in the event that one has a great protest finder and a ten megapixel picture, at that point one would attempt to utilize the locator at all ten million areas in the picture which could without much of a stretch expect minutes to weeks contingent on the many-sided quality of the question identifier and the quantity of picture changes being viewed as, for example, turn and scale (Kashyap & Gautam, 2016).

On account of programmed picture division, rather than trying utilizing the protest finder at all pixel areas, now just need to attempt it for the quantity of fragments in the picture which is regularly somewhere in the range of 10 and 100 and surely requests of size not as much as the quantity of areas in a picture (Juneja & Kashyap, 2016). Moreover, one may likewise have a go at utilizing the question locator at various introductions which can likewise be mitigated by the picture division. The advantages are not constrained to only computational speed, but rather likewise to upgrading exactness. When one performs window-based question recognition, one regularly additionally needs to manage foundation clamor and distracters. On the off chance that the programmed picture division calculation functions admirably, at that point it will have naturally expelled the foundation commotion which will fundamentally expand the precision of the protest acknowledgment (Kashyap & Tiwari, 2018).

Moreover, programmed picture division can give us bits of knowledge into how the human visual framework can play out a similar assignment. It can give hypothetical defenses to the qualities and shortcomings of visual data frameworks; it can give us profound knowledge into the conditions when visual data frameworks won't have the capacity to effectively comprehend visual ideas or protests on the planet (Juneja & Kashyap, 2016). Robotized division can go past question acknowledgment and location in that it isn't required to know the protest or visual ideas heretofore. This can prompt real achievements as a rule computer vision since it enables new questions is found out by the framework. At the point when an obscure question is found and isn't ordered by the current database, at that point another passage can be made for the new obscure protest and this can prompt a genuinely broad computer vision framework (Kashyap & Tiwari, 2017). So the principle advantages of programmed picture division are as per the following: It can enhance computational effectiveness. It can enhance precision by taking out foundation commotion. It can give both hypothetical and profound bits of knowledge into both how visual frameworks function and what the constraints are. It can be broader than question location and acknowledgment, Figure 5 shows how data acquisition and IoT works together.

IoT gadgets have the capacity of information gathering, moving and handling in savvy applications. This information composes spread to numerous zones, for example, wellbeing, transportation, military and so on. Security of the touchy information, that is the greatest danger of IoT, comes into conspicuousness. This hazard establishes in two primary vulnerabilities. First; heterogeneous gadgets furthermore, between operable associations makes the administration of IoT frameworks more mind boggling. Second; numerous gadgets have asset constraints, absence of computational ability, low idleness. Second reason likewise makes the recognition of conceivable and obscure assaults to IoT gadgets troublesome (Lee & Lee, 2015). These reasons make the steering conventions powerless for instance, WSN comprise of hubs that incorporate at least one sensor which have minimal effort and constrained power. These sensors' goals are detecting nature and speaking with the base station, the base station has more vitality,

Figure 5. Images and data acquisition and Internet of Things

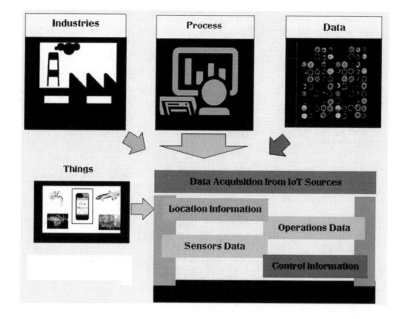

correspondence and computational power than different hubs to guarantee the system between different hubs and end client, figure 6 shows fault identification process from collected data.

These capacities guarantee checking natural conditions by hubs. WSN has general attributes for example; having modest number of hubs, control constrained hubs, dynamic system topology and huge size of sending. WSN has critical issues as delicate information insurance, protection and validation. Lamentably, the customary answers for these issues, as cryptography or key circulation conventions, couldn't be relevant due the specified limitations of sensor devices. There are various steering conventions in WSN. Some of them based on asset mindfulness or vitality decrease; however, none of them are hearty directing conventions against the IoT assaults, system of IoT is shown in Figure 7.

There are many sort of assaults to IoT that are physical assaults, observation assaults, DoS, get to assaults, assaults on security, digital wrongdoings, destructive assaults and SCADA. Steering assaults are performed at organize layer and they are more basic than other assaults, in other saying, they can be an initialize for rest of the assaults to IoT. RPL assaults can be analyzed under three classes relying upon the weakness which they expect to misuse. These classes are asset based, topology based and movement based. Asset based assaults intend to devour vitality, power and over-burden the memory. Topology-based assaults intend to upset the typical procedure of the system. This could cause that at least one hub are severed from the system. Moreover these assaults undermine the first topology of the system. Movement based assailant hubs point to join the system as a typical hub. At that point these assailants utilize the data of the organize activity to lead the assault directing assaults happen at the system layer. IoT frameworks are for the most part powerless against directing assaults (Fattah, Sung, Ahn, Ryu & Yun, 2017). Among the most noteworthy directing assaults is diminished rank, hi surge and form number assaults.

Figure 6. Fault identification and prediction using IoT and deep learning

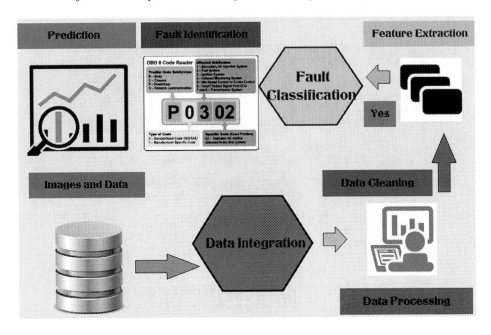

Figure 7. Deep learning and its role after processing IoT data

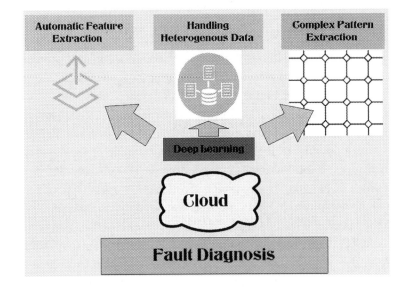

Security Problems of Internet of Things

IoT is under hazard because of its heterogeneous structure which thus empowers collaboration of digital space and physical area. Vulnerabilities of IoT are recorded and inadequate validation, unreliable system administrations, absence of transport encryption furthermore, uprightness confirmation, security concerns, unreliable programming or firmware, poor physical security are in the rundown, moreover, and lacking directing conventions can be added to the rundown and the situation of meeting up close and personal with the results of these specified vulnerabilities. In October of 2016, the biggest DDoS assault was completed by utilizing IoT botnets. PayPal, The Guardian, Netflix, Reddit and CNN, especially, turned into the objective. The botnets were made by a malware called Mirai. This malware misused the security weakness of IoT gadget's login information's. Abused gadgets were coordinated to the objectives. Utilizing default username, secret word, and non-special passwords also, absence of programming and firmware refreshes caused the Mirai assault.

The term of IoT is an arrangement of interconnected gadgets, machines and related programming administrations. It has been assuming an essential part in the cutting edge society since it empowered vitality effective robotization for upgrading personal satisfaction. Anyway IoT frameworks are an evident focus for digital assaults due to their impromptu and asset compelled nature. In this way, nonstop observing and examination is required for anchoring IoT frameworks (Weber, 2010). As a result of the huge measure of system and detecting information created by IoT gadgets and frameworks, big data and ML strategies are very viable in consistent checking and examination for the security of IoT frameworks. It is acquired a high level of preparing precision (up to 99.5%) and F1-scores (up to 99%). In this examination the main concentration is on particular IoT directing assaults, to be specific, diminished rank, rendition number change and hi surge. Frameworks security prerequisites depend to strength against steering assaults and profound learning based for discovery for directing assaults to IoT figure 8 shows IoT system. There are three principle interruption recognition approaches in the writing; abuse location, inconsistency discovery, and particular based location. Moreover, cross breed based framework is additionally situated under the interruption discovery subject and it's, quickly, a blend of abuse identification and oddity recognition (Jha & Kwon, 2017).

Abuse identification is exceptionally viable in identifying known assaults anyway it is deficient against obscure or novel assaults in light of the fact that their marks are not yet known. Furthermore, any alteration to the marks can cause an expansion in false caution rate and that will diminish viability and unwavering

Figure 8. Systems of Internet of Things

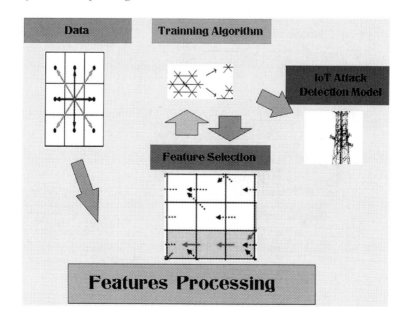

quality of the recognition framework. Particular based location plans to set specific conduct in light of the default deny standards. On the off chance that the determinations are abused, the framework will think there is an irregular circumstance. This approach is successful to covert the concealed assault that might be completed later on. Notwithstanding, setting specific details to the framework is a staggering errand in thinking about each extraordinary issue (Shaoshi Yang, Tiejun Lv, Maunder & Hanzo, 2013).

Abnormality based recognition approach is, essentially, developed on typical action profile and it expect that any foe activity will strife with the typical movement. Peculiarity based identification is analyzed under four subheadings; progressed measurable models, control based systems, organic models and learning models. The learning models, in view of that regardless of whether abuse recognition can give quicker reaction. Learning models have a more hearty structure against obscure assaults than others. Customary ML strategies, for example, Bayesian Belief Networks (BBN), Support Vector Machines (SVM) have been connected for digital security, anyway the huge scale information age in IoT requires a profound learning based strategy which performs better with huge information sizes and is versatile to distinctive assault situations (Datta & Das, 2015). IPv6 is a generally utilized convention in IoT and IPv6 based remote sensor systems (WSNs) are especially defenseless to steering assaults. IPv6 over Low-fueled Wireless Individual Area Networks (6LoWPAN) is an IPv6 based WSN convention. 6LoWPAN displays a few focal points as low power utilization, little, little impression, modest structure and simple support. In addition, WSNs incorporate numerous sensors which have constrained assets, for example, low memory, little transmission capacity and low vitality (Ahmed & AL-Shaboti, 2018). Areas of steering assaults in IoT are additionally appeared in Figure 9.

In our examination practicality of our system with reenactments up to 1000 hubs while the current investigations, for example the strategy with minimal number of hubs (up to 50), which is definitely not a reasonable approach for an IoT situation and to utilize the information created by genuine identical recreations in view of an absence of accessibility of open IoT assault datasets. The Cooja recreation

Figure 9. Overview of IoT attack

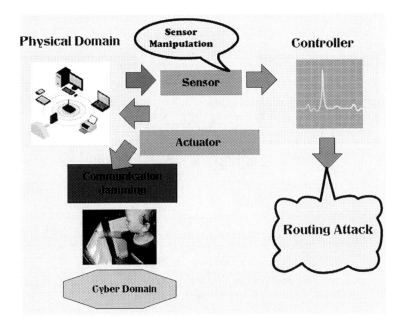

produces crude bundle catch documents, which are first changed over into Comma Separated Values (CSV) records for content based handling. The CSV documents are then contribution to the component pre-handling module of our framework. The highlights are ascertained in light of the activity stream data in the CSV documents. In the first place, include discussion process is connected to a few highlights, which is situated in crude datasets, at that point, recognized 12 includes as an starting hopeful list of capabilities. Subsequently, include standardization is connected to all datasets to lessen the negative impacts of minor qualities. In the pre-highlight choice advance, examined the significance of highlights by randomized decision trees, histograms and pearson rate estimation because of this examination, a portion of the highlights are dropped in pre-include determination process after element preprocessing (Roh, Kim, Son & Kim, 2011), the datasets comparing to every situation is named and blended to deliver a preprocessed dataset, comprising of a blend of assault and kindhearted information. These datasets are nourished into the profound learning calculation. Profound layers are prepared with regularization and dropout instruments, their weights are balanced and the IoT attack detection models are made.

Profound Learning Based Detection of Steering Attacks

In this area, our profound learning based steering assault recognition will be clarified and assess the significance of the highlights because of the dataset's record for choosing highlights to influence the figuring out how to process more exact. The highlights with too high and low significances are dropped with a specific end goal to avert over fitting. The datasets are standardized by a component standardization procedure to influence the preparation to process speedier (Subbulakshmi, 2017). The yield of the element preprocessing steps is preprocessed datasets which are taken into the profound learning calculation. The learning calculation is actualized by the assistance of Python libraries such as Keras, Scikit and Numpy. The learning procedure yields the IoT assault location show and tried the model against various test situations for more exact estimation of exactness and review.

Routing Attack Detection

Directing assaults can be distinguished by signature based arrangements and abnormality arrangements. Mark based arrangements are better against directing assaults that have little difference in its temperament. So abnormality based arrangements are superior to anything mark based arrangements about the recognition exactness of new assaults (Lachdhaf, Mazouzi & Abid, 2018). The examination that profound learning has preferable execution over shallow learning in the light of this brief data; utilized profound figuring out how to distinguish steering assaults as shown in Figure 10.

Neural Systems and Profound Learning

The fundamental engineering of neural systems goes back to the 1950s and the quintessence has not changed much since. A neural system contains interconnected layers of neurons. The knowledge of the network is stored in the weights of the connections between the nodes This hypothesis expresses that these basic neural systems can speak to each conceivable capacity at the point when given proper weights; it does, be that as it may, not state how to discover these parameters or what number of weights are required. Advances in innovation, for example, productive GPU usage and the accessibility of colossal marked datasets permitted to prepare progressively more profound and complex system designs.

Figure 10. Attacks detection model in Internet of Things

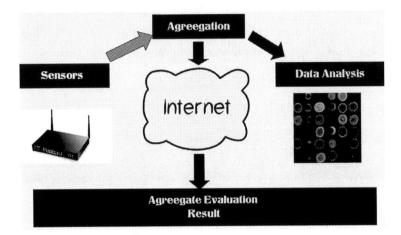

As of now to a great degree profound systems are the best in class procedure for picture furthermore, discourse acknowledgment for a more inside and out review of the historical backdrop of neural systems what's more, profound realizing.

Resource Obliged Machine Learning

Both neural systems and other machine learning calculations and procedures require huge measures of assets, particularly memory and handling power. The preparation period of a neural system is the most computationally costly. The inclination drop calculation used to tune the weights of the system needs various disregards the preparation set and every cycle requires various framework increases and augmentations. A significant part of the examination on disseminated neural systems has in this way been centered around models for the circulated preparing of profound systems on immense measures of information. The most well known case of this is the Google Map Belief framework, fit for preparing to great degree vast neural systems on 1000s of machines and 10,000s of CPU centers (Titanto & Dirgahayu, 2014). While the assets accessible when preparing a system are relatively boundless, the assessment of the prepared system is frequently done on a financial plan need to include the knowledge of a profound neural system to a compelled gadget. Here, inherent confinements on battery limit, handling force and memory, confine the size and many-sided quality of the system. Different works have proposed strategies to limit the cost while assessing a machine learning model.

Researchers show different topologies in which machine learning models can be joined to limit the cost while assessing the models. They portray how to develop a tree of classifiers where tests can take after an individual way. Every way takes a gander at particular highlights of the info information. A course can be viewed as a unique instance of a tree topology. The method exhibit here varies from past employments of a course topology in a machine learning model. Our course does not contain an arrangement of free element extractors but rather is prepared all in all, as one major model. By including an early-halting component in the shape of middle yield layers can reuse parts of the enormous model as a littler model. As of late, different systems have been proposed to pack a prepared neural system, making it more reasonable for asset obliged gadgets, for example, cell phones, robots or rambles. The creators demonstrate that a shallow system can figure out how to mirror an extensive, profound system, adequately compacting the profound engineering in a little system with comparable properties. This enables the little system to get a superb execution at a much lower cost, both in memory required to store the weights and in preparing power expected to assess the system. It is additionally conceivable to pack a troupe of neural systems into one system to make a model more appropriate for dispersed assessment by presenting an early-halting system.

CONCLUSION

This proposal is the evidence of idea that profound learning can effectively manage IoT security. The steering assaults diminished rank assault; hi surge assault and form number assault are effortlessly distinguished by our proposed assault identification models. This proposition additionally fills an exceptionally vital hole of the steering assault location for IoT. The greatest issue of this sort of regions is the absence of datasets and furthermore the information isn't best when it has impossible substance. The significant preferred standpoint of this method is that it takes into consideration a runtime exchange off between precision and speed. An appropriate limit can be chosen in light of the required precision what's more, on the accessible assets as opposed to having one system with a settled precision and computational cost. The time expected to process one picture relies upon the multifaceted nature of the picture, though an ordinary usage of a neural system utilizes precisely the same for each picture paying little respect to the distinctive complexities. This idea of contingent calculation has been as of late proposed in different fills in too. The most important of these methodologies are the Big-Little neural systems where somewhat, quick to execute arrange is utilized to attempt to group an information test. The huge system is just utilized when the certainty of the little organize is not exactly a predefined limit. The falling engineering could be viewed as an extraordinary instance of a Big-Little system where a piece of the huge system is utilized as the little system, along these lines keeping away from the overhead of putting away two totally autonomous systems. Another favorable position of the course thought about to the Big-Little design is that the calculations done by the principal organize in the course are utilized by the last stages when required. The Big system in the Big-Little engineering on the other hand needs to begin again starting with no outside help when the little system can't characterize the info.

REFERENCES

Addo, P., Guegan, D., & Hassani, B. (2018). Credit Risk Analysis Using Machine and Deep Learning Models. *Risks, 6*(2), 38. doi:10.3390/risks6020038

Ahmed, A., & Al-Shaboti, M. (2018). Implementation of Internet of Things (IoT) Based on IPv6 over Wireless Sensor Networks. *International Journal Of Sensors. Wireless Communications And Control, 7*(2). doi:10.2174/2210327907666170911145726

Arnold, T. (2017). kerasR: R Interface to the Keras Deep Learning Library. *The Journal of Open Source Software, 2*(14), 296. doi:10.21105/joss.00296

Bendre, M., & Thool, V. (2016). Analytics, challenges and applications in big data environment: A survey. *Journal Of Management Analytics*, *3*(3), 206–239. doi:10.1080/23270012.2016.1186578

Campbell, C., & Ying, Y. (2011). Learning with Support Vector Machines. *Synthesis Lectures On Artificial Intelligence And Machine Learning*, *5*(1), 1–95. doi:10.2200/S00324ED1V01Y201102AIM010

Carta, J., Cabrera, P., Matías, J., & Castellano, F. (2015). Comparison of feature selection methods using ANNs in MCP-wind speed methods. A case study. *Applied Energy*, *158*, 490–507. doi:10.1016/j.apenergy.2015.08.102

Chae, J., & Quick, B. (2014). An Examination of the Relationship Between Health Information Use and Health Orientation in Korean Mothers: Focusing on the Type of Health Information. *Journal of Health Communication*, *20*(3), 275–284. doi:10.1080/10810730.2014.925016 PMID:25495418

Datta, S., & Das, S. (2015). Near-Bayesian Support Vector Machines for imbalanced data classification with equal or unequal misclassification costs. *Neural Networks*, *70*, 39–52. doi:10.1016/j.neunet.2015.06.005 PMID:26210983

Deng, L. (2014). A tutorial survey of architectures, algorithms, and applications for deep learning – ERRATUM. *APSIPA Transactions On Signal And Information Processing*, *3*. doi:10.1017/atsip.2014.4

Despotovic, V., & Tanikic, D. (2017). Sentiment Analysis of Microblogs Using Multilayer Feed-Forward Artificial Neural Networks. *Computer Information*, *36*(5), 1127–1142. doi:10.4149/cai_2017_5_1127

Fattah, S., Sung, N., Ahn, I., Ryu, M., & Yun, J. (2017). Building IoT Services for Aging in Place Using Standard-Based IoT Platforms and Heterogeneous IoT Products. *Sensors (Basel)*, *17*(10), 2311. doi:10.339017102311 PMID:29019964

Fu, R., Li, B., Gao, Y., & Wang, P. (2018). Visualizing and analyzing convolution neural networks with gradient information. *Neurocomputing*, *293*, 12–17. doi:10.1016/j.neucom.2018.02.080

Gomes, C., & Mayes, A. (2014). The kinds of information that support novel associative object priming and how these differ from those that support item priming. *Memory (Hove, England)*, *23*(6), 901–927. doi:10.1080/09658211.2014.937722 PMID:25051200

Guo, Y., Liu, Y., Georgiou, T., & Lew, M. (2017). A review of semantic segmentation using deep neural networks. *International Journal of Multimedia Information Retrieval*, *7*(2), 87–93. doi:10.100713735-017-0141-z

Hong, S., & Lee, Y. (2013). CPU Parallel Processing and GPU-accelerated Processing of UHD Video Sequence using HEVC. *Journal Of Broadcast Engineering*, *18*(6), 816–822. doi:10.5909/JBE.2013.18.6.816

Jang, Y. (2015). Big Data, Business Analytics, and IoT: The Opportunities and Challenges for Business. *Journal of Information Systems*, *24*(4), 139–152. doi:10.5859/KAIS.2015.24.4.139

Jha, D., & Kwon, G. (2017). Alzheimer's Disease Detection Using Sparse Autoencoder, Scale Conjugate Gradient and Softmax Output Layer with Fine Tuning. *International Journal Of Machine Learning And Computing*, *7*(1), 13–17. doi:10.18178/ijmlc.2017.7.1.612

Juneja, P., & Kashyap, R. (2016). Energy based methods for medical image segmentation. *International Journal of Computers and Applications*, *146*(6), 22–27. doi:10.5120/ijca2016910808

Juneja, P., & Kashyap, R. (2016). Optimal approach for CT image segmentation using improved energy based method. *International Journal of Control Theory and Applications*, *9*(41), 599–608.

Kashyap, R., & Gautam, P. (2016). Fast level set method for segmentation of medical images. In *Proceedings of the International Conference on Informatics and Analytics (ICIA-16)*. ACM. 10.1145/2980258.2980302

Kashyap, R., & Piersson, A. (2018). Big Data Challenges and Solutions in the Medical Industries. In Handbook of Research on Pattern Engineering System Development for Big Data Analytics. IGI Global. doi:10.4018/978-1-5225-3870-7.ch001

Kashyap, R., & Tiwari, V. (2017). Energy-based active contour method for image segmentation. *International Journal of Electronic Healthcare*, *9*(2–3), 210–225. doi:10.1504/IJEH.2017.083165

Kashyap, R., & Tiwari, V. (2018). Active contours using global models for medical image segmentation. *International Journal of Computational Systems Engineering*, *4*(2/3), 195. doi:10.1504/IJC-SYSE.2018.091404

Kim, D., Jeong, Y., & Kim, S. (2017). Data-Filtering System to Avoid Total Data Distortion in IoT Networking. *Symmetry*, *9*(1), 16. doi:10.3390ym9010016

Koakutsu, S. (2018). Deep Learning - Current Situation and Expectation of Deep Learning and IoT. *The Journal Of The Institute Of Electrical Engineers Of Japan*, *138*(5), 270–271. doi:10.1541/ieej-journal.138.270

Ksiezopolski, B. (2012). QoP-ML: Quality of protection modelling language for cryptographic protocols. *Computers & Security*, *31*(4), 569–596. doi:10.1016/j.cose.2012.01.006

Lachdhaf, S., Mazouzi, M., & Abid, M. (2018). Secured AODV Routing Protocol for the Detection and Prevention of Black Hole Attack in VANET. *Advanced Computing: An International Journal, 9*(1), 1-14. doi:10.5121/acij.2018.9101

LeCun, Y., Bengio, Y., & Hinton, G. (2015). Deep learning. *Nature*, *521*(7553), 436–444. doi:10.1038/nature14539 PMID:26017442

Lee, I., & Lee, K. (2015). The Internet of Things (IoT): Applications, investments, and challenges for enterprises. *Business Horizons*, *58*(4), 431–440. doi:10.1016/j.bushor.2015.03.008

Li, H., Ota, K., & Dong, M. (2018). Learning IoT in Edge: Deep Learning for the Internet of Things with Edge Computing. *IEEE Network*, *32*(1), 96–101. doi:10.1109/MNET.2018.1700202

Li, H., Ota, K., & Dong, M. (2018). Learning IoT in Edge: Deep Learning for the Internet of Things with Edge Computing. *IEEE Network*, *32*(1), 96–101. doi:10.1109/MNET.2018.1700202

Mazzei, D., Baldi, G., Montelisciani, G., & Fantoni, G. (2018). A full stack for quick prototyping of IoT solutions. *Annales des Télécommunications*, *73*(7-8), 439–449. doi:10.100712243-018-0644-5

Rayner, M. (2011). The curriculum for children with severe and profound learning difficulties at Stephen Hawking School. *Support for Learning*, *26*(1), 25–32. doi:10.1111/j.1467-9604.2010.01471.x

Roh, Y., Kim, J., Son, J., & Kim, M. (2011). Efficient construction of histograms for multidimensional data using quad-trees. *Decision Support Systems, 52*(1), 82–94. doi:10.1016/j.dss.2011.05.006

Senov, A. (2015). Improving Distributed Stochastic Gradient Descent Estimate via Loss Function Approximation. *IFAC-Papersonline, 48*(25), 292–297. doi:10.1016/j.ifacol.2015.11.103

Sezer, O., Dogdu, E., & Ozbayoglu, A. (2018). Context-Aware Computing, Learning, and Big Data in Internet of Things: A Survey. *IEEE Internet Of Things Journal, 5*(1), 1–27. doi:10.1109/JIOT.2017.2773600

Subbulakshmi, T. (2017). A learning-based hybrid framework for detection and defence of DDoS attacks. *International Journal of Internet Protocol Technology, 10*(1), 51. doi:10.1504/IJIPT.2017.083036

Titanto, M., & Dirgahayu, T. (2014). Google Maps-Based Geospatial Application Framework with Custom Layers Management. *Applied Mechanics and Materials, 513-517*, 822-826. Retrieved from www.scientific.net/amm.513-517.822

Vlajic, N., & Zhou, D. (2018). IoT as a Land of Opportunity for DDoS Hackers. *Computer, 51*(7), 26–34. doi:10.1109/MC.2018.3011046

Vu, H., Gomez, F., Cherelle, P., Lefeber, D., Nowé, A., & Vanderborght, B. (2018). ED-FNN: A New Deep Learning Algorithm to Detect Percentage of the Gait Cycle for Powered Prostheses. *Sensors (Basel), 18*(7), 2389. doi:10.339018072389 PMID:30041421

Weber, R. (2010). Internet of Things – New security and privacy challenges. *Computer Law & Security Review, 26*(1), 23–30. doi:10.1016/j.clsr.2009.11.008

Yang, S., Tiejun, L., Maunder, R., & Hanzo, L. (2013). From Nominal to True A Posteriori Probabilities: An Exact Bayesian Theorem Based Probabilistic Data Association Approach for Iterative MIMO Detection and Decoding. *IEEE Transactions on Communications, 61*(7), 2782–2793. doi:10.1109/TCOMM.2013.053013.120427

Yao, S., Zhao, Y., Zhang, A., Hu, S., Shao, H., Zhang, C., ... Abdelzaher, T. (2018). Deep Learning for the Internet of Things. *Computer, 51*(5), 32–41. doi:10.1109/MC.2018.2381131

Yao, S., Zhao, Y., Zhang, A., Hu, S., Shao, H., Zhang, C., ... Abdelzaher, T. (2018). Deep Learning for the Internet of Things. *Computer, 51*(5), 32–41. doi:10.1109/MC.2018.2381131

Chapter 6
Transfer Learning in 2.5D Face Image for Occlusion Presence and Gender Classification

Sahil Sharma
Thapar Institute of Engineering and Technology, India

Vijay Kumar
Thapar Institute of Engineering and Technology, India

ABSTRACT

Face depth image has been used for occlusion presence and gender prediction by transfer learning. This chapter discusses about the overfitting problem and how augmentation helps overcoming it. Pre-processing of the dataset includes converting a 3D object image into depth image for further processing. Five state-of-the-art 2D deep learning models (e.g., AlexNet, VGG16, DenseNet121, ResNet18, and SqueezeNet) have been discussed along with their architecture. The effect of increasing the number of epochs on the top-1 error rate has been presented in the experimental section. The result section consists of error rates in comparison of with and without augmentation on the datasets.

INTRODUCTION

Face recognition is the oldest problem which has been worked in the field of computer vision. Many researchers have contributed to build robust face recognition systems since more than a three decade now. Transfer learning has come handy when comparing the efficiency of the face recognition systems. Using Labelled Faces in Wild face benchmark dataset multiple deep learning-based models have given human level accuracy. Some of the methods are DeepFace (Taigman et al., 2014), DeepID3 (Sun et al., 2015), FaceNet (Schroff et al., 2015), Baidu (Liu et al., 2015), VGGface (Parkhi et al., 2015), light-CNN (Wu et al., 2018), SphereFace (Liu et al., 2017), Cosface (Wang et al., 2018), Arcface (Deng et al., 2018) and Ring loss (Zheng et al. 2018). All the mentioned face recognition methods are done on two dimensional faces. No work has been done with deep learning for depth images of faces.

DOI: 10.4018/978-1-5225-7862-8.ch006

There are various ways to implement face recognition using facial modalities, 2D face images (Liu et al., 2017), 2.5D depth face images (Lee et al., 2016), and 3D face images (Liu et al., 2018). The capturing of depth images is the key for the next level problems in the field of computer vision. Plethora of work has been done in the field of 2D face recognition (Xu et al., 2017; Ranjan et al., 2017; Grm et al., 2017; Hu et al., 2015). There are various challenges that need to be worked for building a robust face recognition system which can deal with real-world problems of occlusion, low-lightening, makeup, augmented reality and low-resolution image etc. To handle these kinds of challenges, there is need for a robust face detection algorithm that has to be implemented in spatial region. Considering the challenges in depth face images, this becomes more tough. Considering the most famous viola-jones face detection algorithm (Viola et al., 2003) to be state-of-the-art for two dimensional algorithms, face detection can be extended for depth images to handle real world scenarios. The lack of depth image face datasets makes the recognition problem challenging. Augmentation can be used to counter the challenge of overfitting because of less number of images. Augmentation is the concept of improving the number of images by variations of the same image (Perez et al., 2017).

The motivation of the current work is the enormous amount of work being done in the field of deep learning for two dimensional images, but no work has been done on depth face images. Pose and expression normalization has been done on depth images by Feng, & Zhao, 2018 for the purpose of face recognition but not for occlusion presence and gender recognition. Occlusion and gender prediction of depth facial images has not been implemented using transfer learning. In real time, quadcopters having depth sensors coupled with these models can be used to track head count of male and female for attendance purposes or in public gatherings. Counting the number of people in crowds by correctly segmenting different people can be done if presence of occlusion can be identified. Detection of faces in depth images is a challenging task.

In current work, the problem of occlusion classification as well as gender recognition is discussed in detail. The face image can have different types of occlusion viz. glasses, hand, paper, cap, cigarette, bottle, and cropping etc. Deep learning is used for classifying the face image into occluded image or the non-occluded image. The gender binary classification into male and female is presented on the two datasets. The transfer learning is implemented for the task of binary classification in both type of problems.

The following sections are as follows: Section 2 discusses the background of the work. Section 3 presents the types of transfer learning as well as architecture of five deep neural networks. Section 4 presents the experimentation and results section. The last Section 5 presents the conclusion.

BACKGROUND

This section discusses the basics of two-dimensional deep learning.

Occlusion and Gender Prediction From Face Depth Image

The phases of face recognition with depth image for the classification of presence of occlusion and gender can be seen in Figure 1.

It can be seen in Figure 1 that the initial dataset images are converted from the 3D face object images to pre-processed depth images of size 224x224. The size is set to 224x224 because the input layer of the deep learning models is set to default 224x224 in AlexNet [20] and other models viz. VGG16 (Simonyan

Figure 1. Depth image based face occlusion and gender binary classification using transfer learning

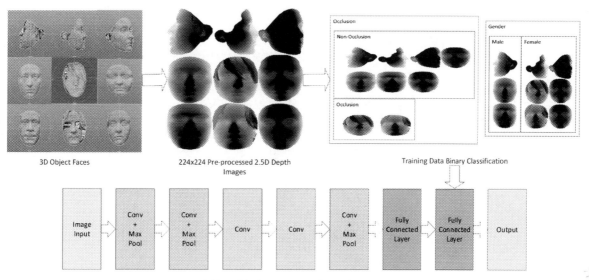

& Zisserman, 2014), DenseNet-121 (Oiao et al., 2018), ResNet-18 (He et al., 2016), and SqueezeNet (Iandola et al., 2016) etc. The pre-processed images are divided according to their classes. In case of occlusion classification, two directories viz. Occlusion and Non-Occlusion were made. In case of gender classification, male and female directories were made for further processing in transfer learning.

Overfitting

Figure 2 presents the example of classifying two different type of stars. A kernel function is trained to fit the model perfectly. This overfitting results in optimizing the prediction just for the training set. Overall this model performs bad because it would be taking more time even for binary classification.

Pooling

Pooling layers are added in between the convolution layers to down-sample the size of spatial size for reducing the number of parameters, hence contributing in reduction of overfitting (Karpathy et al., 2016). There are two types of pooling viz. max pooling and average pooling. There are two types of hyperparameters namely filter size and stride in pooling. The main feature of the pooling layer is that there is no parameter to learn.

Max Pooling

In max pooling technique, the pooling filter is convoluted on the feature map on the basis of filter size and stride, fetching the maximum number out of filter for filling up the feature map. It can be visualized in Figure 3.

Figure 2. Overfitting the kernel for binary classification

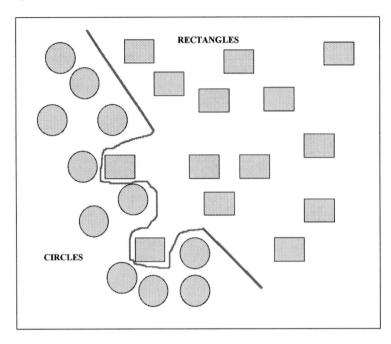

Figure 3. Max pooling

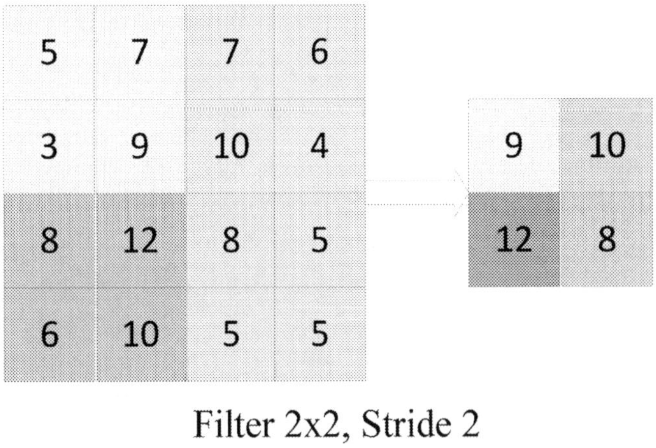

Filter 2x2, Stride 2

Average Pooling

In average pooling technique, the pooling filter is convoluted on the feature map on the basis of filter size and stride, fetching the average of numbers in the filter for filling up the feature map. It can be visualized in Figure 4.

Figure 4. Average pooling

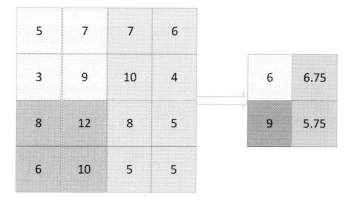

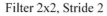

Filter 2x2, Stride 2

Dropout

Srivastava et al., 2014 introduced the concept of dropout. Dropout is a regularization technique in which random neuron weights along with their connections are dropped from the deep neural network. Dropout technique helps in overcoming overfitting problem.

Softmax Function

Softmax function is the generalization of S-shaped logistic function, which improves the log-loss value and converts n-dimensional array into one dimensional array (Christopher, 2016).

ReLu

ReLu is an activation function which is applied on each element of the volume with a function of max(0, x). It does not affect the size of the volume. The concept can be visualized in Figure 5.

Fire

Expansion of the convolution layers of 1x1 and 3x3 filters is termed as fire module in SqueezeNet.

Transfer Learning

In application of deep learning for convolutional neural networks, training of a whole new network is time consuming and needs huge number of images in practice. Due to lack of resources for the training of a deep neural network from scratch, the concept of transfer learning is used.

There are three major scenarios for the use of transfer learning.

Figure 5. ReLu activation function

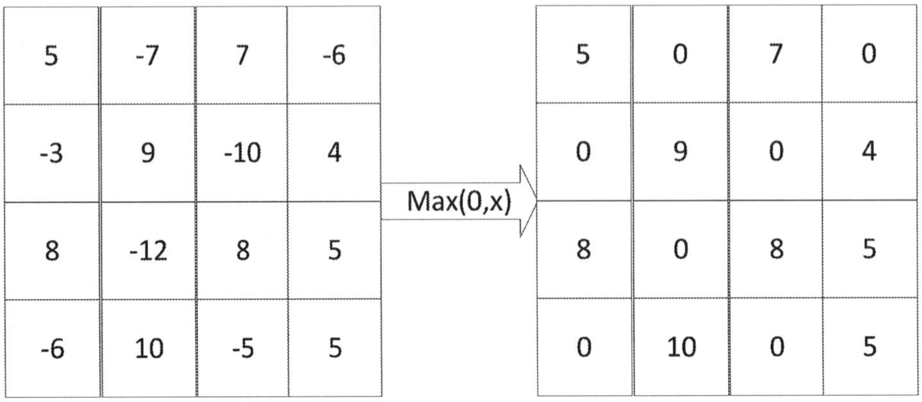

5	-7	7	-6
-3	9	-10	4
8	-12	8	5
-6	10	-5	5

Max(0,x)

5	0	7	0
0	9	0	4
8	0	8	5
0	10	0	5

Scenario 1: Using the convnet pre-trained on ImageNet (Deng et al., 2009), removing the last fully connected layer and treating the feature map as fixed feature extractor for new dataset.

Scenario 2: The second more effective way is to fine tune the original model for backpropagation in addition to removing the last fully-connected layer.

Scenario 3: The training of ImageNet takes several days to complete with the need of multiple GPUs, which is very computation expensive. People share the weights of their models at ModelZoo (Jia & Shelhamer, 2015) for the help of other researchers.

AlexNet

A deep convolutional neural network trained on 1.2 million images of ImageNet LSVRC-2010 with 1000 unique classes. AlexNet achieved 15.3% top-5 error rate in doing the assigned task. A total of five convolutional layers and three fully connected layers were used for training the network along with max-pooling layers and softmax layer. There are 60M parameters and 6,50,000 neurons that are trained according to the training dataset during transfer learning. About 95% of the total parameters in Alexnet are in the fully connected layers. Architecture of AlexNet can be seen in Table 1.

VGG-16

Input image of size 224x224 is given into the training model. Visual Geometric Group (VGG) trained a deep learning model using 16 layers in their work along with other variations. In pre-processing, mean RGB value of whole dataset is subtracted from each image. 3x3 and 1x1 filters have been used for the convolutions in linear and non-linear transformations. Max pooling has been done using 2x2 filters and stride of 2.

In MATLAB version of VGG-16 model, there are 41 layers. These layers can be seen in the form of table below. This version has 134 million parameters and take a lot of power and time consumption to process the data. Architecture of VGG-16 can be seen in Table 2.

Table 1. Architecture of AlexNet

Layers	Image Size for One of Two GPUs
1. Input Image	224x224x3
2. 11x11x3 Convolution, Stride 4	55x55x48
3. 5x5x48 Convolution → MaxPooling	27x27x128
4. 3x3x128 Convolution → MaxPooling	13x13x192
5. 3x3x192 Convolution	13x13x192
6. 3x3x192 Convolution	13x13x128
7. MaxPooling → Fully Connected Layer	1x2048
8. Fully Connected Layer	1x2048
9. Fully Connected Layer → Softmax	1x1000
10. Output	1x1000

Table 2. Architecture of VGG-16

Layers
1. Input Image
2. Convolution → ReLu → Convolution → ReLu
3. MaxPooling → Convolution → ReLu → Convolution → ReLu
4. [MaxPooling → Convolution → ReLu → Convolution → ReLu → Convolution → ReLu] x 3
5. MaxPooling
6. [FullyConnected → ReLu → Dropout] x 2
7. FullyConnected → Softmax
8. Output Image

DenseNet-121

This deep learning model is a few shot learning techniques using one, two or three images of each subject for the purpose of training the model. Input image size for this model is 224x224. There are 120 convolution layers and one softmax layer in this architecture.

DenseNet-121 architecture can be seen in the Table 3.

ResNet-18

This model of residual network with 18 layers has been proposed by Microsoft. There are 17 convolutional layers and one softmax layer in this architecture. The initial input size of the image is 224x224.

ResNet-18 architecture can be seen in Table 4.

Table 3. Architecture of DenseNet-121

Layers	Image Size
1. Input Image	224x224
2. 7x7 Convolution, Stride 2	112x112
3. 3x3 MaxPooling, Stride 2	56x56
4. [1x1 Convolution → 3x3 Convolution] x 6	56x56
5. 1x1 Convolution	56x56
6. 2x2 Average Pool, Stride 2	28x28
7. [1x1 Convolution → 3x3 Convolution] x 12	28x28
8. 1x1 Convolution	28x28
9. 2x2 Average Pool, Stride 2	14x14
10. [1x1 Convolution → 3x3 Convolution] x 24	14x14
11. 1x1 Convolution	14x14
12. 2x2 Average Pool, Stride 2	7x7
13. [1x1 Convolution → 3x3 Convolution] x 16	7x7
14. 7x7 Global Average Pool	1x1
15. Fully Connected Layer → Softmax	1x1000
16. Output Image	1x1000

Table 4. Architecture of ResNet-18

Layers	Image Size
1. Input Image	224x224
2. Convolution 7x7, 64, Stride 2	112x112
3. 3x3 MaxPooling, Stride 2 → (3x3, 64 Convolution → 3x3, 64 Convolution) x 2	56x56
4. (3x3, 128 Convolution → 3x3, 128 Convolution) x 2	28x28
5. (3x3, 256 Convolution → 3x3, 256 Convolution) x 2	14x14
6. (3x3, 512 Convolution → 3x3, 512 Convolution) x 2	7x7
7. Average Pool → Fully Connected Layer → Softmax	1x1
8. Output Image	1x1

SqueezeNet

The primary focus of this model was to reduce the size of the standard deep learning architectures. This model size is 510 times smaller than AlexNet model. The main advantage of this model is that it is faster to execute, easier to deploy and requires lesser resources to train itself.

SqueezeNet architecture can be seen in the form of table below.

Table 5. Architecture of SqueezeNet

Layers	Image Size
1. Input Image	224x224x3
2. Convolution 7x7, Stride 2	111x111x96
3. 3x3 MaxPooling, Stride 2	55x55x96
4. Fire2 → Fire3	55x55x128 → 5x55x128
5. Fire4	55x55x256
6. 3x3 MaxPooling, Stride 2	27x27x256
7. Fire5 → Fire6 → Fire7 → Fire8	27x27x256 → 27x27x384 → 27x27x384 → 27x27x512
8. 3x3 MaxPooling, Stride 2	13x12x512
9. Fire9	13x13x512
10. 1x1 Convolution, Stride 1	13x13x1000
11. 13x13 Average Pooling, Stride 1	1x1x1000
12. Output Image	1x1000

EXPERIMENTATION AND RESULTS

This section presents the detailed description of the experimentation, including dataset information, the experimental setup, and the performance comparison.

Dataset Used

The experimentation for the occlusion classification of faces has been performed on the two datasets namely Bosphorus (Sarvan et al., 2008) and University of Milano Bicocca Database (UMBDB) (Colombo et al., 2011).

Table 6 describes the characteristics of these datasets.

Experimental Setup

The simulation results have been done on workstation with Intel(R) Core(TM) i7-8700K CPU @ 3.70GHz with 32G RAM. The testing software is MATLAB 2017a and PyTorch 9.0 in Ubuntu 16.04 Linux environment.

Table 6. Dataset description

Dataset Name	Number of Images	Number of Image with Augmentation	Number of Subjects	Number of Males	Number of Females	No. of Occluded Images	No. of Occluded Images with Augmentation
Bosphorus	4666	13998	105	60	45	381	1143
UMB DB	1473	4419	143	98	45	590	1770

Performance Comparison

All the results have been shown in the form of top-1 error rates using augmentation technique with transfer learning. Total of five two-dimensional deep learning models are implemented for the purpose of experimentation. Different number of epochs/iterations are done for the comparison purposes. More the number of epochs, more number of times the backpropagation is done for the improvement of the performance of the models.

Occlusion Binary Classification

Experiment 1: Comparison of Top-1 error rates for Bosphorus Occlusion Classification

Table 7 presents the top-1 error rates for the Bosphorus dataset occlusion presence classification without augmentation. The best error rates provided are 3.9946% (for 5 epochs), 3.0723% (for 10 epochs), 3.2735% (for 15 epochs), 2.9452% (for 20 epochs), and 3.2359% (for 25 epochs). All the best error rates in this case have been achieved by the SqueezeNet model in comparison to other models.

Table 8 presents the top-1 error rates for the Bosphorus dataset occlusion presence classification with augmentation. Number of images are three times the original number of images in the dataset. The best error rates provided are 2.0386% (for 5 epochs), 1.073% (for 10 epochs), 1.2876% (for 15 epochs), 0.8584% (for 20 epochs), and 1.1493% (for 25 epochs). All the best error rates in this case have been achieved by the SqueezeNet model in comparison to other models.

Experiment 2: Comparison of Top-1 error rates for UMBDB Occlusion Classification

Table 7. Top-1 error rates for bosphorus occlusion classification without augmentation

Model Name	#Epochs = 5	#Epochs = 10	#Epochs = 15	#Epochs = 20	#Epochs = 25
AlexNet	4.2733	4.1723	4.3623	4.3732	4.2945
VGG16	4.3473	3.5632	3.9754	4.0634	3.9618
SqueezeNet	**3.9946**	**3.0723**	**3.2735**	**2.9452**	**3.2359**
DenseNet121	5.4326	4.3264	4.0756	3.9238	3.6182
ResNet18	5.0365	3.9425	4.6843	4.9994	3.2407

Table 8. Top-1 error rates for bosphorus occlusion classification with augmentation

Model Name	#Epochs = 5	#Epochs = 10	#Epochs = 15	#Epochs = 20	#Epochs = 25
AlexNet	2.2532	2.1459	2.3605	2.3605	2.3605
VGG16	2.1459	1.5021	1.9313	1.824	1.824
SqueezeNet	**2.0386**	**1.073**	**1.2876**	**0.8584**	**1.1493**
DenseNet121	3.4335	2.5751	2.0386	1.9313	1.6094
ResNet18	3.0043	2.2532	2.6824	3.1116	1.1803

Table 9. Top-1 error rates for UMBDB occlusion classification without augmentation

Model Name	#Epochs = 5	#Epochs = 10	#Epochs = 15	#Epochs = 20	#Epochs = 25
AlexNet	24.5293	21.8337	18.2423	19.9734	20.2264
VGG16	12.7423	10.3834	12.2458	12.7234	9.7234
SqueezeNet	**11.7234**	**8.3473**	**9.4337**	**10.1573**	**9.7233**
DenseNet121	16.7233	19.8732	16.2773	15.2436	16.7322
ResNet18	14.7237	12.7421	13.8324	14.2353	14.2346

Table 9 presents the top-1 error rates for the UMBDB dataset occlusion presence classification without augmentation. The best error rates provided are 11.7234% (for 5 epochs), 8.3473% (for 10 epochs), 9.4337% (for 15 epochs), 10.1573% (for 20 epochs), and 9.7233% (for 25 epochs). All the best error rates in this case have been achieved by the SqueezeNet model in comparison to other models.

Table 10 presents the top-1 error rates for the UMBDB dataset occlusion presence classification with augmentation. The best error rates provided are 8.5324% (for 5 epochs), 6.4846% (for 10 epochs), 6.4846% (for 15 epochs), 8.1911% (for 20 epochs), and 7.8498% (for 25 epochs). All the best error rates in this case have been achieved by the SqueezeNet model in comparison to other models.

Experiment 3: Comparison of Top-1 error rates for Bosphorus + UMBDB Occlusion Classification

Table 11 presents the best top-1 error rates for the binary occlusion presence classification in Bosphorus and UMBDB datasets combined depth images without augmentation. The best error rates provided are 5.2953% (for 5 epochs), 4.6418% (for 10 epochs), 4.7104% (for 15 epochs), 4.2653% (for 20 epochs),

Table 10. Top-1 error rates for UMBDB occlusion classification with augmentation

Model Name	#Epochs = 5	#Epochs = 10	#Epochs = 15	#Epochs = 20	#Epochs = 25
AlexNet	21.5017	19.1126	16.041	16.7235	18.43
VGG16	10.2389	8.5324	9.215	9.215	7.8498
SqueezeNet	**8.5324**	**6.4846**	**6.4846**	**8.1911**	**7.8498**
DenseNet121	13.3106	16.3823	14.6758	12.9693	13.6519
ResNet18	12.628	9.8976	10.2389	11.2628	11.2628

Table 11. Top-1 error rates for bosphorus + UMBDB occlusion classification without augmentation

Model Name	#Epochs = 5	#Epochs = 10	#Epochs = 15	#Epochs = 20	#Epochs = 25
AlexNet	7.6234	8.6263	7.7346	7.6754	8.2652
VGG16	7.3845	6.8714	5.7242	5.8356	5.3734
SqueezeNet	**5.2953**	**4.6418**	**4.7104**	**4.2653**	**4.5672**
DenseNet121	9.2108	7.8149	7.3346	7.6123	7.4272
ResNet18	9.1835	8.4279	7.2642	6.7213	8.2734

and 4.5672% (for 25 epochs). All the best error rates in this case have been achieved by the SqueezeNet model in comparison to other models.

Table 12 presents the best top-1 error rates for the binary occlusion presence classification in Bosphorus and UMBDB datasets combined depth images with augmentation. The best error rates are 3.1837% (for 5 epochs), 2.7755% (for 10 epochs), 2.8571% (for 15 epochs), 2.3673% (for 20 epochs), and 2.6939% (for 25 epochs). All the best error rates in this case have been achieved by the SqueezeNet model in comparison to other models.

Gender Binary Classification

Experiment 4: Comparison of Top-1 error rates for Bosphorus Gender Classification

Table 13 presents the best top-1 error rates for the gender binary classification in Bosphorus dataset combined depth images without augmentation. The best error rates provided are 18.2677% (for 5 epochs), 15.4337% (for 10 epochs), 12.3278% (for 15 epochs), 11.3834% (for 20 epochs), and 11.2357% (for 25 epochs). All the best error rates in this case have been achieved by the SqueezeNet model in comparison to other models.

Table 14 presents the best top-1 error rates for the binary gender classification in Bosphorus dataset depth images with augmentation. The best error rates provided are 16.2017% (for 5 epochs), 13.0901% (for 10 epochs), 10.4077% (for 15 epochs), 9.9785% (for 20 epochs), and 10.0858% (for 25 epochs). All the best error rates in this case have been achieved by the SqueezeNet model in comparison to other models.

Experiment 5: Comparison of Top-1 error rates for UMBDB Gender Classification

Table 12. Top-1 error rates for bosphorus + UMBDB occlusion classification with augmentation

Model Name	#Epochs = 5	#Epochs = 10	#Epochs = 15	#Epochs = 20	#Epochs = 25
AlexNet	6.5306	6.9388	5.8776	6.1224	6.3673
VGG16	5.2245	4.9796	4.5714	4.3265	4.1633
SqueezeNet	**3.1837**	**2.7755**	**2.8571**	**2.3673**	**2.6939**
DenseNet121	7.1837	5.9592	5.3878	5.6327	5.3061
ResNet18	7.102	6.3673	5.9592	5.3061	6.1224

Table 13. Top-1 error rates for bosphorus gender classification without augmentation

Model Name	#Epochs = 5	#Epochs = 10	#Epochs = 15	#Epochs = 20	#Epochs = 25
AlexNet	22.2634	23.8554	20.3467	19.2768	19.8534
VGG16	19.7536	18.4368	20.8452	18.8437	21.2578
SqueezeNet	**18.2677**	**15.4337**	**12.3278**	**11.3834**	**11.2357**
DenseNet121	19.7433	17.2346	18.8625	15.2846	15.8724
ResNet18	22.3467	19.9758	19.9863	19.7234	18.3247

Table 14. Top-1 error rates for bosphorus gender classification with augmentation

Model Name	#Epochs = 5	#Epochs = 10	#Epochs = 15	#Epochs = 20	#Epochs = 25
AlexNet	19.5279	20.1717	18.6695	17.8112	17.9185
VGG16	16.9528	16.309	17.4893	15.5579	19.4206
SqueezeNet	**16.2017**	**13.0901**	**10.4077**	**9.9785**	**10.0858**
DenseNet121	17.382	15.3433	15.0215	13.3047	13.6266
ResNet18	19.4206	16.7382	17.382	17.9185	15.5579

Table 15. Top-1 error rates for UMBDB gender classification without augmentation

Model Name	#Epochs = 5	#Epochs = 10	#Epochs = 15	#Epochs = 20	#Epochs = 25
AlexNet	**11.3491**	**9.8434**	**9.4578**	**9.2357**	**8.2147**
VGG16	14.1257	11.2685	10.3457	12.8432	10.8257
SqueezeNet	12.8434	12.8439	13.2384	9.2357	9.2467
DenseNet121	18.3273	17.4565	17.7563	15.5843	16.7323
ResNet18	15.8447	16.8645	14.5786	15.7235	15.2137

Table 15 presents the best top-1 error rates for the gender binary classification in UMBDB dataset combined depth images without augmentation. The best error rates provided are 11.3491% (for 5 epochs), 9.8434% (for 10 epochs), 9.4578% (for 15 epochs), 9.2357% (for 20 epochs), and 8.2147% (for 25 epochs). All the best error rates in this case have been achieved by AlexNet model in comparison to other models.

Table 16 presents the best top-1 error rates for the binary gender classification in UMBDB dataset depth images with augmentation. The best error rates provided are 8.1911% (for 5 epochs), 7.5085% (for 10 epochs), 7.8498% (for 15 epochs), 7.8498% (for 20 epochs), and 6.1433% (for 25 epochs). All the best error rates in this case have been achieved by AlexNet model in comparison to other models.

Experiment 6: Comparison of Top-1 error rates for Bosphorus + UMBDB Gender Classification

Table 17 presents the best top-1 error rates provided for the binary gender classification in Bosphorus and UMBDB datasets combined depth images without augmentation. The best error rates provided

Table 16. Top-1 error rates for UMBDB gender classification with augmentation

Model Name	#Epochs = 5	#Epochs = 10	#Epochs = 15	#Epochs = 20	#Epochs = 25
AlexNet	**8.1911**	**7.5085**	**7.8498**	**7.8498**	**6.1433**
VGG16	12.2867	8.8737	8.8737	9.5563	8.8737
SqueezeNet	10.5802	9.8976	10.5802	7.8498	7.8498
DenseNet121	16.7235	15.3584	14.6758	12.9693	13.3106
ResNet18	13.9932	13.6519	11.9454	13.3106	12.628

Table 17. Top-1 error rates for bosphorus + UMBDB gender classification without augmentation

Model Name	#Epochs = 5	#Epochs = 10	#Epochs = 15	#Epochs = 20	#Epochs = 25
AlexNet	17.7353	18.5257	17.4712	19.1267	18.7323
VGG16	18.2364	20.8423	19.8324	18.7232	18.8232
SqueezeNet	**16.9709**	**14.2734**	**13.3752**	**13.1263**	**13.2146**
DenseNet121	18.8944	18.3278	17.7832	16.7332	17.2732
ResNet18	19.8436	19.9458	18.2133	18.5732	19.1473

are 16.9709% (for 5 epochs), 14.2734% (for 10 epochs), 13.3752% (for 15 epochs), 13.1263% (for 20 epochs), and 13.2146% (for 25 epochs). All the best error rates in this case have been achieved by the SqueezeNet model in comparison to other models.

Table 18 presents the best top-1 error rates provided for the binary gender classification in Bosphorus and UMBDB datasets combined depth images with augmentation. The best error rates provided are 15.0897% (for 5 epochs), 12.8874% (for 10 epochs), 11.5824% (for 15 epochs), 11.9086% (for 20 epochs), and 11.2561% (for 25 epochs). All the best error rates in this case have been achieved by the SqueezeNet model in comparison to other models.

CONCLUSION

The presented work discusses the transfer learning techniques for occlusion presence and gender classification for 2.5D face depth images. Architectures of five deep learning models have been discussed in the paper. Depth images from Bosphorus and UMBDB datasets have been used for the purpose of occlusion presence and gender classification. Experimentation and results section presents the results for occlusion presence classification as well as gender binary classification for two cases viz. with augmentation, and without data augmentation. It has been observed that the top-1 error decreases in all experiments with data augmentation.

Table 18. Top-1 error rates for bosphorus + UMBDB gender classification with augmentation

Model Name	#Epochs = 5	#Epochs = 10	#Epochs = 15	#Epochs = 20	#Epochs = 25
AlexNet	16.8026	15.6607	14.9266	16.6395	15.8238
VGG16	17.4551	17.7814	17.292	16.721	15.7423
SqueezeNet	**15.0897**	**12.8874**	**11.5824**	**11.9086**	**11.2561**
DenseNet121	17.4551	15.0082	15.0082	13.8662	14.4372
ResNet18	18.3524	17.3736	16.8842	16.0685	16.6395

REFERENCES

Christopher, M. B. (2016). *Pattern Recognition and Machine Learning.* Springer-Verlag New York.

Colombo, A., Cusano, C., & Schettini, R. (2011, November). UMB-DB: A database of partially occluded 3D faces. In *Computer Vision Workshops (ICCV Workshops), 2011 IEEE International Conference on* (pp. 2113-2119). IEEE.

Deng, J., Dong, W., Socher, R., Li, L. J., Li, K., & Fei-Fei, L. (2009, June). Imagenet: A large-scale hierarchical image database. In *Computer Vision and Pattern Recognition, 2009. CVPR 2009. IEEE Conference on* (pp. 248-255). IEEE. 10.1109/CVPR.2009.5206848

Deng, J., Guo, J., & Zafeiriou, S. (2018). *Arcface: Additive angular margin loss for deep face recognition.* arXiv preprint arXiv:1801.07698

Grm, K., Štruc, V., Artiges, A., Caron, M., & Ekenel, H. K. (2017). Strengths and weaknesses of deep learning models for face recognition against image degradations. *IET Biometrics, 7*(1), 81–89. doi:10.1049/iet-bmt.2017.0083

He, K., Zhang, X., Ren, S., & Sun, J. (2016). Deep residual learning for image recognition. In *Proceedings of the IEEE conference on computer vision and pattern recognition* (pp. 770-778). IEEE.

Hu, G., Yang, Y., Yi, D., Kittler, J., Christmas, W., Li, S. Z., & Hospedales, T. (2015). When face recognition meets with deep learning: an evaluation of convolutional neural networks for face recognition. In *Proceedings of the IEEE international conference on computer vision workshops* (pp. 142-150). IEEE. 10.1109/ICCVW.2015.58

Iandola, F. N., Han, S., Moskewicz, M. W., Ashraf, K., Dally, W. J., & Keutzer, K. (2016). *Squeezenet: Alexnet-level accuracy with 50x fewer parameters and < 0.5 mb model size.* arXiv preprint arXiv:1602.07360

Jia, Y., & Shelhamer, E. (2015). *Caffe model zoo.* Academic Press.

Karpathy, A. (2016). Cs231n convolutional neural networks for visual recognition. *Neural Networks, 1.*

Krizhevsky, A., Sutskever, I., & Hinton, G. E. (2012). Imagenet classification with deep convolutional neural networks. In Advances in neural information processing systems (pp. 1097-1105). Academic Press.

Lee, Y. C., Chen, J., Tseng, C. W., & Lai, S. H. (2016, September). Accurate and robust face recognition from RGB-D images with a deep learning approach. BMVC. doi:10.5244/C.30.123

Liu, F., Zhu, R., Zeng, D., Zhao, Q., & Liu, X. (2018, March). Disentangling features in 3D face shapes for joint face reconstruction and recognition. In *Proceedings of the IEEE Conference on Computer Vision and Pattern Recognition* (pp. 5216-5225). IEEE. 10.1109/CVPR.2018.00547

Liu, J., Deng, Y., Bai, T., Wei, Z., & Huang, C. (2015). *Targeting ultimate accuracy: Face recognition via deep embedding.* arXiv preprint arXiv:1506.07310

Liu, W., Wen, Y., Yu, Z., Li, M., Raj, B., & Song, L. (2017, July). Sphereface: Deep hypersphere embedding for face recognition. In *The IEEE Conference on Computer Vision and Pattern Recognition (CVPR)* (Vol. 1, p. 1). IEEE. 10.1109/CVPR.2017.713

Parkhi, O. M., Vedaldi, A., & Zisserman, A. (2015, September). Deep face recognition. In BMVC (Vol. 1, No. 3, p. 6). Academic Press. doi:10.5244/C.29.41

Perez, L., & Wang, J. (2017). *The effectiveness of data augmentation in image classification using deep learning.* arXiv preprint arXiv:1712.04621

Qiao, S., Liu, C., Shen, W., & Yuille, A. L. (2018). Few-shot image recognition by predicting parameters from activations. In *Proceedings of the IEEE Conference on Computer Vision and Pattern Recognition* (pp. 7229-7238). IEEE. 10.1109/CVPR.2018.00755

Ranjan, R., Patel, V. M., & Chellappa, R. (2017). Hyperface: A deep multi-task learning framework for face detection, landmark localization, pose estimation, and gender recognition. *IEEE Transactions on Pattern Analysis and Machine Intelligence.* PMID:29990235

Savran, A., Alyüz, N., Dibeklioğlu, H., Çeliktutan, O., Gökberk, B., Sankur, B., & Akarun, L. (2008, May). Bosphorus database for 3D face analysis. In *European Workshop on Biometrics and Identity Management* (pp. 47-56). Springer. 10.1007/978-3-540-89991-4_6

Schroff, F., Kalenichenko, D., & Philbin, J. (2015). Facenet: A unified embedding for face recognition and clustering. In *Proceedings of the IEEE conference on computer vision and pattern recognition* (pp. 815-823). IEEE. 10.1109/CVPR.2015.7298682

Simonyan, K., & Zisserman, A. (2014). *Very deep convolutional networks for large-scale image recognition.* arXiv preprint arXiv:1409.1556

Srivastava, N., Hinton, G., Krizhevsky, A., Sutskever, I., & Salakhutdinov, R. (2014). Dropout: A simple way to prevent neural networks from overfitting. *Journal of Machine Learning Research, 15*(1), 1929–1958.

Sun, Y., Liang, D., Wang, X., & Tang, X. (2015). *Deepid3: Face recognition with very deep neural networks.* arXiv preprint arXiv:1502.00873.

Taigman, Y., Yang, M., Ranzato, M. A., & Wolf, L. (2014). Deepface: Closing the gap to human-level performance in face verification. In *Proceedings of the IEEE conference on computer vision and pattern recognition* (pp. 1701-1708). IEEE. 10.1109/CVPR.2014.220

Viola, P., & Jones, M. J. (2004). Robust real-time face detection. *International Journal of Computer Vision, 57*(2), 137–154. doi:10.1023/B:VISI.0000013087.49260.fb

Wang, H., Wang, Y., Zhou, Z., Ji, X., Li, Z., Gong, D., . . . Liu, W. (2018). *CosFace: Large margin cosine loss for deep face recognition.* arXiv preprint arXiv:1801.09414

Wu, X., He, R., Sun, Z., & Tan, T. (2018). A light CNN for deep face representation with noisy labels. *IEEE Transactions on Information Forensics and Security, 13*(11), 2884–2896. doi:10.1109/TIFS.2018.2833032

Xu, X., Dou, P., Le, H. A., & Kakadiaris, I. A. (2017). *When 3D-Aided 2D Face Recognition Meets Deep Learning: An extended UR2D for Pose-Invariant Face Recognition.* arXiv preprint arXiv:1709.06532

Zheng, Y., Pal, D. K., & Savvides, M. (2018, February). Ring loss: Convex feature normalization for face recognition. In *Proceedings of the IEEE Conference on Computer Vision and Pattern Recognition* (pp. 5089-5097). IEEE. 10.1109/CVPR.2018.00534

Chapter 7
Deep Learning:
Architectures and Applications

Kamaljit I. Lakhtaria
Gujarat University, India

Darshankumar Modi
Shantilal Shah Engineering College, India

ABSTRACT

Deep learning is a subset of machine learning. As the name suggests, deep learning means more and more layers. Deep leaning basically works on the principle of neurons. With the increase in big data or large quantities of data, deep learning methods and techniques have been widely used to extract the useful information. Deep learning can be applied to computer vision, bioinformatics, and speech recognition or on natural language processing. This chapter covers the basics of deep learning, different architectures of deep learning like artificial neural network, feed forward neural network, CNN, recurrent neural network, deep Boltzmann machine, and their comparison. This chapter also summarizes the applications of deep learning in different areas.

INTRODUCTION

Deep Learning has been emerged as new concept of Machine Learning since 2006. Deep learning is a part of machine learning algorithm that tries to get the details from multiple based on based on abstraction level. In other it can be also defined as machine learning sub-field where there be better understanding of underlying layers based on their features and characteristics. Here, higher level concepts have been defined from lower level representations and these lower level concepts are useful in defining other higher level concepts. One example to denote is an image. Image is higher level representation whereas group of pixels denotes the lower levels. Following sections elaborates how data has been emerged in huge amount.

DOI: 10.4018/978-1-5225-7862-8.ch007

Figure 1 shows the relationship between artificial intelligence, machine learning and deep learning. Artificial intelligence is referred as machine that tends to perform the tasks which requires human intelligence. It provides a machine a capability to behave like a human. While machine learning is using algorithms to process the data, analyze from the data and then make the prediction about related things. The machine is trained using large amounts of data and procedures provide them ability to perform the new task. Deep learning has been defined from machine learning. It was inspired by human neurons. It contains basically multiple layers of information. In each layer, more and more features or information extracted.

Rise of Huge Amount of Data

In today's world, the rise of data is due to development of newly created devices that generates different kind of data. Nowadays each and every user is connected with a smartphone to make life smarter. Each operation with smartphone generates data. Applications in the smartphone like temperate and humidity too generates data in large size.

Another factor for development of huge amount of data is IOT. Internet of Things connects your physical device to make it smarter and faster. Smart ACs, Smart TVs, Smart Car are example of IOT. Let us take simple example of Smart ACs. Smart ACs controls temperature of the room from the details room temperature, surrounding temperature and from global data as well. To accumulate this data, it has get details of temperature from sensors which provides room and surrounding temperature. Based on this data, Smart ACs set the temperature of room. In another example of smart car, Sensors attached to the smart car measures whatever the obstacle is, size of obstacle and speed of the obstacle. After analyzing huge amount of data, smart car can run. There are so many applications which processing and generating huge amount of data every day.

Figure 1. AI vs machine learning vs deep learning

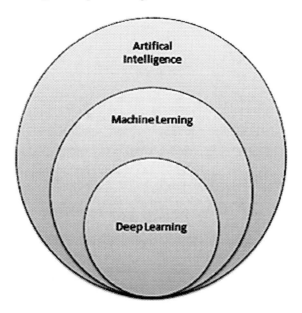

Medical devices are also responsible for generating data. These telemetry devices can measure blood pressure, oxygen saturation, heart beat at some regular intervals. The information collected or typically measured from these devices will be stored to a database located remotely. By analyzing such kind data, we can prevent and core measure health issues.

Data collected from various sources in the form of structured or unstructured format. In telemetry, data integration is critical. The data generated from different remote points must be stored within any transactional or analytical database. As data from different point comes to us, size or volume of data is growing exponentially. Thus need arises to efficiently and effectively manages such kind of huge data and retrieve useful information.

Artificial Neural Network

Artificial Neural Networks (hereby referred to as neural networks) are machine learning algorithms which recently have seen a surge in research and industry applications due to the boom of big data and increasing relevance of artificial intelligence and machine learning. Neural networks are connected layers of 'nodes', each of which have several input data values and a single duplicated output which depends on the multiple values which are given to it as input. Figure 2 shows multi-layer neural network comprising of 3 input and output nodes each with multiple hidden layers.

The main idea behind a neural network is to create some architecture/pattern of a number of nodes in each layer of the network and then provide a set of input 'training' data, along with a predetermined output data. We start the network learning which consists of cycling through all the input data and compares the end result to the predetermined output data. This training mode comparing the acquired output with the desired output. The end result is a set of node biases and paired weighting values which have been optimized such that the output of the neural network is as close as possible to the desired output. It is necessary to train the network many times on the same input training data and each pass of this training data is referred to as an epoch. In this sense, the network automatically learns how to parse the input data in order to obtain a desired output.

Once the network has been trained, it can be saved as a model and then used to run against new 'test' data which it has never seen before thereby providing genuine new data output. As a simple example, consider feeding a neural network a sequence of ordered time series values and suppose the output of

Figure 2. Multi-layer neural network

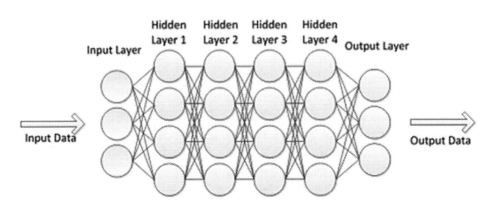

the neural network should be the same sequence. This implies the network will attempt to learn an 'identity' function. By feeding the network with many consecutive sequences, each time providing the same time sequence as desired output, it is able to learn a general identity function for this particular set of time series data (up to some reconstruction accuracy). Now, when we have trained a model and feed it a new sequence of time series data, if the reconstruction error is high based on the network output then one can say the input data was different relative to all the input data the model was trained on - thereby indicating that an anomaly occurred within this input time sequence.

Feed-Forward Neural Networks

In machine learning, artificial neural network is a group of nodes that are interconnected. This neural network basically learns patterns from readings. The first ever neural network consisting of input layer and output layer is perceptron (Rosenblatt, 1958). A perceptron, or a modified perceptron with multiple output units, is termed as a linear model, prohibiting its application in tasks involving complicated data patterns, despite the use of nonlinear activation functions in the output layer. This limitation can be overcome by introducing a so-called hidden layer between the input layer and the output layer. Note that in neural networks the units of the neighboring layers are fully connected to one another, but there are no connections among units in the same layer. Feed Forward Neural Networks are bad in predicting what is going to be next as they are memory less. Flow of the information in this neural network is straight.

Convolutional Neural Network

Convolutional Neural Networks are used in processing the data that could be in the form of multiple arrays i.e. 1D, 2D and 3D. Examples of 1D, 2D and 3D are signal & sequences, images and Videos respectively. The aim of a CNN is to learn higher-order features from the data via different layers. They are well suited in computer vision and object recognition. With help of CNN with can identify human

Figure 3. Feed forward neural network

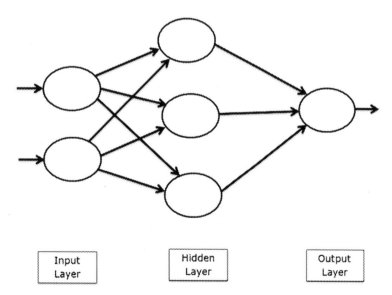

faces, street signs and many more. CNNs are very good at machine vision which can be deployed in many applications for robotics, smart driving cars, etc. Convolutional deep neural networks are used in computer vision. CNNs also have been applied to acoustic modeling for automatic speech recognition (ASR). Architecture of CNN is shown in below Figure 4.

CNNs transform the input data from the input layer through all connected layers into a set of class scores given by the output layer. There are basically three types layers available in the CNN: 1) Input Layer 2) Feature Extraction Layer and 3) Classification Layer.

Input layer will be feed with 3D data in the form Geospatial images containing Red, Green and Blue color channels. Color channel refers to RGB values for each and every pixel. Feature extraction layer is composing with sequences of convolutional layers and pooling layers. Convolutional layers transform the input data into units of feature map. It creates the patch of locally connected units from previous layers. Generally output of CN has same or larger dimensions compared to input. Pooling layers are used to progressively reduce the spatial dimension. It does so by merging similar features into one. For example if you have supplied image of 32*32 (Width*Height), output image may have smaller width and height. It can be applied to Natural language processing or graph data.

Recurrent Neural Networks

Recurrent Neural Networks allow sequential as well as parallel computation. Recurrent Neural Networks are trained to generate sequences, in which the output at each time-step is based on both the current input and the input at all previous time steps. In RNN, data flows in only one direction. RNN process an input sequence one element at a time while preserving the information about the previous elements of sequence. The outputs of all hidden layers are considered as if they were output of different neurons. RNNs are particularly used in applications such as language modeling. They are very good in predicting next character in the text. Long short-term memory is particularly effective for this use. Architecture of Neural Network is shown in below Figure 5.

Figure 4. Layers of convolutional network

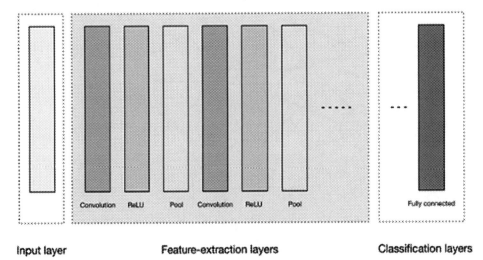

Figure 5. Recurrent neural network

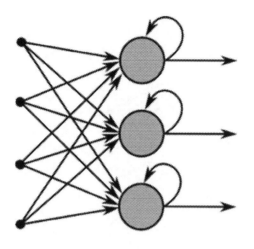

It is difficult to train RNNs because back propagation may shrink or grow at each time step. The recurrent neural network faces Vanishing Gradient Problem. It is being solved by LSTM network which is variation of Recurrent Neural Network.

Deep Boltzmann Network

Boltzmann learning is statistical in nature, and is derived from the field of thermodynamics. It is similar to error-correction learning and is used during supervised training. In this algorithm, the state of each individual neuron, in addition to the system output, are taken into account. In this respect, the Boltzmann learning rule is significantly slower than the error-correction learning rule. Neural networks that use Boltzmann learning are called Boltzmann machines.

Boltzmann learning is similar to an error-correction learning rule, in that an error signal is used to train the system in each iteration. However, instead of a direct difference between the result value and the desired value, we take the difference between the probability distributions of the system.

DBMs (Deep Boltzmann Machines) can learn complex and abstract internal representations of the input in tasks such as object or speech recognition, using limited, labelled data to fine-tune the representations built using a large supply of unlabeled sensory input data. Deep Boltzmann adopts the inference and training procedure in both directions, bottom-up and top-down pass, which allow the machine to better unveil the representations of the input structures.

The main purpose of Boltzmann Machine is to optimize the solution of a problem. It is the work of Boltzmann Machine to optimize the weights and quantity related to that particular problem.

It is type of recurrent neural network. They are having stochastic neurons with two possible values either 0 or 1. Neurons in Boltzmann Networks have two kinds of state available. Free state and Frozen State. In other words some neurons will be having free states other might have frozen state. Discrete Hopfield network can be transformed into Boltzmann machine by applying simulated annealing.

Figure 6. Deep Boltzmann network

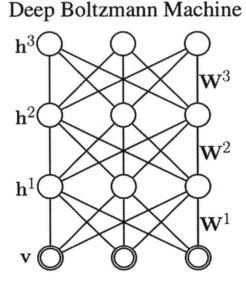

Deep Autoencoder

An auto-encoder is a neural network that has three layers: an input layer, a hidden (encoding) layer, and a decoding layer. The network is trained to reconstruct its inputs, which forces the hidden layer to try to learn good representations of the inputs.

An autoencoder neural network is an unsupervised Machine learning algorithm that applies back-propagation, setting the target values to be equal to the inputs. An autoencoder is trained to attempt to copy its input to its output. Internally, it has a hidden layer that describes a code used to represent the input. Figure 7 (Stanford, n.d.) represents the architecture of Autoencoder network.

Autoencoders belong to the neural network family, but they are also closely related to PCA (principal components analysis). Autoencoder is an unsupervised machine learning algorithm that is similar to PCA. Autoencoders although is quite similar to PCA but its Autoencoders are much more flexible than PCA. Autoencoders can represent both liners and non-linar transformation in encoding but PCA can only perform linear transformation. Autoencoders can be layered to form deep learning network due to its Network representation.

Categorization of Deep Learning

Unsupervised Feature Representation Learning

Compared with shallow architectures that require a good feature extractor designed mostly by hand on the basis of expert knowledge, deep models are useful for discovering informative features from data in a hierarchical manner (i.e., from fine to abstract). Here, we introduce three deep models that are widely used in different applications for unsupervised feature representation learning.

Figure 7. Autoencoers

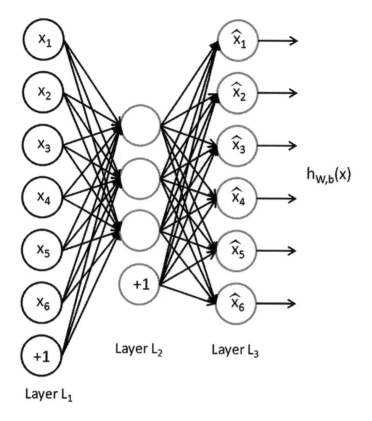

Deep networks for unsupervised learning, which are intended to capture high-order correlation of the observed or visible data for pattern analysis or synthesis purposes when no information about target class labels is available. Unsupervised feature or representation learning in the literature refers to this category of the deep networks. When used in the generative mode, may also be intended to characterize joint statistical distributions of the visible data and their associated classes when available and being treated as part of the visible data. In the latter case, the use of Bayes rule can turn this type of generative networks into a discriminative one for learning.

Deep Networks for Supervised Learning

It is intended to directly provide discriminative power for pattern classification urposes, often by characterizing the posterior distributions of classes conditioned on the visible data. Target label data are always available in direct or indirect forms for such supervised learning. They are also called discriminative deep networks.

Hybrid Deep Networks

Here the goal is discrimination which is assisted, often in a significant way, with the outcomes of generative or unsupervised deep networks. This can be accomplished by better optimization or/and regularization of the deep networks in category (Gibson & Patterson, 2017). The goal can also be accomplished when discriminative criteria for supervised learning are used to estimate the parameters in any of the deep generative.

Comparisons of Deep Learning Architectures

See Table 1.

Barriers of Deep Learning

Unavailability of Dataset

Deep learning requires massive amount of training dataset as classification accuracy of deep learning classifier is largely dependent on the quality and size of the dataset, however, unavailability of dataset is one the biggest barrier in the success of deep learning in medical imaging. On the other hand, development of large medical imaging data is quite challenging as annotation requires extensive time from medical experts especially it requires multiple expert opinion to overcome the human error. Furthermore,

Table 1. Overall summary of different deep learning neural networks

Type of Network	Detail	Advantages	Disadvantages
Deep Neural Network	Consisting of two or more layers which allows complex non linear relationships. Can be used for regression and classification	Provides higher level of accuracy	Training process is not trivial. Error may propagate through previous layers as well. Learning Process is too slow.
Convolution Neural Network	It is good for 2 Dimensional data. Comprising of convolution filters which transform from 2D to 3D.	High performance Learning process is fast.	Required large amount of labeled data for classification.
Recurrent Neural Network	Capability of learning sequences.	Can learn sequential events Can model time dependencies Provides accuracy in Speech Recognition and Character Recognition	Requires large amount of datasets for learning
Deep Boltzmann Machine	Capable of learning internal representations Complex and Fully Connected neural network	Deal robustly with ambiguous inputs	Difficult to train well Approximate interference is hard.
Deep Belief Network	Unidirectional connection between top two layers. Can be used supervised and unsupervised learning	Hierarchical representation of training data	Due to initialization, training process becomes more expensive.
Deep Auto Encoder	Can be used in Supervised learning Mainly designed for extraction and reduction of dimensionality feature	Does not required labeled data for classification. More robust	Required pre training.

annotation may not be possible due to unavailability of qualified expert or availability of sufficient cases are also issue in case of rare disease. Another issue major issue is unbalancing of data that is very common in health sector i.e.rare diseases, by virtue of being rare, are underrepresented in the data sets. If not accounted for properly, the class imbalance that ensues.

Heterogeneity in Dataset

Heterogeneity in Dataset is another barrier in deep learning. Currently, nature of data differ from hardware to hardware thus there exist large variation in images due to sensors and other factors. Furthermore, the breadth of any applications medical sector requires to combine several different datasets for better algorithms learning and accuracy.

Legal Issues

Data collected from various sources are much more complicated to share as compared other information. With the increase in healthcare data, scientists face big challenges that how to hide the personal details while disclosing the data. Other issues remains with that how to share data which is more sensitive and limit the amount of data sharing.

Applications of Deep Learning

Use of deep learning has rapidly evolved the field of object recognition in an image. Convolutional neural network have been used for applications like Traffic sign recognition, biological image recognition and face recognition. Deep learning is also useful in Speech recognition. Nowadays many technologies are available that enable the recognition and translation of the spoken language into text. Deep leaning have been used in medical area with good results. Below are the some applications of Deep Learning.

Automatic Speech Recognition

Large-scale automatic speech recognition is the first and most convincing successful case of deep learning. LSTM RNNs can learn "Very Deep Learning" tasks that involve multi-second intervals containing speech events separated by thousands of discrete time steps, where one time step corresponds to about 10 ms. LSTM with forget gates is competitive with traditional speech recognizers on certain tasks. All major commercial speech recognition systems (e.g., Microsoft Cortana, Xbox, Skype Translator, Amazon Alexa, Google Now, Apple Siri, Baidu and iFlyTek voice search, and a range of Nuance speech products, etc.) are based on deep learning.

Image Recognition

A common evaluation set for image classification is the MNIST database data set. MNIST is composed of handwritten digits and includes 60,000 training examples and 10,000 test examples. As with TIMIT, its small size lets users test multiple configurations. A comprehensive list of results on this set is available.

Visual Art Processing

With the increase in various deep learning techniques, it can be also applied to visual art tasks. Deep Neural Networks have proven themselves capable of identifying the style period of a given painting, "capturing" the style of a given painting and applying it in a visually pleasing manner to an arbitrary photograph and generating striking imagery based on random visual input fields.

Natural Language Processing

Google translate neural machine translation system which ANN to provide accuracy and fluency. It improves translation quality by giving thousands or millions of examples to the system. It learns the same by encoding the semantics of the input rather than memorising phrase.

Customer Relationship Management

Deep neural networks can be able to extract features from unstructured data. For Customer Relationship Management would use that cause they might have received data in the form of customer feedback and in the form of logs. From these feedback and responses, one can create labelled dataset. Then we can apply the deep learning neural network on that available dataset. Deep reinforcement learning can be used to approximate the value of possible direct marketing actions.

Recommendation System

Recommendation systems have used deep learning to extract meaningful features for a latent factor model for content-based music recommendations. Recommendation lists are generated based on user preferences, item features, user-item past interactions.

Bio-Informatics

Deep learning architecture like convolution network is extensively used in Biomedical informatics. Brain tumor segmentation, segmentation of pancreas, Segmentation Magnetic Resonance brain images uses CNN. Auto encoder ANN and Deep neural networks are used in predicting gene behaviour and gene function relationships.

Mobile Advertising

Deep learning algorithms have highly impacted Mobile arena. Nowadays speech recognition systems which are based on the deep learning algorithm is available on all major smartphone. It helps us to precisely understand the text, web content. As deep learning based system can run on highly parallel fashion, it provides faster response time. Based on the content used, day time and weather, geographic location, deep learning can track usage of the content.

Financial Fraud Detection

Deep learning is being successfully applied to financial fraud detection and anti-money laundering. "Deep anti-money laundering detection system can spot and recognize relationships and similarities between data and, further down the road, learn to detect anomalies or classify and predict specific events". The solution leverages both supervised learning techniques, such as the classification of suspicious transactions, and unsupervised learning, e.g. anomaly detection.

Healthcare

Due to success in computer vision, the first applications of deep learning to clinical data were on image processing, mostly for analyzing MRI images to predict the disease. To refer a knee MRI images, deep learning can be also applied. Deep learning was also applied to multi-channel 3D MRIs for the detection of breast cancers. Deep learning gathers a massive volume of data, including patients' records, medical reports, and insurance records, and applies its neural networks to provide the best outcomes.

Drug Discovery and Toxicology

Drug discovery and development is considered to be a tedious process, often consuming a significant amount of time and resources. To design a new drug with some specific requirements requires a huge amount of time, as well as computing power. In one or other way, deep learning algorithms are being developed to accelerate this process. It is anticipated that digital solutions for drug discovery may save significant time and capital. Companies like AiCure, Atomwise, Benevolent, InSilico Medicine, etc. uses deep learning technologies to develop the drugs.

Medical Imaging

Medical imaging techniques such as MRI scans, CT scans, ECG, are used to diagnose dreadful diseases such as heart disease, cancer, brain tumor. Hence, deep learning helps doctors to analyze the disease better and provide patients with the best treatment.

Insurance Fraud

Deep learning is used to analyze the medical insurance fraud claims. With predictive analytics, it can predict fraud claims that are likely to happen in the future. Moreover, deep learning helps insurance industry to send out discounts and offers to their target patients.

Alzheimer's Disease

Alzheimer is one of the significant challenges that medical industry faces. Deep learning technique is used to detect Alzheimer's disease at an early stage.

Genome

Deep learning technique is used to understand a genome and help patients get an idea about disease that might affect them. Deep learning has a promising future in genomics, and also insurance industry. Entilic says that they use deep learning technique to make doctors faster and more accurate. Cellscope uses deep learning technique and helps parents to monitor the health of their children through a smart device in real time, thus minimizing frequent visits to the doctor. Deep learning in healthcare can provide doctors and patients with astonishing applications, which will help doctors to make better medical treatments.

Image Restoration

Deep learning for image restoration is on the rise. Vincent et al. (n.d.) proposed the stacked denoising auto-encoder. A multi-layer perceptron can be applied to image denoising. Convolutional neural networks are also applied to natural image denoising, inpainting, matting and colorization.

Pixel Restoration CSI Style

In the show CSI they often zoom into videos beyond the resolution of the actual video. This seemed completely unreliable and there are even a few videos on YouTube like the one below where people explain they don't watch CSI because that is unrealistic.

Well, it was unrealistic until Deep Learning. Early in 2017, Google Brain researchers trained a Deep Learning network to take very low resolution images of faces and predict what each face most likely looks like. They call the method Pixel Recursive Super Resolution which enhances resolution of photos significantly.

In the image below you can see the original 8x8 photos, the ground truth (which was the real face originally in the photos) and in the middle the guess of the computer. Obviously it is not perfect, as it cannot be, but it is pretty unbelievable that the computer can guesstimate so well many of the features of the person in the photo.

Real-Time Multi-Person Pose Estimation

Deep Learning networks can now greatly aid animators in estimating the poses of people. Nowadays they can even do it in real-time. A work by Zhe Cao et al taught a neural network to estimate the position of human's skeleton. In the video below you can see over a dozen people dancing, while the network knows where they are and how they move. This is done without having any devices on them, only by analyzing the video!

Real-Time Analysis of Behavior

So Deep Learning networks know how to recognize and describe photos and they can estimate people poses. DeepGlint is a solution that uses Deep Learning to get real-time insights about the behavior of cars, people and potentially other objects. This is an application of Deep Learning that is on the sketchy side, but it is worth being familiar with.

Generating Photos of Galaxies

We don't really have to stop in terrestrial object when studying the natural world using Deep Learning. Astronomers are now using Deep Learning to create photos of galaxies as well as volcanoes.

Figure 8. 8x8 pixel photos were inputted into a Deep Learning network which tried to guess what the original face looked like. As you can see it was fairly close (the correct answer is under "ground truth") (Hadad, 2017)

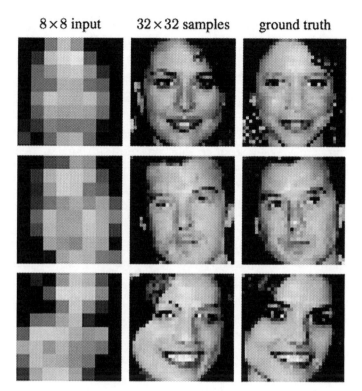

Figure 9. Computer generated galaxies and volcanoes. The architecture used here is called Generative Adversarial Networks (GANs) (Hadad, 2017)

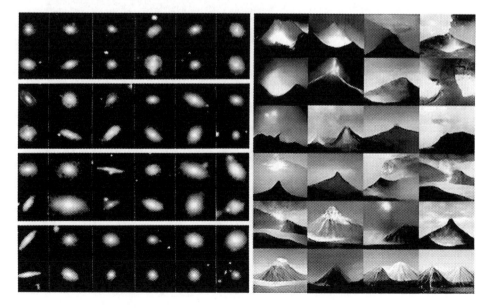

Music Composition

The same technology used for voice recognition can also be used to train a Deep Learning network to produce music compositions. Below is one example by Francesco Marchesani who trained the computer to compose music like my favorite classical composer Chopin. After the computer learns the patterns and statistics that are unique to the music of Chopin, it creates a completely new piece!

Estimate Solar Savings Potentials

Google Sunroofs uses aerial photos from Google Earth to create a 3-D model of your roof. The project uses Deep Learning neural networks to separate your roof from surrounding trees and shadows. It then uses the sun's trajectory and weather patterns to predict how much energy can be produced by installing solar panels on your roof.

Translation

Google Translate app can now automatically translate images with text in real-time to a language of your choice. Just hold the camera on top of the object and your phone runs a deep learning network to read the image, OCR it (i.e. convert it to text) and then translate it. Languages will gradually stop being a barrier and we will be able to communicate with other humans universally.

Figure 10. Google Sunroof predicts how much money you can save if you install solar panels. It uses Deep Learning to analyze the Google Earth aerial images (Hadad, 2017)

CONCLUSION

Recently, deep learning has achieved significant progress. Deep learning is a kind of representation learning that provides a machine with a capability to process the raw data such that it automatically detects different representations. Deep learning methods are comprising of multiple layers with each layer providing more abstract view of data. In this article, we have presented different neural networks of deep learning. We have also shown the comparison of different deep learning neural networks. The article also displays how these neural networks are used in variety of applications.

REFERENCES

Ackley David, H., Hinton Geoffrey, E., & Sejnowski Terrence, J. (1985). A Learning Algorithm for Boltzmann Machines. *Cognitive Science*, 9(1), 147–169. doi:10.120715516709cog0901_7

Battenberg, E., Schmidt, E., & Bello, J. (2014). *Deep learning for music*. International Conference on Acoustics Speech and Signal Processing (ICASSP).

Bengio, Y. (2009). Learning deep architectures for AI. *Foundations and Trends in Machine Learning*, 2(1), 1–127. doi:10.1561/2200000006

Chen, Engkvist, Wang, Olivecrona, & Blaschke. (2018). The rise of deep learning in drug discovery. Drug Discovery Today, 23(6), 1241-1250.

Cheng, J.-Z., Ni, D., Chou, Y.-H., Qin, J., Tiu, C.-M., Chang, Y.-C., ... Chen, C.-M. (2016). Computer-aided diagnosis with deep learning architecture: Applications to breast lesions in US images and pulmonary nodules in CT scans. *Scientific Reports*, 6(1), 24454. doi:10.1038rep24454 PMID:27079888

DeepMind Health. Google DeepMind. (2016). Retrieved from: https://www.deepmind.com/health

Deng, L., Abdel-Hamid, O., & Yu, D. (2013). A deep convolutional neural network using heterogeneous pooling for trading acoustic invariance with phonetic confusion. *Proceedings of International Conference on Acoustics Speech and Signal Processing*. 10.1109/ICASSP.2013.6638952

Deng, L., & Yu, D. (2013). Deep Learning Methods and Applications. Foundations and Trends in Signal Processing, 7(3-4).

Diez, A. (2013). *Automatic language recognition using deep neural networks* (Thesis). Universidad Autonoma de Madrid, Spain.

Gibson, A., & Patterson, J. (2007). *Deep Learning*. Sebastopol, CA: O'Reilly Media.

Goodfellow, Mirza, Courville, & Bengio. (2013). Multi-prediction deep Boltzmann machines. *Proceedings of Neural Information Processing Systems*.

Hadad, Y. (2017). *30 amazing applications of deep learning*. Retrieved from: http://www.yaronhadad.com/deep-learning-most-amazing-applications/

Liua, W., Wang, Z., Liua, X., Zeng, N., Liu, Y., & Alsaad, F. E. (2017). A survey on deep neural network architectures and their applications. *Neurocomputing, 234*, 11-26.

Min, S., Lee, B., & Yoon, S. (2017). Deep learning in bioinformatics. *Briefings in Bioinformatics, 18*(5), 851–869. PMID:27473064

Miotto, R., Wang, F., Wang, S., Jiang, X., & Dudley, J. T. (2017). Deep learning for healthcare: Review, opportunities and challenges. *Briefings in Bioinformatics*, 1–11. PMID:28481991

O'Meara, Schlag, & Wickler. (2018). *Applications of Deep Learning Neural Networks to Satellite Telemetry Monitoring*. SpaceOps Conference, Marseillef, France.

Rosenblatt, F. (1958). The perceptron: A probabilistic model for information storage and organization in the brain. *Psychological Review, 1958*, 65–386. PMID:13602029

Schmidhuber, J. (2015). Deep learning in neural networks: An overview. *Neural Networks, 61*, 85–117. doi:10.1016/j.neunet.2014.09.003 PMID:25462637

Schuler, C. J., Christopher Burger, H., Harmeling, S., & Scholkopf, B. (2013). A machine learning approach for non-blind image deconvolution. *IEEE Explore*. Retrieved from: http://citeseerx.ist.psu.edu/viewdoc/download?doi=10.1.1.378.7602&rep=rep1&type=pdf

Shatnawi, A., Al-Bdour, G., Al-Qurran, R., & Al-Ayyoub, M. (n.d.). A Comparative Study of Open Source Deep Learning Frameworks. *Conference: International Conference on Information and Communication Systems*.

Shen, Wu, & Suk. (2017). Deep Learning in Medical Image Analysis. *Annual Review of Biomedical Engineering, 19*, 221–248.

Stanford. (n.d.). Autoencoders. *UFLDL Tutorial*. Retrieved from: http://ufldl.stanford.edu/tutorial/unsupervised/Autoencoders/

Vincent, P., Larochelle, H., Bengio, Y., & Manzagol, P.-A. (n.d.). *Extracting and composing robust features with denoising autoencoders*. Retrieved from: http://www.cs.toronto.edu/~larocheh/publications/icml-2008-denoising-autoencoders.pdf

Yoo, Y., Brosch, T., & Traboulsee, A. (2014). Deep learning of image features from unlabeled data for multiple sclerosis lesion segmentation. *International Workshop on Machine Learning in Medical Imaging*, 117–24. 10.1007/978-3-319-10581-9_15

Zhang, S., Yao, L., Sun, A., & Tay, Y. (2018). Deep Learning based Recommender System: A survey and New Perspectives. *ACM Computing Surveys, 1*(1).

Chapter 8
A Survey on Deep Learning Techniques Used for Quality Process

Vanyashree Mardi
Alva's Institute of Engineering and Technology, India

Naresh E.
Jain University, India & Ramaiah Institute of Technology, India

Vijaya Kumar B. P.
Ramaiah Institute of Technology, India

ABSTRACT

In the current era, software development and software quality has become extensively important for implementing the real-world software application, and it will enhance the software functionality. Moreover, early prediction of expected error and fault level in the quality process is critical to the software development process. Deep learning techniques are the most appropriate methods for this problem, and this chapter carries out an extensive systematic survey on a variety of deep learning. These techniques are used in the software quality process along with a hypothesis justification for each of the proposed solutions. The deep learning and machine learning techniques are considered to be the most suitable systems for software quality prediction. Deep learning is a computational model made up of various hidden layers of investigation used to portray of information with the goal that researchers can better understand complex information issues.

INTRODUCTION

Software quality is the amount of a system or the standard that measures the system performance. There are two types of software quality measurement. First, the internal quality is measured during the process of software development life cycle (SDLC), while the external quality is related to the functionality that could depend on some of the internal quality attributes. The quality models allow for prediction of the

DOI: 10.4018/978-1-5225-7862-8.ch008

external quality attributes as a function of different internal quality attributes. The tasks involved in prediction of quality attributes are:

1. Recognition of the internal quality attributes,
2. Description of the relationship between the internal and external attributes.

Many research scholars have proposed different models for software quality prediction. The deep learning approach for predicting the software quality is more efficient than any other methodology.

In this survey, we focused on a variety of deep learning methods used for quality prediction process proposed by different investigators. These deep learning can be defined as neural network with a large number of attributes and hidden layers in one of four essential network architectures:

1. Convolutional Neural Networks
2. Recurrent Neural Networks
3. Recursive Neural Networks
4. Unsupervised Pre-training Networks

Software quality plays an important role in our day to day life as constantly require better quality product with more functionality. So to detect the product quality we used neural networks which is very efficient method. The neural network will observes the learning features and match into the target output and actual output. Deep learning method solves the problem of quality prediction by providing better quality of software. The Convolutional Neural Network is a kind of Neural Network which is designed from biologically driven model. The research has been found how humans perceive a quality in different layer. It is very prominent for the quality process kind of application. Convolutional Neural Network which learns pccr to peer mapping between low-quality and high qualities. This is absolutely achieved via hidden layers. The entire process of software quality is obtained through learning with pre-processing.

Convolutional Neural Network is designed in such a way that it provides superior quality accuracy. It requires moderate number of layers and filters. Therefore the proposed methods are faster as compared to other methods and also achieve fast rate for online usage. It does not need to solve any optimization problem because it is a feed-forward model. When large amount of dataset are available then improved the quality of network. The Convolutional Neural Network is trained in a supervised manner to generate high quality product using perceptual loss function which is not based on differences between qualities but instead on differences between high level features extracted from pre-trained convolution Neural Network. During training perceptual loss measures the similarity between output product and target quality product. The proposed method is relatively accurate and fast as compared to other method. This method is efficient as it produces high quality software products.

There are three aspects of this survey:

1. Convolutional Neural Network be trained with peer to peer mapping between low to high product with modest preprocessing.
2. The idea of designing network structure comes from the relation among the deep learning method and traditional method.
3. A Deep learning method is useful in computer vision problem of software application and achieves speed and good quality.

Figure 1. "Convolutional Neural Network (CNN)

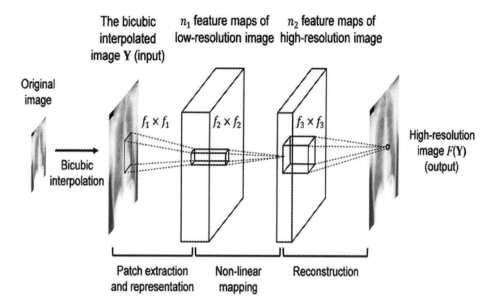

Artificial Neural Network (ANN)

Artificial Neural Network is one of the fascinating trending topics in this era. With the evolution of this Artificial Neural Network the unpredictable tasks can be conveniently can be done now. In some situations the machine learning models fails to learn the features when several variables are included. So in such situation the deep learning makes a fantasy in such situation. The Below Figure 2 shows the architecture of the Neural Networks.

Deep Neural Network

Now days, mimic of human brains is efficiently works in each and every area helps for the complex problems in the different domains. It designed basis on to recognize the complex patterns. This patterns are capable to recognize the video, audio and real world data and also it's translates into machine level language. Deep Neural Network (Amasaki et al., 2005) is one which is composed of several layers or stacked Networks which are composed like human brain. Compared to single Neural Network, the deep Neural Network consists of multi layers to process the data. Here the Deep Neural Network is composed of more than three layers which show the Deep learning. Figure 3 shows the diagram of Deep Neural Network (Challa et al., 2011), Based on previous layers output each layer inherently trains the same set of features which are distinct.

Deep Neural Network is efficient to find out the different latent structures which include the unlabeled and unstructured data. This type of unstructured data has enormous unlabeled data in the world. In some media types like audio, video, texts and pictures which has unstructured labeled data and this type of data can't recognized by human brains and which can't be organized the relational database.

Figure 2. Artificial neural networks

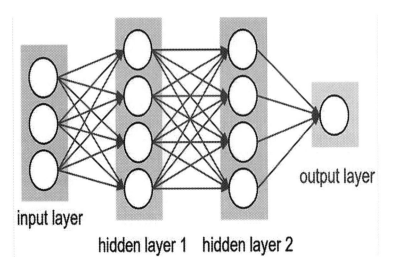

Figure 3. Deep neural networks

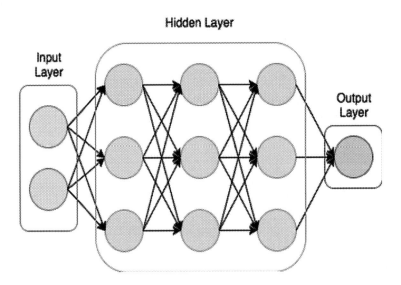

Motivation

Computer software is a collection or a set of programs that perform specific tasks. From a small digital smart watch to the large complex behemoths which manage space shuttle launches, none of the machines will work without programming it. During software maintenance phase software program must be checked for error, faults or failures before delivering it to the customer to ensure high quality and reliable outcome. Software developers or testers receive bug reports through various issues management tools such as Jira or Bugzilla. If the tester is new to the team or new to the domain it becomes very difficult for him to comprehend the application.

Super quality images are used in many fields. There are various computer vision areas like Medical field, Surveillance camera, Satellite imaging etc where analysis are extremely difficult. There are multiple low-resolution images available with the same scene but different perspective, value of high-resolution is obtained by combining the information present in low-resolution image. Non-uniform deblurring for dynamic view is one of the major challenging problems of computer vision as blur arises not only from object motions but also from camera and scene depth variation. High resolution frame in camera contains different kind of blurring. It is difficult to extract the information from blurry images. But multiple low-resolution based super-resolution algorithms faces many challenges like image registration error, poor blur filter estimation. In real world applications it is not easy to get multiple low-resolution images with the same scene thus generating high-resolution image is very important. The main goal of using super-resolution image is to generate high quality images from low quality resolution images by using low cost imaging device. Many techniques are available for super-resolution each of them have their own strengths and limitations.

BACKGROUND

The background work in the area with their applications and methods/algorithms used are described in the above Table 1.

Key Issues in Super-Quality Images

Deep learning method is one of the techniques used to improve the quality of image. Deep learning can prove to be a boon to address the everyday challenges that are faced in visual industry. But there are some issues that are faced in deep learning techniques for super-resolution image:

1. Image registration is one of the major issues facing in deep learning algorithm.
2. When the images are aligned geometrically there may be chances of lighting variation because of different lighting level.
3. Blur identification is difficult if the blur varies spatially across the images.

Table 1. Background work and its applications

Author	Application	Method/ Algorithm
Mohamed, Abdel-rahman, George Dahl, Geoffrey Hinton	Deep Belief Networks for phone recognition	Back propagation and associative memory architecture
Silver David, et al	Mastering the Game of Go with Deep Neural Networks and Tree Search	Supervised learning and reinforcement learning
Francesco Marra, Giovanni Poggi, Carlo Sansone Kiran B. Raja, R. Raghavendra, Vinay Krishna Vemuri, Christoph Busch	Iris sensor model identification Iris Recognition by using smartphones' cameras smartphones' cameras	Convolutional neural networks Deep sparse filtering

4. Understanding the features extracted from the training model is sometimes difficult.
5. Computational complexity is one of the major issues facing in deep learning techniques.
6. It is hard to get consistent conclusion from different super-resolution techniques in terms of performance evaluation.
7. Prediction performance of high quality images can be degraded.

Challenges

1. In recent years researchers have used different techniques to improve the quality of products from the low-quality software. But still they are facing some challenges which prevent the algorithm to practice in real time applications. One of the challenges is image registration in image processing. During the super-resolution process it causes registration error which generates wrong, low quality results.
2. Computational efficiency is the second challenge for super-resolution techniques. In super-resolution algorithms the high-resolution quality of the image that is recovered after processing depends upon the similarity among input image and training dataset. Training dataset should contain large number of images and it should be trained on that but it causes high computation cost.
3. Robustness of super-resolution is another challenge due to the presence of noise, inaccurate blur models, moving scene, motion blur etc. It cannot be estimated perfectly and may result in visual degradation which is not acceptable by many applications.
4. Deblurring of dynamic scenes is a challenging problem in computer vision as blur arises in images not only due to multiple objects but also from camera motion and scene depth variation.

Objectives

The main objectives of the survey are as follows:

1. To develop the method which generates the high quality application
2. To train the model which is capable of predicts early fault or error in software.
3. To improve the visual quality of products.
4. To extract the detail features from training model.
5. To design the method in such a way that it provides superior accuracy.
6. To overcome the hardware limitation in order to achieve best results.
7. To provide efficient computational methodologies for reconstruction of product.
8. To achieve efficient results with high quality, speed and accuracy.

DEEP LEARNING MODELS

Deep learning allows computational models to learn the representation of information for multiple level of abstraction. Modern deep learning frameworks are available for supervised learning and unsupervised learning. Deep Neural Network allows adding more number of layers but it increases the complexity.

Feed Forward Neural Networks

Feed Forward Neural Networks form the basis of many significant Neural Networks being used in the recent times, such as Convolutional Neural Networks (CNN) and Recurrent Neural Network (RNN). Feed-Forward Neural Networks are a kind of directed acyclic graph which means that there are no feedback connections or loops in the Network. Generally, these Networks are known by multiple names such as vanilla Neural Network, multilayer or fully connected Networks. Single layer Neural Network without any activation function is capable to learn a linear function (y = xW) and this Network corresponds to linear regression problem. If an activation function is added to output nodes of this Network, a logistic regression model, which is also a linear classification method (y = f (xW)) (Amasaki et al., 2005), is learned from this Network. Since two Networks learn a linear function, the problem of finding the best weight parameters turns to a concave optimization problem and only one local minimum point occurs in function space. For this reason, optimizing linear Networks are relatively easier than deeper Networks.

On the other hand, if at least one hidden layer is added to the Network, the optimization problem turns to a convex problem and function space has multiple local minimum points. Therefore, due to convergence to the local minimum problem, optimizing the Network turns to a harder problem. Although the difficulty of the training, multilayer Networks are capable to learn nonlinear functions y = f (f (xW 1)W 2) that increase the performance of the applications.

Convolutional Neural Network

Convolutional Neural Network is parallel to Feed-Forward Neural Networks. They are made up of neurons and having learnable biases and weight. Each layer receives some inputs, perform product and follow non-linearity. It uses loss functions with all training and optimization techniques for learning Feed Forward Neural Networks.

- **Forward Pass**: Network learning is usually done in sample of batches. It is denoted by x_i^t which is ith feature map of sample t and y_j^t is the jth output feature map of sample t. The filters denoted by k$_{ij}$. During the forward pass of Convolutional layer, features map output is calculated using the Convolutional operator (Amasaki et al., 2005).

$$y_j^t = \sum k_{ij} * x_i^t \tag{1}$$

- **Backward Pass:** Convolution layer computes the gradient of network loss function during the backward pass (Amasaki et al., 2005) .

$$\frac{\partial l}{\partial k_{ij}} = \sum_j \frac{\partial l}{\partial y_j^t} * k_{ij} \tag{2}$$

where * is representing the convolution with zero padding. Back-propagation algorithm is used so that value of gradient passed to the previous layer which computed x_j^t (Amasaki et al., 2005).

$$k_{ij} = k_{ij} - \alpha \frac{\partial l}{\partial k_{ij}}$$

(3)

where α : learning rate.

Layer of Convolutional Neural Network

Input product goes through different phases of layers. It takes the patch from the input and passes it to Convolutional layer. The Convolutional layer is a set of filters which can be applied through input layer. Same input product passes through number of filters. The processed data goes through another layer i.e., pooling layer. There are different aspects of pooling layer. This process will go on, again this patch will go to Convolutional layer and get more information from it and down sampled further. At the end there is a layer called fully connected layer. Here each node is connected to next node in the coefficient so it is a heavy data driven model. Convolutional Neural Network is divided among two phases training phase and inference phase. Training phase is taking lots of input data which is going through feed forward form and creating set of filters. Dataset which are used by inference phase can be used in real time application. Convolutional Neural Network uses little preprocessing as compared to other prediction algorithm.

Convolutional Layer

Convolutional Layer is the core block of Convolutional Neural Network. It takes bunch of filters which applied to input and create different activation features in that input data (Ahmed & Al-Jamimi, 2013). The output received by convolving the data with a particular filter is called feature map.

Parameters of Convolutional layer as follows:

1. Input dimension - W * H * D
2. Filters - 3 * 3 * D
3. Number of filters - N
4. Output - W * H * N

Figure 4. General structure of CNN

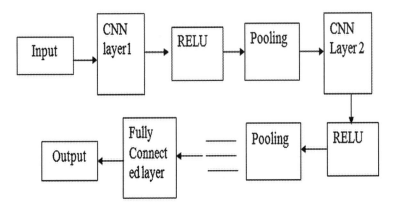

where W = width, H = Height, D = depth

Basically Convolutional layer extracts the feature from the given data. One filter can extract the edge of image; other can extract the color of image and so on.

RELU

RELU is also known as non linear activation layer. It is used to bring non linearity in network. It removes the over fitting probability and makes it more adaptive for real time cases.

Pooling Layer

When the products are too large there is a need to reduce the number of trainable parameters. Pooling is done to reduce the size of products or size of data. Pooling layer makes the representation of input smaller and more manageable. It is also responsible for controlling the over fitting. It also reduces the computational complexity and extracts prominent features. The size of pooling is defined to reduce the width and height of activation volume. For example, pooling size is defined as 2×2 to halve the width and height of input activation volume. Larger pool size should be selected to reduce it further. The most common pooling size is 2×2, to perform some computation, and then slide it over so it doesn't overlap and repeat.

Fully Connected Layer

To detect final output categories. After processing previous step, pick the top three using some probability distribution algorithm examples and detect the output.

Recurrent Neural Network (RNN)

A Recurrent Neural Network (RNN) is a category of Artificial Neural Network (ANN). Here there is a directed graph throughout a sequence for the connections between nodes. This property helps it to model dynamic behavior for continuous time sequence.

Long Short-Term Memory (LSTM) blocks are building blocks for different layers of a Recurring Neural Network. A Recurring Neural Network consisting of Long Short Term Memory blocks called as 'LSTM Network'. A Deep network is a class of Artificial Neural Network composed of numerous invisible layers in between layers of inputs and outputs. DNNs can imitate complicated irregular relationships. These DNNs basically the Networks which are feed forward in nature where the data flow from input layers to output layers is straight forward without any loops (Ahmed & Al-Jamimi, 2013; Aguilar-Ruiz et al., 2001).

RNNs are not similar to feed forward Networks because they use their internal memory state to operate on the input sequences. This behavior makes them used in applications like speech recognition or handwriting recognition. Recurring Neural Network randomly refers to two large categories of Neural Networks such as finite impulse and infinite impulse where both of these categories show dynamic behavior.

An infinite impulse Recurrent Network will not unrolled, as it is directed cyclic graph. Finite impulse and Infinite impulse Recurrent Networks are capable of having supplementary storage state whose control is solely dependent on Neural Network. Another network is the other substitute for storage if it comprises of delays, time and feedback loops. These kinds of controlled states often called as gated memory or gated state that are segment of Long Short-Term Memories (LSTM) and gated recurrent units. By unrolling, simply mean that we write out the network for the entire sequence.

Recurrent Neural Network involves learning the data to predict the output words. Recurrent Neural Network has application in Image Processing. However, with the applications of Natural Language Processing (NLP) techniques like Text Normalization and Text Transliteration from one language to other languages.

Recurrent Neural Network consists of three layers:

1. **Input Layer:** The input layer consists of words or images as input data.
2. **Hidden Layer:** This Layer describes the learning mechanism of the input data.
3. **Output Layer:** The output layer is set of well-formed words.

Text Processing Using RNN

1. The text data created by collecting the raw text from various sources like information centres and other dictionaries.
2. The collected text data is then loads to train using Recurrent Neural Network approach.
3. Keras and Tensor flow are the basic packages used to train the text data.
4. The prediction of words starts in a sequential way based on previous sequence of characters.

Mathematical Model

A Comparative model developed to compare the results that obtained by using N-gram approach and Recurrent Neural Network approach. A better quality achieved by using Recurrent Neural Network approach. By using the deep learning technique, character level training can be done for the input data that taken as input to predict the words. A model developed to train the data using Recurrent Neural Network Approach. In Recurrent Neural Network Approach, learning is done in sequential way based

Figure 5. RNN network

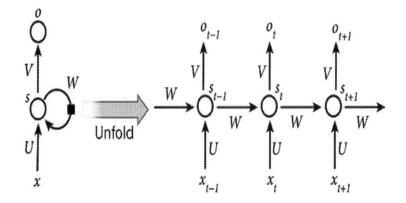

on previous predictions. The sequence range of ten previous characters considered to predict the next words in the sequence.

An accuracy calculated by comparing the results obtained by using N-gram approach and RNN approach language modeling. Accuracy is used to evaluate the performance or efficiency in learning method; it is used to reckon how the test was worthy and consistent. In order to calculate the accuracy, we need to measure some of metrics like true negative (TN), true positive (TP), false negative (FN) and false positive (FP). Accuracy has calculated by using following formulae (Challa et al., 2011):

$$Accuracy = \frac{TN + TP}{TN + TP + FN + FP} \tag{4}$$

The Table 2 illustrates the confusion matrix of the learning models. If predicted value is false and actual value is also false then doesn't have defect it comes under case True Positive. If predicted value is true and actual value is false then it cannot predict correct result it comes under case False Negative. The False Negative is also called as Type I error. It will reject the null hypothesis (H_0) when it is true. If predicted value is false and actual value is true then it cannot predict correct result it comes under case False Positive. It is also called as Type II error. If predicted value is true and actual value is also true then product has a defect comes under case True Negative.

Language Modelling: Recurrent Neural Network

Create a Language Model to train the text data to predict the words. We are using Long Short Term Memory (LSTM) model to train the corpus. The Classic approach of Recurrent Neural Language Modelling incorporated. The corpus along with a user defined sequential character length is given as input to a Language Model to train the data and to create a sequential model in it RNN is a type of Neural Network which is best suited for learning patterns from temporal data. Keras package is a high-level python API that used to quickly build and train Neural Networks using Tensor flow and Theano as back-end. In addition, Keras is a collection of different libraries used to perform many data mining and training the Neural Networks written in Python Language. Keras is having dependency on h5py, numpy, Scipy, pillow, Dense, LSTM and other libraries.

PERFORMANCES AND MODEL EVALUATION

We evaluate the quality process with the standard Evaluation metrics like Precision, recall and F-measure etc. These are common evaluation metrics for an Information retrieval system. For any Information re-

Table 2. Confusion matrix

Result of the Test		Predicted Value	
		False	True
Actual Value	**False**	True Positive	False Negative
	True	False Positive	True Negative

trieval system, the selection of the evaluation metrics mainly relies on the outcome of the Information system. For a bug retrieval system, we generally need input documents and a test suite serving as a query and a set of actual documents to judge the resulted file. Many Information retrieval forums provide this requirement.

Evaluation Metrics

Here several metrics for performance evaluation are identified. We first discuss some standard measure like precision. Then we talk about different evaluation measures. efficiency of the bug localization system is depends on the relevancy of the retrieved systems.

Precision

Precision is an important metrics which determines performance of the bug localization system in terms of the retrieved files. Precision of the system measures the "Degree of soundness" of the system. Precision can be considered for all the retrieved files in the system or can take a cut off at n ranked files i.e., Precision at nth rank. TP is True Positive FP is False Positive. Precision of the system is given by below equation.

Recall

Recall is a metric which measures the performance as a fraction of number of relevant files that are retrieved successfully. Recall measures the "Degree of completeness of the system". To achieve the good performance the system must achieve high recall value. 100% recall value indicates that all the relevant files are retrieved successfully. Recall is also known as sensitivity" or "Positive Predictive Value". TP being True Positive and FN being False Negative the Recall of the system is given by below equation.

Mean Average Precision (MAP)

Mean Average Precision is calculated by taking mean of all Average precision for each query description in the data set. MAP is the known standard metric for measuring the system performance. In our system the similarity between the bug description and the source code to calculated to retrieve the top ranked files. Average Precision for each file is calculated at rank of every relevant document retrieved. General Formula for calculating the Average Precision is given below. M denotes the Number of Relevant files for the given query. Pm denotes the precision at the mth relevant file retrieved. MAP is then calculated by taking mean of all calculated average precision divided by total number of bug reports in the experimental data set given by N.

F-Score

F-Score is generally used to measure the performance of any information retrieval system. F-Score considers both precision P and recall R to calculate the accuracy of the bug localization system. F score is the average of precision and recall. The performance of the system is best when F-Score value is 1 and is at worst condition at 0. The F-Score is given by the below formula:

Score

Score metric represents the number of buggy files that needs correction. Score metric is directly relative to accuracy metric more the value of score metric more is the accuracy of the system. Score metric was evaluated on file system consisting of 132 files and tested on 10 query descriptions. Suppose the score value for the first query is 85% then it means Bug resided in 15% of the overall file system. The score value is calculated using the formula given below.

Two evaluation metrics have been used for the performance of quality reconstructed image. We are using PSNR and SSIM are used as the performance metrics to evaluate the visual quality of super-resolved image. For super-resolution problem, it is preferable to obtain high PSNR and SSIM values from models. However, high PSNR or SSIM value does not always mean high perceptual quality.

Peak Signal to Noise Ratio (PSNR)

PSNR is a metric which is used to measure the quality difference between two images (Khoshgoftaar et al., 1997). Image with better image quality is having high PSNR. It is calculated as:

$$PSNR = 10log_{10}(S^2/(1/C_i * H_i * W_i \sqrt{\sqrt{\varphi}}\left(I'_{HR}\right) - \varphi\left(I_{HR}\right) \tag{5}$$

where s is maximum possible value that exists in original image, maximum possible value is 255. For color image first image is converted from RGB to YCbCr color space and PSNR is calculated on luminance channel due to sensitivity of human eye.

Structural Similarity Index (SSIM)

SSIM is a metric which is used to measure the similarity between two images. This assessment is based on three terms, luminance, contrast and structural (Klein, Wolf & Afek, 2015). The overall index is achieved by the multiplication of combination of three terms.

PACKAGES FOR DEEP LEARNING MODELS

Since python is the user-friendly language, it has some of the packages which are very essential for building the deep learning model. For efficient Deep Neural Network some of the packages installed are Theano, Lasagne, Numpy, Pandas, Tensor flow and Scipy. These are essential packages to build a Deep Neural Network which effectively produces reconstructed quality software products. Python is a high level interpreted programming language. Python language has some emphasizing reliability of code and it uses the whitespaces. Python coding language has some features such as:

1. It will change automatically
2. Some of the challenging and standard library
3. It's Time efficient
4. It's Efficient and Functional

5. It's Imperative and procedure
6. Automatic multiple memory management

Python is an open-source environment and it's a capable of interpreting for many operating systems. In the industry type it's oriented for community based model. Here we are using python language for coding because,

1. Efficient Testing Result
2. Metrics can be done by using the python language
3. Commenting section for coding
4. It has Coding guidelines for good programming
5. Fast execution of Results
6. Time efficiency
7. Good Analytical model can be done by using python

Anaconda Python Distribution

Anaconda is open software centre for the Python, R and Julia computing distribution. It's free software for the field of data science, machine learning and deep learning. The applications related to the anaconda packages are used in the field of Predictive Analytics, Scientific Computing and Data Processing. Anaconda is helpful for the efficient deployment of software and package management. Its inherently manages the different versions of the package. Over 6 million users are efficiently using the anaconda packages with respect to the different operating system such as Windows, Linux and Mac operating system.

Anaconda distribution includes an Anaconda Navigator which is version of Graphical user interface (GUI) which is desktop based versions which allows launching different anaconda packages and environments. Anaconda has a local repository which can be further installed in the environment. Some of the python coding background can be seen such as Spyder, Jupyter etc are some of the python programming tool for the efficient and classic output based results. The packages for deep learning models as follows:

Theano

Theano is a deep learning package essential to build the Neural Network. This library is mainly used for computing the mathematical functions using multiple arrays. Inherently here the Neural Networks are the building blocks and higher level wrappers are used to build the efficient Deep Neural Network. Theano is also considered as compiler for mathematical expressions in python. It knows how to take structure and to turn them in efficient code and uses Numpy to run as fast as possible on CPU or GPU.

Functions of Theano are following:

1. Automatically builds the symbolic graph for computing gradients.
2. It compiles the parts of expression graph into CPU or GPU instruction and optimizes the speed.
3. It also recognizes numerically unstable expression and computes them with more stable algorithms.

Lasagne

Lasagne is a frivolous library used to train and build the Neural Network in Theano. One of the functions of Lasagne is to make convenient the use of functions of Theano and able to write the Theano methods very effectively.

1. It supports Feed Forward Networks such as Convolutional Neural Network, Recurrent Network etc.
2. It allows the use of many optimization methods like ADAM.
3. It allows the architecture of multiple inputs and outputs.
4. Due to Theano's symbolic differentiation, it freely defines the cost functions.

Numpy

Numpy is an array processing python package. It provides high performance multi-dimensional array object. It is also known as fundamental package of scientific computing in python.

1. An N-dimensional array and powerful object.
2. It has sophisticated functions so it can be used in Fourier transformation and linear algebra etc.

Tensor Flow

Tensor flow is one which is an open source package in the anaconda which shows the dataflow graphs by using the numerical computation. This library has open sourced for the entire user and made available for public. It is developed by the Google Brain Team with in the research organization.

Scipy

Scipy is an extension of Numpy; it has relative functions and mathematical methods. It gives more power to the python interactive session by providing the end-user with high-level instructions, visualizing data and classes for manipulating. With the help of Scipy we can process data and system prototyping. It contains the modules of linear algebra, optimization, integration and interpolation etc.

Pillow (PIL Fork)

Pillow is a python imaging library which is used for opening, manipulating, and saving images. It allows to programmatically handling images in python.

VggNet

VggNetwork is a Convolutional Neural Network for image classification. It is using 3 * 3 kernel size filters which are stacked on top of each other in increasing depth. Instead of large size kernel multiple small size kernels is better as it allows the network to learn more complex feature at lower cost. First it is trained with smaller version of data consisting of less weight layers. This smaller network is used as initialization for the larger deeper network. This process is called pre-training. It helps in designing network architecture. It is used to define loss function. One of the advantages of deeper network is that it gives better results.

Pandas

Pandas is open source python libraries which giving superior, simple to utilize information structures and information examination apparatuses for the Python programming language. Pandas expand on packages like Numpy and Matplotlibto give you a solitary, advantageous, place to do the greater part of visualization and data analysis.

HOW DO WE CHOOSE QUALITY SOFTWARE?

We should implement Quality software whenever we need to enhance the quality of our system or product. Regardless of whether you are creating expectations as a feature of a task or operational group, a viable quality administration and quality assurance process will be useful.

The Quality Process is consist of material, organization of people, equipment and rules into work activities designed to produce a specified final result. The Quality Assurance (QA) is ensured and analyzed by performing a sequence of activities. These activities are step by step process and result analysis is conducted for final evaluation process.

- **Quality Definition:** Quality is very important for business software and organizational process.
- **Process Selection:** Process selection is one which selects the appropriate tools and methods.
- **Quality Evaluation:** This model is evaluates the quality of product and process relative to the specific system and business goals.
- **Quality Organization:** Initially for each stage organize the quality assurance to improve the evaluation and improvement through planning.

Goal /Question /Metric Paradigm for Quality Process

A software process development paradigm tailored for the business Improvement paradigm. Associate in managerial structure approach for building code competencies and supply them to expertise works.

Quality Improvement Paradigm Characterize its surroundings with relevance metrics. The quantitative aim for this survey is to quality improvement and high performance. Select the appropriate method for model building and tools. Execute the method, construct the product, data collection, validate the product and analyze the information and give feedback for corrective action.

Implementing the Quality Cycle and Quality Improvement

The process improvement models is also known as PDSA cycle, which stands Plan, Do, Check or Study and Act as illustrates in Figure 6. The improvement cycle is a efficient stage for learning the quality improvement process.

The PDSA cycle has consist of four steps as follows:

Figure 6. Quality improvement cycle

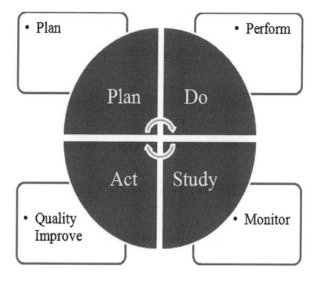

- **Plan:** This stage consists of identifying a purpose or aim, defining and formulating the metrics and plan.
- **Do:** This step which tells the product of the plan is implemented.
- **Study:** This stages involves monitoring results to test the validity of the plan for process, progress and success and quality improvement.
- **Act:** This is last stage of cycle, it will integrate and learning by entire process, which should be used in goal, change techniques and reformulate the intrusion.

SOFTWARE TESTING

Software Testing is process of checking the completeness of the quality software by validating expected output against actual results. Software testing involves the process of executing the software to check the correctness of feature in interest. Software testing also helps in identifying errors, flaws and any missing requirements. Software testing can be done wither manually or can be automated. Here White Box testing is chosen to test the bug or error in the software. The main aim of testing is to identify faults by testing individual modules separately. During testing these modules are combined to perform integration testing. During testing it must ensure that system should not show unexpected behavior.

1. **Unit Testing:** Unit testing is defined as the first basic phase or level of the software testing process where single components of the software in elaborated. It is done to check whether all the components are working as per the description done during design. It increases the confidence for in elaborating code. It is basically followed with the help of white box testing method.
2. **Integration Testing:** Integration testing is a phase that comes after unit testing where the combination of units are done in a group and tested to check the compatibility and adoptability to different units of the whole system. It is done to correct or the check the faults that are appeared due to the

combination or integration of different testing units. Any method such as black box, grey box or white box testing method is helpful for integration testing.

3. **System Testing:** It is the third phase of testing level where it is done on the complete integrated software system. It is basically done to check the software obedience as per described requirements. This process is done with the help of black box testing method and it is carried out by the separate software testers.

4. **Acceptance Testing:** This is the final phase of testing system which is done on the complete system to check whether it is complete with business requirement and is in a phase of delivery to the customers. It is done with the help of black box testing.

Importance of Software Testing

1. Software Testing ensures customer satisfaction and reliability by validating software application.
2. Testing ensures fewer faults which minimizes major bugs in the future.
3. Testing helps in delivering high quality software to the customers.
4. Testing is necessary to achieve high performance of the system.

Types of Software Testing

Functional Testing

Functional testing includes testing main functionality of the testing. Two types of functional testing are black box testing and white box testing. Other types of testing are interface testing, unit testing, smoke testing and regression testing etc.

Non-Functional Testing

Non-functional testing includes testing of non-functional components of the system like How the system behaves when too many users check in, can the software be ported from one environment to another, can the software handle stress, is the software more secure, how is the performance of the system under normal circumstances etc. Some of the non-functional testing includes performance testing, load testing, Endurance testing and so on.

Maintenance Testing

Maintenance Testing is done at the stage of enhancement of software system or migration of the software system. Two types of maintenance testing are regression and maintenance testing.

Statistical Testing

The Statistical Testing is mainly used for estimate the results. Hypothesis Testing is a statistical procedure to determine whether hypothesis should be accepted or rejects based on collected data. The following methods are used to test the hypothesis:

1. **Null Hypothesis (H$_0$):** No significant difference between particular populations, in any observed reason.
2. **Alternative Hypothesis (H$_1$):** ~H$_0$. There is significant difference between specific populations; in some observed reason (Adline & Ramachandran, 2014).

P-value and Significance levels (α) is a tool that helps to measure the type I error in a hypothesis testing. The significance level is nothing but a probability of accepting the null hypothesis (H$_0$). The P-value is nothing but a probability of obtaining an effect at least as extreme as the one in our sample data, assuming the truth of the null hypothesis (Adline & Ramachandran, 2014). When a P-value is greater than or equal to the significance level (α), we should accept the null hypothesis (H$_0$). The P-value has some range between 0 and 1. If P-value is less ($\leq \alpha$) then it indicates strong evidence against the null hypothesis (H$_0$). If P-value is greater ($> \alpha$) then it indicates weak evidence against the null hypothesis (H$_0$), so we should accept the null hypothesis.

APPLICATIONS OF DEEP LEARNING TECHNIQUES

1. Automatically Adding Sounds to Silent Movies
2. Automatic Machine Translation
3. Automatic Text Generation
4. Predicting Earthquakes
5. Neural Networks for Brain Cancer Detection
6. Winning Atari Breakout
7. Changing gazes of people in photos
8. Healthcare monitoring for pets
9. Predicting high quality products etc.

CONCLUSION

In this survey, the deep learning techniques are used to improve the quality of the software. In deep neural network there is one input layer and multiple of hidden layers; output depends on the hidden layers. Due to the multiple hidden layers the process execution of the software improved significantly. So the deep learning techniques show high performance and accurate result.

REFERENCES

Abouelela, M., & Benedicenti, L. (2010). Bayesian network based XP process modeling. *International Journal of Software Engineering and Its Applications*, *1*(3), 1–15. doi:10.5121/ijsea.2010.1301

Abouelela, M., & Beneficent, L. (2010). Bayesian network based XP process modeling. *International Journal of Software Engineering and Its Applications*, *1*(3), 1–15. doi:10.5121/ijsea.2010.1301

Adline, A., & Ramachandran, M. (2014). Predicting the software fault using the method of genetic algorithm. *International Journal of Advanced Research in Electrical, Electronics and Instrumentation Engineering, 3*(2), 390–398.

Adline, A., & Ramachandran, M. (2014). Predicting the software fault using the method of genetic algorithm. *International Journal of Advanced Research in Electrical, Electronics and Instrumentation Engineering, 3*(2), 390–398.

Adline, A., & Ramachandran, M. (2014). Predicting the software fault using the method of genetic algorithm. *International Journal of Advanced Research in Electrical, Electronics and Instrumentation Engineering, 3*(2), 390–398.

Aguilar-Ruiz, J., Ramos, I., Riquelme, J. C., & Toro, M. (2001). An evolutionary approach to estimating software development projects. *Information and Software Technology, 43*(14), 875–882. doi:10.1016/S0950-5849(01)00193-8

Ahmed, M. A., & Al-Jamimi, H. A. (2013). Machine learning approaches for predicting software maintainability: A fuzzy-based transparent model. *IET Software, 7*(6), 317–326. doi:10.1049/iet-sen.2013.0046

Amasaki, S., Takagi, Y., Mizuno, O., & Kikuno, T. (2005). Constructing a Bayesian belief network to predict final quality in embedded system development. *IEICE Transactions on Information and Systems, 88*(6), 1134–1141. doi:10.1093/ietisy/e88-d.6.1134

Azar, D., & Vybihal, J. (2011). an ant colony optimization algorithm to improve software quality prediction models: Case of class stability. *Information and Software Technology, 53*(4), 388–393. doi:10.1016/j.infsof.2010.11.013

Challa, J. S., Paul, A., Dada, Y., Nerella, V., Srivastava, P. R., & Singh, A. P. (2011). Integrated software quality evaluation: A fuzzy multi-criteria approach. *Journal of Information Process System, 7*(3), 473–518. doi:10.3745/JIPS.2011.7.3.473

Dong, C., Loy, C. C., He, K., & Tang, X. (2014). Learning a deep convolutional network for image super-resolution. In *European Conference on Computer Vision (ECCV)* (pp. 184–199). Springer. 10.1007/978-3-319-10593-2_13

Guo, P., & Lyu, M. R. (2000). Software quality prediction using mixture models with EM algorithm. *Proceedings of Quality Software in First Asia-Pacific Conference on IEEE*, 69–78.

Gupta, D., Mittal, H.K., & Goyal, V. (2011). Comparative study of soft computing techniques for software quality model. *International Journal of Software Engineering Research Practices, 1*(1), 33–37.

Kapur, P. K., Khatri, S. K., & Goswami, D. N. (2008) 'A generalized dynamic integrated software reliability growth model based on neural-network approach', *Proceedings of International Conference on Reliability, Safety and Quality Engineering*, pp.831–838.

Karayilan & Kilic. (2017). Prediction of Heart Disease Using Neural Network. In *2nd International conference on Computer Science & Engineering (UBMK'17)*. Department of Computer Engineering Yildirim Beyazit University. doi:10.1109/CVPR.2015.7299117

Karunanithi, N., Whitley, D., & Malaiya, Y. K. (1992). Using neural networks in reliability prediction. *Software, IEEE, 9*(4), 53–59. doi:10.1109/52.143107

Khoshgoftaar, T. M., Allen, E. B., Halstead, R., Trio, G. P., & Flass, R. (1997a). Process measures for predicting software quality. *Proceedings of High-Assurance Systems Engineering Workshop, Proceedings on IEEE*, 155–160.

Khoshgoftaar, T. M., Ganesan, K., Allen, E. B., Ross, F. D., Munikoti, R., Goel, N., & Nandi, A. (1997b). Predicting fault-prone modules with case-based reasoning. *Proceedings of Software Reliability Engineering, The Eighth International Symposium on IEEE*, 27–35. 10.1109/ISSRE.1997.630845

Khoshgoftaar, T. M., & Seliya, N. (2002). Tree-based software quality estimation models for fault prediction. *Proceedings of Software Metrics of Eighth IEEE Symposium*, 203–214. 10.1109/METRIC.2002.1011339

Khoshgoftaar, T. M., & Seliya, N. (2002). Software quality classification modeling using the SPRINT decision tree algorithm. *International Journal of Artificial Intelligence Tools, 12*(3), 207–225. doi:10.1142/S0218213003001204

Khoshgoftaar, T. M., Seliya, N., & Sundaresh, N. (2006). An empirical study of predicting software fault with case-based reasoning. *Proceedings of Software Quality Journal, 14*(2), 85–111.

Khoshgoftaar, T. M., Shan, R. M., & Allen, E. B. (2000). Improving tree-based models of software quality with principal components analysis. *Proceedings of Software Engineering Reliability Engineering, ISSRE 2000 of 11th International Symposium on IEEE*, 198–209. 10.1109/ISSRE.2000.885872

Klein, B., Wolf, L., & Afek, Y. (2015). A Dynamic Convolutional Layer for short range weather prediction. *2015 IEEE Conference on Computer Vision and Pattern Recognition (CVPR)*.

Mittal, H., Bhatia, P., & Goswami, P. (2008). Software quality assessment based on fuzzy logic technique. *International Journal of Soft Computing Applications, 1*(3), 105–112.

Pizzi, N. J., Summers, R., & Pedrycz, W. (2002). Software quality prediction using median-adjusted class labels. *Proceedings of International Joint Conference on Neural Networks, 3*, 2405–2409.

Puri, A., & Singh, H. (2014). Genetic algorithm based approach for finding faulty modules in open source software systems. *International Journal of Computer Science & Engineering Survey, 5*(3), 29–40.

Radliński, L. (2011). A conceptual Bayesian net model for integrated software quality prediction. *Annales UMCS Informatica, 11*(4), 49–60.

Rashid, E., Bhattacherjee, V., & Patnaik, S. (2012). The application of case-based reasoning to estimation of software development effort. *International Journal of Computer Science and Informatics, 1*(3), 29–34.

Rashid, E., Patnaik, S., & Bhattacherjee, V. (2012). Software quality estimation using machine learning: case-based reasoning technique. *International Journal of Computer Applications, 58*(14), 43–48.

Wagner, S. (2010). A Bayesian network approach to assess and predict software quality using activity-based quality model. *Information and Software Technology, 52*(11), 1230–1241. doi:10.1016/j.infsof.2010.03.016

Xing, F., Guo, P., & Lyu, M. R. (2005). A novel method for early software quality prediction based on support vector machine. *Proceedings of Software Reliability Engineering (ISSRE), 16th IEEE International Symposium on IEEE*, 10–15.

Yuan, X., Khoshgoftaar, T. M., Allen, E. B., & Ganesan, K. (2000). An application of fuzzy clustering to software quality prediction. *Proceedings of Application-Specific Systems and Software Engineering Technology in 3rd IEEE Symposium on IEEE*, 85–90. 10.1109/ASSET.2000.888052

Chapter 9
Deep Learning in Early Detection of Alzheimer's:
A Study

Anitha S. Pillai

https://orcid.org/0000-0002-3883-8234
Hindustan Institute of Technology and Science, India

Bindu Menon
Apollo Hospitals, India

ABSTRACT

Advancement in technology has paved the way for the growth of big data. We are able to exploit this data to a great extent as the costs of collecting, storing, and analyzing a large volume of data have plummeted considerably. There is an exponential increase in the amount of health-related data being generated by smart devices. Requisite for proper mining of the data for knowledge discovery and therapeutic product development is very essential. The expanding field of big data analytics is playing a vital role in health-care practices and research. A large number of people are being affected by Alzheimer's Disease (AD), and as a result, it becomes very challenging for the family members to handle these individuals. The objective of this chapter is to highlight how deep learning can be used for the early diagnosis of AD and present the outcomes of research studies of both neurologists and computer scientists. The chapter gives introduction to big data, deep learning, AD, biomarkers, and brain images and concludes by suggesting blood biomarker as an ideal solution for early detection of AD.

INTRODUCTION

The huge amount of data being generated by healthcare industry has great future to support a variety of healthcare and medical functions. The digitization of this voluminous data generated by the healthcare industry is the Big Medical data. This data includes physicians' prescription, laboratory test data, X-ray, scan reports, pharmacy data, patient data in Electronic Health records, sensor data, social media posts

DOI: 10.4018/978-1-5225-7862-8.ch009

which includes tweets, Facebook messages and status updates, news feeds, newspaper, magazines and medical journals.

The digitization of medical data, the field of genomics and use of wearable sensors to monitor patient health are some of the factors that have contributed to the growth of Big Data in Health Care/Biomedicine (Mathew & Pillai, 2016).

Big Medical Data can be used by researchers to identify patterns which can be used for predictions. For example, in the case of Alzheimer's, disease (AD) by analyzing the MRI images of the brain certain patterns can be identified. This knowledge can be used in identifying the ones who are at the greatest risk of getting this disease.

Big data analytics has helped in medical research as we have the necessary software and algorithms capable of analysing cognitive functions and help doctors to easily identify such patients. Lumosity is a brain game platform wherein user score data is used for early detection of Alzheimer's before a permanent neuronal loss occurs (Krishnan, 2018). High-dimensionality research in the future is likely to create intelligent analytical systems that are capable of generating effective disease diagnostic and drug development deliverables. Biomedical datasets are growing daily and a plethora of high-dimensionality datasets are now freely accessible for neurodegenerative diseases, such as AD (Maudsley, Devanarayan, Martin & Geerts, 2018). The convergence of advanced computing and numerous Big Data technological options has paved the way to attain high performance and scalability at a relatively low cost. Big data solutions usually come with a set of innovative data management solutions and analytical tools, and when effectively implemented can transform the healthcare outcomes (Mathew & Pillai, 2015).

Deep Learning

Deep learning is an artificial intelligence function in machine learning that enables computers to learn from experience and understand the world in terms of a hierarchy of concepts. Deep Learning (DL) is a subfield of machine learning concerned with algorithms inspired by the structure and function of the brain called artificial neural networks (Browniee, 2016). In Deep learning neural network composed of several layers are used. The node combines input from the data with an associated weight or coefficient. The product of input and weight are summed and sent to the activation function. Depending on the value of the summation, the signal progresses further through the network to identify the final outcome. The earlier versions of Neural Networks had one input, one output, and one hidden layer. In deep learning, there is more than one hidden layer and each layer of nodes is trained on a different set of features based on the previous layer's output. One main benefit of deep learning is as there are several layers, and as we go deep into the network, nodes will be capable of identifying complex features as they aggregate and recombine features from the previous layer.

Supervised learning algorithms used are:

- Logistic Regression
- Multilayer perceptron
- Deep Convolutional Network

Semi-Supervised / Unsupervised Learning algorithms are:

- Auto Encoders
- Restricted Boltzmann Machines
- Deep Belief Networks

DL can be applied to Biology and medicine as they are rich in data that are complex and difficult to understand. DL is used for the diagnosis of a number of diseases including Cancer and Alzheimer's. Literature survey reveals that some of the challenges faced by DL researchers in applying to Medical / Biomedical studies is the unavailability of the Biomedical dataset, privacy issues, guidance from medical experts etc. Though deep learning based application has provided good results, however, due to the sensitivity of healthcare data and challenges, more sophisticated deep learning methods that can deal complex healthcare data efficiently is required. Most researchers believe that within few years, deep learning based applications will take over human and not only most of the diagnosis will be performed by intelligent machines but will also help to predict disease, prescribe medicine and guide in treatment (Razzak, Nazb & Zaib, 2017).

Alzheimer's Disease

Alzheimer's disease is a progressive neurological disorder which causes cognitive decline involving memory loss and behavioural changes due to the death of brain cells. It is the most common type of dementia, accounting for 60 to 80 percent of cases of dementia in the United States and In 2013, 6.8 million people in the U.S. had been diagnosed with dementia (MacGill, 2018) also according to MacGill (2018), Of these, 5 million had a diagnosis of Alzheimer's and according to the author By 2050, the numbers are expected to double. Alzheimer's is a neurodegenerative disease with mild symptoms at the beginning and progresses over the years.

Fast facts on Alzheimer's disease (MacGill, 2018)

- Alzheimer's disease is the most common type of dementia.
- AD usually occurs when plaques containing beta- amyloid form in the brain.
- As time progresses symptoms also worsen and becomes difficult for AD subjects to remember recent events, to recognize people they know, use appropriate words/spellings.
- Mostly, a person with AD will need full-time assistance to carry out their day to day activities.

Biomarkers

The term "biomarker" or "biological marker", are a set of medical signs – which are medical states observed from outside the patient – which can be measured accurately. Some examples of biomarkers include pulse and blood pressure through basic chemistries to more complex laboratory tests of blood and other tissues (Strimbu & Tavel, 2010). According to the WHO, biomarkers includes "almost any measurement reflecting an interaction between a biological system and a potential hazard, which may be chemical, physical, or biological. Biomarkers can be classified based on different parameters, including their characteristics, such as imaging biomarkers (computed tomography, positron emission tomography, magnetic resonance imaging) or molecular biomarkers (Huss, 2015).

According to Ralf Huss (2015), Molecular biomarkers have biophysical properties, which permit them to be measured in biological samples, and include nucleic acid–based biomarkers such as gene mutations or polymorphisms and quantitative gene expression analysis, peptides, proteins, lipids metabolites, and other small molecules.

Brain Imaging / Neuroimaging

One of the most encouraging areas of research focused on prompt detection of AD is Neuroimaging. Structural imaging with MRI or computed tomography (CT) is usually used to detect tumours, small or large strokes, damage from severe head trauma or a fluid in the brain.

The following are taken from https://www.alz.org/research/science/earlier_alzheimers_diagnosis.asp

- Studies related to Structural imaging has shown that the brains of people with Alzheimer's shrink considerably as the disease advances and shrinkage in some specific brain regions such as the hippocampus may be an initial sign of Alzheimer's. But standardized values for brain volume has not been identified so as to conclude the presence of AD.
- Using Functional imaging with positron emission tomography (PET) and other methods it has been noticed that patients with AD typically have less brain cell activity in certain regions. Lessening of glucose in areas of the brain which are important in memory, learning and problem solving is also associated with AD.
- Another active area of research namely Molecular imaging helps in detecting biological clues specifying Alzheimer's is underway even before the disease alters the brain's structure or function.
- Pittsburgh compound B (PIB) was the first radiotracer capable of highlighting deposits of beta-amyloid—one identifier of AD.
- Florbetaben (Neuraceq®), Florbetapir (Amyvid®) and Flutemetamol (Vizamyl®) also help in identifying beta-amyloid in the brain.

Cerebrospinal fluid (CSF) biomarkers (Aβ peptides and tau proteins). *Amyloid-β precursor protein (AβPP)*, *presenilin 1 (PSEN1)*, and *presenilin 2 (PSEN2)* genes are strongly involved in early-onset Alzheimer's disease (EOAD).

Late-onset Alzheimer's disease (LOAD) has been linked with other genes including *apolipoprotein E-ε4 (APOEε4)*, *bridging integrator 1 (BIN1)* region, *clusterin (CLU)*, *phosphatidylinositol clathrin assembly lymphoid-myeloid (PICALM)*, and *complement receptor 1*, mostly identified through genome-wide association studies (GWAS).

LITERATURE REVIEW

Korolev et al. (2017) proposed deep 3D convolutional neural network architectures for classification of brain Magnetic Resonance Imaging (MRI) scans. Their study compared the performance of the residual and plain convolutional neural networks with their proposed model based on the Alzheimer's Disease National Initiative (ADNI) dataset with Alzheimer's disease and normal controls. The comparative study revealed that their proposed model performed better in comparison with the earlier methods and one advantage of the model according to the authors was ease of use and no need for handcrafted feature generation. Authors used label propagation and classified MRI images in a manifold-based semi-supervised learning framework and used voxel morphometry analysis to extract some of the most critical AD-related features of brain images from the original MRI volumes and also grey matter (GM) segmentation volumes. Their main focus was to identify the features that differentiate between a healthy and Alzheimer-affected brain. Next dimension reduction of the extracted features was done using Principal Component Analysis (PCA) for faster and accurate analysis. Using the subset of labelled training data and using the label propagation method the labels of the remaining images were predicted and classified into two groups namely mild Alzheimer's and normal condition. According to the authors, the accuracy of the classification using their proposed method is 93.86% for the Open Access Series of Imaging Studies (OASIS) database of MRI brain images which when compared to the best existing methods, provided a 3% lower error rate (Korolev et al., 2017).

Using data from healthy people getting scopolamine, Simpraga et al. (2017) developed an index of the muscarinic acetylcholine receptor antagonist (mAChR) consisting of 14 EEG biomarkers. Authors reported that the mAChR index developed produced higher classification performance than any single EEG biomarker with precision ranging from 88–92%. Their research reported that the mAChR index also helped to differentiate between healthy elderly from patients with Alzheimer's disease (AD). Their study further stated the importance of integrating multiple EEG biomarkers to improve the accuracy of identifying disease or drug interventions, which was important for clinical trials.

Lu et al. (2018) proposed a novel deep neural network to identify individuals at risk of developing Alzheimer's disease. Their multi-scale and multi-modal deep neural network (MMDNN) was designed to integrate different scales of information from various regions of the brain taken from several modalities. Initially, the authors demonstrated the efficiency of the proposed MMDNN approach by comparing with the existing methods in differentiating between stable MCI and progressive MCI individuals. Later the classifier was trained to distinguish subjects of a probable AD. Authors observed that MMDNN had the overall classification accuracy of 82.4% in identifying the individuals with mild cognitive impairment (MCI) who will convert to AD at 3 years prior to conversion, a 94.23% sensitivity in classifying individuals with clinical diagnosis of probable AD, and a 86.3% specificity in classifying non-demented controls (Lu et al., 2018). By performing this study, the authors suggest that deep neural network classifiers have a great potential for providing evidence in support of the clinical diagnosis of a probable AD.

Li et al. (2017) presented a deep ordinal ranking model for classifying AD's different stages using structural imaging data focusing on the hippocampus, built on CNNs and ordinal ranking techniques. Then on comparison with the traditional multi-category classification methods based on the ADNI dataset authors demonstrated that their method could achieve better classification performance by utilising inherent ordinal severity of brain degeneration associated with AD's different stages. The study also pointed out that the deep learning features of the hippocampus outdid hand-crafted imaging features, like shape. Authors suggested that the performance of the flexible architecture of proposed deep model could be further improved if multimodality information is taken into account, e.g., PET imaging and cerebrospinal fluid (CSF) biomarkers.

3D convolutional neural networks (3D-CNNs) to learn the multi-level imaging features for classification of AD using PET brain images was done by Cheng and Liu (2017). Initially, they constructed multiple deep 3D-CNNs on different local image patches to transform the local image into more compact high-level features and then a deep 3D CNNs was trained to learn the high-level features for final classification. According to the authors, the proposed method could automatically learn the generic features from PET imaging data for classification. The proposed method was evaluated on the PET images from

193 people which consisted of 93 AD patients and 100 normal controls (NC) taken from Alzheimer's Disease Neuroimaging Initiative (ADNI) database. Results of the experiment indicated that the proposed method achieved an accuracy of 92.2% for the classification of AD versus NC, establishing a very promising classification performance (Cheng & Liu, 2017).

A study to show the importance of deep learning techniques for the classification of CT brain images, using a convolutional neural network (CNN), for providing information on the early diagnosis of Alzheimer's disease was conducted by Gao, X. W., & Hui, R, 2016. CT images (N=285) are clustered into three groups namely, AD, Lesion (e.g. tumour) and Normal ageing. In order to handle images with a larger thickness along the direction of depth (z) (~3-5mm), an advanced CNN architecture was used integrating both 2D and 3D CNN networks. According to Gao and Hui (2016), the classification accuracy rates obtained by this CNN architecture are 85.2%, 80% and 95.3% for classes of AD, Lesion and Normal respectively with an average of 87.6%.

A deep learning method using 8-layer 3D Convolutional Network (3D ConvNet) was used for automatic feature learning and Alzheimer's disease classification by Backstrom et al (2018). The study was performed on the ADNI dataset containing 1198 MRI brain scans from 199 AD patients and 141 NC subjects. Authors claim that by using the random data partitioning strategy, the proposed scheme yielded 98.74% accuracy on the test dataset, with 100% for AD detection with false alarm 2.4%.

According to LeWitt, Li, Lu, et al. (2017) Biomarkers in the blood and cerebrospinal fluid (CSF) of patients with Parkinson's disease (PD) show strong correlations to disease progression, according to a report in the February 8 online issue of *Neurology*. Le Witt PA et.al, reports that as on date, neurologists rely on clinical rating scales or radioisotope neuroimaging results and, no additional biological indicators have emerged that can help in predicting how a patient will do over time, or whether an experimental treatment is neuroprotective. They also suggested that biomarkers could provide information about subtypes of PD and would aid in assessing the effectiveness of neuroprotective treatments.

According to Buckley, Schultz, Hedden et al. (2017) Among healthy adults, those with the lowest default mode network (DMN) connectivity — the network of interacting brain regions — and a positive amyloid scan shown via the PET radiotracer scan, Pittsburgh compound PiB, had poorer cognitive outcomes and were more likely to progress from preclinical Alzheimer's disease to the symptomatic phase of the disease. The authors predicted that in healthy older adults who had lower functional brain connectivity and presence of amyloid as per the scan reports were prone to cognitive decline within three years.

Fluorodeoxyglucose (FDG) positron emission tomography (PET) measures the decline in the regional cerebral metabolic rate for glucose, offering a reliable metabolic biomarker even on presymptomatic Alzheimer's disease (AD) patients (Singh et al., 2017). This model made use of probabilistic principal component analysis on max-pooled data and mean-pooled data for dimensionality reduction, and to perform binary classification multilayer feed forward neural network was used. According to the authors, 186 cognitively unimpaired (CU) subjects, 336 mild cognitive impairment (MCI) subjects with 158 Late MCI and 178 Early MCI, and 146 AD patients from Alzheimer's Disease Neuroimaging Initiative (ADNI) dataset was used for this study and the study reported that deep model-based research as an effective imaging biomarker of AD in comparison with FDG-PET.

Various researchers are working on blood, cerebrospinal fluid and brain images to detect Alzheimer's as early as possible. A team of researchers from the University of Bari in Italy used an algorithm based on Artificial Intelligence (AI) that can spot tiny structural changes in the brain caused by the disease a decade before symptoms even appear (Moon, 2017). They made use of 67 MRI scans ie 38 from Alzheimer's patients and 29 from healthy controls to train their AI. Initially the researchers divided the scans into small regions and had their AI analyze the neuronal connectivity. After training, the algorithm was tested with 148 brain scans from 148 people. According to Moon (2017) AI was able to diagnose Alzheimer's 86 percent of the time and detect mild cognitive impairment 84 percent of the time.

Rachmadi, Hernández, Agan, Perri, and Komura (2018) proved the effectiveness of the 2D CNN scheme by comparing its performance against those obtained from another deep learning approach like Deep Boltzmann Machine (DBM), two conventional machine learning approaches: Support Vector Machine (SVM) and Random Forest (RF), and a public toolbox: Lesion Segmentation Tool (LST) and concluded that Deep learning algorithms perform much better than the traditional machine learning algorithms.

According to Xiaonan Liu, Kewei Chen, Teresa Wu, David Weidman, Fleming Lure, Jing Li, (2018), most of the studies concentrate only on building classifiers that used multi-modality imaging and non-imaging data to predict MCI conversion to AD and obtained accuracy which was generally below or barely above 80%. They suggested that in order to monitor the progression of the disease, a binary classification was not sufficient and a multi-class model was the need of the hour. Xiaonan et.al also felt that machine learning algorithms are mostly used in the existing studies and DL-based algorithms have not been used for early AD diagnosis though DL is very popular in other areas of computer vision.

CASE STUDIES

Studies have shown that many people with mild cognitive impairment go on to develop Alzheimer's, which is much more severe. People with this condition forget words, spellings, stop recognizing close relatives, lose basic self-care skills and eventually become entirely dependent on caregivers. But not all people with mild cognitive impairment develop AD. So, it would be really great if AD can be detected at an early stage and treated, and one way of doing it is by studying positron emission tomography (PET) scans of the brain. Alzheimer's is generally characterized by the unwanted growth of protein clumps called amyloid plaques and slow brain metabolism which is usually measured by the rate at which the brain uses glucose. Certain types of PET scans can reveal signs of both these conditions and can, therefore, be used to identify people with mild cognitive impairment who are most at risk of developing Alzheimer's (Choi & Jin, 2018). Choi and Jin (2018) developed a deep-learning neural network to train brain images of people with and without Alzheimer's to recognize the difference between them. The data set had brain images of 182 people in their 70s with normal brains and brain images of 139 people of roughly the same age who have been diagnosed with AD. With conventional training, the machine was taught to differentiate between normal brain images and the ones diagnosed with AD with an accuracy of almost 90 percent. The authors then used their deep learning machine on a different dataset which had brain images of 181 people in their 70s with mild cognitive impairment of which 79 developed AD within three years and wanted their network to identify those 79 people. According to Choi and Jin (2018), their neural network identified those at risk of developing AD with an accuracy of 81 percentage. That according to them was significantly higher than what was done manually. Their study results proved that deep learning could be used as a tool for predicting disease outcome using brain images and the network was useful in spotting people at risk of developing Alzheimer's and those who could benefit by early diagnosis and treatment.

A question that has been in existence for a long time is how best to use brain morphometric and genetic data to distinguish AD patients from cognitively normal (CN) subjects and how to predict those who will progress from MCI to AD (Ning, Chen, Sun, Hobel, Zhao, Matloff, & Toga, 2018). Ning et al. (2018) used a Neural Network (NN) on both structural brain measures and genetic data to address this question. They tested the effectiveness of neural networks in classifying and predicting AD. Data used for the study was from ADNI which included baseline structural MRI data and single nucleotide polymorphism (SNP) data for 138 AD patients, 225 CN subjects, and 358 MCI patients. NN models with both brain and SNP feature as predictors perform significantly better than models with either alone in classifying AD and CN subjects, (Ning et al., 2018). Their work also proved that NN models to not only classify and predict AD occurrence but can also be used to identify important AD risk factors.

CONCLUSION

From the literature review it is very clear that many researchers have used Deep Learning for early prediction of AD. Though some of them have received good results there is still a long way to go in early prediction of the disease. We should be able to develop a good biomarker. A biomarker for the biological diagnosis of AD needs to have sensitivity and specificity especially form differentiating from other neurodegenerative disorders. MRI can assess a sequential and regional imaging of the brain for anatomical details. However, this tool of assessment can be vague with less precision. The diagnostic accuracy needs to be high for continued clinical utility and for further research for newer drug discoveries. A blood biomarker would be an ideal scenario however as the concentration of CSF analytes are less in peripheral blood due to its inability to pierce the blood-brain barrier, this method remains a challenge. The pathology of AD is predominantly extracellular deposition of beta amyloid-Aβ and intracellular accumulation of tau protein. A good biomarker would be non-invasive detection of these pathological biomarkers. Imaging brain amyloid in the brain is probably the best imaging diagnostic tool.

REFERENCES

Backstrom, K., Nazari, M., Gu, I. Y., & Jakola, A. S. (2018). An efficient 3D deep convolutional network for Alzheimer's disease diagnosis using MR images. *2018 IEEE 15th International Symposium on Biomedical Imaging (ISBI 2018).* doi:10.1109/isbi.2018.8363543

Benedictus, M. R., Leeuwis, A. E., Binnewijzend, M. A., Kuijer, J. P. A., Scheltens, P., Barkhof, F., ... Prins, N. D. (2017). Lower cerebral blood flow is associated with faster cognitive decline in Alzheimer's disease. *European Radiology*, 27(3), 1169–1175. doi:10.100700330-016-4450-z PMID:27334014

Browniee, J. (2016, September 22). *What is Deep Learning?* Retrieved from https://machinelearningmastery.com/what-is-deep-learning/

Buckley, R. F., Schultz, A. P., & Hedden, T. (2017). *Functional network integrity presages cognitive decline in preclinical Alzheimer's disease.* Retrieved from http://http://www.neurology.org/content/early/2017/06/07/WNL.0000000000004059.short

Cheng, D., & Liu, M. (2017). Classification of Alzheimer's Disease by Cascaded Convolutional Neural Networks Using PET Images. In Q. Wang, Y. Shi, H. I. Suk, & K. Suzuki (Eds.), Lecture Notes in Computer Science: Vol. 10541. *Machine Learning in Medical Imaging. MLMI 2017.* Cham: Springer. doi:10.1007/978-3-319-67389-9_13

Choi, H., & Jin, K. H. (2018). Predicting cognitive decline with deep learning of brain metabolism and amyloid imaging. *Behavioural Brain Research, 344,* 103–109. doi:10.1016/j.bbr.2018.02.017 PMID:29454006

Fox, N. C., & Schott, J. M. (2004). Imaging cerebral atrophy: Normal ageing to Alzheimer's disease. *Lancet (London, England), 363*(9406), 392–394. doi:10.1016/S0140-6736(04)15441-X PMID:15074306

Gao, X. W., & Hui, R. (2016). A deep learning based approach to classification of CT brain images. *2016 SAI Computing Conference (SAI).* 10.1109/SAI.2016.7555958

Huss, R. (2015). *Biomarkers.* Translational Regenerative Medicine. Retrieved from https://www.sciencedirect.com/science/article/pii/B9780124103962000190

Korolev, S., Safiullin, A., Belyaev, M., & Dodonova, Y. (2017). Residual and plain convolutional neural networks for 3D brain MRI classification. *2017 IEEE 14th International Symposium on Biomedical Imaging (ISBI 2017).* doi:10.1109/isbi.2017.7950647

Krishnan, S. (2018). How Big Data Can Help in Treating Alzheimer's Disease. *Analytics Insight.* Available at: https://www.analyticsinsight.net/big-data-can-help-treating-alzheimers-disease/

LeWitt, P. A., Li, J., Lu, M., & the Parkinson Study Group-DATATOP Investigators. (2017). *Metabolomic biomarkers as strong correlates of Parkinson disease progression.* Retrieved from http://http://www.neurology.org/content/early/2017/02/08/WNL.0000000000003663.short

Liu, X., & Chen, K. (2018). Teresa Wu, David Weidman, Fleming Lure, & Jing Li, Use of multi-modality imaging and artificial intelligence for diagnosis and prognosis of early stages of alzheimer's disease. *Translational Research; the Journal of Laboratory and Clinical Medicine.* doi:10.1016/j.trsl.2018.01.001

Long, X., Chen, L., Jiang, C., & Zhang, L. (2017). Prediction and classification of Alzheimer disease based on quantification of MRI deformation. *PLoS One, 12*(3), e0173372. doi:10.1371/journal.pone.0173372 PMID:28264071

Lu, D., Popuri, K., Ding, G. W., Balachandar, R., & Beg, M. F. (2018). Multimodal and Multiscale Deep Neural Networks for the Early Diagnosis of Alzheimer's Disease using structural MR and FDG-PET images. *Scientific Reports, 8*(1). doi:10.103841598-018-22871-z PMID:29632364

MacGill, M. (2018, February 13). *Alzheimer's disease: Symptoms, stages, causes, and treatment.* Retrieved from https://www.medicalnewstoday.com/articles/159442.php

Mathew, P. S., & Pillai, A. S. (2015). Big Data solutions in Healthcare: Problems and perspectives. *2015 International Conference on Innovations in Information, Embedded and Communication Systems (ICIIECS).* 10.1109/ICIIECS.2015.7193211

Mathew, P. S., & Pillai, A. S. (2016). Big Data Challenges and Solutions in Healthcare: A Survey. In V. Snášel, A. Abraham, P. Krömer, M. Pant, & A. Muda (Eds.), *Innovations in Bio-Inspired Computing and Applications. Advances in Intelligent Systems and Computing* (Vol. 424). Cham: Springer. doi:10.1007/978-3-319-28031-8_48

Maudsley, S., Devanarayan, V., Martin, B., & Geerts, H. (2018). Intelligent and effective informatic deconvolution of "Big Data" and its future impact on the quantitative nature of neurodegenerative disease therapy. *Alzheimer's & Dementia, 14*(7), 961–975. doi:10.1016/j.jalz.2018.01.014 PMID:29551332

Moon, M. (2017, September 17). *AI can detect Alzheimer's 10 years before symptoms show up*. Retrieved from https://www.engadget.com/2017/09/17/ai-alzheimers-early-detection/

Ning, K., Chen, B., Sun, F., Hobel, Z., Zhao, L., Matloff, W., & Toga, A. W. (2018). Classifying Alzheimers disease with brain imaging and genetic data using a neural network framework. *Neurobiology of Aging, 68*, 151–158. doi:10.1016/j.neurobiolaging.2018.04.009 PMID:29784544

Payan, A., & Montana, G. (2015). *Predicting Alzheimer's disease: a neuroimaging study with 3D convolutional neural networks*. ICPRAM.

Rachmadi, M.F., Hernández, M.D., Agan, M.L., Perri, C.D., & Komura, T. (2018). Segmentation of white matter hyperintensities using convolutional neural networks with global spatial information in routine clinical brain MRI with none or mild vascular pathology. *Computerized Medical Imaging and Graphics, 66*, 28-43.

Razzak, M. I., Naz, S., & Zaib, A. (2017). Deep Learning for Medical Image Processing: Overview, Challenges and the Future. *Lecture Notes in Computational Vision and Biomechanics Classification in BioApps*, 323-350. doi:10.1007/978-3-319-65981-7_12

Simpraga, S., Alvarez-Jimenez, R., Mansvelder, H. D., Gerven, J. M., Groeneveld, G. J., Poil, S., & Linkenkaer-Hansen, K. (2017). EEG machine learning for accurate detection of cholinergic intervention and Alzheimer's disease. *Scientific Reports, 7*(1). doi:10.103841598-017-06165-4

Strimbu, K., & Tavel, J. A. (2010, November). What are Biomarkers? *Current Opinion in HIV and AIDS, 5*(6), 463–466. doi:10.1097/COH.0b013e32833ed177 PMID:20978388

Section 2
Advanced Deep Learning Techniques

Chapter 10
Deep Clustering

M. Parimala Boobalan
VIT University, India

ABSTRACT

Clustering is an unsupervised technique used in various application, namely machine learning, image segmentation, social network analysis, health analytics, and financial analysis. It is a task of grouping similar objects together and dissimilar objects in different group. The quality of the cluster relies on two factors: distance metrics and data representation. Deep learning is a new field of machine learning research that has been introduced to move machine learning closer to artificial intelligence. Learning using deep network provides multiple layers of representation that helps to understand images, sound, and text. In this chapter, the need for deep network in clustering, various architecture, and algorithms for unsupervised learning is discussed.

INTRODUCTION

Growth in digital data and storage methodologies has resulted in collection of a huge database. The process of extracting or finding relevant and hidden information from large databases in the field of Data Mining is a powerful technology with great potential for analysis of meaningful information in data warehouse. Knowledge discovery task involves various steps, selection of target data, pre-processing of data, transformation, extracting meaningful pattern and interpreting discovered pattern. It also involves the process of extracting hidden information from large databases, which is a powerful tool to help companies to focus on predicting behavior of future trends and improve performance of the organization by analyzing future market trends.

The process of clustering involves grouping similar objects into one cluster and dissimilar objects into different cluster. The quality of clusters is evaluated based on two measures namely, intra-cluster similarity and inter-cluster similarity. The similarity among objects within the cluster is defined as intra-cluster similarity whereas the similarity of objects in different clusters is called as inter-cluster similarity. The cluster with low inter-cluster similarity and high intra-cluster similarity is considered to be a quality cluster. Clustering is classified into different types namely Partition based clustering, Hierarchical clustering, Model-based Clustering, Density based clustering and Graph clustering.

DOI: 10.4018/978-1-5225-7862-8.ch010

The important task in partition based clustering is to group set of objects into k disjoint points such that points within group are similar. Given a set of n data points $\left\{x_1, x_2 \ldots x_n\right\}$, the algorithm partition into k clusters $\left\{C_1, \ldots, C_k\right\}$ such that each data point x_i is assigned to a unique cluster C_i. There are two types of Hierarchical clustering namely Agglomerative (merge) and Divisive (divide). In the Agglomerative method, clusters are measured on the basis of distance. Initially, each object is formed as a cluster and then cluster centroids that are close to each other are merged. The Divisive method starts with a single cluster that consists of all data points and iteratively splits into various subgroups. This process continues until each cluster contains single object.

Density based clustering is a method that groups objects on the basis of density. DBSCAN algorithm is a widely used density based algorithm that detects clusters with arbitrary shape and varied density. The main idea of this algorithm is that the number of objects within neighborhood must be greater than or equal to the threshold points.

Clustering technique finds extensive application in the field of business and financial data, bioinformatics, telecommunication and health applications. Credit card holders can be grouped on the basis of usage of card, purchase pattern, money spent on card, frequency of use and location of a card used. This information can be very useful for market analysis to find a group to which promotional activities can be targeted that might be of interest. This analysis can be of mutual benefit to both card holders and sellers. Market analysis is based on lifestyle, past purchase behavior or their demographic characteristics.

Clustering can also be applied in a chain store which wants to examine profit of outlets similarly placed, on the basis of variables like social neighborhood, purchase pattern, vicinity to other shops and so on. Cluster analysis has also been used widely in areas of medicine such as psychiatry, disease modelling, gene modelling and disease diagnostics. The other applications of clustering are grouping policy holders with average claim cost, creating thematic maps by grouping feature space, document classification and cluster weblog data to discover groups of similar patterns.

Search engines initially try to group similar objects in one cluster and dissimilar objects in different cluster. The result of searching for an object is based on the nearest similar object of key data. Efficient searching depends on quality of cluster derived. Clustering algorithm can also be applied in Wireless Sensor Network by detecting the cluster head which collects the complete information from the nodes in a cluster. It can also be effectively used in academic community to monitor the progress of students in academics where each group denotes different levels of performance.

Clustering process is widely utilized in Health applications to group cancerous data set and to locate people with similar symptoms. Clustering plays an essential role behind the search engines that initially try to group similar objects in one cluster and dissimilar objects in other cluster. The result of search for an object is based on nearest similar object of key data and depends on quality of cluster derived.

Over the last few years Deep Learning was applied to hundreds of problems, ranging from computer vision to natural language processing. In many cases Deep Learning outperformed previous work. Deep Learning is heavily used in both academia to study intelligence and in the industry in building intelligent systems to assist humans in various tasks. Both machine and deep learning are subsets of artificial intelligence, but deep learning represents the next evolution of machine learning. In machine learning, algorithms created by human programmers are responsible for parsing and learning from the data. They make decisions based on what they learn from the data. Deep learning learns through an artificial neural network that acts very much like a human brain and allows the machine to analyze data in a structure very much as humans do. Deep learning machines don't require a human programmer to tell them what to do with the data. This is made possible by the extraordinary amount of data we collect and consume—data is the fuel for deep-learning models.

The task of providing labels to the millions of training data in deep neural networks is becoming complex to achieve the current state-of-the-art results. In this chapter, various deep networks for unsupervised learning technique is discussed. In massive datasets like ImageNet and Twitter, supervised learning has been successfully trained over past few years in the research field. Recently, enormous amount of video datasets are becoming popular in the context of deep learning for object identification, image recognition and pattern analysis. When supervised technique is applied on all these datasets, labelling of data becomes a quite complex and time-consuming work. To avoid this problem, the research community needs a large breakthrough in the use of unlabelled data. As it is obvious that the unlabelled data is available abundantly in the industry, extensive research has been carried out to learn the hierarchy in the applications. Some deep learning techniques use filters to extract the multiple input features and connections to combine the extracted feature and provide them as an input for the next layer.

Convolutional Neural Network (CNN) is a widely used neural network for labelled data as these networks can scale them with more number of layers and filters. CNN improves the accuracy by increasing the depth and width off the network. By contrast, unsupervised algorithms are not able to scale them deep into many layers such as convolution and pooling in each layer. Therefore recent studies use large network with more number of layers. Constructing deep network is not simply adding layers to neural network. The main drawback in deep network is vanishing gradient problem that influence the convergence of results. This problem can be overcome by normalized initialization and intermediate layers that start converging using backpropagation algorithm. Another drawback is the problem of degradation, accuracy of result gets saturated and degrades rapidly when the depth of the network increases.

This chapter is organized as follows. The basic concepts of Machine Learning is discussed initially. Comparison of machine learning with deep learning is done. Then Deep Neural Network used for unsupervised learning is presented followed by set of Deep Clustering Algorithms.

MACHINE LEARNING

The popularly quoted definition of Machine Learning by Tom Mitchell explains, "*A computer program is said to learn from experience E with respect to some class of tasks T and performance measure P if its performance at tasks in T, as measured by P, improves with experience E* ". Classical examples are predicting weights based on height and predicting storm based on weather conditions. Some of the machine learning algorithms are decision tree, linear/logistic regression, support vector machine, Nearest Neighbor, Naive Bayesian and neural network. Three broad categories of learning are based (Kononenko, 2007) on supervised, unsupervised and reinforcement learning.

Supervised Learning

Supervised learning is a method of learning process based on labelled objects. The results and the data are known in prior to the training of system. A network consists of set of neurons and interconnection weights which is adjusted during the learning phase. The process of learning phase includes processing of input, comparing the output with desired outcome and minimizing the error by adjusting the weights. Then the network can analyze unknown training set to deliver the correct output. One of the drawbacks of CNN method is overfitting which occurs due to large number of parameters or providing the dataset that cannot be trained in the network. Convolutional neural network and recurrent neural network are categorized under supervised learning approach.

Unsupervised Learning

Unsupervised learning is a method based on unlabelled and unstructured data and so the output of the analysis is not predictable. This type of learning method identify the pattern based on deviations of unstructured data and by adjusting weights of neurons based similarities of input values. Clustering is one of the main unsupervised learning technique where the pattern are recognised based on the similarities of the objects. Similar objects form a group and dissimilar objects are present in different group. Clustering is a popular and widely used unsupervised technique in many applications.

Supervised learning categorizes the data based on class labels and so number of groups to be formed is known in prior to the analysis. Since the unsupervised learning is not based on any class labels, number of groups formed is known only in the result. For example, classifying the people who are interested in reading comic and historical books is a supervised technique. In contrast, studying the reading interest of customer is unsupervised pattern.

Reinforcement Learning

Reinforcement Learning (RL) is similar to human learning (Degris, 2012) methods. The system learns automatically based on trial and error method. Each step generates certain output and it evaluates itself based on the feedback it receives from the environment till the system achieves the target. The main drawback of this system is that it requires huge memory to save each value to each state of complex problems like game theory and genetic algorithms.

DEEP LEARNING VS. MACHINE LEARNING

- **Artificial Intelligence:** Human Intelligence Exhibited by Machines
- **Machine Learning:** An Approach to Achieve Artificial Intelligence
- **Deep Learning:** A Technique for Implementing Machine Learning

The main task of clustering is to group a given collection of unlabelled data into meaningful clusters such that objects within a cluster are more similar than the objects outside the other clusters. Deep learning (DL) is a subset of machine learning whereas machine learning (ML) is a subset of AI as shown in Figure 1 In other words, all machine learning algorithms are AI but not all AI is machine learning. ML is an approach to achieve AI Machine learning uses algorithms to parse data, learn from the parsed data and make informed decisions based on what it has learned while deep learning structures algorithm in layers to create a neural network model that can learn and make intelligent decisions on it own. Both deep and machine learning falls under the broad category of Artificial intelligence.

For a couple of years deep learning is getting more attention. *"Deep learning is a particular kind of machine learning that achieves great power and flexibility by learning to represent the world as nested hierarchy of concepts, with each concept defined in relation to simpler concepts, and more abstract*

Table 1. Comparison of machine learning with deep learning

	Machine Learning	Deep Learning
Data Dependencies	Even works for small amount of data	Needs large amount of data
Hardware dependencies	Works on low-end machine	Requires high end machine
Feature Engineering	Feature need to be identified by an expert and hand-coded	Try to learn high level feature from data
Problem Solving approach	Breaks the problem into different parts, solve and combine to get result	Solves the problem end-to-end
Execution time	Takes less execution time and more testing time	Takes more time to train and less time for testing
Interpretability	Simple to interpret the results	Complex to interpret the result

representations computed in terms of less abstract ones." For example, animal recognizer deep network recognize whether the given image is a cat or a dog. To solve this problem in Machine Learning, features of animal has to be pre-defined and let the system identify the objects based on the features identified. Deep learning is one step more than ML because DL automatically finds out the features whereas in ML we had to manually give the features. Comparison of ML with DL based on certain properties is explained in Table 1.

Andrew Ng, the chief scientist of China's major search engine Baidu and one of the leaders of the Google Brain Project, shared a great analogy for deep learning: "I think AI is akin to building a rocket ship. You need a huge engine and a lot of fuel. If you have a large engine and a tiny amount of fuel, you won't make it to orbit. If you have a tiny engine and a ton of fuel, you can't even lift off. To build a rocket you need a huge engine and a lot of fuel. The analogy to deep learning is that the rocket engine is the deep learning models and the fuel is the huge amounts of data we can feed to these algorithms

ARTIFICIAL NEURAL NETWORK

Artificial neural network is an artificial simulation of human brain and a programming paradigm to process the information similar to the biological neural system. The cell present in the biological network is considered as 'Neurons' in ANN, dendrites as Weights or interconnection, cell body as net input and axon as net ouput. For this simple neuron network, net input is calculated as,

$$y_{in} = x_1 w_1 + x_2 w_2 + \ldots x_n w_n = \sum_{i=1}^{n} x_i w_i \tag{1}$$

where x_1 and x_2 are the input neurons and the output neuron y can be obtained by applying activations over the net input y_{in}

$$y = f\left(y_{in}\right) \tag{2}$$

Figure 1. Relation between artificial intelligence, machine learning, deep learning
Ref. https://blogs.nvidia.com/blog/2016/07/29/whats-difference-artificial-intelligence-machine-learning-deep-learning-ai/

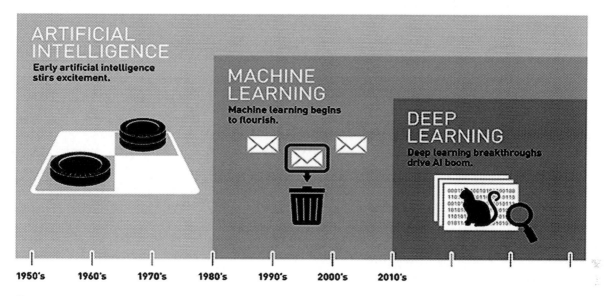

Since an early flush of optimism in the 1950s, smaller subsets of artificial intelligence – first machine learning, then deep learning, a subset of machine learning – have created ever larger disruptions.

The speed, size and complexity of ANN modelled using computer is faster than the biological neuron. ANN is a neutrally implemented model where there exist highly interconnected elements like neuron. The weighted interconnection holds the information or knowledge. The processing elements of ANN have the ability to learn, recall, generalize from the given data by suitable adjustments of weights. ANN is a random approximation tool which is more cost-effective for arriving complex solutions. Instead of taking the entire data sets it takes a random sample for solving problems that saves both time and money. Simple ANN as shown in Figure 2 have three layers namely input layer, hidden layer and output layer. Hidden layer receives the output of input layer as the input and the output of hidden layer is given as input to the output layer. The application decides the number of hidden layers needed for ANN.

The working principle of ANN is discussed in detail. Initially random weights are assigned to all the linkages in the network and then the activation rate of hidden nodes is identified using the inputs and the

Figure 2. Three layers of artificial neural network

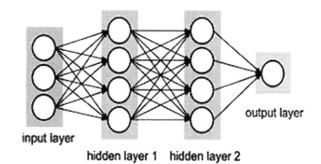

linkages. The activation rate of the output nodes are calculated using the activation rate of hidden node and linkages to output. Error rate is calculated from the actual output and the predicted output. Based on this error rate the weights between the hidden and the output node are adjusted. Error for the hidden nodes is cascaded down by using the weights and error in output node. The weights between the hidden and the input node are adjusted. The above process is repeated until the network converges.

In general, sigmoidal function is used between the input variables and activation rate of hidden nodes or between the hidden nodes and the activation rate of output nodes. In the same way, recalibration of weights is also a lengthy process. The error rate of the output node in the network is known by finding the difference between the actual and predicted value. Adjustment of weights on the linkage between hidden and the output node is a function of this error rate on output nodes. Using these errors linkage between hidden and input nodes are adjusted in a similar fashion. So, it is inferred that ANN performs multiple re-calibration for each linkage weights. Therefore the time taken by the ANN is much faster than traditional algorithm for the same size of data. Generally, ANN works well for image and voice recognition.

DEEP NEURAL NETWORK

Convolutional Neural Network

LeCun et. al., (1998) proposed Deep Convlutional Neural Network (CNN) have been a successful network over vision problems such as semantic segmentation, edge detection and recognition. Borji and Dundar(2017) used U-Net one of the CNN network and states that CNN's can be used for clustering process for the following reaasons

- The nearby pixels are highly correlated in natural scenes and also the natural objects are compositional. This property is convinient for applying the same filters across spatial locations.
- Building complex filters from simpler ones to detect high level patterns.
- When two clusters overlap with different shape, the problem can be solved by having filters responding to each shape.
- Incorporating domain knaowledge while clustering wuld not give a general soution to solve all clusterring problems but these deep network is a general system with rich set of learned and trained filters.

Convolutional Neural Network (CNN) consists of more number of hidden layers compared to simple network. CNN (Dundar,2015) are built in three dimensions namely width, height and depth as shown in Figure 3 below.

Any trained network will identify the solution on its own, adjust and optimize by itself whereas the CNN solves the problem by instructing the system with minimized and optimized defined tasks. This is the reason CNN becoming more popular in large companies and research community. Applications of CNN are more remarkable in terms of video analysis, image and speech recognition and computer vision. The main advantage of CNN is that it processes the image or sound easily inspite of distortion in image, differences in camera lenses and lightning conditions. It also performs dimensionality reduction, feature extraction and therefore reduced training time and memory is achieved.

Figure 3. Convolutional Neural Network

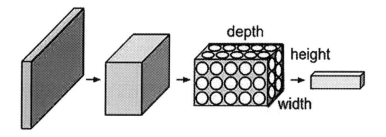

In general convolutional neural networks are used to train supervised learning but they can also be used for unlabelled data sets. Some of the Convolutional Neural Network (CNN) are like Autoencoders are discussed. CNN is the best network to deal with processing of images which mainly focus on mathematical operation called convolution (Hershey, 2016). Two dimensional filters are considered to be the training parameters. Feature map (Tzanakou, 1999) is created by applying filter to the image that contains information about the relative position in the image. Fully connected network is not required because the features belongs to spatial position of the image. The perceptrons are analyzed according to the weights and also processed by non-linearity and rectification. Finally, deep learning leads to multiple training stages do that the internal feature representation is hierarchically structured. "Low-level stages are used to detected primary edges. High-level stages lastly connect information on where and how objects are positioned regarding the scene".

The first application of Convolutional Neural Network LeNet-5 is developed by LeCun in 1990's. He states that "Multilayer Neural Networks trained with back propagation algorithm constitutes the best example of a successful Gradient-Based Learning technique. Given an appropriate network architecture, Gradient-Based Learning algorithms can be used to synthesize a complex decision surface that can classify high-dimensional patterns such as handwritten characters, with minimal preprocessing." LeNet is the first convolutional networks designed to focus on 2D shapes specifically for handwritten recognition (Browne, 2003). The various components of basic convolutional neural network are discussed below,

1. **Convolutional Layer**: The main task of convolutional layer is to find local conjunction of features from the previous layer and mapping their appearance to feature map. In convolutional neural network the image is partitioned into perceptrons, creating local feature and finally reducing the perceptrons in feature map. This map stores the information about each feature of the image and how it resembles to the filter. In each layer, there is a collection of filters. The number of filters required for each layer depends on the depth of volume of output feature. Each filter finds specific feature at every location on the input. So the pixels are assembled into edglets, edglets into motifs, motifs into parts, parts into objects and objects into scenes.

2. **Non-Linearity Layer**: Non-Linearity layer comprises of activation function required for CNN. Activation function takes the feature map generated by CNN as the input and produces activation map as the output. The dimensions of input and output in CNN are identical because the activation function performs element-wise operation over the input.

3. **Rectification Layer**: This layer performs element-wise absolute value calculation on the input volume. Similar to Non-Linearity layer, it also performs element-wise operation these two layers can be merged together. As this layer plays a major role in performance of CNN it is also called as "crucial component".

4. **Rectified Linear Units (ReLU):** ReLU is the combination of Non-Linear and Rectification layer in CNN. As ReLU propagate the gradient efficiently, it likely reduces the vanishing gradient problem which is a common drawback deep neural networks.

5. **Pooling Layer**: This layer is also called as down sampling layer that is responsible reducing the spatial dimensions of activation maps. Pooling aims to preserve the detected features in smaller representation by removing less significant data. Two methods of pooling are Max pooling and Average pooling. Finding the highest value within window region is called max pooling whereas using the mean value is Average pooling. Research has shown that max pooling shows faster and better performance compared to average pooling.

6. **Fully Connected Layer**: Multilayer perceptron with two or three layers forms fully connected layer. Input layer of standard multilayer perceptron uses vector whereas fully connected layer accepts activation volume as input. AlexNet is a classic example of CNN that generates activation volume of 512*7*7

Autoencoders

Autoencoder is one of the convolutional neural networks [7] used for unsupervised learning method. Network consists of two layers namely encoding and a decoding layer. The main aim of the network is to identify function within the structure. Encoding is the process of denoting a data of size n in the input layer to m parameters. Decoding is the method converting the representation of size m to the original input x in the output layer as depicted in Figure 4.

- Encoding: $f : \mathbb{R}^n \to \mathbb{R}^m, x \mapsto f(x)$
- Decoding: $g : \mathbb{R}^m \to \mathbb{R}^n, f(x) \mapsto g(f(x))$
- Minimizing the Loss: $L(x, g(f(x)))$

The expansion of input size (m) from the original input (n) can be achieved without loss. The more tedious task is to reduce the input pattern, as it may lead to loss of information. CNN network identifies and recreates the reduced representation to the possible nearest original input. Simple backpropagation network is computationally expensive to train for deep neural net structures. So, autoencoders efficiently handles this problem by performing layerwise training with unlabeled objects. Further, the network can accelerate the convergence speed to reduce the computational cost and can be combined with backpropagation to improve the accuracy.

Multi-Column Deep Neural Networks Architecture

Multi-column deep neural networks (MCDNN) **is** a common deep neural (Ciregan,2012) networks (DNN) that performs close human pattern for recognizing handwritten signs. This architecture produce high performance compared to other traditional methods which is commonly used in Machine learning

Figure 4. Autoencoder

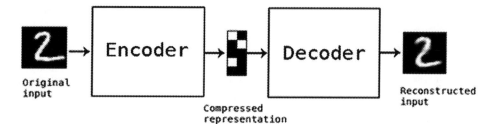

and computer vision. The goal of this architecture is to iteratively reduce the error on labelled training objects from initially random weights. Main drawback of this network is they are difficult to train and increase in computational power. DNN comprises shared weights with 2-dimensional fully connected layers. The DNN architecture aims to train only the winner neurons where the weights are updated only after each gradient step. Finally, several DNN columns are combined to form MCDNN where columns are trained on same input and averaged.

Recurrent Neural Networks (RNN)_

Recurrent Neural Network (RNN) is a type of neural network that become popular [9] in recent years. RNN is a combination of feedforward network that is able to remember the last state. The main difference between feed forward and recurrent neuron. Normal feed forward neuron has two weights for input and output neuron. In RNN it has three neurons for input, output and one for connection from output given as input. This extra edge or a loop is called "feed-back" connection. Neural network with more number feed forward and recurrent neurons form RNN.

The two major advantage of RNN are their ability to store previous state information and to handle sequential data of various length. Feedback connection store information in form of activations whereas RNN stores these information in some form of memory. RNN follows different ways of mapping between input to output such as one to many, many to one, one to one and many to many. RNN is more useful compared to other neural network specifically in terms of image recognition. It can work on large regions in the input space as it focuses more on neighbourhood with increase in time step. In CNN it is limited when it goes to higher layers of network. RNN reduces the input parameters as it is based weight sharing thereby increasing the network depth. They also handle sequential data and the neurons connected to the network are biologically inspired where such connections can improve the artificial network to bring interesting pattern. RNN is used in many applications such as speech recognition, clinical decision support system, speech recognition and also used to control dynamic systems.

Mixed CNN and RNN-RCNN

The positive features of RNN are combined with CNN to from a network called RCNN. CNN is a feedforward network while in recent applications recurrent connections are abundant. This recurrent CNN (RCNN) can be used in object recognition by combining the recurrent connections in each convolutional layer. The key factor in RCNN is recurrent convolution layer (RCL) and recurrent connections evolving over time through which each unit is influenced by its neighbouring units. This property of RCNN integrates the context information of image which is most important key factor for object detection. RCNN performs better than CNN with same number of layers. For example, recurrent convolutional layer in RCNN uses four time steps for unfolding whereas CNN is implemented with four added feed forward layer. The results of comparison show that RCNN is less prone to overfitting and performs better than the extended CNN.

DEEP CLUSTERING ALGORITHMS

In recent years, motivated by the success of deep neural network in supervised learning, unsupervised learning approaches are becoming widely popular for dimensionality reduction performed before clustering. Many approaches has been defined to combine clustering methods with Deep Neural Network which is becoming popular in the field of research. These methods can be categorized (Borji,2017) into two groups, (i) sequential methods that apply clustering on the learned DNN representations (ii) unified approaches that jointly optimize the deep representation learning and clustering objectives. In the first group, CNN such as Deep belief network and stacked auto encoders is the first trained unsupervised network to approximate non-linear feature space mapped embedded feature space. Then, any clustering algorithms can be applied on the feature space to partition the data. As the feature learning and clustering are separated from each other this method is not effective for clustering. In the second group, deep embedded clustering method simultaneously learns feature representation with stacked encoder and cluster assignments. Some of the popularly used deep clustering algorithms are discussed in Table 2

Deep Embedded Clustering (DEC)

Clustering is an important visualization tool that has been studied extensively in unsupervised machine learning from different perspectives. Euclidean distance measure is used to represent the data in feature space. The choice of selecting the distance measure depends on the application used by the end-user. Clustering with Euclidean distance measure in simple image dataset on raw pixels is completely ineffective. A unsupervised clustering algorithm Deep Embedded Clustering (DEC) performs a parametrized non-linear mapping from the data space X to a lower-dimensional feature space. Stochastic Gradient Descent (SGD) with backpropagation is used on clustering objective to learn the mapping, which is parametrized by a deep neural network. Cluster assignment and underlying feature representation is

Table 2. Comparison of deep clustering algorithms

	Deep Embedded Clustering (DEC)	Discriminatively Boosted Clustering (DBC)	Deep Clustering Network (DCN)
Author	Xie et al.,2016	Li et al.,2017	Yang et al.,2016
Deep Neural network	Multilayer Perceptron	Convolutional Neural Network	Multilayer Perceptron
Clustering Algorithm	Soft assignment	K-means	k-means
Application	Image and text	Image	Text
Combining loss term	Pre-training & fine tuning	Pre-training & fine tuning	Alternatively between joint training and cluster updates

simultaneously solved. Moreover, unlike supervised learning, deep network cannot be trained with la-belled data. The clusters are refined iteratively with auxillary target distribution derived from the current soft cluster assignment. Thereby, gradually improving the clustering as well as feature representation.

A set of n points $\left\{x_i \in X\right\}_{i=1}^{n}$ is grouped into k clusters with a centroid $u_j, j = 1,...,k$. Initially the data points are transformed and mapped to a non-linear mapping $f_\theta : X \rightarrow Z$, where Z is the feature space and θ is a learnable parameter, instead of clustering directly on the data space X. In order to avoid the "curse of dimensionality", data space X is mapped into Z feature space. Deep Neural Network (DNN) is the best choice to parametrize f_θ due to their feature learning capabilities and theoretical function approximation. DEC has two phases: (i) Parameter initialization using deep autoencoder (ii) parameter optimization by minimizing Kullback-Leibler (KL) divergence.

DEC is initialized with stacked autoencoder (SAE) layer by layer with each layer being denoising au-toencoder trained to reconstruct the previous layer output after random distribution. Training is performed in each layer by minimizing the least-squares loss. After training of one layer, the output of previous layer is taken as the input to train the next layer. Then all the encoder layers are followed by all decoder layers in reverse layer-wise training order to construct a deep autoencoder and then optimize to minimize the loss of reconstruction. The final multilayer deep encoder is formed by discarding the decoder layers and use only the encoder layers as initial mapping between the data space and the feature space. DEC works iteratively by optimizing a KL divergence based clustering objective with a self-training target distribution. This algorithm can be viewed as unsupervised extension of semisupervised self- training that performs clustering without ground truth cluster member-ship labels.

Discriminatively Boosted Clustering (DBC)

Li et al., (2017) has stated Discriminatively Boosted Clustering (DBC) which is almost similar to DEC except for using convolutional auto encoders. DBC uses k-means clustering algorithm like DEC and also uses the same training method like pretraining with auto encoder reconstruction loss and fine tun-ing using the cluster assignment hardening loss. Additionally the same advantage and disadvantages are shared by both the methods. Since DBC uses convolutional layer, it outperforms DEC's cluster quality on image dataset which is obviously expected. There are two steps involved in DBC. In the first step, fully conventional encoder-decoder network is used for feature extraction. Then the decoder part is discarded and a soft k-means model is added on top of the encoder to form a unified clustering model. The model

Figure 5. Deep Embedded Clustering (DEC)

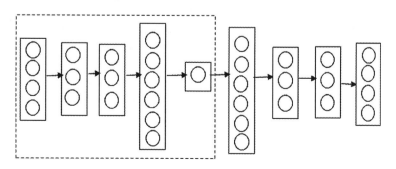

is also trained with gradually boosted discrimination where assignments with high score are highlighted and low score are de-emphasized.

Deep Clustering Network (DCN)

DCN proposed by Yang et al., (2017) is an autoencoder-based model that uses k-means for clustering. Clustering framework is modelled by using dimensionality reduction and k-means together where dimensionality reduction is implemented through learning a DNN rather than linear model. Similar to DEC, first phase trains the network using autoencoder reconstruction. The second step is different from DEC, the network is jointly trained using a mathematical combination of the autoencoder reconstruction loss and the k-means clustering loss function. Instead of probabilities used in DEC, a strict cluster assignments were used in DCN to train the network and to perform cluster updates.

APPLICATION

Deep Learning is going to play a major role in near future in all field and area of research. It is predicted that in next five to ten years Deep Learning based tools, packages, libraries would become a standard component in every software applications. Some of the vital deep learning applications that will be predominant in 2018 and beyond are listed below.

1. **Healthcare:** Deep learning is extensively used in Breast or Skin Cancer diagnostics and also in prediction of personalized medicine on the basis of Biobank-data. Artificial Intelligence is completely reforming life sciences, medicine, and healthcare as an industry. Innovations in AI are succeeding the future medicine and population health management in incredible ways. Computer-aided detection, decision support tools, quantitative imaging, and computer-aided diagnosis will play a major role in years to come.

2. **Voice Search and Voice-Activated Assistants**: One of the most prevalent usage areas of deep learning is voice-activated intelligent assistants and voice search. Voice-activated assistants are present nearly in every smartphone. Apple's Siri is one of the model which is on the market since October 2011. Google has launched voice-activated assistant for Android less than a year after Siri. Cortana is the newest voice-activated intelligent assistants by Microsoft.

3. **Automatically Adding sounds to Silent Movies**: The task of synthesizing the sound to match the silent video is an interesting task. The system is trained using 1000 examples of video with sound of a drumstick hitting various surfaces and creating diverse sounds. A deep learning model links the video frames with a database of pre-rerecorded sounds in order to select a sound to play that matches best with the scene. scene. The system is then evaluated using a turing-test like setup where humans had to determine which video is having the real or fake (synthesized) sounds. This uses application of both convolutional neural networks and Long short-term memory (LSTM) recurrent neural networks (RNN).

4. **Automatic Machine Translation**: The process of converting the words, phrases or sentence automatically from one language to another language is called Automatic Machine Translation. Deep learning has proved in these two specific areas:
   a. Automatic Translation of Text

b.   Automatic Translation of Images

Text translation can be achieved without any pre-processing of the sequence, permitting the algorithm to learn the dependencies between words and their mapping to a new language.

5.   **Automatic Text Generation**: Generating the text automatically is an interesting task, where a mass of text is learned and new text, character-by-character or word-by-word is generated based on the designed model. The model is capable of learning how to spell, punctuate, form sentences and even capture the style of the text in the database. Large recurrent neural networks are used to learn the relationship between items in the sequences of input strings and then generate text. In the same manner deep network is also used to automatically recognize the handwriting and generate the sequence of input text.

6.   **Image Recognition**: Another widely used area regarding deep learning is image recognition. The main motive is to identify people and objects in images and also understands the content and context. Image recognition is already being used in several applications like gaming, retail, social media, tourism, etc. This task requires the classification of objects within a photograph as one of a set of previously known objects. A difficult variation of this task called object detection involves exactly identifying one or more objects within the scene of the photograph and drawing a box around them.

7.   **Automatic Image Caption Generation**: Automatic image captioning is the task where given an image the system must generate a caption that describes the contents of the image. In 2014, there was an explosion of deep learning algorithms achieving very impressive results on this problem, leveraging the work from top models for object classification and object detection in photographs. Once objects are detected in photographs, labels are generated for those objects, in turn those labels change into a coherent sentence description. Generally, the systems involve the use of very large convolutional neural networks for the object detection in the photographs and then a recurrent neural network (RNN) like Long short-term memory (LSTM) to turn the labels into a coherent sentence.

8.   **Automatic Colorization**: Image colorization is the task of adding color to black and white Images. Deep learning can be used to identify the objects and their context within the photograph to color the image, similar like a human operator might solve the problem. This capability leverage the high quality and large convolutional neural networks trained for ImageNet and co-related for the problem of image colorization. Generally, the process involves the use of very large convolutional neural networks and supervised layers that reconstruct the image with the addition of color.

9.   **Predicting Earthquakes**: Harvard scientists used Deep Learning for a computer to learn visco-elastic computations that are used in predictions of earthquakes. In general, these computations are very computer intensive but the applications of deep learning has improved the computation time. When it come natural calamities timing is more important and this improvement can vitally save the people life.

10.   **Neural Networks in Finance**: Futures markets have seen a remarkable success since their initiation both in developed and developing countries during the last four decades. This study analyzes a trading strategy which benefits from this leverage by using the **Capital Asset Pricing Model (CAPM)** and cost-of-carry relationship. The team applies the technical trading rules developed from spot market prices, on futures market prices using a CAPM based hedge ratio. Historical daily prices of twenty stocks from each of the ten markets (five developed markets and five emerging markets) are used for the analysis.

FUTURE RESEARCH DIRECTIONS

The scope of deep learning concept is growing exponentially in all the fields. Since it has attracted the attention of so many researchers and academicians, the process of deep learning process is getting its shape in all the applications. For example in the process of restoring the blurred image, currently they focus on grey scale but this can be enhanced in future for color and real time images. The image classification model can be enhanced by including the low-level features such as shape and spatial location. There is high scope in unsupervised learning than the supervised learning. So many work has been done over classification but limited research has been done on clustering and prediction.

CONCLUSION

There is multiple complex tasks in everyday life that involves unsupervised learning like grouping and sequencing of event. For example, grouping similar feature and gene expression, sequence of words defines their meaning, time defines the occurrence of events and every genome sequence has different meaning. Different deep neural networks with deep clustering algorithms help to handle all these task effectively using different layers for unlabeled data for huge sized dataset. The recent applications and development has proved that deep learning plays a major role in solving most complex problems. The other main advantage of deep clustering is the process involved in grouping similar object is very similar to the way the human brain solves the problem. In this chapter we have discussed about various deep networks, various deep clustering algorithm and the applications of deep clustering in real time scenarios. Deep learning is going to be the future for atleast five to ten years. Deep network provide the accurate output for huge amount of data when compared with the traditional models.

REFERENCES

Analytics Vidhya. (n.d.). Retrieved from: https://www.analyticsvidhya.com/blog

Borji, A., & Dundar, A. (2017). *Human-like Clustering with Deep Convolutional Neural Networks*. Academic Press.

Browne, M., & Ghidary, S. S. (2003). Convolutional neural networks for image processing: an application in robot vision. In *Australasian Joint Conference on Artificial Intelligence* (pp. 641-652). Springer. 10.1007/978-3-540-24581-0_55

Ciregan, D., Meier, U., & Schmidhuber, J. (2012). Multi-column deep neural networks for image classification. In *Computer Vision and Pattern Recognition (CVPR), 2012 IEEE Conference on 2012 Jun 16* (pp. 3642-3649). IEEE.

Degris, T., Pilarski, P. M., & Sutton, R. S. (2012). *Model-free reinforcement learning with continuous action in practice. In American Control Conference (ACC)* (pp. 2177–2182). IEEE.

Dundar, A., Jin, J., & Culurciello, E. (2015). *Convolutional clustering for unsupervised learning*. arXiv preprint arXiv:1511.06241

Hershey, J. R., Chen, Z., Le Roux, J., & Watanabe, S. (2016, March). Deep clustering: Discriminative embeddings for segmentation and separation. In *Acoustics, Speech and Signal Processing (ICASSP), 2016 IEEE International Conference on* (pp. 31-35). IEEE.

Kononenko, I., & Kukar, M. (2007). *Machine learning and data mining: Introduction to principles and algorithms*. Horwood Publishing. doi:10.1533/9780857099440

LeCun, Y., Bottou, L., Bengio, Y., & Haffner, P. (1998). Gradient-based learning applied to document recognition. *Proceedings of the IEEE, 86*(11), 2278–2324. doi:10.1109/5.726791

The Keras Blog. (2016). Building autoencoders in Keras. *The Keras Blog*. Retrieved from: https://blog.keras.io/building-autoencoders-in-keras.html

Tzanakou, E. M. (Ed.). (1999). *Supervised and unsupervised pattern recognition: feature extraction and computational intelligence*. CRC Press. doi:10.1201/9781420049770

Xie, J., Girshick, R., & Farhadi, A. (2016, June). Unsupervised deep embedding for clustering analysis. In *International conference on machine learning* (pp. 478-487). Academic Press.

Yang, B., Fu, X., Sidiropoulos, N. D., & Hong, M. (2016). *Towards k-means-friendly spaces: Simultaneous deep learning and clustering*. arXiv preprint arXiv:1610.04794

Chapter 11
Deep Reinforcement Learning for Optimization

Md Mahmudul Hasan
 https://orcid.org/0000-0003-2543-3112
Anglia Ruskin University, UK

Md Shahinur Rahman
Daffodil International University, Bangladesh

Adrian Bell
Anglia Ruskin University, UK

ABSTRACT

Deep reinforcement learning (DRL) has transformed the field of artificial intelligence (AI) especially after the success of Google DeepMind. This branch of machine learning epitomizes a step toward building autonomous systems by understanding of the visual world. Deep reinforcement learning (RL) is currently applied to different sorts of problems that were previously obstinate. In this chapter, at first, the authors started with an introduction of the general field of RL and Markov decision process (MDP). Then, they clarified the common DRL framework and the necessary components RL settings. Moreover, they analyzed the stochastic gradient descent (SGD)-based optimizers such as ADAM and a non-specific multi-policy selection mechanism in a multi-objective Markov decision process. In this chapter, the authors also included the comparison for different Deep Q networks. In conclusion, they describe several challenges and trends in research within the deep reinforcement learning field.

INTRODUCTION

Nowadays it is more important to train up a machine and interact with environment to determine potential behaviours. Deep reinforcement learning is a powerful and most usable technique for communicate between an agent and an environment. Reinforcement Learning is a technique to understand how an agent can communicate with the environment and find out which action is best based on every step by trial and error (H. Li, Wei, Ren, Zhu, & Wang, 2017). In machine learning there are three main categories

DOI: 10.4018/978-1-5225-7862-8.ch011

which are supervised learning, Unsupervised Learning and Reinforcement Learning. In this chapter, we are given an overview about one of the most exciting topic of Machine learning is Reinforcement Learning. It is more important to find out the best solution of a problem but most of this process it's so much difficult to find the exact solution without any reaction. RL can take a decision which action is best and how can an agent learn behaviour in environment by action and seeing result. To overcome this problem one of most important step is using optimization with RL. Optimization is movement process to take the best compromising solution based on a set of all possible solution reduce leftover. Let think about a robots movement. A robot may take a long step in front and it can fall. Again the robot may take a short step and can hold balanced ("Reinforcement learning explained - O'Reilly Media," 2016). So here using RL we can get a possible solution set based on environment and from the possible solution set using optimization we can extract the best compromising solution. If we go through the definition of Reinforcement Learning then we can say that in initial position a robot doesn't know anything but when train up the robot how to walk, take action, keep balanced based on Environment this is called the Reinforcement Learning.

The following Figure 1 shows a reinforcement learning model where an agent takes action for an environment for each states and earned some rewarding points (Zoltán Gábor, Zsolt Kalmár, & Csaba Szepesvári, 1998).

There are several ways to solve the control or sequential decision making problems using reinforcement learning techniques. They are as follows (Watkins & Dayan, 1992):

1. Markov Decision Process
2. Dynamic Programming
3. Temporal difference learning
4. Q Learning
5. Deep Learning
6. Monte-Carlo Tree Search (MCTS)

To know about RL is firstly we need to know about State, Action, Reward function and Environment.

- **State**: To learn about environment it's maintained by Agent
- **Action**: Based on environment and situation a set of possible solution which is done by Agent
- **Reward Function**: It's a model to give instruction agent how to behave.
- **Environment**: Environment defines the scenario what is the agent seen.

Figure 1. Reinforcement learning model

Based on this observation scenario Deep reinforcement Learning take a decision. In this paper are we mainly focused on Optimization for Deep reinforcement Learning. Though Deep Reinforcement make a decision by agent to seen the scenario. But it may have side loss. Using optimization we can get the maximizing or minimizing result. If we think about a system then optimization can help to get in lost cost having the best result. To apply optimizing in a problem to get maximizing result we have to follow three steps. Make a significant model then select the problem type and last one is selecting optimizing software based on the problem ("Introduction to Optimization | NEOS," 2018).

- **Model**: Model is a way to describe how it work. An optimization model is a process to identify and exposed of mathematical term. An optimization model has three parts- An objective function, variables and Constrains.
- **Problem Type**: In this step optimization process select the problem type which is associate to the model. Most of the common problem is Continuous problem, unconstrained problem, none, one or many objectives, Deterministic optimization etc.
- **Optimizing Software**: The last step of Optimizing is select optimizing software based on the optimizing problem that will be solve. Solver software and Modeling solver are highly used here.

The computational intelligence researchers will involve more into simulation using robots, augmented & virtual reality and gaming environment. In this whole process, games or gaming environment will be one of the key components to analyse different algorithms and simulate the problems and provide solutions. Deep learning and deep reinforcement learning will be the integral part of this changes. Therefore, it is essential to discuss thoroughly different DRL algorithms and optimisation techniques.

In this chapter, section 2 describes the common applications for optimisation. Deep reinforcement learning and different deep learning algorithms (i.e. Deep Q Networks) have been analysed in section 3. In this section, we also describe the optimisers that are available in deep learning area with challenges and trends. Finally, the concluding remarks have been presented in the last section.

DEEP REINFORCEMENT LEARNING

In recent years, deep neural network or deep learning has been major focus in reinforcement learning area. It is an influential method for interaction between an agent and environment. We witnessed innovations, like deep Q network (Mnih et al., 2015), AlphaGo (Silver et al., 2016), unsupervised reinforcement and auxiliary learning (Jaderberg et al., 2016; Mirowski et al., 2016). Deep RL has significantly reduced the dependence of the domain knowledge and enables highly efficient feature engineering which is usually time-consuming, over-specified or incomplete (Y. Li, 2017). The following figure 2 shows a basic structure for deep reinforcement learning

The successful implementation for deep reinforcement learning is emerged different areas such as:

- **Robotics**: Black-Box Data-efficient Policy Search for Robotics (Chatzilygeroudis et al., 2017)
- **Games**: Human-level Control through Deep Reinforcement Learning (Mnih et al., 2015)
- Spoken dialogue system (Su et al., 2016)
- Information extraction (Narasimhan, Yala, & Barzilay, 2016)

Figure 2. Deep reinforcement learning architecture

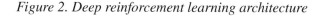

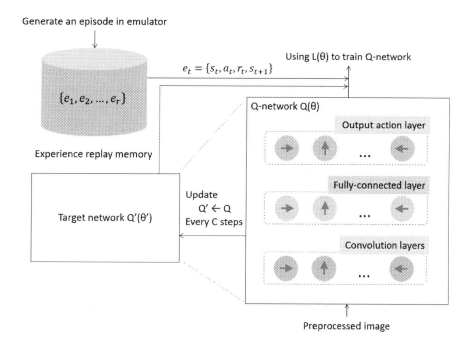

Applications of the Optimisers

Traffic Flow Optimization

Now a days in modern era traffic overcrowd is one of the most common problem faced by whole world. For this problem not only pollution environment but also increase the fuel erosion. Beside of this it also impact in economy. To reduce this problem as a part of artificial intelligence Traffic flow optimization is play a vital role. Based on so many algorithm it could reduce traffic jam, fuel problem, traffic signal problem, suffering of humans. There is several method for traffic flow optimization such as through GPS.

The goal of the traffic flow optimization issue is to limit the ideal opportunity for a given arrangement of different vehicles to movement between their individual sources and reaching points. It utilized the streamlining presumption that opportunity to cross a road is relative to a component of the quantity of vehicles at present involving the road. So, Traffic Flow Optimization minimize total time for all cars and other vehicles by minimizing total congestion over all road segments. Overcrowding or blockage on an individual section is dictated by a quadratic capacity of the quantity of different types of vehicles crossing it in a particular time. Here we outlined the steps for traffic flow optimization:

- Pre-process map and GPS data.
- Identify areas where overcrowded traffic.
- Determine spatially and temporally valid alternative routes for each vehicle in the dataset.
- Minimization problem.
- Find a solution that reduces overcrowd among routes assignments in the whole traffic graph.
- Redistribute the vehicles based on the results.

- Iterate steps 2–6 till no overcrowded traffic is identified.

Combinational Optimization

Combinational optimization issues over years emerging from various application areas, for example, transportation, communications and planning, are NP-hard, and have in this manner pulled in significant enthusiasm from the hypothesis. Combinatorial optimization problem is an optimization problem, where an optimal solution has to be identified from a finite set of solutions. The solutions are normally discrete or can be formed into discrete. This is an important topic studied in operations research, software engineering, artificial intelligence, machine learning, and so on. Travelling sales man problem is one of the popular combinatorial optimization problem. Such as the travelling salesman problem:

- The Traveling Salesman Problem: given the (x, y) positions of N different cities, find the shortest possible path that visits each city exactly once.
- Bin-Packing: given a set of N objects each with a specified size s_1, fit them into as few bins (each of size B) as possible.
- Integer Linear Programming: maximize a specified linear combination of a set of integers X1 ... XN subject to a set of linear constraints each of the form

$$a_1 X_1 + ... a_n X_n <= c.$$

- **Job-Shop Scheduling**: Given a set of jobs that must be performed, and a limited set of tools with which these jobs can be performed, find a schedule for what jobs should be done when and with what tools that minimizes the total amount of time until all jobs have been completed.
- **Boolean Satisfiability**: Assign values to a set of Boolean variables in order to satisfy a given Boolean expression. (A suitable objective function might be the number of satisfied clauses if the expression is a CNF formula.)

Figure 3. Example of combinatorial optimisation

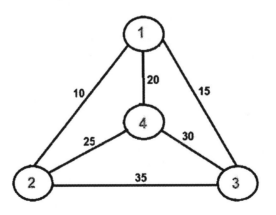

The space of conceivable arrangements is regularly too extensive to look thoroughly utilizing unadulterated beast compel. At times, issues can be tackled precisely utilizing Branch and Bound strategies. Nonetheless, in different cases no correct calculations are practical, and randomized pursuit calculations must be utilized.

Transforming Cooling Optimization

In modern era based on information technology data centre plays a very important role. From microtik server to cloud based server in every sphere data centre is very much needed. So the data centre is always heated up because of so many uses. We need to make it cool as much as it (data centre) possible. That is why everyone uses a cooling system for data centre. With AI we build an automated air-conditioner could be the best solution for data centre's heat consummation. It will deliver the output taking four types of input. From the outputs by using optimization it will determine or deliver the best possible room temperature of the data centre. The following steps are shown below about how it works:

- Difference between data set and current room temperature
- Data set is changing in a time interval. (Here the date set is collection of room temperature and server temperature)
- From the data set it is determining the number of temperature change occurs.
- Now it will determine best possible temperatures.
- By using optimization it will provide appropriate temperature.

Control Optimization

Basically, all designing issues are optimization issues. If a system engineer going to design a system then one of the most important objective to make it in cheap way or that can be implemented most rapidly, where obviously a few particulars and imperatives, for example, measure, quality, security, and so on must be considered. When building up another kind of system, we search for the most sparing design, the least expensive outline, or the plan with the most elevated execution.

A standout amongst other known household cases of automatic controls would be the cruise control of an engine auto. The journey control keeps the auto's speed steady, regardless of street inclination and wind heading. At the point when the street runs tough or downhill, the voyage control consequently changes the quickening agent position to keep the auto's speed steady. In control, which is a field of designing, the objective is to think of a component (this is typically a bit of programming) that has ongoing basic leadership ability. In optimization, which is a field of science, the objective is to think of the individual from a set that is the best as indicated by some standard. Based on this a system can make a best decision.

Warehouse Optimization

Warehouse optimization is critical to the productive activity of warehouses all things considered. A restrained procedure, warehouse optimization incorporates mechanization and an assurance of how to reduce time, space, and assets while decreasing blunders and enhancing adaptability, correspondence, administration, and consumer loyalty. Other warehouse optimization contemplations incorporate warehouse stream, item situation, stockpiling, and recovery frameworks. Warehouse optimization is fundamental to lean warehouses and dexterous supply chains. The most productive warehouses are those that have been advanced to beat the opposition on each level.

In warehouse optimization, there is some common challenge identified with mistakes, wastefulness, and absence of straightforwardness. Some people use some technique like warehouse optimization, barcoding, automated data collection to recover this problem. There are some challenge is:

- **Inventory Accuracy:** Organizations regularly don't realize what they have in stock and have too little permeability into their distribution centers when they do not have a robotized framework.
- **Inventory Location:** Without precise understanding of the stock area, pickers can't work proficiently, which results in slower stacking procedures and reinforcements in dock booking.
- **Space Utilization and Warehouse Layout:** In the event that capacity frameworks and distribution center racking isn't advanced, space required to house stock and work required inside the stockroom increment.
- **Picking Optimization:** Such a large number of warehouses need normal courses for picking things for shipment in light of the fact that their manual procedures are wasteful.

There are so many areas and procedures you can center on when endeavoring to optimize your warehouse, the technique recorded underneath can be connected to all regions of your warehouse in some frame.

A GENERAL FRAMEWORK FOR DEEP Q NETWORK

A common settings of an RL agent is that interacts with an environment. At each time step t, the agent receives a state s_t in a state space S and selects an action a_t from an action space A, following a policy $\pi(a_t | s_t)$, which is the agent's behaviour. In an episodic problem, the reward function can be defined as in Equation 1:

$$R_t = \sum_{k}^{\infty} \gamma^k r_{t+k+1} \tag{1}$$

where $\gamma \in (0,1]$. The agent aims to maximize the expectation of such long term return from each state. The problem is set up in discrete state and action spaces. The following figure 4 shows a Deep Q network architecture (Deep Q Network, 2018).

Comparisons of the Different Deep Q Networks

This section describes the common DQN algorithms' aim, description, advantages and disadvantages which is one of the crucial part to implement various DRL algorithms.

Figure 4. Q value selection in a Deep Q network

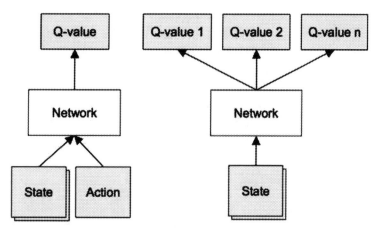

Optimisers for Deep Reinforcement Learning

Gradient descent (GD) is common algorithm to perform optimization of deep learning. There are many deep learning libraries that contains various gradient descent algorithms such as Keras, Chainer, Tensorflow, Theano and so on. The problem of using these optimisers are they used as a black-box and users are often not clear what's going inside. In the following section, we will be describing the pros and cons for this.

Stochastic Gradient Descent Optimiser

SGD optimisers are normally much faster than gradient descent optimisers. In addition, this can be used to learn online. The following algorithm 1 shows the SGD.

On the other hand, it caused high variance where the objective functions fluctuate frequently.

Adam Optimizer

Adam is an optimization algorithm of gradient descent that can utilized rather than the established stochastic inclination plunge methodology to refresh arrange weights iterative situated in preparing information. Adam optimization algorithm is one of those calculations that function admirably over an extensive variety of profound learning designs. It is prescribed by some notable neural network algorithm specialists. Adam was introduced by two researcher Diederik Kingma and Jimmy Ba. They presented Adam in their paper which title was "Adam: A Method for Stochastic Optimization" (Kingma & Ba, 2014). I will cite generously from their paper in this post except if expressed something else.

While presenting the algorithm, the author lists the alluring advantages of utilizing Adam on non-curved streamlining issues, as takes after

- Direct to actualize.
- Computationally productive.

Table 1.

Policy Optimisation	
Aim	To optimize policies in an episodic or stochastic environment where values are yet to be explored. It is noted that policy π optimization can be simpler than finding Q and value V.
Description	Step 1: Set the policy parameters Step 2: Fix policy rules in accordance with policy variations Step 3: Compute gradient to determine policies Step 4: Find optimum policy
Pros	Performs better in converging properties Can learn stochastic process
Cons	Usually converge to a local rather than in global optimum Challenging to find out a good estimator policy gradient Validating policies are typically inefficient and high variance
Actor-Critic Method	
Aim	To seek for a parameter vector which maximizes the return by using a policy gradient approach where actor deals with the policy and critic evaluates the current policy.
Description	Step 1: Initialise state and policy factors Step 2: Set critic learning rate and actor learning rate Step 3: Get sample reward, transitions and actions Step 4: Observe reward and evaluates policies prescribed by the actor Step 5: Repeat until the terminated state
Pros	Reducing high variance and effective in high dimension Evaluated policy by critic
Cons	This method may introduces bias
DQN	
Aim	Define function Q (s,a)which refers to the maximum discounted future reward for each action a in state s and optimize continuously from that point.
Description	Step 1: At first, define Q value and policy π which set the rules of how we choose different action in states. Step 2: After set the Q value, pick the highest q value and fix Q function using Bellman equation (Bellman, 1958). Step 3: Sample random transitions from a set of temporary experiences Step 4: As Q-function converges, the network gets more appropriate Q values and thus, exploration decreases Step 5: Train the Q network until terminated state
Pros	a) It performs faster while training the network considering it uses random minibatches from temporary memory instead of recent transitions. b) In the episodic environment, if the space is too big then Q-table can be replaced instead of deep neural network.
Cons	a) As the agent follows greedy approaches to fix the Q value, it often may lead to less optimized policy and increase time complexity.
Double DQN Algorithm	
Aim	The idea of Double Q-learning is to reduce overestimations which is often caused by standard Q learning algorithm by decomposing the max operation in the target into action selection and action evaluation
Description	Step 1: Take inputs of empty and replay buffer, initialise the network parameters, training batch size and target network Step 2: For each episode, initialise frame sequences Step 3: Set state and sample actions Step 4: Append new frame and delete the old one Step 5: Sample minibatch and set the target network Step 6: Compute the gradient descent step with loss and replace target parameters for each step.
Pros	It performs better to reduce observed overestimations compare to Q learning. Double DQN finds better policies and it is more stable and reliable in terms of learning.
Cons	Single stream double DQN performs worse than DuDQn.

continued on following page

Table 1. Continued

Dueling Q Network (DuDQN)	
Aim	It is a model-free reinforcement learning algorithm aims to represent two separate estimators such as state-value function and state-dependant action advantage function to generalise learning across actions
Description	Step 1: Set one stream of fully-connected layers output a scalar V (s; θ,β), and the other stream output an $\|A\|$-dimensional vector A(s, a; θ,α). θ for the parameters of the convolutional layers, while α and β are the parameters of the two streams of fully-connected layers. Step 2: Then it can be integrated with Double DQN [shown above] or Prioritised Experience Replay
Pros	It provides better results for policy evaluation. The dueling architecture can learn which states are valuable or not without having to learn the effect of each action for each state. It uses two separate streams to that are combined to produce single output Q function which can be used to train some other RL algorithms such as DDQN and SARSA.
Cons	It performs better than standard Q network only with the large set of actions.
Continuous DQN	
Aim	It aims to provide better performance with normalised advantage functions as an alternative of policy gradient and actor-critic method for continuous actions.
Description	Step 1: Initialise normalise Q network, target network and replay buffer Step 2: For each episode, initialise random process for action exploration Step 3: After getting initial observation, select action and store the transition Step 4: Sample random minibatch from replay memory Step 5: Update the target network by minimising loss until the terminal state
Pros	It substantially improve performance on a set of simulated robotic control tasks.
Cons	Continuous DQN performs worse than DDPG for finding better policies in the continuous domain spaces.
Deep Deterministic Policy Gradient (DDPG)	
Aim	It is a model free RL algorithm that can learn competitive policies using low-dimensional observations and often can achieve good policies direct from pixels with the same network structure.
Description	Step 1: Initialise critic network, actor with weights Step 2: Initialise target network and replay buffer Step 3: For each episode, initialise a random process for action exploration Step 4: For each time, select actions according to the current policy and exploration noise Step 5: Store transitions and sample a random minibatch Step 6: Update critic, actor and target network
Pros	It can learn better policy among several competitive policies DDPG can treat the problem of exploration in the continuous spaces independently from the learning algorithm.
Cons	It requires a large number of training episodes to find solutions.
Asynchronous N-step Q Learning (ANSQ)	
Aim	To design a RL algorithm that can train the deep neural network policies faster and reliably with minimum resource requirements
Description	Step 1: Initialise counter, target network thread specific parameters and network gradients Step 2: Select actions using exploration policy until state reaches its final state or up to t_{max}. Step 3: Compute gradients for each state-action pairs for n-steps Q-learning updates Step 4: Update asynchronously global shared parameter vector θ Step 5: The accumulated updates are applied in a single gradient step
Pros	Learning process becomes faster by propagating rewards faster after n steps Propagating rewards to relevant state-action pairs that potentially makes the algorithm efficient
Cons	Explicit computing of n-steps returns may increase computational complexity

continued on following page

Table 1. Continued

Prioritised Experience Replay	
Aim	It is an online reinforcement learning algorithm aims to provide faster and effective learning by using replay memory for experiences based on priority
Description	Step 1: Initialise replay memory and store the experience(s,a,t,r,s′) into it Step 2: Select actions from state and store transition with the highest priority Step 3: Compute importance sampling and TD-error Step 4: Update transition priority and weights into the target network Step 5: Choose optimal action A_t from $\pi_\theta(S_t)$
Pros	It requires less experiences to be trained due to prioritisation and can utilise more computation and memory Outperforms with sampling using Double DQN
Cons	This can introduce bias for non-uniform sampling for experiences
Asynchronous Advantage Actor-Critic (A3C)	A3C aims to provide simple and robust solution in the domain of RL by using a global network and several sub-networks which performs asynchronously and update the global network.
Description	Step 1: Initialise global network and sub-network Step 2: Sub-networks interact with the environment Step 3: Compute value and policy-loss by the sub-networks Step 4: Sub-network gets gradient from losses asynchronously Step 5: Sub-network updates global network with gradients after t_{max} actions or a terminal state is reached Step 6: After each update global network propagates new weights to the sub-network to share a common policy
Pros	This can be implemented for continuous and discrete action spaces It can perform better on GPU.
Cons	Employing too many agents or sub-networks can cause computational delay which leads to reduction to the convergence speed.
Actor-Critic With Experience Replay (ACER)	
Aim	ACER is an off-policy RL algorithm that aims to achieve stable and efficient learning by minimising the cost of simulation steps by using experience replay buffer.
Description	Here, the algorithm is associated with a master algorithm that is responsible to call the associated algorithm for discrete actions. Step 1: Reset the gradients and initialise the parameters Step 2: Sample the trajectory from the replay memory Step 3: Compute the function for on-policy and quantities for trust region updating Step 4: Accumulate gradients and update the retrace target network asynchronously Step 5: Update the average policy network.
Pros	It can performs both in discrete and continuous domain spaces. It performs faster compare to standard actor-critic.
Cons	Rare and infrequent experiences may lead bias.

- Little memory necessities.
- Invariant to corner to corner rescale of the angles.
- Appropriate for issues that are huge regarding information and additional parameters.
- Suitable for non-stationary goals.
- Suitable for issues with exceptionally loud/or inadequate angles.
- Hyper-parameters have instinctive translation and normally require small tuning.

Adam Configure Parameters:

Algorithm 1. Adam optimizer

- Computes update for **each** example $x^{(i)}y^{(i)}$.
- Update equation: $\theta = \theta - \eta \cdot \nabla_\theta J(\theta; x^{(i)}; y^{(i)})$

```
for i in range(nb_epochs):
  np.random.shuffle(data)
  for example in data:
    params_grad = evaluate_gradient(
      loss_function, example, params)
    params = params - learning_rate * params_grad
```
Listing 2: Code for stochastic gradient descent update

- **Alpha:** Likewise alluded to as the learning rate or step measure. The extent that weights are refreshed. Bigger qualities results in speedier introductory learning before the rate is refreshed. Littler qualities back adapting appropriate off amid preparing
- **beta1:** The exponential rot rate for the principal minute appraisals
- **beta2.** The exponential rot rate for the second-minute appraisals. This esteem ought to be set near 1.0 on issues with an inadequate slope (e.g. NLP and PC vision issues).
- **Epsilon:** Is a modest number to keep any division by zero in the execution.

Pros & Cons:

Algorithm 2. Adam optimizer

Algorithm 1: *Adam*, our proposed algorithm for stochastic optimization. See section 2 for details, and for a slightly more efficient (but less clear) order of computation. g_t^2 indicates the elementwise square $g_t \odot g_t$. Good default settings for the tested machine learning problems are $\alpha = 0.001$, $\beta_1 = 0.9$, $\beta_2 = 0.999$ and $\epsilon = 10^{-8}$. All operations on vectors are element-wise. With β_1^t and β_2^t we denote β_1 and β_2 to the power t.

Require: α: Stepsize
Require: $\beta_1, \beta_2 \in [0, 1)$: Exponential decay rates for the moment estimates
Require: $f(\theta)$: Stochastic objective function with parameters θ
Require: θ_0: Initial parameter vector
  $m_0 \leftarrow 0$ (Initialize 1st moment vector)
  $v_0 \leftarrow 0$ (Initialize 2nd moment vector)
  $t \leftarrow 0$ (Initialize timestep)
  while θ_t not converged **do**
    $t \leftarrow t + 1$
    $g_t \leftarrow \nabla_\theta f_t(\theta_{t-1})$ (Get gradients w.r.t. stochastic objective at timestep t)
    $m_t \leftarrow \beta_1 \cdot m_{t-1} + (1 - \beta_1) \cdot g_t$ (Update biased first moment estimate)
    $v_t \leftarrow \beta_2 \cdot v_{t-1} + (1 - \beta_2) \cdot g_t^2$ (Update biased second raw moment estimate)
    $\hat{m}_t \leftarrow m_t/(1 - \beta_1^t)$ (Compute bias-corrected first moment estimate)
    $\hat{v}_t \leftarrow v_t/(1 - \beta_2^t)$ (Compute bias-corrected second raw moment estimate)
    $\theta_t \leftarrow \theta_{t-1} - \alpha \cdot \hat{m}_t/(\sqrt{\hat{v}_t} + \epsilon)$ (Update parameters)
  end while
  return θ_t (Resulting parameters)

- + Adaptive learning rate and force for every parameter.
- + Learning rate does not reduce as in AdaGrad.
- - Does not "look forward" like NAG.

Stochastic gradient-based optimization is of centre functional significance in numerous fields of science and designing. Numerous issues in these fields can be given a role as the optimization of some scalar parameterized target work requiring expansion or minimization as for its parameters. On the off chance that the work is differentiable w.r.t. its parameters, gradient plunge is a generally productive optimization the technique, since the calculation of first-arrange fractional subordinates w.r.t. every one of the parameters is of the same computational many-sided quality as simply assessing the capacity [4].

```
Require: α: Stepsize
Require:), ∈ [0, 1): Exponential decay rates for the moment estimates
Require:: Stochastic objective function with parameters θ
Require:: Initial parameter vector
← 0 (Initialize 1st moment vector)
← 0 (Initialize 2nd moment vector)
t ← 0 (Initialize timestep)
while not converged do
t ← t + 1
← (-1) (Get gradients w.r.t. stochastic objective at timestep t)
← · mt-1 + (1 -) · (Update biased first moment estimate)
← · vt-1 + (1 -) · (Update biased second raw moment estimate)
← /(1 -) (Compute bias-corrected first moment estimate)
← /(1 -) (Compute bias-corrected second raw moment estimate)
← -1 - α · /(√ +) (Update parameters)
end while
return (Resulting parameters)
```

Keras Implementation:

```
keras.optimizers.Adam(lr=0.001, beta_1=0.9, beta_2=0.999, epsilon=None, de-
cay=0.0, amsgrad=False)
```

Non-Specific Policy Optimiser

This algorithm represents a multi-objective optimisation approach in a dynamic environment which is defined by multi-objective Markov decision process (MOMDP) (Parisi, Pirotta, & Restelli, 2016). In this algorithm, the objectives are divided into several sub-problems and each objective is assigned to work with a particular DQN. Then an objective relation mapping (ORM) is established to map with the different objectives to form a meta-policy. The following figure 5 shows the basic structure of the non-specific policy-optimiser.

Pros:

Figure 5. Basic structure of the non-specific policy optimiser

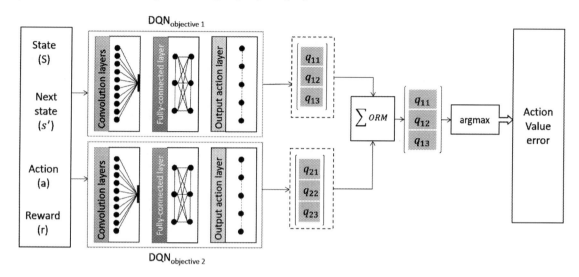

Algorithm 3. Non-specific policy selection mechanism

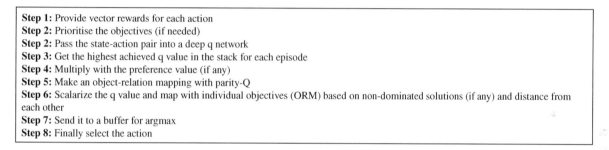

Step 1: Provide vector rewards for each action
Step 2: Prioritise the objectives (if needed)
Step 2: Pass the state-action pair into a deep q network
Step 3: Get the highest achieved q value in the stack for each episode
Step 4: Multiply with the preference value (if any)
Step 5: Make an object-relation mapping with parity-Q
Step 6: Scalarize the q value and map with individual objectives (ORM) based on non-dominated solutions (if any) and distance from each other
Step 7: Send it to a buffer for argmax
Step 8: Finally select the action

- This optimiser is able to learn more properties and complex features by interacting within the environment using vector rewards.
- This technique can be fitted into unstructured data as well.

Cons:

- Generally MOMDP requires a lot of parameters and pre-defined models.
- Interpreting the learning pattern is often hard to interpret and fine-tuning in the deep layer is difficult considering different objectives.

Apart from these, there are several gradient descent algorithms such as Momentum, Nesterov, accelerated gradient, Adagrad, Adadelta and RMSprop.

Challenges in Deep Reinforcement Learning

It is instructive to emphasize some challenges faced in DRL for optimisation:

- Choosing a learning rate.
- Defining an annealing schedule.
- Avoiding suboptimal minima.
- Setting up the vector reward for multi-objective environment
- The observations of the agent can have over or under estimations
- Can suffer from temporal credit assignment problem (SUTTON, 1984).

Trends in Deep Reinforcement Learning

The followings are the recent trends in deep reinforcement learning domain:

- Deep layer fine-tuning to get more insights and meaningful behaviours of the deep Q networks
- Self-learning and human-agent teamwork for the optimisation problem
- Off –policy and model-free integration for an on-demand service providing the agent

CONCLUSION

With the review of the RL and DRL, it can be concluded that it is one the most promising techniques to train the machine to respond to a changing environment and then take evolutionary actions based on the policy. In this chapter, we argued on the approaches to solve the RL problem and discussed three prominent solutions as optimisers. However, in the context of the MORL, the vector rewards are important if the agent aims to achieve a compromising solution based on different objectives. As a result, this approach would be suitable for creating an AI for autonomous devices. Therefore, implementing the RL agent in various computer vision problems can have serious impacts so that it can be proliferating to solve in various problems. Therefore, we need to plan to find out a lot more success using RL and of course, with quicker operation in terms of time complexity.

In our opinion, the AI community has observed a different dimension of solving the problem using RL. By combining the RL approach and traditional supervised machine learning, it is possible to augment machine learning with expert knowledge. As a result, embedding the deep neural network with RL can be fed with the expert input and the RL can provide the flexibility to use the knowledge in the new context respectively. Besides, RL agents are expected to be outperforming humans in many situations such as playing Go, Chess, Atari 2600 and so on.

Despite the successes of DRL, a proper investigation needs to be made before applying it to solve a real-world and complex problem because of its overwhelming computational costs. A deep learning amalgamation with other traditional AI approaches can significantly improve the performance and achieve the desired goal. Possibly, then, we are not too far away from AI systems that acquire knowledge and act in more human-like ways in increasingly complicated environments. Furthermore, multi-agents implementation can be utilised to solve a particular problem in the future which has not been considered in this study to identify the better policy.

As an ending note, we have analysed several optimisers in deep reinforcement learning domain and identified their merits and demerits. We also described three algorithms that can be used in single objective and multi-objective scenarios. We also analysed some challenges that yet to be addressed in the DRL. Finally we mentioned some trends in deep reinforcement learning area which may help readers to explore further and implement in real-world scenarios. We hope and believe that mankind will be more beneficial from AI and the self-learning ability of the machines. We would like to conclude this chapter with the quote of the famous British scientist and the computer science pioneer:

The original question, 'Can machines think?' I believe to be too meaningless to deserve discussion.
—— *Alan Turing*

REFERENCES

Bellman, R. (1958). Dynamic programming and stochastic control processes. *Information and Control,* *1*(3), 228–239. doi:10.1016/S0019-9958(58)80003-0

Chatzilygeroudis, K., Rama, R., Kaushik, R., Goepp, D., Vassiliades, V., & Mouret, J.-B. (n.d.). *Black-Box Data-efficient Policy Search for Robotics.* Retrieved from https://hal.inria.fr/hal-01576683

Deep Q-network - Deep Learning with Theano. (2018). Retrieved September 23, 2018, from https://www.oreilly.com/library/view/deep-learning-with/9781786465825/ch11s04.html

Gábor, Z., Kalmár, Z., & Szepesvári, C. (1998). Multi-criteria Reinforcement Learning. *Proceedings of the Fifteenth International Conference on Machine Learning,* 24–27. Retrieved from https://dl.acm.org/citation.cfm?id=657298

Introduction to Optimization | NEOS. (2018). Retrieved September 23, 2018, from https://neos-guide.org/content/optimization-introduction

Jaderberg, M., Mnih, V., Czarnecki, W. M., Schaul, T., Leibo, J. Z., & Silver, D. … London, D. (2016). *Reinforcement learning with unsupervised auxiliary tasks.* Retrieved from https://youtu.be/Uz-zGYrYEjA

Kingma, D. P., & Ba, J. (2014). *Adam: A Method for Stochastic Optimization.* Retrieved from http://arxiv.org/abs/1412.6980

Li, H., Wei, T., Ren, A., Zhu, Q., & Wang, Y. (n.d.). *Deep Reinforcement Learning: Framework, Applications, and Embedded Implementations Invited Paper.* Retrieved from https://arxiv.org/pdf/1710.03792.pdf

Li, Y. (2017). *Deep Reinforcement Learning: An Overview.* Academic Press. doi:10.1007/978-3-319-56991-8_32

Mirowski, P., Pascanu, R., Viola, F., Soyer, H., Ballard, A., Banino, A., … Hadsell, R. (2016, November 4). *Learning to Navigate in Complex Environments.* Retrieved from https://openreview.net/forum?id=SJMGPrcle

Mnih, V., Kavukcuoglu, K., Silver, D., Rusu, A. A., Veness, J., Bellemare, M. G., ... Hassabis, D. (2015). Human-level control through deep reinforcement learning. *Nature*, *518*(7540), 529–533. doi:10.1038/nature14236 PMID:25719670

Narasimhan, K. R., Yala, A., & Barzilay, R. (2016). Improving Information Extraction by Acquiring External Evidence with Reinforcement Learning. *Narasimhan*. Retrieved from https://dspace.mit.edu/handle/1721.1/105337

Parisi, S., Pirotta, M., & Restelli, M. (2016). Multi-objective Reinforcement Learning through Continuous Pareto Manifold Approximation. *Journal of Artificial Intelligence Research*, *57*. Retrieved from https://core.ac.uk/download/pdf/74313357.pdf

Reinforcement learning explained - O'Reilly Media. (2016). Retrieved September 23, 2018, from https://www.oreilly.com/ideas/reinforcement-learning-explained

Silver, D., Huang, A., Maddison, C. J., Guez, A., Sifre, L., Van Den Driessche, G., ... Hassabis, D. (2016). *Mastering the game of Go with deep neural networks and tree search*. Academic Press. doi:10.1038/nature16961

Su, P.-H., Gaši'c, G., Mrkši'c, N. M., Rojas-Barahona, L., Ultes, S., Vandyke, D., ... Young, S. (n.d.). *On-line Active Reward Learning for Policy Optimisation in Spoken Dialogue Systems*. Retrieved from http://www.aclweb.org/anthology/P16-1230

Sutton, R. S. (1984). Temporal credit assignment in reinforcement learning. *Doctoral Dissertations Available from Proquest*. Retrieved from https://scholarworks.umass.edu/dissertations/AAI8410337

Watkins, C. J. C. H., & Dayan, P. (1992). Q-learning. *Machine Learning*, *8*(3–4), 279–292. doi:10.1007/BF00992698

Chapter 12
A Similarity–Based Object Classification Using Deep Neural Networks

Parvathi R.
VIT University Chennai, India

Pattabiraman V.
VIT University Chennai, India

ABSTRACT

This chapter proposes a hybrid method for classification of the objects based on deep neural network and a similarity-based search algorithm. The objects are pre-processed with external conditions. After pre-processing and training different deep learning networks with the object dataset, the authors compare the results to find the best model to improve the accuracy of the results based on the features of object images extracted from the feature vector layer of a neural network. RPFOREST (random projection forest) model is used to predict the approximate nearest images. ResNet50, InceptionV3, InceptionV4, and DenseNet169 models are trained with this dataset. A proposal for adaptive finetuning of the deep learning models by determining the number of layers required for finetuning with the help of the RPForest model is given, and this experiment is conducted using the Xception model.

1. INTRODUCTION

Machine Learning has a specialized branch called Deep learning. In machine learning features which are relevant are extracted manually from the images. From the extracted features, various objects in an image is to be classified by creating a model. In different to machine learning process,deep learning automatically extracts relevant features from the images and also it achieves "end-to-end learning" in which network is trained and then learned to do classification automatically by giving raw data. Machine learning support two types of learning paradigms i) Supervised Learning and ii) Unsupervised Learning (Agrawal, Carreira, & Malik, 2015). Supervised Learning is categorized into Classification and Regression. Support Vector Machine, Discriminant Analysis,Naïve Bayes, Nearest Neighbor and Neural Networks

DOI: 10.4018/978-1-5225-7862-8.ch012

Figure 1. Difference between machine learning and deep learning

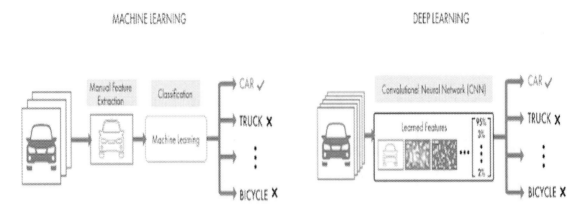

are the major classification algorithms in machine learning. Under Regression Model, Linear Regression, Generalized Linear Models, Support Vector Regressor, Ensembling methods, and Decision Tree are known methods. Similarly, Kmeans, Kmediods, Fuzzy C- means, Hierarchical, Gaussian Mixture, Hidden Markov Model are the famous clustering algorithms. Another key contrast appeared in Figure 1. is a profound learning calculations scale with information, though shallow learning coverages. Shallow learning alludes to machine learning strategies that level at a specific level of execution when clients include more illustrations and training data to the system. The major pro of deep learning networks is it's directly proportional to the size of data i.e networks endure to expand as the size of data rises.

Python and the Keras library of deep learning is used to pre-train the dataset by which1000 various catagories of objects and other objects in real time environment can be recognized with high accuracy. This chapter consists of 8 sections. Section 2 describes about the various deep learning image classifiers, Section 3 elaborates various search techniques, Section 4 explains the Approximate Nearest Neighbor Search with Random Projection Forest Building an ANN Search Tree. Section 5 deals with Fitness-Scaled Chaotic Artificial Bee Colony (FSCABC) algorithm, Section 6 gives about Classification of Objects Using Multiclass Support Vector Machine and Computer Vision, Section 7 explains the Automatic Object classification using random forest algorithm and Section 8 is the Conclusion

2. DEEP LEARNING IMAGE CLASSIFIERS

ImageNet

Different types of research are being carried out for object classification, especially computer vision uses this ImageNet which has the collection of 23,000 separate object categories discussed by He, K., Zhang (2015). In the context of deep learning and Convolutional Neural Networks, it can be called as Imagenet Large Visual Recognition Challenge (ILSVRC). The Objective of this task is to prepare a prototype which accurately arrange the picture into 1000 different object categories. About 1.2 million of pictures are considered as training phase and 50,000 pictures are taken for approval and 100,000 pictures utilized for testing. The full rundown of questionable classifications is given in Imagenet Large Visual Recognition Challenge(ILSVRC). The cutting edge pre-trained networks incorporated into the Keras center library speak to a portion of the most astounding carrying out Convolutional Neural Networks on the ImageNet task in the course of recent decades. This kind of networks likewise exhibits solid capacity to generalize to images outside these datasets by means of exchange learning, for example, include feature extraction and fine tunning.

Deep learning image classifiers in Keras. Keras have different CNN On ImageNet dataset which are pre-trained

1. LeNet5
2. VGG16
3. VGG19
4. ResNet50
5. Inception V3
6. Xception

LeNet5

The LeNet5 architecture shown in Figure 2 is essential model, in particular the understanding that image highlights are spread all through the picture and learnable parameters of the convolutions are utilized to extract the similary highlights which are available in the diverse areas. Around then, there was not GPU for training and CPU speed additionally moderate Therefore being able to save parameters and computation was a key advantage. This is in contrast to using each pixel as a separate input of a large multi-layer neural network. LeNet5 may not be helpful as first layer, since pictures are spatially related and individual pixel of the picture is considered as discrete feature. This would not exploit these correlation. Summary of LeNet5 features

1. To extract spatial features by convolution image subsample,three layers of convolutional neural network namely Convolution,pooling, non-linearity of deep learning is used.
2. Non-linearity in the form of tanh or sigmoids
3. To avoid large computational cost, sparse connection matrix between layers

Figure 2. LeNet5

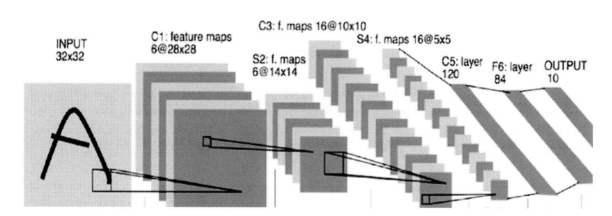

4. Multi-layer neural network (MLP) is a final classifier
5. Image subsample using spatial average of maps

Dan Ciresan Net

Ciresan, Meier, and Schmidhuber (2012) have published very first implementation of GPU Neural nets. It has forward and backward implementation of NVIDIA GTX 280 graphic processor with nine layers neural network.

AlexNet

Krizhevsky, Sutskever, and Hinton (2012) released AlexNet is extended version of LeNet.

AlexNet scaled the bits of knowledge of LeNet into a substantially bigger neural system that could be utilized to learn significantly more complex objects and object hierarchies of importance. The contribution of AlexNet are:

- Use of rectified linear units (ReLU)) as non-linearities
- use of dropout system to specifically overlook single neurons amid preparing which abstain from overfitting of the model
- overlapping max pooling, evading the averaging impacts of normal pooling
- utilization of GPUs NVIDIA GTX 580 to decrease preparing time

GPU consists of higher number of core than CPUs and perform ten times quicker training time and larger datasets, biggest images can be processed using GPU. The success of AlexNet (Idanola et al., 2016) leads to the large neural networks .

VGG16 and VGG19

The VGG organize architecture presented by Simonyan and Zisserman (2014) is portrayed by its effortlessness, utilizing just 3×3 convolutional layers stacked over each other in increasing depth. Lessening volume estimate is taken care of by max pooling. Two completely connected layers, each with 4,096 hubs are then trailed by a softmax classifier (above). The "16" and "19" remain for the quantity of weight layers in the system .

The VGG frameworks from Oxford were the first to use impressively littler 3 * 3. cnnels in each convolutional layers and besides went along with them as a gathering of convolutions. This is from every angle contrary to the gauges of LeNet, where far reaching convolutions were used to get practically identical features in a photo. As opposed to the 9 * 9 or 11 * 11 channel of AlexNet, channels started to wind up more diminutive, too perilously close to the famous 1 * 1 convolutions that LeNet expected to avoid, in any occasion on the principle layers of the framework. Regardless, the impressive ideal position of VGG was the understanding that various 3 * 3 convolution in course of action can emulate the effect of greater open fields, for outlines 5 * 5 and 7 * 7 These contemplations will be also used as a piece of later framework outlines as Inception and ResNet (Targ, Almeida & Lyman, 2016). The VGG frameworks uses different 3 * 3 convolutional layers to speak to complex features. Notice squares 3, 4, 5 of VGG-E: 256 * 256 and 512 * 512 channels are used different conditions in game plan to remove all the more confusing features and the mix of such features. This is feasibly like having enormous 512 * 512 classifiers with 3 layers, which are convolutional. This clearly means countless, what's more learning power. In any case, preparing of these structures was troublesome, and must be part into more diminutive frameworks with layers included one by one. This in view of the nonattendance of solid approaches to manage regularize the model, or to some way or another farthest point the immense intrigue space advanced by the extensive measure of parameters.

VGG used gigantic segment sizes in various layers and along these lines derivation was extremely extravagant at run-time. Diminishing the amount of features, as done in Inception bottlenecks, will save a bit of the computational cost. In 2014, 16 and 19 layer frameworks were viewed as significant (ignoring the way that we starting at now have the ResNet building which can be satisfactorily organized of significance of 50-200 for ImageNet and more than 1,000 for CIFAR-10). Simonyan and Zisserman (2014) discovered getting ready Visual Geometry Group (VGG16 and VGG19) testing (particularly concerning gathering on the more significant frameworks), to make planning simpler, they at first arranged smaller modifications of VGG with less weight layers (portions A and C) first. The more diminutive frameworks joined and were then utilized as introductions for the more noteworthy, more significant networkss — this system is called pre-getting ready.

While seeming well and good, pre-training ready may be an awfully time overwhelming, bleak task, requiring a whole framework to be set up before it will function Associate in Nursing low-level sorting out for a more deeper network. User directly not use pre-training ready (almost) and rather like Xavier/ Glorot low-level formatting or Microsoft Research Asia (MSRA) low-level planning (all over known as He et al. low-level outlining from the paper, Delving Deep into Rectifiers: Surpassing Human-Level Performance on ImageNet Classification). The centrality of weight low-level formatting and moreover the converging of significant neural frameworks inside all may be a sensible in it, Mishkin and Matas (2017).

There are two noteworthy downsides with VGGNet:

1. It's agonizingly ease back to train.
2. The detail weights themselves area unit very monster (as far as disk/band width).

Because of its depth and variety of completely associated nodes, VGG is more than 533MB for VGG16 and 574MB for VGG19. This makes sending VGG a tedious undertaking. Scientists still utilize VGG in a few deep learning image order issues; at the same time, littler system designs territory unit ordinarily extra entrancing, (for example, SqueezeNet, GoogLeNet, and so on.).

Network-in-Network

Network-in-network (NiN) had the great and simple insight of abuse 1 * 1 convolutions to supply extra combinatory capacity to the choices of a convolutional layer. The NiN configuration utilized spatial MLP layers once every convolution, to raised blend choices before another layer. afresh one will assume the 1x1 convolutions is against the main principles of LeNet, anyway to a great degree they instead encourage to blend convolutional alternatives in an exceedingly higher approach, that isn't attainable by only stacking extra convolutional layers. this can be totally not the same as abuse crude pixels as input to consequent layer by Lin, Chen, Yan (2013). Here 1 * 1 convolution is utilized to spatially combine choices crosswise over choices maps once convolution, with the goal that they successfully utilize just a couple of parameters, shared over all pixels of those highlights .

NiN also utilized a normal pooling layer as a piece of the last classifier, another apply which will wind up normal. This was done to normal the reaction of the network to different of the input picture before arrangement

ResNet

Unlike ancient sequential network architectures like AlexNet, OverFeat, and VGG, ResNet is instead a type of "exotic architecture" that depends on micro-architecture modules (also known as "network-in-network architectures") shown in Figure 3.

The term micro-architecture refers to the set of "building blocks" accustomed construct the network. a set of micro-architecture building blocks (along with your standard CONV, POOL, etc. layers) results in the macro-architecture (i.e,. the end network itself).

Despite the fact that ResNet might be a ton more profound than VGG16 and VGG19, the model size is genuinely significantly littler because of the utilization of worldwide normal pooling rather than completely associated layers — this chops the model size directly down to 102MB for ResNet50.

RESNET50: In Targ, Almeida, and Lyman (2016) the field of image classification deep convolutional neural networks have always resulted in many great discoveries. It's understood that the profundity of the neural network takes on a really significant part in the resulting accuracy. It is anticipated to have lower training error by increasing the depth of network layers, but this is not always the case and it sometimes results in degradation of training accuracy. He, K., Zhang, X., et al. (2016) tried to address the degradation problem caused by deeper neural networks by following the residual learning principle. In ResNet a residual mapping is being fit to the stacked layers and the authors claim that it's easier to optimize the residual mapping than the original function. Shortcut connections are brought out to the normal architecture which neither adds extra parameters nor increase the computational complexity. These shortcut connections are connections formed by bypassing one or more layers. These shortcut connections perform only identity mapping in case of ResNet. The output from these shortcut connections then

Figure 3. The residual module in ResNet

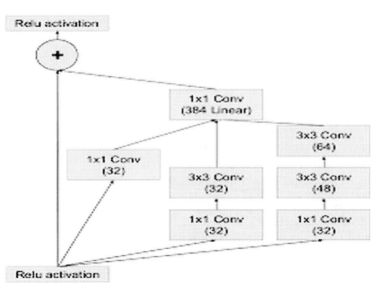

gets added to the output from the stacked layers. The training errors of these networks are lower when compared to the normal plain stacked layer network architecture. In normal plain networks the training error is not getting reduced as it's supposed to be when the network gets deeper, whereas with residual nets, though its deep it is easy to optimize the network and lead to a better accuracy gain as the network depth increases. Here instead of the normal mapping the layers are mapped with shortcut connections and thus form $f(x) + x$ which can be considered as feedforward networks with shortcut connections. The building block of the residual net is defined as: $y = f(x, \{W_i\}) + x$ with $f(x, \{W_i\})$ representing the residual mapping to be learned, x and y are input and output vectors of the corresponding layer.

The size of image that can be passed to a ResNet is formally 224x224. After every convolution in the network a batch normalization is applied, batch normalization is also applied after activation. Mostly 3x3 filters were used in the convolutional layers in the network. A global-average-pooling layer and a 1000 way fully connected network with softmax marks the end of the network. For ImageNet, an end-to-end training was done using SGD with a mini-batch size of 256, with learning rate initialized to 0.1 and the learning rate was cut down to its 10 percent when the error plateaus. The models were trained for 600000 iterations, with a weight decay of 0.0001, momentum of 0.9 and this 152-layer residual net achieved an overall 3.57% top-5 error on the ImageNet test set in the Imagenet Large Visual Recognition Challenge- ILSVRC 2015. This won them the first place in the competition in that year (LeCun, Bottou, Bengio, & Haffner, 1998).

Inception V3

The "Inception" micro-architecture was first introduced by Szegedy et al. (2015), *Going Deeper with Convolutions*. The goal of the inception module is to act as a "multi-level feature extractor" by computing 1×1, 3×3, and 5×5 convolutions within the same module of the network — the output of those filters area unit then stacked on the channel dimension and before being fed into the next layer within the network.

The original incarnation of this design was known as GoogLeNet, however sequent manifestations have merely been known as inception vN wherever N refers to the version range place out by Google. The inception V3 architecture included within the Keras core comes from the later publication by Szegedy et al (2015)., Rethinking the inception architecture for computer Vision that proposes updates to the origination module to further boost ImageNet classification accuracy. The weights for inception V3 are smaller than each VGG and ResNet, coming in at 96MB.

The main improvement that Szegedy, C et al. (2017) have setforth in this architecture is that of the improved utilization of the computing resources within the network. They designed the architecture of the network in such a way that it allows to make the network have increased depth and width but still keeps the computational budget constant. The Hebbian principle was used to create the architectural decisions which helped them to optimize the quality. The most frequently used method for improving the accuracy of deep neural network was by increasing the size of the network, by size it includes both the number of layers used, depth and the number of units in each layer, width. This solution comes along with two major drawbacks that is with a larger size of network it will contain more number of parameters thus the network becomes more prone to the problem of overfitting. The possibility of which is more with lesser amount of the training data, but creation of good quality training sets requires experts in the field to help in fine-grained visual category distinction. Another main pain-point is the increased use of the computational resources. IF the added capacity of the network is not used efficiently then large amount wasted computation may occur.

To resolve these issues sparsely connected architectures should be used. The well known work of Arora et al. has proved that the probability distribution of the dataset can be depicted by a large very sparse deep neural network, this will help to construct the optimal network topology layer by layer after analyzing the correlation statistics of the activations of the last layer and grouping the neurons with highly correlated outputs.

The key idea behind the Inception architecture is on finding how optimal local sparse structure in a CNN can be approximated and covered by promptly available dense segments. All that is required to be done is to find out the optimal local construction and then to repeat it spatially. It is assumed that the each unit from the early layer corresponds to some region inside the input image and these units are clustered to into the filter banks. In the early layers that are the layers close to the input layer correlated units would concentrate in solitary regions and these can be covered by using a layer of 1x1 convolutions into the next layer. There is also the chance of having fewer number of spatially spread out clusters and clusters can be secured by larger convolutions. To avoid the patch-alignment problems the design of inception architecture is currently confined to filters of sizes 1 * 1, 3* 3, and 5 * 5. Thus in this architecture a combination of all layers with their output filter banks concatenated to form a single output vector and this vector forms the input to the following stage. With even an unobtrusive number of 5 * 5 convolutions it can be restrictively costly over a convolutional layer. Thus there is a need of applying the dimension reduction and projection wherever the computational cost would else be high. So 1 * 1 convolutions are used to calculate the reductions before the 3* 3 or 5 * 5 convolutions are applied.

Commencement design is along these lines framed of such modules as specified above stacked on each other, with occasional max-pooling layers with walk 2 to such an extent that the determination of the network is divided. These beginning modules are utilized just in the higher layer with bring down layers kept as the same of the customary convolutional organize layers. This design takes into consideration growing the quantity of units at each stage yet this won't prompt an uncontrolled increment in the computational precision. This design was given group name as GoogleNet in 2014 and this could get the title of best in class classification engineering for the Imagenet Large Visual Recognition Challenge that year.

Bottleneck Layer

Inspired by NiN, the bottleneck layer of inception was reducing the quantity of highlights, and in this manner activities, at each layer, in this manner the inference time may well be kept low. Before passing information to the costly convolution modules, the quantity of highlights was lessened by, say, 4 times. This prompted mammoth savings in computational cost, and furthermore the accomplishment of this architecture.

We should examine this completely. Suppose you have 256 highlights coming in, and 256 coming out, and suppose the origin layer exclusively performs 3x3 convolutions. that is 256 x 256 x 3x3 convolutions that should be performed (589,000s increase amass, or mac operation). that might be over the computational spending plan, to run this layer in zero.5 milli-seconds on a Google Server. as opposed to doing this, to diminish the quantity of highlights which should be convolved, guidance 64 or 256/4. during this case, first perform 256 → 641 x 1 convolutions, at that point sixty four convolution on all inception branches, so we utilize again a 1x1 convolution from sixty four - > 256 choices back yet again. The activities are right now

- $256 \times 64 \times 1 \times 1 = 16{,}000s$
- $64 \times 64 \times 3 \times 3 = 36{,}000s$
- $64 \times 256 \times 1 \times 1 = 16{,}000s$

For an aggregate of around 70,000 versus the just about 600,000 previous result. Right around 10x less activities! Besides, in spite of the way that we are doing less errands, we are not losing clearing proclamation in this layer. Frankly the bottleneck layers have been exhibited to perform at state of-workmanship on the ImageNet dataset, for example, and will be in like manner used as a piece of later structures, for instance, ResNet. The reason behind the accomplishment is that the information features are connected, and in this way overabundance can be cleared by joining them reasonably with the 1x1 convolutions. By then, after convolution with less features, they can be broadened again into meaningful combination for next layer.

GoogLeNet Architecture

Unique GoogLeNet engineering gives significantly more detail on the outline decisions. Arrangements of the first thoughts are:

- maximize data stream into the system can be acquired via painstakingly developing systems which adjusts profundity and width. Highlight guide should increment before each pooling.
- The number of highlights or width of the layer is expanded as for profundity
- Increase in width prompts increment the blend of highlights in the following layer utilize just 3x3

  convolution, filter 5x5 and 7x7 is decomposed into multiple 3x3

INCEPTION V3 AND INCEPTION V4

The goal of the inception module is to act as a "multi-level feature extractor" by computing 1 x 1, 3 x 3, and 5 x 5 convolutions within the same module of the network the output of these filters are then stacked along the channel dimension and before being fed into the next layer in the network. The original incarnation of this architecture was called GoogLeNet, but subsequent manifestations have simply been called Inception vN where N refers to the version number put out by Google. The weights for Inception V3 are smaller than both VGG and ResNet, coming in at 96MB.

This is similar to older ideas like this one. But here they bypass two layers and are applied to large scales. Bypassing after 2 layers is a key intuition, as bypassing a single layer did not give many improvements. By 2 layers can be thought as a small classifier, or a Network-In-Network.

ResNet with a large number of layers started to use a bottleneck layer similar to the Inception bottleneck shown in Figure 4.

This layer diminishes the amount of features at each layer by first utilizing a 1 x 1 convolution with a humbler yield (commonly 1/4 of the information), and after that a 3 x 3 layer, and after that again a 1 x 1 convolution to a greater number of features. Like by virtue of Inception modules, this licenses to keep the computation low, while giving rich blend of features. See "bottleneck layer" fragment after "GoogLeNet and Inception".

Figure 4. Inception Bottleneck

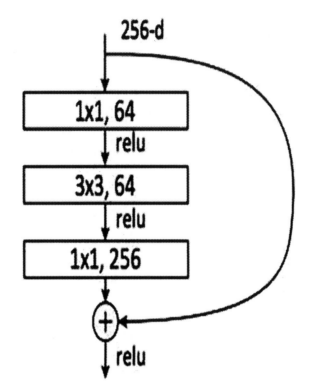

ResNet uses a genuinely fundamental starting layers at the info (stem): a 7 x 7 conv layer took after with a pool of 2. Contrast this to more mind boggling and less instinctive stems as in Inception V3, V4. ResNet furthermore uses a pooling layer notwithstanding softmax as definite classifier. Additional bits of information about the ResNet architecture are seeming every day:

- ResNet can be seen as both parallel and serial modules, by essentially thinking about the inout as going to various modules in parallel, while the yield of each module interface in game plan
- ResNet can in like manner be thought as different gatherings of parallel or serial modules
- It has been found that ResNet as a general rule takes a shot at blocks of low significance ~20– 30 layers, which act in parallel, instead of serially stream the entire length of the framework.
- ResNet, when the yield is sustained back to the commitment, as in RNN, the framework can be seen as a predominant bio-possible model of the cortex. An investigation of modules

ResNet, when the yield is maintained back to the responsibility, as in RNN, the structure can be viewed as an unrivaled bio plausible model of the cortex. An examination of modules An exact evaluation of CNN modules has been shown. It is advantageous to use:

1. use ELU non-linearity without batchnorm or ReLU with it.
2. apply a learned colorspace transformation of RGB.
3. use the linear learning rate decay policy.

4. use a sum of the average and max pooling layers.
5. use mini-batch size around 128 or 256. If this is too big for your GPU, decrease the learning rate proportionally to the batch size.
6. use fully-connected layers as convolutional and average the predictions for the final decision.
7. when investing in increasing training set size, check if a plateau has not been reach. • cleanliness of the data is more important then the size.
8. if you cannot increase the input image size, reduce the stride in the con- sequent layers, it has roughly the same effect.
9. if your network has a complex and highly optimized architecture, like e.g. GoogLeNet, be careful with modifications.

Densely Connected Convolutional Networks

DenseNet: Huang et al. (2017) proposed a new architecture in the name of DenseNet. Here the network connects each layer to every other layer in the network and this connection is in a feedforward manner. Thus in this architecture if there is L layers then there will a total of $(L(L + 1))/2$ direct connections. Thus with this network the input for each layer would be the feature maps of all the layers preceding it and the layer following it will have feature maps of all the preceding layers with its own feature map as well. One of the main advantages with this network is that it helps to limit the problem of vanishing gradient to an extend as all the layers have direct connections from all of its preceding layers (Huang et al. 2017). This also means that it strengthens the propagation of feature through the network, and improves the feature reuse. This all improvement comes along with the added advantage of a generously reduced number of parameters.

The DenseNet makes use of the networks power of reusing the features. This has the additional use of getting a condensed model that would be easier to train and efficiency of parameters will also be high. With DenseNet it can be seen that there is an improved row of information and gradients throughout the network, and this also makes it training easier. Each layer gets the input as the gradients from the loss function and also gets the real input signal. This helps in a profound deep supervision. All these factors help in training of the deeper network architectures. Overfitting in smaller training set sizes are also re-duced by the regularization effect observed as part of the dense connections. Adding more feature maps that are learned by different layers would help to increase the variety in the input of following layers and this would thus help to improve the overall efficiency of the network.

Though the structure of a DenseNet architecture is similar to that of a ResNet with the difference being that in the ResNet the input to the next layer is obtained by summing up the output of previous layers but with DenseNet concatenation of the same is being done. This still helped the architecture to provide the layers with accessibility to any of the feature maps of the previous layers and this in turn helped achieve feature reuse and thus a more compact model. It is easy to scale the DenseNet architec-ture to hundreds of layers without creating any optimization barriers. Also to increase of the number of parameters it was able to achieve consistent improvement in its accuracy as well. It performs less computation and uses a lesser number of parameters but still was able to be one of the state-of-the-art network architectures of deep learning.

Xception DeepLearning With Depthwise Separable Convolutions

Xception enhances the initiation module and architecture with a straightforward and more exquisite architecture that is as successful as ResNet and Inception V4. This system can be anybody's most loved given the straightforwardness and tastefulness of the architecture, introduced here . The architecture has 36 convolutional stages, influencing it to shut in likeness to a ResNet-34. In any case, the model and code is as basic as ResNet and significantly more intelligible than Inception V4.It is fascinating to take note that the ongoing Xception architecture was likewise propelled by our work on distinguishable convolutional filters

Chollet (2017) is an extension of the Inception architecture shown in Figure 5 which replaces the standard Inception modules with depthwise separable convolutions. In this deep convolutional neural network architecture Inception modules have been replaced with depthwise separable convolutions. Two minor differences between and "extreme" version of an Inception module and a depthwise separable convolution are depthwise separable convolutions as usually implemented (e.g. in TensorFlow) perform first fliter-wise spatial convolution and then perform 1 x 1 convolution, whereas Inception performs the 1 x 1 convolution first. The presence or absence of a non-linearity after the first operation. In Inception, both operations are followed by a ReLU non-linearity, however depthwise separable convolutions are usually implemented without non-linearities.

Chollet (2017) proposes an architecture in which the convolutional network layers are based completely on the depthwise convolutional layers. The hypothesis proposed is that the mapping of cross-fliters correlations and spatial correlations in the feature maps in a CNN can be entirely decoupled. The architecture is given name to depict the meaning of "Extreme Inception" and hence the name Xception. It has a total of 36 convolutional layers that is spread across 14 blocks or modules. All these connections have residual connections around them except for the first and the last module. This architecture can

Figure 5. The Xception architecture

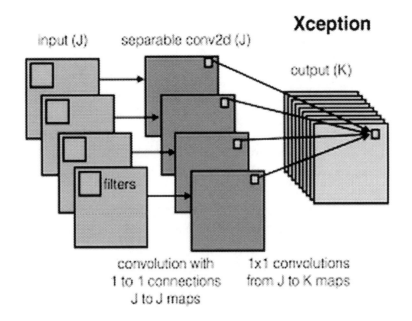

hence be considered as a stack of depthwise convolutional layers having residual connections. This can be easily formed using the Keras or Tensorflow libraries.

On comparing Xception and Inception V3 it can be seen that the number of parameters used by both the networks are relatively same in number hence any gap in the performance of both these architecure will not be accounted to the capacity of the network. Experiments were conducted using Tensorflow framework to compare the performances of both these networks with hyperparameters tuned for the best performance of the Inception V3 architecture on both ImageNet and JFT dataset. Results for ImageNet were collected based on the test with the validation set and for JFT after 30 million iterations. With ImageNet results it was seen that the Xception was able to outperform the Inception marginally and also in JFT the Xception architecture achieved a 4.3% relative improvemnt on the FastEval14k MAP@100 metric. The architecture was also able to give better results than that reported by the ResNet-50, ResNet-101, ResNet152. It achieved a top-1 accuracy of 79% with ImageNet results where Inception had 78.2% and a top-5 accuracy of 94.5% where Inception V3 gave 94.1%. Also with JFT results, using Xception with fully connected layers it got a FastEval14K MAP@100 of 6.78, Inception V3 in the same had 6.50. Thus, by experiments they were able to prove that the performance of Xception architecture is better than that of the Inception by replacing the inception modules with depthwise separable convolution layers.

Squeeze Net

The SqueezeNet architecture can obtain AlexNet-level accuracy (~57% rank-1 and ~80% rank-5) at only 4.9 MB through the usage of "fire" modules that "squeeze" and "expand" which is shown in Figure 6.

Figure 6. Squeeze net

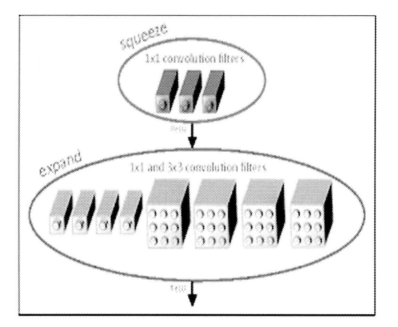

Figure 7. Nearest neighbor search structure

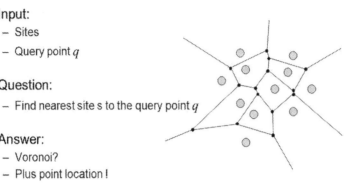

3. SEARCH TECHNIQUES

Nearest Neighbour Search

It is a technique for vicinity seek, and is an enhancement issue of finding point in each set that is nearest to some given point. The closeness is ordinarily expressed as far as disparity work: less comparable items have bigger capacity esteems. Lets consider M is a metric space and the divergence is expressed as separation metric, which has symmetricity and satisfies triangle imbalance. Further, M is d-dimensional vector space where uniqueness are estimated utilizing Manhattan separate, Euclidean separation or some other separation metric. However, this uniqueness capacity might be discretionary (Nene & Nayar, 1997). A few answers to NNS issue have been proposed. Quality and handiness of these calculations are controlled by time multifaceted nature of inquiries, alongside space intricacy of any gave look information structures. A casual perception ordinarily alluded to as revile of dimensionality expresses that quite is no universally useful correct answer for the NNS in the high-dimensional Euclidean space by methods for polynomial preprocessing and the polylogarithmic look time.NNs structure is shown in Figure 7.

Methods Used as a Solution to Nns

Linear Search

The unassuming answer to NNS issue is to register separate from inquiry point to the each other point in database, along these lines monitoring best up until this point". The calculation is frequently alluded to as guileless approach and has running time of $O(d(N))$ where N remains for the cardinality of S, and further d is dimensionality of M. As, there are no search information structures to be kept up, consequently linear search is having no space complexity past capacity of the database. The naive search by and large can beat the space dividing strategies on the higher dimensional spaces.

Space Partitioning

Prior in 1970s, the branch and bound technique have been connected to issue. While thinking about the Euclidean space, the approach is identified as spatial index or the spatial access strategies. Various space-partitioning approaches have been produced for taking care of NNS issue. In spite of the fact that the most straightforward is k-d tree, iteratively bisecting look space in two locales, in this way containing half of purposes of parent district. The inquiries are made through traversal of tree from root to leaf hub by assessing query point at each split. Contingent upon separate specified in query, the neighboring branches that may contain hits may likewise should be assessed. For the constant dimension query time, in case of the randomly distributed points,the average complexity is 0(log N) worst being 0(kN(1-(1/k))).

Then again, the R-tree data structure was intended for supporting the closest neighbor look in some unique setting, since it has efficient calculations for the inclusions and erasures for example the R* tree. These R-trees can yield the closest neighbors for the Euclidean distance, as well as can be utilized with some different distances.

On account of general metric space, the branch and bound technique are known under the name of metric trees, the illustrations are vp-tree and BK-tree. Further, utilizing an arrangement of focuses gathered from some 3-dimensional space and put into the BSP tree, likewise given some inquiry point gathered from same space, some conceivable answer for issue of finding closest point-cloud point to question point is given in the depiction of the algorithm. Henceforth, entirely, no such point may exist, as it won't not be interesting. Despite the fact that practically speaking, regularly we just think about the finding of any of subsets of all the point-cloud focuses which exist at the most limited separation to the given question point. The thought is that for each fanning of tree, figure that nearest point in cloud dwells into equal parts space containing question point. This will not be the situation, however it's a decent heuristic. Accordingly recursively experiencing all inconvenience of taking care of issues for speculated half-space, examination of separation returned by this outcome with the briefest separation from that question point to parceling plane is finished. The last separation is between question point and nearest conceivable point that may exist into equal parts space which isn't sought. Further, if this separation is bigger than that separation, returned in prior outcome, at that point by then, obviously there is no compelling reason to look other half-space. Also, if there is such need, at that point the inconvenience of taking care of an issue for other half space is considered, contrasting its outcome with previous outcome, consequently restoring the correct outcome. The Performance of the algorithm is subsequently, closer to the logarithmic time than the direct time when question point is close to the cloud, as separation between inquiry point and nearest point-cloud point nears to zero, algorithm needs just to play out some gaze upward by utilizing inquiry point as key to get right outcomes.

- **Approximation Methods**: The approximation algorithm is allowed to restore some point, whose separation from the question is the most extreme c times remove from an inquiry to the closest focuses. The request of the approach is that in a few cases, the surmised closest neighbor is by and large in the same class as correct one. On the off chance that the separation measure catches the thought of client quality precisely, at that point the little differences in separation ought not make any difference.
- **Locality Sensitive Hashing:** Locality sensitive hashing (LSH) is method for the grouping of points present in space in 'buckets' based on a distance metric operating on points. Here, the

points that are close to one another under some chosen metric are mapped to the same bucket with the highest probability.

- Nearest Neighbor Search in the spaces with some small intrinsic dimension. A cover tree has theoretical bound which is based on dataset's doubling constant.

- Projected radial search In the extraordinary situation where the information is thick 3D-guide of the geometric focuses, projection geometry of detecting procedure could be utilized to significantly streamline seek issue. The approach requires that 3D information is requested by projection to two dimensional network and henceforth expect that information is spatially smooth over the neighboring matrix cells with a special case of the protest limits. These suspicions we made are legitimate when working with 3D sensor information in applications like looking over, stereo vision and apply autonomy, yet won't not hold for the sloppy information for the most part Canziani,et. al (2016). For all intents and purposes, the system has a normal search time of:

$O(1)$ or $O(K)$ for k-nearest neighbor issues

- Vector approximation file When considering high dimensional spaces, the tree indexing structures turn out to be useless as an increasing percentage of nodes are needed to be examined. Hence, to speed up linear search, the compressed version of feature vectors kept in the RAM is used to pre-filter dataset in first run. Final candidates are determined in the second stage by using uncompressed data from disk for the distance calculation. Two other techniques which can be applied to solve nearest neighbor problem, using approximation methods are compression/clustering based search and the greedy walk search in small-world graphs.

4. APPROXIMATE NEAREST NEIGHBOR SEARCH WITH RANDOM PROJECTION FOREST

Building an ANN Search Tree

Suppose we have set of points. We start with all these points in space and try to divide it in recursion into smaller and smaller buckets that contain points that are closer to each other or are similar. To find the similarity between a query point and a set of points instead of calculating its distance from all the other points, we divide the search space into smaller buckets by drawing random lines and we search only within the bucket in which the query point. That is, we draw an arbitrary vector bringing up from the origin (the red arrow) (shown in Figure 8)

Red dot denotes the query point,blue dots are the other points in the search space. Source https:/making.lyst.com/2015/07/10/Ann/. Obviously a portion of the blue points point in the same direction of arrow from the arrow (to one side of the red line), and some indicate far from it (its left). That is our first split: all the dark red points are doled out to one bucket, and the blue points to the next.

Numerically, we take the dot product result of the arbitrary vector and our focuses: in the event that it is larger than zero, we relegate the focuses to one side subtree; in the event that it is smaller, we dole them out to the right subtree.

Figure 8. Creating random projection tree

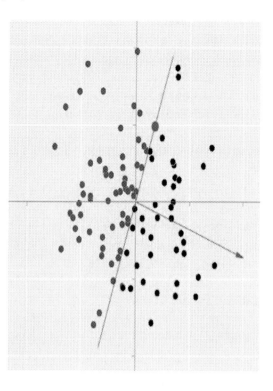

Figure 9. Dividing Points into smaller buckets based on their position in RPForest. Source https:/making.lyst.com/2015/07/10/ann/

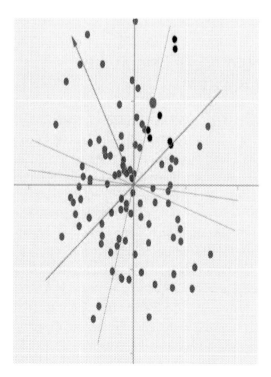

At this stage, Figure 9 explains each bucket still contains an excessive number of focuses, thus we proceed with the procedure by drawing another random vector, and doing the split once more. After these two parts, just the dull red focuses are in an same bucket as the query point.

We proceed with the parts until the point when we are happy with the number of points contained in a bucket. In the last picture, just 7 out of the underlying 100 focuses are in the ANN bucket, giving us a 10x accelerate while querying. The resulting data structure is a binary tree: at each internal node, we split our arrangement of focus into two. The leaf nodes contain the points themselves.

Querying in Aritifical Neural Networks With Random Projection Tree

Once the tree is being formed, querying it is exceptionally direct. If the point that is queried is in the tree then the bucket of that query point is been look up and a brute force search is done in that bucket alone.

If a new query point is to be searched we first need to traverse the tree to locate the suitable leaf node. Recursively take the dot product of the query point with the internal node vectors, moving down the right subtree at each split until the point that we hit a leaf hub.

Building Random Projection Forest

Up until this point, we have created just one tree. By and by, we construct numerous such trees a random projection forest. Since we are utilizing a probabilistic calculation, it is likely, yet not ensured, that a leaf node will contain a query point's closest neighbors. If we look at the figure we can see that some of the points that are very close to our query point fell into the other bucket. In the event that we have only a single tree, these points would be (wrongly) never retrieved. We create numerous trees to make this occurrence more improbable, such that candidate sets returned from each of these trees are checked and maximum reoccurring neighbors arc returned from all these as the neighbors.

5. FITNESS-SCALED CHAOTIC ARTIFICIAL BEE COLONY (FSCABC) ALGORITHM

Zhang, et al. (2014; 2012) proposed the system of utilizing a feed forward neural network to fathom the test of organic product classification. They have utilized Fitness-Scaled Chaotic Artificial Bee Colony (FSCABC) algorithm alongside a feed forward neural network for classification. The pictures of their tests were caught utilizing a computerized camera and for expelling the foundation they utilized the split-and-consolidation algorithm. The various features highlights the organic product pictures of every class were extricated to make an element space. At that point the dimensionality reduction strategy, Principle part examination was connected in the this component space to lessen the measurements. At that point these decreased highlights were utilized as a contribution to the FNN, the weights and inclinations of this Feedforward Neural Network (FNN) was prepared by the FSCABC algorithm. The stratified k-overlay cross approval method was then connected with the goal that it will enhance the age capacity of FNN.

The experiments were conducted on 1653 images belonging to 18 different categories. The background of the images were first removed with help of image segmentation techniques, split-and-merge technique. Color histogram was used to denote the distribution of colors in the image. Local binary pattern and the gray level co-occurrence matrix though are good texture features, but it would consume time, hence they used Unser's texture feature vectors for denoting the texture features of the images. Eight morphological measures were used to describe the shape features.Thus, from a 256 x 256 image 64 color features, 8 shape features and 7 texture features were extracted. The original image space has 196608 dimensions from which the features were reduced to a 79 feature space. The color,texture and shape features were extracted from the color images to form a hybrid feature set and dimensionality reduction of these features were done with the help of the principal component analysis technique and the reduced feature were fed as input to the FNN and FSCABC is used as algorithm to train its weights. Overfitting problem is handled by stratified K-fold cross validation technique .From their experiment results it was proved that the classification accuracy based on FSCABC-FNN method was higher than the method that used Genetic Algorithm FNN, Particle Swarm Optimization FNN, Artificial Bee Colony- FNN and kernel support vector machines. The FSCABC-FNN method was able to achieve an accuracy of 89.1%.

6. CLASSIFICATION OF OBJECTS USING MULTICLASS SUPPORT VECTOR MACHINE AND COMPUTER VISION

The dataset comprised of 1653 pictures having a place with 18 different natural product classes is used A hybrid feature extraction method (Chollet, 2017) that uses the shading features, Unser's surface, and shape features were considered by Yudong Zhang and Lenan Wu (2012) in their paper. Main part investigation was connected in the wake of removing the shape, shading and surface features to decrease the quantity of features. They utilized three different Support Vector Machine, Winner-Take-All Support Vector Machine (WTA-SVM), Max-Wins-Voting Support Vector Machine (MWV-SVM) (Zhang & Wu, 2012), and Directed Acyclic Graph Support Vector Machine (DAG-SVM) for multi class classification. Three different kernels were utilized as a part of this investigation, specifically, direct kernel, Homogeneous Polynomial kernel, and Gaussian Radial Basis kernel. Shading histograms were utilized to find the dispersion of hues. Flightiness, Area, Perimeter, Euler, Convex, Solidity, MinorLength, MajorLength were the different morphological measures considered. Three different multi-class SVM were utilized in the wake of applying PCA on the separated features for acknowledgment of the different natural products. These SVMs were prepared with help of the 5-overlap stratified cross approval procedure with diminished feature set as information. The best outcomes accomplished was utilizing the GRB (Gaussian Radial Basis) kernel MWV-SVM with a classification precision of 88.2%. At the point when the calculation time was consider over the Directed Acyclic Graph Support Vector Machine s performed well.

The shading histograms were utilized to speak to the shading features while Unser's surface features were utilized to signify the surface features. For the shape features Eccentricity, Area, Perimeter, Euler, Convex, Solidity, MinorLength, MajorLength were the features thought about so the major morphological features of the organic products are being gathered and spoken to. Unser demonstrated that the total and difference of two arbitrary factors that has similar fluctuations are de-connected and the foremost tomahawks of their related joint likelihood work are defined. Subsequently, they have utilized the aggregate S and difference D histograms for the surface depiction of the organic products. Subsequent to applying dimensionality lessening method an aggregate of 79 features was utilized to shape the feature space to speak to every one of the picture.

Kernel traps are connected onto Support Vector Machine to sum up the confounded circulated information to nonlinear hyperplanes. This Kernel Support Vector Machine calculation is like the typical Support Vector Machine, with the main difference is that each speck item is supplanted by a nonlinear kernel work. In Winner-Takes-All Support Vector Machine in the first place 'c' unmistakable parallel SVMs are ready, each one arranged to differentiate the information in a solitary class from the information of the remainder of the classes. Exactly when tried with another test information, all the C classifiers are run, and the classifier which yields the greatest regard is picked. On the off chance that there are two vague yield regards, Winner-Take-All (WTA) picks the class with the smallest record. In WVM-SVM, a twofold SVM for each match of classes is manufactured, so in supreme we will get c(c-1)/2 binary SVMs. Exactly when connected to another test information, each SVM gives one vote to the triumphant class, and the test information are set apart with the class having the most marks. In the event that two same votes is there by possibility, that is there are two indistinct votes, MWV picks the class with the smallest list. From the trials they found that Gaussian Radial Basis kernel on MWV-SVM gives the most noteworthy precision of all with an exactness of 88.2%.

7. AUTOMATIC OBJECT CLASSIFICATION USING RANDOM FOREST ALGORITHM

Three kinds of natural products to be specific orange, strawberry and apples were utilized as a part of trials by Bosch, Zisserman, and Munoz (2007). In their paper, Bosch, Zisserman, and Munoz (2007) tried the approach of using Random Forest for classifying the fruit images (Kontschieder, Fiterau, Criminisi, & Rota Bulo, 2015; Garcia, Cervantes, Lopez & Alvarado, 2016). Pictures were caught with the assistance of advanced camera and MATLAB was utilized to do all picture controls. Pictures were first resized to 90x90 pixels in order to lessen the shading list. They utilized natural product's shape, shading qualities and Scale Invariant Feature Transform (SIFT) as the organic product picture features. Color is considered as a feature with high significance for picture portrayal on account of the reason that shading is invariant concerning picture scaling,translation and pivot. Henceforth, the rest feature extraction system incorporate use of shading and shape ascribes to make the feature vector for each natural product picture in the dataset. The used shading features to depict the pictures are shading fluctuation, shading kurtosis, shading skewness and shading mean. The shape traits are spoken to using Eccentricity, Centroid, and Euler Number features. Scale Invariant Feature Transform (SIFT) is another strategy used to make feature vector, this calculation is utilized in picture features extraction and is invariant to picture scaling,rotation and interpretation and incompletely invariant to afine projection and lighting up changes (Garcia et al., 2016). Filter contains four essential strides to be specific: scale-space incredible acknowledgment, keypoint confinement, presentation task and keypoint descriptor.

Irregular Forest calculation was utilized for classification. 178 natural product pictures having a place with 3 different classes were utilized. Examinations in view of K-nearest neighours, Support Vector Machines and Random Forest calculations were directed (Kontschieder et al., 2015; Zawabaa, Hazman, Abbass, & Hassanien, 2014). As said two feature extraction strategies were put to utilize: feature vectors are framed utilizing shading and shape attributes in the first technique and in the second Scale Invariant Feature Transform algorithm is used to form feature vector. Color variance, color mean, color kurtosis, and color skewness were used to form color features and eccentricity, centroid, and Euler number are used for shape features. Apple, orange and strawberry were considered as they can be utilized to signify the likenesses and differences in view of shading and shape. Here the organic products were isolated into

3 gatherings to signify the difference in, shading and shape (orange strawberry), same shading different shape (apple-strawberry) and same shape different shading (orange-apple). Various investigations were directed as a blend of feature vectors and classifiers. From their examinations they presumed that the precision of similitudes relying upon the shape features has bring down exactness than shading features and SIFT features and Random Forest calculation gives higher precision than K-NN and SVM. The outcomes of the experiments show that the accuracy of similarities on shape group sets the lower accuracy among the three groups. For orange and strawberry group, the height accuracy is accomplished 100% with SIFT feature extraction and KNN classier. The height accuracy accomplished in the second group is for 96.97% apple-strawberry using Random Forest classfier, and for 78.89% orange-apple using SVM classier. Third group scores 96.97% for apple when used with SIFT feature extraction. While strawberry height accuracy is 92.31% when utilizing SIFT as feature extraction and KNN as classier. Comparing all the experiments, RF based calculation gives better accuracy to the other machine learning strategies.

8. CONCLUSION

In this chapter different deep neural network architecture ResNet50,Inception V4, Inception V3, Xception and DenseNet169 were analysed . A robust classification model which provided better accuracy than the accuracy given by deep learning models. This was done by combining the deep learning network with a nearest neighbour search algorithm along with RP Forest model . The false negative images after classification from the deep neural networks is passed to the RPForest model. This can help the researcher in getting better accuracy than using deep neural network alone for the purpose of classification.

Also a adaptive finetuning model creation method is discussed in which the RPForest model derived neighbors for the new classes is taken and based on the cosine distance deriving the depth of finetuning to be applied to onboard a new class to the existing classifier and tested with Xception Network.

Figure 10. Comparison of various Architectures- Single crop - single model experimental results. Reported on the set of Imagenet Large Visual Recognition Challenge- ILSVRC 2015

Metrics	LeNet 5	AlexNet	Overfeat fast	VGG 16	GoogLeNet v1	ResNet 50
Top-5 error[†]	n/a	16.4	14.2	7.4	6.7	5.3
Top-5 error (single crop)[†]	n/a	19.8	17.0	8.8	10.7	7.0
Input Size	28×28	227×227	231×231	224×224	224×224	224×224
# of CONV Layers	2	5	5	13	57	53
Depth in # of CONV Layers	2	5	5	13	21	49
Filter Sizes	5	3,5,11	3,5,11	3	1,3,5,7	1,3,7
# of Channels	1, 20	3-256	3-1024	3-512	3-832	3-2048
# of Filters	20, 50	96-384	96-1024	64-512	16-384	64-2048
Stride	1	1,4	1,4	1	1,2	1,2
Weights	2.6k	2.3M	16M	14.7M	6.0M	23.5M
MACs	283k	666M	2.67G	15.3G	1.43G	3.86G
# of FC Layers	2	3	3	3	1	1
Filter Sizes	1,4	1,6	1,6,12	1,7	1	1
# of Channels	50, 500	256-4096	1024-4096	512-4096	1024	2048
# of Filters	10, 500	1000-4096	1000-4096	1000-4096	1000	1000
Weights	58k	58.6M	130M	124M	1M	2M
MACs	58k	58.6M	130M	124M	1M	2M
Total Weights	60k	61M	146M	138M	7M	25.5M
Total MACs	341k	724M	2.8G	15.5G	1.43G	3.9G
Pretrained Model Website	[56]‡	[57, 58]	n/a	[57-59]	[57-59]	[57-59]

[†]Accuracy is Measured Based on Top-5 Error on ImageNet [14].
[‡]This Version of LeNet5 has 431000 Weights for the Filters and Requires 2.3 million MACs Per Image, and Uses ReLU Rather Than Sigmoid.

REFERENCES

Agrawal, P., Carreira, J., & Malik, J. (2015). Learning to see by moving. In *Proceedings of the IEEE International Conference on Computer Vision* (pp. 37-45). IEEE.

Bosch, A., Zisserman, A., & Munoz, X. (2007, October). Image classification using random forests and ferns. In *Computer Vision, 2007. ICCV 2007. IEEE 11th International Conference on* (pp. 1-8). IEEE. 10.1109/ICCV.2007.4409066

Canziani, A., Paszke, A., & Culurciello, E. (2016). *An analysis of deep neural network models for practical applications.* arXiv preprint arXiv:1605.07678

Chollet, F. (2017). *Xception: Deep learning with depthwise separable convolutions.* arXiv preprint, 1610-02357

Cireşan, D., Meier, U., & Schmidhuber, J. (2012). *Multi-column deep neural networks for image classification.* arXiv preprint arXiv:1202.2745

Garcia, F., Cervantes, J., Lopez, A., & Alvarado, M. (2016). Fruit classification by extracting color chromaticity, shape and texture features: Towards an application for supermarkets. *IEEE Latin America Transactions, 14*(7), 3434–3443. doi:10.1109/TLA.2016.7587652

He, K., Zhang, X., Ren, S., & Sun, J. (2015). Delving deep into rectifiers: Surpassing human-level performance on imagenet classification. In *Proceedings of the IEEE international conference on computer vision* (pp. 1026-1034). IEEE. 10.1109/ICCV.2015.123

He, K., Zhang, X., Ren, S., & Sun, J. (2016). Deep residual learning for image recognition. In *Proceedings of the IEEE conference on computer vision and pattern recognition* (pp. 770-778). IEEE.

Huang, G., Liu, Z., Weinberger, K. Q., & van der Maaten, L. (2017, July). Densely connected convolutional networks. In *Proceedings of the IEEE conference on computer vision and pattern recognition* (Vol. 1, No. 2, p. 3). IEEE.

Iandola, F. N., Han, S., Moskewicz, M. W., Ashraf, K., Dally, W. J., & Keutzer, K. (2016). *SqueezeNet: AlexNet-level accuracy with 50x fewer parameters and< 0.5 MB model size.* arXiv preprint arXiv:1602.07360.

Kontschieder, P., Fiterau, M., Criminisi, A., & Rota Bulo, S. (2015). Deep neural decision forests. In *Proceedings of the IEEE international conference on computer vision* (pp. 1467-1475). IEEE.

Krizhevsky, A., Sutskever, I., & Hinton, G. E. (2012). Imagenet classification with deep convolutional neural networks. In Advances in neural information processing systems (pp. 1097-1105). Academic Press.

LeCun, Y., Bottou, L., Bengio, Y., & Haffner, P. (1998). Gradient-based learning applied to document recognition. *Proceedings of the IEEE, 86*(11), 2278–2324. doi:10.1109/5.726791

Lin, M., Chen, Q., & Yan, S. (2013). *Network in network.* arXiv preprint arXiv:1312.4400

Mishkin, D., Sergievskiy, N., & Matas, J. (2017). Systematic evaluation of convolution neural network advances on the imagenet. *Computer Vision and Image Understanding*, *161*, 11–19. doi:10.1016/j.cviu.2017.05.007

Nene, S. A., & Nayar, S. K. (1997). A simple algorithm for nearest neighbor search in high dimensions. *IEEE Transactions on Pattern Analysis and Machine Intelligence*, *19*(9), 989–1003. doi:10.1109/34.615448

Simonyan, K., & Zisserman, A. (2014). *Very deep convolutional networks for large-scale image recognition*. arXiv preprint arXiv:1409.1556

Szegedy, C., Ioffe, S., Vanhoucke, V., & Alemi, A. A. (2017, February). Inception-v4, inception-resnet and the impact of residual connections on learning. In AAAI (Vol. 4, p. 12). Academic Press.

Szegedy, C., Liu, W., Jia, Y., Sermanet, P., Reed, S., Anguelov, D., ... Rabinovich, A. (2015). Going deeper with convolutions. In *Proceedings of the IEEE conference on computer vision and pattern recognition* (pp. 1-9). IEEE.

Targ, S., Almeida, D., & Lyman, K. (2016). *Resnet in Resnet: generalizing residual architectures*. arXiv preprint arXiv:1603.08029

Zawbaa, H. M., Hazman, M., Abbass, M., & Hassanien, A. E. (2014, December). Automatic fruit classification using random forest algorithm. In *Hybrid Intelligent Systems (HIS), 2014 14th International Conference on* (pp. 164-168). IEEE. 10.1109/HIS.2014.7086191

Zhang, Y., Wang, S., Ji, G., & Phillips, P. (2014). Fruit classification using computer vision and feedforward neural network. *Journal of Food Engineering*, *143*, 167–177. doi:10.1016/j.jfoodeng.2014.07.001

Zhang, Y., & Wu, L. (2012). Classification of fruits using computer vision and a multiclass support vector machine. *Sensors, 12*(9), 12489-12505.

Zhang, Y., & Wu, L. (2012). Classification of fruits using computer vision and a multiclass support vector machine. *Sensors, 12*(9), 12489-12505.

Chapter 13
Cognitive Deep Learning:
Future Direction in Intelligent Retrieval

Chiranji Lal Chowdhary
VIT University, India

Ashraf Darwish
Helwan University, Egypt

Aboul Ella Hassanien
Scientific Research Group in Egypt, Egypt

ABSTRACT

Deep learning states the scientific algorithms that are accustomed to come through a particular assignment. Such tidy issues could also be meteorology or brain diagnosing wherever records are obtainable as text. In such a state of affairs, cognitive computing can help medical practitioners to diagnose patterns that they might not observe, and they will extend the flexibility to diagnose the brain with efficiency. Deep learning is additionally able to introduce new APIs.

PRELIMINARY NOTE ON AI

Artificial Intelligence (AI) is outlined as the imitation of humanoid intellect developments thru technologies, above all computer systems. Such practices encirclement learning (the attainment of data and rules for discrimination of the info), reasoning (expending the ideologies to be successful in estimated or convinced assumptions), and self-correction. AI is covering all sets of technologies, algorithms, ways and theories that change computer systems to try and do tasks that typically need human intelligence. In keeping with this description, it's understood that computer vision, machine learning, artificial intelligence all are a component of artificial intelligence in a method or the opposite. Artificial intelligence specialist's claim that AI permits a machine to supply increased intelligence and it'd, therefore, surpass human's insight and accuracy, or maybe legerity or strength. Machine learning and massive information hold the key to harnessing the large potential medical information holds. New Applications engineered on machine learning models will facilitate in identification of diseases and in providing an accurate

DOI: 10.4018/978-1-5225-7862-8.ch013

diagnosing of ailments. Machine learning also can facilitate in gene-sequencing, clinical trials, drug discovery and analysis & Development, and epidemic irruption predictions. As an example, Alibaba Cloud's ET Medical Brain recently brought algorithmic program scientists from all elements of the globe to a standard platform in medical competition. They were able to develop a prognostic model for the personalised treatment of polygenic disorder. AI-based systems are serving to hospitals within the improvement of their operational workflows and management of information. It's additionally common for aid professionals to commit mistakes in reading dose directions or nosology information. Good AI systems with image recognition and optical character recognition capabilities will check all this information and guarantee reduction of such errors (Miller, 2019).

Outline Cognitive Computing Technology

Cognitive computing, on the opposite hand, is tough to be expressly outlined. Various technical specialists describe cognitive computing as nothing however computing that's attentive on reasoning and comprehending at a sophisticated level. It should be in an exceedingly means that's quite kind of like human knowledge that has the aptitude of constructing high-level selections in complicated eventualities. Cognitive computing will handle conceptual/symbolic information instead of simply pure information or sensing element streams. in keeping with advocates of cognitive computing – the technology will manage a large quantity of information and thoroughgoing rounds of analytics. Even so, the humans are firmly answerable of higher cognitive process. So, in easier terms – AI empowers a computer to be good to a degree of being smarter than humans. Whereas on the opposite hand – cognitive computing is that the individual technologies that perform specific tasks that facilitate human intelligence (Wang et al., 2010).

Background of Deep Learning

Deep Learning (DL) is such a very important field for information Science, AI, The technology and human lives immediately, and it deserves all of the eye is obtaining. Deep learning could be a definite deputize arena of machine learning, a replacement tackle learning illustrations on or after information that sets a stress scheduled learning serial "layers" of progressively significant depictions. Deep learning permits machine prototypes that remain collected of manifold process layers to be told demonstrations of info by numerous stages of intellection. Such superimposed demonstrations stay learned through prototypes known as neural networks, designed in precise layers arranged one when the opposite. Deep Learning are using a few things like artificial neural network (ANN) which is just a network impressed by genetic neural networks those are accustomed estimation or imprecise tasks that may rely on an outsized variety of contributions which are typically unidentified. Though deep learning could be an impartially previous deputize arena of machine learning, this solely design to distinction within the early 2010-11 (Kindermans et al, 2017).

Reasons of Using Deep Learning

There is still a tendency to miss a consistent mode to sequence appallingly deep neural networks. Consequently, neural networks be situated equitably thin, leverage just 1 or 2 layers of exemplifications, at that juncture those all weren't capable to sparkle in contradiction of a lot of sophisticated thin ways like support vector machines (SVM) or random forests. However during last period of 10 years, through the event of many straightforward however vital recursive enhancements, the developments in hardware (commonly GPU), and therefore the growing very fast cohort and accretion of information, using the assistance of deep learning these days the situation doable to route little deep learning prototypes on laptop computer (or within the cloud). Although such case is often not a replacement area, which are the ways to be able to move by the computer to try and fix Deep Learning. This one in every of the foremost vital instants for such field was the design of TensorFlow. TensorFlow is associate degree open source software system library for mathematical calculation by means of information stream graphs. Nodes within the display signify scientific processes, whereas the graph edges epitomise the flat information arrays (tensors) connected amid them (Xin et al., 2018, Ravi et al, 2016).

Tensors and Keras

Tensors, outlined technically, are merely arrays of facts, or purposes that rework in keeping with bound rules underneath a modification of coordinates. However during that range a tensor could be an oversimplification of directions and matrices to doubtless advanced dimensionality. Inside, TensorFlow signifies tensors as n-dimensional arrays of improper datatypes. So, the tensors result as a NumPy (the elementary compendium for technical calculating with Python) privations is making Tensors. The tensors are converted into NumPy and vice-versa. This doable meanwhile the paradigms are outlined undoubtedly as arrays/matrices. TensorFlow conglomerates the machine pure mathematics of compiling improvement procedures, creating simple the intention of the numerous calculated terminologies that might be tough to estimate, as an alternative. There is often not a web log concerning TensorFlow and they are nice ones. However, it is absolutely necessary to present Keras. Keras could be a sophisticated neural networks application program interface which is inscribed in Python and accomplished of playing on prime of TensorFlow, CNTK, or Theano. This is absolutely technologically advanced with attention on sanctioning quick investigation. Having the ability to travel after plan to result by the smallest amount doable suspension is vital to exploit sensible analysis. Francois Chollet (Chollet, 2017) proposed the primary thoughtful phase for creating Deep Learning simple for the lots. TensorFlow features a Python application program interface that isn't that onerous, however Keras created very easy to induce into Deep Learning for many individuals. Keras is that the winner for currently, it's attention-grabbing to work out that individuals prefers a straightforward interface and usefulness.

Deep Cognition

Thus unremarkably tend to work with deep learning programming and learning of innovative application program interfaces is roughly more durable than others and some are very informal associate degree communicative alike Keras, A few graphical application program interface to form and organise deep learning explanations by the clicking of a button. Such are often the potential of deep cognition. The deep cognition platform was based to "democratize AI". AI is already making vital worth for the globe economy. There's a (big) shortage of AI experience though' that makes a big barrier for organizations able to adopt AI. And this is often what they're resolution. For this we'll be victimization the cloud version of the deep learning approach. This is often single-user answer for making and organising artificial intelligence. The straightforward drag and drop interface assistances in designing deep learning prototypes by simplicity. Pre-trained reproductions use intrinsically helpful options change and accelerate the typical expansion method. This can have importation prototypical code and manage the model with the optical interface. The stand mechanically protects every exemplary form as ingeminate and tune hyper limits to boost routine. This is to compare performance across versions to search out optimum style. Deep learning studio will automagically style a deep learning model for custom dataset due to advance AutoML feature. This may have sensible playacting model up and running in minutes. An affirmative AutoML is what users are thinking that, automatic Machine Learning, which is applied specifically to deep learning, and this produce for you a full pipeline to travel from data into predictions (https://deepcognition.ai/).

Applications of Cognitive Computing in Medicinal Imaginary

Cognitive computing functional to medicinal pictures takes nice probable in each problem-solving and analysis settings, however it additionally aspects vital tests. The big selection of doable helpful consequences comprises helping general practitioner, accompanying general practitioner, rising the standard of treatment and medicinal conclusions, decreasing the prices of providing attention, and emerging novel considerate of sickness procedures and erraticism through numerous inhabitants. General practitioners may well be motor-assisted by quick and comprehensive screening of huge image information sets to apace and accurately determine the foremost vital components (Shaw, 2010).

The mission of medical imaginary is fine matched to cognitive computing since mental image of three and four dimensional information arrangements are not a traditional humanoid visual expertise, and revising massive information arrangements may be period intense and need each operative mental image outfits and knowledgeable about referees. Additionally, cognitive computing may well remain intended for big measure longitudinal contrasts also as associations by different medicinal information not resulting as of pictures that might rather be tough or not possible to try and do at scale. The consequences would possibly find sickness circumstances by previous besides a lot of wieldy phases and permit extensive association of data strenuously and through "comparable" patients. The latent for enhanced carefulness and consequences may be doable because of a lot of pervasive watching and integration from numerous datasets (Adali et al., 2015).

The scale and unpredictability of medicinal images information arrangements are possibly a big defy. It is a good vary of visual sense and proprieties for practical and functional images from 2 dimensional estimate xrays and superficial skin pictures, to a few dimensional capacity pictures from computerized axial tomography (CT) and resonance imaging (MRI), to advanced dimensional imaging sets that embrace time variation for alternative proprieties, distinction trainings, signal trainings, or longitudinal evaluations. Once multimodal assessments or information combination are thought-about, as an example victimization each organisational magnetic resonance imaging and practical magnetic resonance imaging through graphical record information, the spatiality stands any distended experiments to productive request of cognitive computing to medicinal images embrace the information, set dimensions and unpredictability and therefore the attainment of adequate coaching information.

Image information arrangements stand massive associated towards text information groups and lots of kinds of physical extents like blood harmony and Electrocardiograms (Shaw, 2010). In various cases it is found that one three dimensional breast CAT scan imaginary data may have 1024 voxels of nearly two gigabytes, and a hundred sets are given for one check-up victimization distinction of about two hundred gigabytes.

About creating implications aimed at single patient victimization the total framework of all medicinal check-ups intended for the targeted patient, various alternative picture information sets victimization various modalities, such as CAT Scan and positron emission tomography scan, or many scales, like, blood vessels, may likewise be thought-about. Usually medical pictures for a patient remain no inheritable on behalf of the precise native space of maximum apprehension, not a broader setting. Removing info in lieu of such numerous information sets and that can picture totally functional and practical physiognomies of nonridged volumes with dissimilar rules victimization changed scales and alignment grants experiments for coaching. Massive synchronised schemes of information access are required to produce sufficient consistent data for coaching and authentication. Lately the IBM Watson Health Medical Imaging cooperative consumes transported along an outsized variety of healthiness structures and educational medicinal organizations to coach a doubtless personalised medicinal investigation systems.

Impression of Societal Statistics and Cognitive Computing Intellect

Human culture endures to bear wonderful evolution by relevancy of totally features of data admittance besides distribution. This is having a philosophical impact happening on the means which tend to, individuals, and therefore the entire social survives, works and interrelates in commercial and community situations. In present scenario, huge data sharing, likely in terabytes, is also possible over social networks, online societies, games, software development tools, e-mails, blogs, posts, etc. This one furthermore assortments in kind: text, images, hyperlinks, likes, network connections etc. Humanoid community, behaviour and cognitive individualities take develop a lot of visible over interwoven of assorted infrastructures in online and offline sceneries. This development provided respond the increase of a replacement perception: community statistics that tries to grasp and infer tendencies associated with altogether features of humanoid community connections.

A social network existence it an expert, individual or entertaining endeavours. Therefore the mainstream of humanoid people is skilled talents, interests, interests, assets and level travel outlines developed not solely combined, however publically obtainable to an enormous mainstream of populace. Furthermore, uniform such individual things as medicines or favourite makes develop unwittingly a fragment of huge information, and so are conditional on all or any the process, data processing and pattern recognition. This is often significantly noticeable within the cyber world context, wherever human online individualities conspicuously platform themselves. Not shocking, such extents as huge information analytics, decision-making, call fusion, AI, pattern recognition and statistics, currently have a permanent presence within the online domain. The significantly distinguished samples of such analysis are cognitive multimodal sanctuary scheme design, founding individuality of Twitter operators over social networks exploration, and gender acknowledgment of Flickr manipulators supported human aesthetic favourites (Kotseruba et. al. 2018, Keretna et. al. 2013, Azam & Gavrilova 2016).

There takes a moderate increase in investigation targeted on analysis of workers social nets (Facebook, Twitter etc.) by the objective of considerate manipulator inclinations and communications supported the domains of their securities or their affiliation. A replacement field of specific attention for social statistics is machine aesthetics – considerate somebody's favourites and benefits with the aim of structure aesthetic profiles. In huge information analytics domain, internet surfing antiquities, consumer's partialities and online interconnections of countless consumers are being composed and analysed scheduled a routine. Proceeding the opposite influence, in security exploration, community behavioural identification also by way of artificial statistics emerged as powerful analysis tools, supported the fastidiously elect options extracted victimization machine intellect and deep learning after recording the past of manipulator online connections. Ancient opportunity of biometric analysis sometimes undertakes identifying somebody's individuality since biometric information which is historically restricted to biological and behavioral statistics. Biological options (face, iris, retina, and ear) frequently composed by specialised picture or audio-visual apprehending expedients, like infrared sensors, distant temperature measure expedients, etcetera. Social individualities, that historically embrace the means someone strides (gait), the means someone dialogues (speech), the means someone inscribes (keying patterns, keystroke burden), or the means someone validates brochures (monogram), may be attained since style of sensors, like KINECT sensing element or signature tablets (Paul et. al. 2012, Sourin et. al. 2016, Dai et.al. 2017, Azam & Gavrilova 2016, Yampolskiy et al. 2012, Kotseruba et. al. 2018, Jain et al. 2004).

Soft statistics embrace simply composed however not by way of distinctive because the preceding 2 biometric information, that is age, sex, tallness, heaviness, eye colour or hair colour of someone. Unfluctuating the means someone informally interrelates or articulated their likings will turn out to be a chic supply of verification info. To conclude, a societal biometric space of analysis existed planned by way of a replacement thanks to get additional however generally vital for verification info. During this field, societal behaviour options are mined after the means manipulators move over numerous societal online and offline nets. This comprises consumer's online existence configurations (time, day, month), the character of communication (tweets, blogs, chats), the contented of interface (topics, likes, opinions), on-line game enjoying ways, cybernetic biosphere avatar partialities, etc. (Kotseruba et. al. 2018, Sultana et. al 2016, Brinjikji et al 2015, Kotseruba et. al. 2018).

Single in every of the most options, that is vital aimed at analysis scheduled the public behaviour statistics. This is the communiqué configurations within the nets of users and therefore the conformation of this type of nets nearly. This is causing plenty of attention and obtaining grip in biometric analysis. Similarly, when the connected areas trying addicted to humanoid collaboration, physical trainings, manipulator identification, pattern recognition, composition credentials, and cooperative intellect. The thought may remain relocated toward the important biosphere also. For an example, in an exceedingly assumed societal setting approximately public behaviour designs like contacts and associates, everyday monotonous, mental situations, sort of language, gesticulations and sentiments throughout discussions, favourites, spatial info, and activity logs will play vital character vogueish distinguishing someone. This type of patterns also can compromise a novel set of implements to push higher considerate of cooperative developments, work flow undercurrents and threat investigation in cooperative/societal surroundings in actual and simulated domains. Through astounding quantity of data collected and analysed each day, this is not possible to undervalue worth of confidentiality of the info. Therefore, additional side of current analysis is targeted on protective the info and therefore the biometric templet after unsanctioned admission, counterfeit or change of state (Paul et. al. 2012, Kotseruba et. al. 2018, Gavrilova and Yampolskiy 2011).

The advent of societal biometric appears toward the accumulative standing of the step of linked tend people to perceive within the societal on-line surroundings. Modern analysis demonstrations which is operating Deep learning, machine intellect and cognitive science disclose concealed forms of behaviour, that permit to spot the being or its sex as of this type of soft partialities as favourite picture, melody, cinemas, much-loved spaces to go to, diversions, and sort of texting or a loop of families. Joining this societal info thru physical or activity information as a fragment of multi-modal biometric organization will offer associate degree incomparable degree of exactness. The contest remaining is protective this significant info and so in emerging privacy-preserving rules, like templet security, designate a needed half or some protection structure.

Cognitive Science Approaches in Managing Big Data

As the cognitive computing is said to be using or relating to computer setting and mainly encompassed of 5 parts. The first one is: this is having a high-performance calculating substructure driven by superior mainframes. Some good examples are multicore CPUs, GPUs, TPUs, and neuromorphic chips. The second section covering software development environs through inherent provision aimed at parallel and distributed computing which is power-driven via the fundamental calculating setup. The software libraries, machine learning and deep learning procedures intended for mining info and data since structured data bases is just the third section of cognitive computing. Next section is about the data analytics setting where procedures and set of rules impersonator humanoid cognitive developments. Now, coming to the last section of cognitive computing which is based on query languages and application program interfaces. This is aimed at retrieving the facilities of the cognitive computing environs.

Cognitive analytics inducements on the cognitive computing setting to cause actions by analysing various varied data bases by means of cognitive representations that the persons brain employments. Traditional symbolic and rule-based methods to difficulties like machine translation and speech-to-speech translation are actuality outmoded by arithmetic learning methods. The iniquitousness of big data, abundant calculating supremacy, and the renaissance of neural network procedures are provided that scalable keys for many challenging complications. The presentation of novel methods to issues which are having considerable tough for computers like conclusion substances in images and classification of images contending humanoid concert (Gudivada et al., 2015, Russakovsky et al., 2015, Goodfellow et al., 2014, Taigman et al., 2014, Lake et al., 2015)

The principal of all massive information acquaintance queries are just the management of human brain at the scale which is virtually awe-inspiring. The quantity of information that is having endlessly involvement over the senses and as of internal interruption and neural feeds to create which means and effectively. The some questions which arises in mind about the neural signal are transmitted and answering psychosomatic and neurologic philosophy by suggesting 2 parallel apparatuses as unitization, for sensual, and abstract or declarative information, and automatic for behaviour or routine data (Wang et al., 2016, Gobet & Lane, 2012; Moors, 2016). Each procedures include information density. Unitization existence decreases of sensual info addicted to less significant components of which means and automaticity actuality the connecting of behaviours to definite sensory decorations in behaviours in which eradicate in-between stages amongst the involvement and behaviour; so manufacturing the stimulant–response (S-R) associates intentional in characteristic behaviour scientific discipline. Over these info density, unitization permits quick recovery of huge volumes of data on the distant side whatever may be obtainable agreed the stowage limits of reminiscence, and automaticity permits fast activity response toward instant sensual information while not the requirement for aware discussion or downside resolution.

Neural assemblage's action by way of incidence securities, record the recurrence or non-repetition of characteristics diagonally manifold sensual involvements. Because the variety of sensual practises (examples) will increase, the frequency counts of attributes within the neural assemblages can exchange nearer and nearer to the particular occurrences of characteristics within the item or incident thru the "rule of huge statistics". Therefore, the neural assembly could be an information density apparatus that decreases the large quantity of knowledgeable about sensual information to a probabilistic statistical supply which gives the simplest illustration of the knowledge that remained within the unique sensual data. once functional to ranked neural arrangements, the neural reinforcement and snipping through Hebb neural physical property implies that the neural assemblies in every ranked step are adjusted to produce the feeds of the very best likelihood incidences to the following advanced level, like every level transfers concerning the foremost penurious information compression (Hebb, 1949, Shell et al., 2010, Chiriacescu, Soh, & Shell, 2013).

It tend to show that unitization immensely will increase potency of learning and productive task answer among the celebrated limitations of humanoid memory. Such unitization and automaticity mechanism remain whatever permit persons by terribly restricted memory and really deliberate process promptness to make behaviours and reach levels of data and experience that equivalent and in several belongings outdo what processer schemes by immensely a lot of power are able to do. though support centred mostly deep learning develops reiteration throughout coaching and downside resolution and therefore the results are accustomed choose that solutions turn out the simplest, or a minimum of acceptable, outcomes, these ways don't do the intensive information density of chunks or decreases of process stages typical of automaticity. Deep learning in addition to different neural net alternatives utilized in cognitive science, reply the nearest to on behalf of true unitization. They are containing ranked strata which may and mirror the operational unitization seen among the data structure of the brain (Chiriacescu, Soh, & Shell, 2013, Mohri, Rostamizadeh, & Talwalkar, 2012, LeCun, Bengio, & Hinton, 2015).

Genetically informative studies of cognitive talents and different individual characteristics associated with mathematical performance. A twin study is underneath means, assembling a good vary of measures from the dual pairs. Participants of the study perform activity tests and questionnaires, so participate in encephalogram experiment. We tend to additionally collect their secretion and social science measures. There's additionally a test-retest singleton (non-twin) cluster of the participants WHO participate within the study doubly in order that we are able to live the steadiness of the tests.

Simulation study of the bias introduced by unsupportive variables in twin analysis. Adjustment of the phenotypical variables for the consequences of sex and age is wide accepted follow in twin analysis. Such variables could increase phenotypical similarity of twins introducing bias to the estimates of genetic and environmental effects. The aim of this study is to estimate the bias underneath numerous conditions (sample size, genetic and environmental effects, impact of unsupportive variable). Deep learning ways in analysis of brain activity information. There's a replacement field of Machine Learning, Deep Learning, which might cash in of the graphical nature of encephalogram derived information and that has shown to exceed several ways for a good vary of applications (REF). cc ways and AI ways as well as Deep Learning can permit researchers world-wide to create higher use of current and future encephalogram derived information. We've samples large enough and machine capacities (cluster computer resources) to deal with this downside (McGue & Bouchard, 1984).

CONCLUSION

Cognitive computing is having huge prospective to donate to a novel cohort of solicitations. This is just an established knowledge which is thorough for requests. Cognitive computing remain additional than objective of the artificial intelligence. Cognitive computing approaches develop apace. Progresses in machine learning and deep learning are interacted intellectual machines and sensors can yield a large revolution where due to exponential developments in computing control, digital storing, and information measure. Machine learning is one in every of the foremost troubled technologies of the twenty first century. Though this technology will still be thought-about to be emerging, its future is bright. The higher than 5 predictions have simply damaged the surface of what may well be doable with machine learning. Within the returning years, we tend to are seemingly to work out a lot of advanced applications that stretch its capabilities to inconceivable levels. Cognitive services include a group of machine learning SDKs, APIs, and services, which permit developers to incorporate intelligent capabilities into their applications. With such services, developers will empower their applications to hold out numerous duties, like vision recognition, speech detection, and speech understanding. As this technology is constant to evolve, we tend to are seemingly to witness the event of extremely smart applications that may progressively speak, hear, see, and even reason with their surroundings. Therefore, developers are able to build a lot of partaking and ascertainable applications that may effectively interpret users' wants supported natural communication techniques.

REFERENCES

Azam, S., & Gavrilova, M. L. (2017). Biometric Pattern Recognition from Social Media Aesthetics. *Journal of Cognitive Informatics and Natural Intelligence, 11*(3), 1–16. doi:10.4018/IJCINI.2017070101

Brinjikji, W., Luetmer, P. H., Comstock, B., Bresnahan, B. W., Chen, L. E., Deyo, R. A., ... Jarvik, J. G. (2015). Systematic literature review of imaging features of spinal degeneration in asymptomatic populations. *AJNR. American Journal of Neuroradiology, 36*(4), 811–816. doi:10.3174/ajnr.A4173 PMID:25430861

Calhoun, V. D., Miller, R., Pearlson, G., & Adalı, T. (2014). The Chronnectome: Time-Varying Connectivity Networks as the Next Frontier in fMRI Data Discovery. *Neuron, 84*(2), 262–274. doi:10.1016/j.neuron.2014.10.015 PMID:25374354

Cervantes, J. A., Rodriguez, L. F., Lopez, S., & Ramos, F. (2013). A biologically inspired computational model of moral decision making for autonomous agents. In *Proceedings of the 12th IEEE International Conference on Cognitive Informatics & Cognitive Computing (ICCI*CC'2013)* (pp. 111-117). IEEE CS Press. 10.1109/ICCI-CC.2013.6622232

Chakraborty, A., Harrison, B., Yang, P., Roberts, D., & St. Amant, R. (2014). Exploring key-level Analytics for Computational Modeling of typing Behavior. *Proceedings of the 2014 Symposium and Bootcamp on the Science of Security.* 10.1145/2600176.2600210

Chiriacescu, V., Soh, L.-K., & Shell, D. F. (2013). Understanding Human Learning Using a Multi-agent Simulation of the Unified Learning Model. *International Journal of Cognitive Informatics and Natural Intelligence, 7*(4), 143–152. doi:10.4018/ijcini.2013100101

Chollet, F. (2017). *Deep Learning with Python*. Manning Publications.

Dai, H., & Hao, J. (2017). Mining social media data for opinion polarities about electronic cigarettes. *Tobacco Control, 26*(2), 175–180. doi:10.1136/tobaccocontrol-2015-052818 PMID:26980151

Eliasmith, C., Stewart, T. C., Choo, X., Bekolay, T., DeWolf, T., Tang, C., & Rasmussen, D. (2012). A large-scale model of the functioning brain. *Science, 338*(6111), 1202–1205. doi:10.1126cience.1225266 PMID:23197532

Gavrilova, M.L. & Azam, S. (2017). Biometric Pattern Recognition from Social Media Aesthetics. *International Journal of Cognitive Informatics and Natural Intelligence Archive, 11*(3), 1-16.

Gavrilova, M.L & Yampolskiy, R. (n.d.). Applying biometric principles to avatar recognition. *Transactions on Computational Science, 12*, 140-158.

Gobet, F., Gobet, F., & Lane, P.C.R. (2012). *Chunking mechanisms and learning*. Academic Press.

Goodfellow, I.J., Bulatov, Y., Ibarz, J., Arnoud, S., & Shet, V. (2014). *Multi-digit number recognition from street view imagery using deep convolutional neural networks*. Academic Press.

Gudivada, V., Baeza-Yates, R., & Raghavan, V. (2015). Big data: Promises and problems. *IEEE Comput., 48*(3), 20–23. doi:10.1109/MC.2015.62

Gudivada, V. N., Irfan, M. T., Fathi, E., & Rao, D. L. (2016). Cognitive Analytics: Going Beyond Big Data Analytics and Machine Learning. Handbook of Statistics, 35, 169-205.

Hebb, D. O. (1949). *The Organization of Behavior: A Neuropsychological Theory*. New York: Wiley. Retrieved from https://deepcognition.ai/

Jain, A. K., Ross, A., & Prabhakar, S. (2004). An Introduction to Biometric Recognition, IEEE Trasaction. *IEEE Transactions on Circuits and Systems for Video Technology, 14*(1), 1. doi:10.1109/TCSVT.2003.818349

Keretna, S., Hossny, A. H., & Creighton, D. (2013). Recognize User Identity in Twitter Social Networks via Text Mining. *IEEE International Conference on Systems, Man, and Cybernetics*, Manchester, UK. 10.1109/SMC.2013.525

Kindermans, P-J, Schutt, K-T, Alber, M, Muller, K-R, Erhan, D., Kim, B., & Dahne, S. (2017). *Learning how to explain neural networks: PatternNet and PatternAttribution*. Academic Press.

Kotseruba, I., & Tsotsos, J. K. (n.d.). 40 years of cognitive architectures: core cognitive abilities and practical applications. *Artificial Intelligence Review*, 1-78.

Lake, B. M., Salakhutdinov, R., & Tenenbaum, J. B. (2015). Human-level concept learning through probabilistic program induction. *Science, 350*(6266), 1332–1338. doi:10.1126cience.aab3050 PMID:26659050

LeCun, Y., Bengio, Y., & Hinton, G. (2015). Deep learning. *Nature, 521*(7553), 436–444. doi:10.1038/nature14539 PMID:26017442

McGue, M., & Thomas, J. (1984). Adjustment of twin data for the effects of age and sex. *Behavior Genetics, 14*(4), 325–343. doi:10.1007/BF01080045 PMID:6542356

Miller, T. (2019). Explanation in artificial intelligence: Insights from the social sciences Author links open overlay panel. *Artificial Intelligence, 267*, 1–38. doi:10.1016/j.artint.2018.07.007

Mohri, M., Rostamizadeh, A. & Talwalkar, A. (n.d.). *Foundations of Machine Learning*. Academic Press.

Moors, P., Boelens, D., Overwalle, J. V. & Wagemans, J. (2016). *Scene Integration without Awareness: No Conclusive Evidence for Processing Scene Congruency during Continuous Flash Suppression*. Academic Press.

Paul, J., Baker, H. M., & Cochran, J. D. (2012). Effect of Online Social Networking on Student Academic Performance. *Computers in Human Behavior, 28*(6), 2117–2127. doi:10.1016/j.chb.2012.06.016

Ravi, D., Wong, C., Deligianni, F., Berthelot, M., Andreu-Perez, J., Lo, B., & Yang, G.-Z. (2016)... *Deep Learning for Health Informatics, 21*(1), 4–21.

Roediger, H. L. III, & Smith, M. A. (2012). The "pure-study" learning curve: The learning curve without cumulative testing. *Memory & Cognition, 40*(7), 989–1002. doi:10.375813421-012-0213-5 PMID:22644774

Rosales, J. H., Jaime, K., & Ramos, F. (2013). An emotional regulation model with memories for virtual agents. In *Proceedings of the 12th IEEE International Conference on Cognitive Informatics & Cognitive Computing (ICCI*CC'2013)*. IEEE. 10.1109/ICCI-CC.2013.6622253

Russakovsky, O., Deng, J., Su, H., Krause, J., Satheesh, S., Ma, S., ... Fei-Fei, L. (2015). ImageNet large scale visual recognition challenge. *International Journal of Computer Vision, 115*(3), 211–252. doi:10.100711263-015-0816-y

Shaw, R. L. (2010). Embedding reflexivity within experiential qualitative psychology. *Qualitative Research in Psychology, 7*(3), 233–243. doi:10.1080/14780880802699092

Shell, D.F., Brooks, D.W., Trainin, G., Wilson, K.M., Kauffman, D.F., & Herr, L.M. (n.d.). *The Unified Learning Model, How Motivational, Cognitive, and Neurobiological Sciences Inform Best Teaching Practices*. Academic Press.

Sourin, A., Earnshaw, R., Gavrilova, M.L., & Sourina, O. (2016). Problems of Human-Computer Interaction in Cyberworlds. *Transactions on Computational Science, 28*.

Sultana, Tabassum, Sultana, Al-Ghanim, Shah, Shahid, & Mahboob. (n.d.). *A Cytogenic Monitoring Approach of Hospital Workers Occupationally Exposed to Ionizing Radiations Using Micronucleus Assay*. Academic Press.

Sultana, Tabassum, S., Sultana, T., Al-Ghanim, K. A., Shah, K., Shahid, T., & Mahboob, S. (2016). A cytogenic monitoring approach of hospital workers occuptionally exposed to ionizing radiations using micronucleus assay. *African Journal of Traditional, Complementary, and Alternative Medicines, 13*(2), 185–190. doi:10.4314/ajtcam.v13i2.22

Taigman, Y., Yang, M., Ranzato, M., & Wolf, L. (2014). DeepFace: closing the gap to human-level performance in face verification. In *Proceedings of the 2014 IEEE Conference on Computer Vision and Pattern Recognition, CVPR'14*. IEEE Computer Society. 10.1109/CVPR.2014.220

Wang, Y., Baciu, G., Yao, T., Kinsner, W., Chan, K., Zhang, B., ... Zhu, H. (2010). Perspectives on cognitive informatics and cognitive computing. *International Journal of Cognitive Informatics and Natural Intelligence, 4*(1), 1–29. doi:10.4018/jcini.2010010101

Wang, Y., Pedrycz,W., Baciu,G., Chen, P., Wang, G., & Yao, Y., (2010). Perspectives on Cognitive Computing and Applications. *International Journal of Software Science and Computational Intelligence, 2*(4).

Wang, Y., Widrow, B., Zadeh, L. A., Howard, N., Wood, S., Bhavsar, V. C., ... Shell, D. F. (2016). Cognitive Intelligence: Deep Learning, Thinking, and Reasoning by Brain-Inspired Systems. *International Journal of Cognitive Informatics and Natural Intelligence*, *10*(4), 1–20. doi:10.4018/IJCINI.2016100101

Wilson-Doenges, G., & Gurung, R. A. R. (2013). Benchmarks for scholarly investigations of teaching and learning. *Australian Journal of Psychology*, *65*(1), 63–70. doi:10.1111/ajpy.12011

Xin, Y., Kong, L., Liu, Z., Chen, Y., Li, Y., Zhu, H., ... Wang, C. (2018). Machine Learning and Deep Learning Methods for Cybersecurity. *IEEE Access: Practical Innovations, Open Solutions*, *6*, 35365–35381. doi:10.1109/ACCESS.2018.2836950

Yampolskiy, R., Cho, G., Rosenthal, R., & Gavrilova, M. L. (2012). *Experiments in Artimetrics: Avatar Face Recognition*. Academic Press.

Section 3
Security in Deep Learning

Chapter 14
Malware Classification and Analysis Using Convolutional and Recurrent Neural Network

Yassine Maleh

ⓘ https://orcid.org/0000-0003-4704-5364

Hassan 1st University, Morocco

ABSTRACT

Over the past decade, malware has grown exponentially. Traditional signature-based approaches to detecting malware have proven their limitations against new malware, and categorizing malware samples has become essential to understanding the basics of malware behavior. Recently, antivirus solutions have increasingly started to adopt machine learning approaches. Unfortunately, there are few open source data sets available for the academic community. One of the largest data sets available was published last year in a competition on Kaggle with data provided by Microsoft for the big data innovators gathering. This chapter explores the problem of malware classification. In particular, this chapter proposes an innovative and scalable approach using convolutional neural networks (CNN) and long short-term memory (LSTM) to assign malware to the corresponding family. The proposed method achieved a classification accuracy of 98.73% and an average log loss of 0.0698 on the validation data.

1. INTRODUCTION

With the rapid development of the Internet, malware has become one of the major cyber threats today. Any software that performs malicious actions, including stealing information, spying, etc. can be called malware. Kaspersky Labs (2017) defines malware as "a type of computer program designed to infect a legitimate user's computer and inflict damage in multiple ways".

As the diversity of malware increases, antivirus scanners cannot meet protection needs, resulting in millions of hosts being attacked. According to malware statistics report, Symantec affirms that more than 357 million new malware variants were observed in 2016. (Symante, 2017). Juniper Research (2016) predicts that the cost of data breaches will rise to $2.1 trillion globally by 2019.

DOI: 10.4018/978-1-5225-7862-8.ch014

In addition, there is a decrease in the level of skill required for malware development, due to the high availability of attack tools on the Internet today. The high availability of anti-detection techniques, as well as the ability to purchase malware on the black market, gives the possibility to become an attacker to anyone, regardless of skill level. Current studies show that more and more attacks are launched by script-kiddies or are automated (Aliyev, 2010).

Therefore, protecting computer systems against malware is one of the most important cybersecurity tasks for individual users and businesses, because even a single attack can compromise important data and cause sufficient losses. Frequent attacks and massive losses dictate the need for accurate and timely detection methods. Current static and dynamic methods do not allow accurate and effective detection, especially when it comes to zero-day attacks. For this reason, techniques and methods based on machine learning can be used (Chumachenko & Technology, 2017).

When classifying malicious code families, it is important to identify the unique characteristics of malicious codes, but it is also important to select the classification algorithms used as classifiers correctly. Recently, one of the most actively studied fields in the study of classification or recognition techniques is the deep neural network (DNN) related research called depth neural network which is made by increasing the number of hidden layers of neural networks. In particular, in the field of image and speech recognition, deep neural network based models have shown excellent performance, and there are moves to use them in other areas as well. Malicious code analysis is one such area. Indeed, various malicious code classification models using deep neural networks have been proposed. There are many research studies that combine classification schemes using recurrent neural networks (NRNs) (Pascanu, Tour, Mikolov, & Tour, 2013) and conventional neural networks in the field of image recognition and processing, but just few in the field of malwares and intrusions detection and classification (Chen, 2015).

This chapter aims to explore the problem of malware classification, and to propose a new approach combining Convolutional Neural Network (CNN) and Long Short-Term Memory Recurrent Neural Network (LSTM). The proposed model has been evaluated on the data provided by Microsoft for the BIG Cup 2015 (Big Data Innovators Gathering).

The main contributions of this chapter are:

1. We explore various deep learning models to solve the proposed malware classification problem;
2. We propose a deep neural network model to classify malicious behavior by combining CNN and LSTM layers;
3. We conduct a case-study using Microsoft Malware Dataset and show that our model has high detection accuracy (98,73%) in comparison with other models.

This chapter presents the research background in the next section. The related work of the malware classification technique in section 3 and the detailed description of the proposed methodology in section 4. Section 5 describes the experiments using the proposed model. Section 6 presents conclusions and future research directions.

2. BACKGROUND

Deep learning has demonstrated powerful function learning capabilities and has achieved remarkable performance in the field of computer vision that extracts the complex features through layer by layer by applying the filters on rectangular area. The deep neural network is a kind of deep learning method (Cui et al., 2018). The difference between a deep neural network (DNN) and a shallow artificial neural network (ANN) is that the former contains multiple hidden layers so that it can learn more complex functions. It has several variants: convolutional neural network, recurrent neural network and recursive neural network. DNNs spread forward and backward. The network parameters are updated according to the learning rate, the cost function per stochastic gradient descent during backscatter. In what follows, we briefly present the structures of the different DNNs applied in NLP tasks.

The complex features represent the hierarchical feature representations in which the features exist in higher level are composed from a set of lower level features. The hierarchical feature representation allows CNN to learn the data in various levels of abstraction. A single or a set of convolution and pooling operations and a non-linear activation functions are primary building blocks of CNN (Athiwaratkun & Stokes, 2017). In recent days, the advantage of using the ReLU as an activation function in deep architectures is widely discussed due to ReLU as an activation function is easy to train in comparison to logistic sigmoid or tanh function (Nair, V., & Hinton, 2010). RNN is mainly used for sequential data modeling in which the hidden sequential relationships in variable length input sequences is learned by them. RNN mechanism has significantly performed well in the field of NLP and SR (LeCun, Y., Bengio, Y., & Hinton, 2015).

In initial time the applicability of ReLU activation function in RNN was not successful due to the fact that RNN results in large outputs. As the research evolved, authors showed that RNN outputs vanishing and exploding gradient problem in learning long-range temporal dependencies of large-scale sequence data modeling. To overcome this issue, research on RNN progressed on the 3 significant directions. One was towards on improving optimization methods in algorithms; Hessian-free optimization methods belong to this category (Martens, 2010). Second one was towards introducing complex components in recurrent hidden layer of network structure. (Schmidhuber, 1997) introduced long short-term memory (LSTM), a variant of LSTM network reduced parameters set;gated recurrent unit (GRU) (Cho, K., Van Merriënboer, B., Gulcehre, C., Bahdanau, D., Bougares, F., Schwenk, H., & Bengio, 2014), and clockwork RNN (CWRNN) (Koutnik, J., Greff, K., Gomez, F., & Schmidhuber, 2014). Third one was towards the appropriate weight initializations. Recently, (Le, Q. V., Jaitly, N., & Hinton, 2015) authors have showed recurrent neural network with ReLU involving an appropriate initialization of identity matrix to a recurrent weight matrix is able to perform closer in the performance in compared to LSTM. This was substantiated with evaluating the 4 experiments on two toy problems, language modeling and speech recognition. They named the newly formed architecture of RNN as identity-recurrent neural network (IRNN). The basic idea behind IRNN is that, while in the case of deficiency in inputs, the RNN stays in same state indefinitely in which the RNN is composed of ReLU and initialized with identity matrix.

The section discusses the concepts of various deep learning algorithms and how they are trained.

2.1. Convolutional Neural Networks (CNN)

A convolutional neural network (CNN) is a type of downstream NN in which the connectivity model between its neurons is inspired by the organization of the animal visual cortex, whose individual neurons are arranged such that they respond to overlapping regions by ploughing the visual field.

The CNN are composed of three types of layers: (i) fully connected, (ii) convolutional and (iii) pooling. All the different implementations of CNN can be described as involving the following process:

- Invite several small filters on the input image.
- Subsample this filter activation space.
- Repeat steps 1 and 2 until you have enough high-level functions left.
- Apply a standard NN feedrate to the resulting characteristics.

Figure 1 describes the architecture used by (Krizhevsky, Sutskever, & Hinton, 2012) that was applied to the ImageNet classification competition. The architecture consists of 8 learning layers, the first five are convolutional and the others are fully connected layers.

2.2. Convolutional Layer

Figure 2 shows how convolution works. If we consider an image of 5x5 pixels as in the figure, where 0 means completely black values and 255 means completely white. In the center of the figure, a 3x3 pixel core has been defined with all eight 0s except one wright set to 1. The output is the result of calculating the kernel at each possible position in the image. Whether the core is convolved or not across all positions, it is determined by the stride. For example, for stride 1, it produces the typical convolution but for stride 2, half of the convolutions are avoided because there should be 2 pixels of distance between the centers.

The size of the output after convolution of a Z size kernel on an N image with S stride is defined as:

$$output = \frac{N - Z}{S} + 1$$

Convolutional layers are the heart of a CNN. A convolutional layer consists of a set of learning cores that are convolved over the width and height of the input characteristics during the forward pass, producing a two-dimensional activation map of the core.

In summary, a core consists of a connection weight layer, the input having the size of a small 2D patch and the output being a single unit.

Figure 1. AlexNet architecture

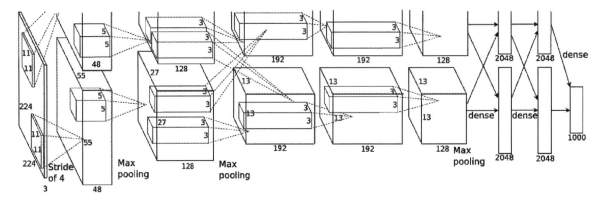

Figure 2. Convolutional Layer

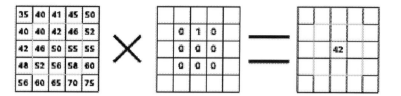

2.3. Pooling Layer

This layer is responsible for subsampling (i.e., reducing the spatial resolution of the input layers) the data produced from the convolution layers so that processing time can be reduced and computing resources can process the scale of the data. This is due to the fact that due to pooling, the number of teachable parameters is reduced in subsequent layers of the network. Max pooling works by dividing the image into a set of rectangles that do not overlap and for each sub-region outputs the maximum value. It's a commonly used pooling technique that keeps the maximum value in a region (for example, 2x2 data regions that do not overlap) and rejects the remaining values as shown in Figure 3.

The max-pooling layer reduces the computation for the upper layers by eliminating non-maximum values, and provides a form of translation invariance and therefore, provides additional robustness to the position being a means of reducing the dimensionality of intermediate representations.

2.4. Fully Connected Layer

Convolutional neural networks always have several layers fully connected by following convolutional layers. The neurons of the fully connected layers have complete connections with all the neurons of the previous layer. The structure of a fully connected layer is the same as that of a layer in a regular neural network. This layer performs the classification on the output generated from the convolution layers and pooling layers. Each neuron in this layer is connected to each neuron in the previous layer. This type of layer is usually followed by a Dropout layer that improves the generalizability of the model by avoiding over-fitting which is a common problem in deep learning.

Figure 3. Max_pooling with 2x2 filter and stride =2

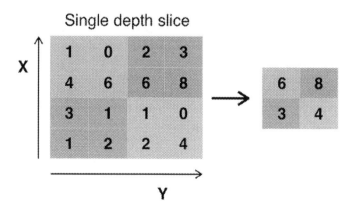

Dropout is a technique to prevent neural networks from being over-fitting and an approximate way to exponentially combine different neural network architectures (Hinton, 2014). When forming the model, the unit to be dropped has a probability p of being temporarily removed from the network, as shown in figure 4. It will be ignored when calculating the input and output in the forward pass and the progression of the backward propagation. Temporarily, this means that this unit is only abandoned when training this specific sample. This prevents the units from adapting too much. A layer with n units can be seen as 2^n possible thinned neural networks. When testing the model, not all units will be dropped and their weights multiplied by *p*. By doing this, 2^n networks with the same parameters are combined into a single neural network.

2.2. Recurrent Neural Network (RNN)

The introduction of long-established neural network in 1980's for sequence data modeling (Elman, 1990) is supplemented by recurrent neural network (RNN). Traditional neural networks do not have the capacity to remember information from the past, which seemed to be a major gap until the advent of the Recurrent Neural Networks (NRNs). Recurrent Neural Network is another type of artificial neural network. Neural networks that have loops, which allows information to stay. RNNNs can be designed as a normal neural network with a chain structure where there are multiple copies of a network and each network transmits the information to its successor and so on. RNNs have received increased attention in the recent past and incredible attention. Results have been obtained by using RNNNs in NLP applications such as speech recognition (Lang, Waibel, & Hinton, 1990), handwriting recognition (Robinson, T., & Fallside, 1991), linguistic translation, linguistic modelling (Robinson, Hochberg, & Renals, 1996) and sometimes also in object detection applications. RNNs are expected to perform the following tasks well in image-based applications, based on the assumption that they might be able to search for past information (say in a past video image) and use that information within the current framework. RNN network architecture is a basic and remained as baseline architecture for the newly introduced architectures.

In general, RNN consider

$$x = \left(x_1, x_2, ..., x_{T-1}, x_T \right)$$

Figure 4. Dropout

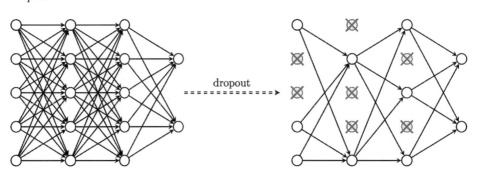

as input and maps them to hidden and *EQUATION MISSING PLEASE SUBMIT* output vector sequences as:

$$hl = (hl_1, hl_2, ..., hl_{T-1}, hl_T) \text{ and } op = (op_1, op_2, ..., op_{T-1}, op_T)$$

from $t = 1$ to T through the following equations in the forward direction.

$$HL(x, hl) = A(w_{xhl}x + w_{hlhl}hl + b)$$

$$HL : \mathbb{R}^m \times \mathbb{R}^n \to \mathbb{R}^n \ \ w_{hx} \in \mathbb{R}^{n \times m} \ \ w_{hh} \in \mathbb{R}^{n \times n} \ \ b \in \mathbb{R}^k$$

where A, b, w denotes activation function, bias vector and weight matrices respectively.

To learn the temporal dependencies, RNN feds the initial step $hl0$ layer value to the next time step hidden layer $hl_1 = HL(x_1, hl_0)$ and this is defined recursively as $hl_T = HL(x_T, hl_{T-1})$. Next, we can feed hl_T to stacked recurrent hidden layer or output layer through $soft$ max or $sigmoid$ as non-linear activation function. At each time-step t, the output node op value is estimated using the hidden node value hl at time-step t as:

$$op_t = sf(w_{ophl}hl_t + b_{op})$$

RNN are converted to FFN using Unfolding or Unrolling. This helps to understand the inherent dynamics of each time-step t. Unfolded RNN contains hl hidden layers for the input sequences of length l.

As shown in Figure 5, the unfolded RNN looks similar to deep neural network except that the weights w_{xh}, w_{hh}, w_{ho} are shared across time steps.

Figure 5. Unfolded over time steps $t = 0, t = 1$ and RNN

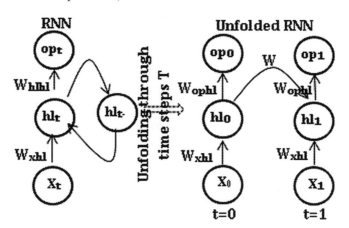

RNN is a parameterized function and to find the right parameters loss function is used. Loss function gives the units of difference between the predicted and target values. This is defined for subnet in unfolded RNN at each time-step t as:

$$L = d(tv, pv) = \sum_{i=1}^{T} d(tv, pv)$$

The full sequence is considered as one training vector for example $(x_1, \cdots, x_{41}, cl)$. So, total loss is estimated by summing the loss at each time-step. Next, to minimize the loss, gradient of the loss with respect to the weight parameters (w) has to be found and the appropriate parameters for weight parameters is selected through stochastic gradient descent (SGD). Like the previously mentioned process of total loss, one training vector require sum of gradient vector at each time step t. A gradient is calculated using backpropagation with a chain rule to iteratively compute the gradient from the unfolded computational graph. However, unfolded RNNs share its weight parameters across time-steps. So this process is called backpropagation through time (BPTT) (Sutskever, 2013). While in the process of backpropagating error across many time-steps, the weight matrix has to be multiplied with the gradient signal. This causes the vanishing issue when a gradient becomes too small and exploding gradient issue when a gradient becomes too large (Cho, K., Van Merriënboer, B., Gulcehre, C., Bahdanau, D., Bougares, F., Schwenk, H., & Bengio, 2014). As results RNN found to be inefficient in learning the long-range context in sequence data modeling. To overcome from these issues, authors recommended regularization to automatically set the appropriate value at each time step (Pascanu, R., Mikolov, T., & Bengio, 2013). They also recommended gradient clipping and a soft constraint for exploding and vanishing issue. Further, Real-time recurrent learning (RTRL) approach is introduced (Williams, R. J., & Zipser, 1989) that estimates the error derivative at each time step to do a single update in forward direction. However, this RTRL was not familiar due to the reason RTRL produces more computational cost in comparison to BPTT. Truncated backpropagation through time (TBPTT) is an amendment of backpropagation through time (BPTT) that offers flexibility in removal of exploding gradient issue in continuously running networks (Williams, R. J., & Peng, 1990). TBTT required setting the number of time steps in which the error can be propagated. As further the research on RNN in handling vanishing and exploding gradient issue.

However, the problem of long-term dependencies would persist in traditional RNNs. When it comes to long-term memory, NRNs cannot remember information from the long past. When the gap between the relevant information and the point where it is needed increases, RNNs cannot remember the connection. This issue was discussed in detail in (Bengio, Y., Simard, P., & Frasconi, 1994). This is where LSTMs are useful. Long Short Short Long-term memory networks (LSTMs) do not have this long-term dependency problem. The LSTMs, which were introduced in (Hochreiter, S., & Schmidhuber, 1997), are explicitly designed to ignore this long period. Like NRNs, LSTMs also have a chain structure, but the difference is that there are cellular states in LSTM cells. The states of these cells can be modified by the use of doors. Doors are structures that eventually allow information to be left to other LSTM cells. Portals control all or part of the information should be transmitted to other cells. This allows LSTMs to control what information needs to be extracted from the past, in order to make effective detection.

LSTM contains a memory block and adaptive multiplicative gating units such as input, forget and output gate to control a memory cell (Gers, F. A., Schraudolph, N. N., & Schmidhuber, 2002). Generally, the forward pass of LSTM is formulated as follows:

$$x_t, hl_{t-1}, mc_{t-1} \rightarrow hl_t, mc_t$$

$$in\_g_t = \sigma(w_{xin\_g}x_t + w_{hlin\_g}hl_{t-1} + w_{mcin\_g}ml_{t-1} + b_{in\_g})$$

$$fr\_g_t = \sigma(w_{xfr\_g}x_t + w_{hlfr\_g}hl_{t-1} + w_{mcfr\_g}ml_{t-1} + b_{fr\_g})$$

$$mc_t = fr\_g_t \odot mc_{t-1} + in\_g_t \odot \tanh(w_{xmc}x_t + w_{hlmc}hl_{t-1} + b_{mc})$$

$$op_t = \sigma(w_{xop}x_t + w_{hlop}hl_{t-1} + w_{mcop}mc_t + b_{op})$$

$$hl_t = op_t \odot \tanh(mc_t)$$

where in_g, fr_g, op are input, forget and output gating functions respectively, mc denotes memory cell, hl output of hidden layer.

As described in Figure 6 shows that a memory cell contains complex set of operations with a single memory cell, 3 adaptive multiplicative units and a self-connection with a fixed weight 1.0. To alleviate the number of units, many variants of LSTM is introduced. CWRNN and GRU is most prominent one.

Gated recurrent unit (GRU) is a variant of LSTM network (Cho, K., Van Merriënboer, B., Gulcehre, C., Bahdanau, D., Bougares, F., Schwenk, H., & Bengio, 2014). Generally, the forward pass of GRU is formulated as follows

$$x_t, hl_{t-1} \rightarrow hl_t$$

$$i\_f_t = \sigma(w_{xi\_f}x_t + w_{hli\_f}hl_{t-1} + b_{i\_f}) \text{ (Update gate)}$$

Figure 6. RNN unit and LSTM memory block Scheme

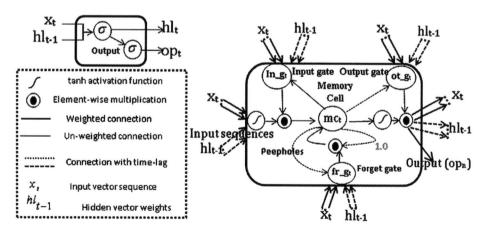

$$f_t = \sigma(w_{xf}x_t + w_{hlf}hl_{t-1} + b_f)\,(\text{Forget or reset gate})$$

$$ml_t = \tanh(w_{xml}x_t + w_{hlml}(fr \odot hl_{t-1}) + b_{ml})\,(\text{Current memory})$$

$$hl_t = f \odot hl_{t-1} + (1-f) \odot ml\,(\text{Updated memory})$$

The GRU comprises of gates (update and forget) which is dissimilar to LSTM memory cell gate list (input, output and forget) that are collaboratively balance the inflow as far as data within the unit.

3. RELATED WORKS

Several methods have been proposed for applying deep learning to malware detection and malware classification. For example, Saxe et al. (Saxe, A. M., McClelland, J. L., & Ganguli, 2013) presented a malware detection method using Deep Neural Network (DNN) on a histogram of byte sequences and metadata extracted from headers. Huang et al. (Huang & Stokes, 2016) used bag-of-words feature consisting of API call n-gram as an input of multi-task DNN, which simultaneously predicts whether a given sample is malware or not and to which family it belongs. Other methods targeting Android apps are also proposed (Yuan, Z., Lyu, Y., Wang, Z., & Xue, 2014) (Yuan, Lu, & Xue, 2016) (Li, J., Sun, L., Yan, Q., Li, Z., Srisa-an, W., & Ye, 2018) (Hou, Saas, Chen, & Ye, 2016). MacLaughlin et al. [20] presented a detection method that applies one-dimensional CNN to instruction sequences of Java Virtual Machine.

Kolsnaji et al. (Kolosnjaji, Zarras, Webster, & Eckert, 2016) combined a convolutional neural network with long-term memory cells (LSTMs). The authors were able to achieve a recall rate of 89.4%, but do not address the binary problem classification of identifying malware from benign software to detect families of malware with deep neural networks, including recurring networks, in order to classify malware into families using API call sequences. Pascanu et al (2013) conducted experiments to

Figure 7. Architecture of Gated recurrent unit

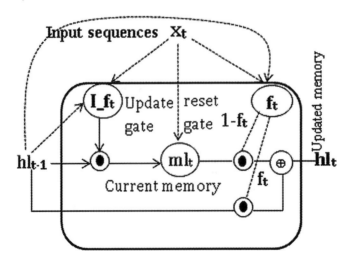

determine whether files was malicious or benign using RNNN and Echo State Networks. Tobiyama et al. (Tobiyama, Yamaguchi, Shimada, Ikuse, & Yagi, 2016) proposed a malware detection method based on process behavior in potential infected terminals. The authors found that Echo State Networks performed better with an accuracy of about 95% (5% error rate), but did not attempt to predict malicious behavior from the initial execution. Rhodea et al. (Rhode, Burnap, & Jones, 2017) explored the possibility of predicting whether an executable is executable or not is malicious based on a short snapshot of behavioral data. Athiwaratkun et al. (Athiwaratkun & Stokes, 2017) proposed a new one-step malware classifier based on a character-level convolutional neural network (CNN). A method proposed by Gibert Llauradó (Gibert, 2016) is also closely related to our proposed method. This work applies a CNN for malware classification. The author experimented with 3 different architectures by adding an extra block (a block consists of a convolutional layer followed by a Max-pooling layer) each time to its base model. However, their model is still very shallow in nature. Meng et al. (Meng et al., 2017) proposed MCSMGS a malware classification model based on static malware genetic sequences, which combines static malware genes with Convolution Neural Network. Drew et al. (Drew, J., Hahsler, M., & Moore, 2017) performed malware classification on the Microsoft Malware dataset using modern gene sequence classification tool and achieved 97.42% of classification accuracy.

In this chapter, we propose a combination of conventional neural network (CNN) and LSTM for classifying malware activity.

4. METHODOLOGY

4.1 . Malware Dataset

The Microsoft malware classification challenge dataset, which was used as the learning and verification data for the proposed artificial intelligence deep learning based malware detection system, was presented at the Kaggle machine learning challenge a machine learning based data analysis contest hosted by Microsoft in 2015 (Ronen, Radu, Feuerstein, & Yom-tov, n.d.). In this challenge, Microsoft released a huge dataset (almost half a terabyte when uncompressed) consisting of 21,741 malware samples. This dataset is divided in two parts, 10,868 samples for training and the other 10,873 samples for testing. Each malware sample had an Id, a 20 character hash value uniquely identifying the sample and a class, an integer representing one of the 9 malware family names to which the malware belong: (1) Ramnit, (2) Lollipop, (3) Kelihos_ver3, (4) Vundo, (5) Simda, (6) Tracur, (7) Kelihos_ver1, (8) Obfuscator. ACY, (9) Gatak. The distribution of classes present in the training data is not uniform and the number of instances of some families significantly outnumbers the instances of other families. Table 1 shows the different malware families.

For each observation, we were provided with a file containing the hexadecimal representation of the file's binary content and a file containing metadata information extracted from the binary content, such as function calls, strings, the sequence of instructions and registers used, etc, that was generated using the IDA disassembler tool. There are two files that represent each malware sample, *.bytes* file that includes the raw hexadecimal representation of the binary content of the file with the executable headers deleted and *.asm* file that contains the disassembled code extracted by the IDA disassembler tool. In our experiments, we only use the *.bytes* files to generate the malware grayscale images. A snapshot of one of these bytes files are shown below.

Table 1. Malware families in the dataset

Family Name	# Train Samples	Type
Ramnit	1541	Worm
Lollipop	2478	Adware
Kelihos_ver3	2942	Backdoor
Vundo	475	Trojan
Simda	42	Backdoor
Tracur	751	TrojanDownloader
Kelihos_ver1	398	Backdoor
Obfuscator.ACY	1228	Any kind of obfuscated malware
Gatak	1013	Backdoor

Figure 8. (a) Snapshot of one-byte file; (b) Snapshot of one assembly code file

4.2 . Data Pre-Processing

This work is inspired by the work of Nataraj (Nataraj, Karthikeyan, Jacob, & Manjunath, 2011), which is based on the observation that images of different samples of malware from the same family appear to be similar while images of samples of malware from a different family are distinct. In addition, if the old malware is reused to create new malware binaries, the resulting binaries would be visually very similar. In their work, they calculated image-based characteristics to characterize malware.

To calculate the texture characteristics, they used GIST (Oliva & Torralba, 2001). The resulting characteristic vectors were used to form a classifier of the nearest neighbor with a Euclidean distance. A given malicious binary file can be read as a vector of unsigned 8-bit integers and organized into a 2D array (Nataraj et al., 2011). This table can then be viewed as a grayscale image in the [0.255] range.

Malware authors usually change a small part of the previously available code to produce new malware (Nataraj, L., Karthikeyan, S., & Manjunath, 2015). If we represent malware as an image then these small changes can be easily tracked. Inspired by this and previous work (Nataraj et al., 2011), we visualize malware binary files as grayscale images.

Firstly, a given malware binary file is read in a vector of 8-bits unsigned integers. Secondly, the binary value of each component of this vector is converted to its equivalent decimal value (e.g. the decimal value for [00000000] in binary is [0] and for [11111111] is [255]) which is then saved in a new decimal vector representative of the malware sample. Finally, the resulting decimal vector is reshaped to a 2D

Figure 9. Visualizing malware as a gray-scale image

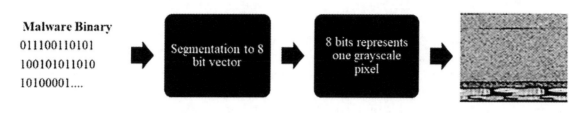

matrix and visualized as a grayscale image. Selecting width and height of the 2D matrix (i.e. the spatial resolution of the image) mainly depends on the malware binary file size. We use the spatial resolution provided by Nataraj et al. (Nataraj et al., 2011) reshaping the decimal vectors. Malware variants belonging to the same family usually have similar texture (i.e. visual appearance).

The main benefit of visualizing malware as an image is that the different sections of a binary can be easily differentiated. In addition, as malware authors only change a small part of the code to produce new variants, images are used to detect small changes while retaining the global structure. In consequence, malware variants belonging to the same family appear to be very similar as images while also being distinct from images of other families. To fulfill CNN's input data requirements, we first pre-process the grayscale image. The CNN takes the input image data with the same sizes, when it performs a task like image classification. As a general rule, the image data should have the same length and width (the length/width ratio is 1:1). This is for the convenience of later convolution surgery. Since the executive files have different file sizes, different grayscale image sizes also have big differences. In fact, a large grayscale image can reach 1.04 MB (2048 × 1036 pixels), while a small image is only 120 KB. (512 × 472 pixels). It is therefore necessary to standardize all grey levels images. We use a bilinear interpolation algorithm, an image scaling for standardization. It uses the four closest pixel values in the original image to determine a virtual pixel of the target image, which results in a better effect than the target image. We finally chose 64×64 as the standard size value for grayscale images.

4.3 . The Proposed Model

Inspired by the work proposed by Tsironi et al. (Tsironi, Barros, Weber, & Wermter, 2017) who analyzed gesture recognition using a recurrent short-term convolutional memory neural network (CNN-LSTM). The proposed deep neural network model for malware classification and analysis has the following design architecture. The Input to our network is a malware image and the output is set of scores for different malware classes. The proposed model involves 2 convolutional layers, each layer subsequently implementing convolution and max-pooling operations. The flattened output of the last convolutional layer is given to the input nodes of a hidden recurrent LSTM neural network, which is finally connected to a

Figure 10. (a) Lollipop samples; (b) Rammit samples

dense layer with a softmax output layer. The CNN and LSTM layers are trained in conjunction with the BackPropagation algorithm based on subsequence. The activation of each output layer unit corresponds to a specific malware class. The one squashing function is used to integrate the convolution layer and the max-pooling layer. This first level is followed by another convolutional and max-pooling layer. To interact with the LSTM layer, the CNN layers must be distributed over time. We have expanded our model to distributed time versions of Convolution2D, MaxPooling2D, and Flatten so that they support the LSTM layer. We experimented with many different network architectures different number and combination of layers and different filter and pooling parameters and found that the CNN-LSTM in figure 11 gave the best performance. Furthermore, we use Dropout (Hinton, 2014) in order to prevent overfitting and a softmax layer to output the label probabilities.

After the pre-processing step, we have 10,868 labeled samples in our dataset. As this is a small number, to obtain a more robust precision measurement, we use a five-step cross-validation. The data set is mixed and divided into 5 equal parts, each with roughly the same class distribution as the main data set. During training, we also applied drop layers after each of the convolutional layers and in the dense layer to avoid over-adjustment and co-dependence between the different filters within the convolutional layer.

The convolution layer and the max-pooling layer are integrated with one squashing function through which the output of a max-pooling layer is transferred in combination with an additive bias:

$$x_j^l = \tanh\left(pooling_{\max}\left(\sum_i^{X_j^{l-1}} * k_{ij}\right) + b_j^l\right)$$

where x_j^l are the feature maps produced by the convolutional layer l, x_j^{l-1} are the feature maps of the previous convolutional layer $l-1$, k_{ij} are the i trained convolution kernels and b_j^l the additive bias. Finally, $pooling_{\max}$ is the max-pooling function and tanh is the hyperbolic activation function.

The minimization was performed using Adaptive Moment Estimation (ADAM), which reduced overfitting of the dataset in the final training epochs by computing adaptive learning rates for each parameter (Kingma, D. P., & Ba, 2014). An additional benefit of ADAM is the parameter wise updates of the learning rate. The CNN and training were implemented using the commonly available Theano (Bergstra et al., 2010) and Lasagne (Dieleman, S., Schlüter, J., Raffel, C., Olson, E., Sønderby, S. K., Nouri, D., ... & De Fauw, 2015) packages for Python to allow for easy replication of the results by other researchers.

We apply LSTM, as network traffic event follows the time series patterns and the current network connection record can be classified based on the past traffic connection records. To capture time series models through time steps of newly formed features from the max-pooling operation in CNN, we feed them to the LSTM layer. The newly built feature map vector is transmitted to an LSTM layer. New feature vectors that are computed from Long short-term memory (CNN-LSTM) is an improved method of recurrent neural networks (RNNs) developed to alleviate the vanishing and exploding gradient issue (Schmidhuber, 1997). In contrast to the conventional simple RNN units LSTM introduces memory blocks. A memory block contains a memory cell and a set of gates. This appears as more effective in capturing long-range dependencies. A recurrent hidden layer function at time step can be generally defined as follows.

Figure 11. The proposed CNN LSTM Model

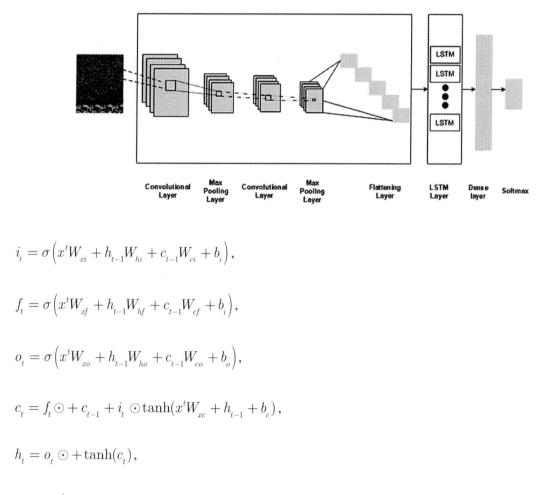

$$i_t = \sigma\left(x^t W_{xi} + h_{t-1} W_{hi} + c_{t-1} W_{ci} + b_i\right),$$

$$f_t = \sigma\left(x^t W_{xf} + h_{t-1} W_{hf} + c_{t-1} W_{cf} + b_i\right),$$

$$o_t = \sigma\left(x^t W_{xo} + h_{t-1} W_{ho} + c_{t-1} W_{co} + b_o\right),$$

$$c_t = f_t \odot + c_{t-1} + i_t \odot \tanh(x^t W_{xc} + h_{t-1} + b_c),$$

$$h_t = o_t \odot + \tanh(c_t),$$

where x^t is the input to the LSTM block, i_t, f_t, o_t, c_t, h_t are the input gate, the forget gate, the output gate, the cell state and the output of the LSTM block, respectively, at the current time step t. W_{xi}, W_{xf}, W_{xo} represent respectively the weights between the input layer and the input grid, the forget grid and the output grid. W_{hi}, W_{hf} and W_{ho} represent respectively the weights between the hidden recurrent layer and the forget gate, the input/output gate of the memory block,. W_{ci}, W_{cf}, W_{co} are respectively the weights between the cell state and the input gate, the forget gate and the output gate, and finally, b_i, b_i, b_o are respectively the additive biases of the input gate, the forget gate and the output gate. The activation functions comprise a sigmoid function. $\sigma(\cdot)$, the hyperbolic activation function $\tanh(.)$, and the element-wise multiplication $\odot$.

To avoid overfitting, we use L2 regularization to constrain the weights of the convolutional layers, and dropout in the dense and LSTM layers. Without regularization measures, representations learned by a neural network may not generalize well. For regularization, we try to use dropout as well as regularization l2 on weight and bias terms in the network in our search space. Dropout (Hinton, 2014) randomly omits a predefined percentage of knots at each training time, which commonly limits overfitting. L2 regularization allows a limited number of weights to become large values.

5. EXPERIMENTS AND RESULTS

In this section, we discuss the malware datasets, experiments and the evaluation scheme.

5.1 . Experimental Setup

We conduct experiments using Microsoft Malware Dataset. In 2015, Microsoft hosted a Kaggle competition for malware classification (Ronen et al., n.d.). In this challenge, Microsoft released a huge dataset (almost half a terabyte when uncompressed) consisting of 21,741 malware samples. This dataset is divided into two parts, 10,868 samples for training and the other 10,873 samples for testing.

The dataset provided by Kaggle for training was divided into two:

- The training set of size $(N - N/10) = 9781$
- The validation set of size $M = N/10 = 1086$

Where N is the total size of the dataset, $N = 10868$ and $M = 1086$. The validation set was used to search the parameters of the networks and to know when to stop training. In particular, we stopped training the network if the validation loss increased in 10 iterations.

All the experiments are conducted on Deep Learning Virtual Machine on Windows Azure environment, with 64-bit Ubuntu 18.04 Intel(R) Core i7–4790K CPU @ 4.00GHz $\rightarrow$ 8 with 64GB RAM and an NVIDIA Titan X GPU with 12GB memory. In order to run experiments on GPU, CUDA driver and CUDA Toolkit are needed for Nvidia's GPU–programming toolchain. Keras (Chollet, 2015) is used as library to build CNN-LSTM model. In the 5-fold cross-validation procedure, we train each model for 100 epochs on our Nvidia 1080 Ti GPU; the weights of the model are modified by the Adam optimization method (Kingma, D. P., & Ba, 2014) to minimize the average log-loss criteria.

To evaluate the performance of the proposed model, we report the performance of different methods in terms of accuracy, which simply refers to the percentage of malware samples that are labeled correctly.

5.2 . Results

Our proposed network CNN-LSTM is trained for 100 epochs with a batch size (a set of training data that is forwarded to the model at once) of 16 when training on Microsoft malware dataset. CNN-LSTM achieved the best performance with a classification accuracy of 98.73% on the validation data of Microsoft malware dataset. Our method outperforms several baseline methods by a huge margin on both of the datasets as can be seen in Table 2. The next figures shows the accuracy and the loss on the training and validation data achieved by the CNN-LSTM final model presented in Figure 12 and Figure 13 until they reached for 100 epochs. The final CNN-LSTM model achieves an average log loss of 0.0698 on the validation data.

5.3 . Testing

Usually, Kaggle provides a test set without label in their competitions and the Microsoft Malware Classification Challenge. Therefore, to evaluate our model using the test set we have to submit a file with the predicted probabilities for each class to Kaggle. Additionally, submissions in Kaggle are evaluated

Figure 12. Training and validation accuracy of CNN-LSTM model

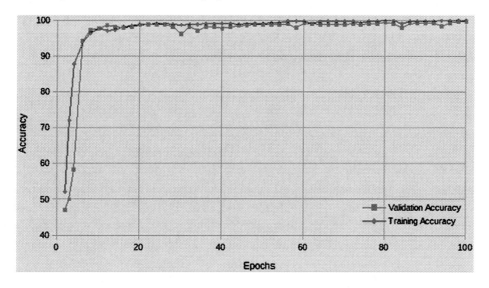

Figure 13. Loss on Training and Validation of CNN-LSTM model

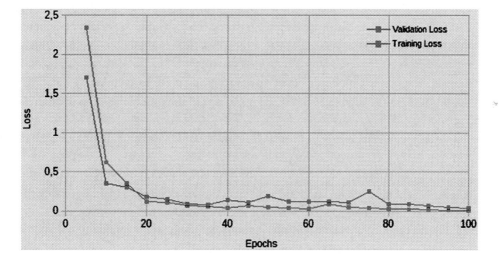

with two scores, the public score and the private score where the first one is calculated on approximately 30% of the test data and the second one is calculated on the other 70%. This submission is evaluated using the multi-class logarithmic loss. The logarithmic loss metric is defined as:

$$\log loss = -\frac{1}{N}\sum_{i=1}^{N}\sum_{j=1}^{M} y_{i,j} \log\left(p_{i,j}\right)$$

where N is the number of malware samples, M is the number of malware classes, $y_{i,j}$ is 1 if the prediction is correct and 0 otherwise, and $p_{i,j}$ is the predicted probability (Ronen et al., n.d.). Upon submitting the predictions of this model for the test malware files to Kaggle, we receive two average log-loss scores: a public score of 0.0691 calculated from 30% of the test dataset and a privates score of 0.0743 calculated from 70% of the test dataset. These results align with the log-loss we obtained on the validation data, which means our final model generalizes well on new data.

5.4 . Comparison Results

We tested the proposed CNN-LSTM against other deep learning models used for malware classification: Nataraj (Nataraj et al., 2011), Meng (Meng et al., 2017), Garcia (Garcia, F. C. C., Muga, I. I., & Felix, 2016), Rieck (Rieck, Holz, Willems, Düssel, & Laskov, 2008), Meng (Meng et al., 2017), kolosnjaji (Kolosnjaji et al., 2016) and Gibert (Gibert, 2016). A brief introduction to each model is provided below. Nataraj's classification model classified malicious codes by visualizing malicious code similar to the proposed model. Gabor filter is used to extract feature points of malicious code images. The extracted feature points are kNN (k-nearest neighbors) algorithm and classified malicious code types. Meng (Meng et al., 2017) proposed a malware classification model that combines static malware genes with deep genes learning methods. The model extracts the gene from the malware sequences that have both a hardware attribute and an informational attribute. Then it makes a distributed representation for each of them malware gene to represent intrinsic correlation and similarity. Finally, the Static Malware Gene Sequences-Convolution Neural Network is used to build the neural network to analyze the malware gene and perform malware classification. Rieck 's (Rieck et al., 2008) classification scheme classified malicious code types into SVMs by using the result of monitoring malicious code' s behavior pattern and executing malicious code in sandbox environment. Han's (Han, B. J., Choi, Y. H., & Bae, 2013) proposed a technique to classify malicious codes by comparing malicious codes with various APIs such as Hash value, AV test result value, and Packer as well as API used in malicious code. Drew (Drew, J., Hahsler, M., & Moore, 2017) performed malware classification on the Microsoft Malware dataset using modern gene sequence classification tool. Garcia (Garcia, F. C. C., Muga, I. I., & Felix, 2016) proposed an approach of converting a malware binary into an image and use Random Forest to classify various malware families. Kolosnjaji (Kolosnjaji et al., 2016) designed a neural network based on convolutional and recurrent layers of the network to obtain the best characteristics for classifying system call sequences. The performance indicators are used based on the most frequently used accuracy in each paper. Table 2 compares the proposed our classification technique with previous research results.

Compared to the existing methods and experiment results, we find that our jointed architecture of CNN and LSTM model performs better than the CNN and RNN models alone in malware classification. We take advantage of both the CNN model and the LSTM model thus get higher classification accuracy than the existing models. CNN extracts the local features of input and LSTM processes sequence input while learning the long-term dependencies and get malware feature representation.

6. CONCLUSION AND FUTURE WORK

Malware is increasingly posing a serious security threat to computer systems. It is essential to analyze the behavior of malware and categorize samples so that robust programs to prevent malware attacks can be developed. Towards this endeavor, we presented a new deep neural network architecture based on CNN and LSTM for malware classification and analysis. We first convert malware samples to grayscale

Table 2. Performance of different methods on validation test

Model	Accuracy
Meng	98%
Nataraj	97.18%
Rjeck	88%
Han	75%
Drew	97.42%
Garcia	95.62
Kolosnjaji	85,6
CNN-LSTM (ours)	**98,73**

images in order to train a CNN for classification. Experimental results on Microsoft malware classification datasets demonstrate that our proposed model achieves better than state-of-the-art performance. We showed the effectiveness of the proposed CNN-LSTM model through extensive experiments. Our deep learning model achieves an accuracy of 98.73% in the cross-validation procedure. The model takes little time to classify the malware class of a binary file, which makes it very convenient to use it in practice.

For future work, we will continue to modify and test our deep learning model on applying more complex deep learning architectures to achieve better performance. Moreover, testing our deep learning approach on larger data sets with more malware classes to achieve a higher accuracy rate.

REFERENCES

Aliyev, V. (2010). Using honeypots to study skill level of attackers based on the exploited vulnerabilities in the network. Chalmers University of Technology.

Athiwaratkun, B., & Stokes, J. W. (2017). Malware classification with LSTM and GRU language models and a character-level CNN. In *2017 IEEE International Conference on Acoustics, Speech and Signal Processing (ICASSP)* (pp. 2482–2486). IEEE. doi:10.1109/ICASSP.2017.795260310.1109/ICASSP.2017.7952603

Bengio, Y., Simard, P., & Frasconi, P. (1994). Learning long-term dependencies with gradient descent is difficult. IEEE Transactions on Neural Networks, 5(2), 157–166. doi:10.1109/72.279181 PubMed doi:10.1109/72.279181 PMID:18267787

Bergstra, J., Breuleux, O., Bastien, F. F., Lamblin, P., Pascanu, R., Desjardins, G., … Bengio, Y. (2010). Theano: a CPU and GPU math compiler in Python. *Proceedings of the Python for Scientific Computing Conference (SciPy)*, 1–7. Retrieved from http://www-etud.iro.umontreal.ca/~wardefar/publications/theano_scipy2010.pdf

Cho, K., Van Merriënboer, B., Gulcehre, C., Bahdanau, D., Bougares, F., Schwenk, H., & Bengio, Y. (2014). *Learning phrase representations using RNN encoder-decoder for statistical machine translation.* ArXiv Preprint ArXiv:1406.1078

Chollet, F. (2015). *Keras: Deep learning library for theano and tensorflow.* Retrieved from https://keras. io/k, 7, 8

Chumachenko, K., & Technology, I. (2017). *Machine Learning for Malware Detection and Classification.* Bachelor's Thesis Information Technology.

Cui, Z., Xue, F., Cai, X., Cao, Y., Wang, G., & Chen, J. (2018). Detection of Malicious Code Variants Based on Deep Learning. IEEE Transactions on Industrial Informatics, 14(7), 3187–3196. doi:10.1109/TII.2018.2822680 doi:10.1109/TII.2018.2822680

Dieleman, S., Schlüter, J., Raffel, C., Olson, E., Sønderby, S. K., Nouri, D., ... & De Fauw, J. (2015). *Lasagne: first release.* Academic Press.

Drew, J., Hahsler, M., & Moore, T. (2017). Polymorphic malware detection using sequence classification methods and ensembles. EURASIP Journal on Information Security. doi:10.1186/s13635-017-0055-6 doi:10.118613635-017-0055-6

Elman, J. L. (1990). Finding structure in time. Cognitive Science, 14(2), 179–211. doi:10.1207/s15516709cog1402_1 doi:10.120715516709cog1402_1

Garcia, F. C. C., Muga, I. I., & Felix, P. (2016). *Random Forest for Malware Classification.* ArXiv Preprint ArXiv:1609.07770

Gers, F. A., Schraudolph, N. N., & Schmidhuber, J. (2002). Learning precise timing with LSTM recurrent networks. Journal of Machine Learning Research, 115–143.

Gibert, D. (2016). *Convolutional Neural Networks for Malware Classification.* Academic Press.

Han, B. J., Choi, Y. H., & Bae, B. C. (2013). Generating malware DNA to classify the similar malwares. Journal of the Korea Institute of Information Security and Cryptology, 23(4), 679–694. doi:10.13089/JKIISC.2013.23.4.679 doi:10.13089/JKIISC.2013.23.4.679

Hinton, G. (2014). Dropout : A Simple Way to Prevent Neural Networks from Overfitting. Journal of Machine Learning Research, 15, 1929–1958.

Hochreiter, S., & Schmidhuber, J. (1997). Long short-term memory. Neural Computation, 9(8), 1735–1780. doi:10.1162/neco.1997.9.8.1735 PubMed doi:10.1162/neco.1997.9.8.1735 PMID:9377276

Hou, S., Saas, A., Chen, L., & Ye, Y. (2016). Deep4MalDroid: A Deep Learning Framework for Android Malware Detection Based on Linux Kernel System Call Graphs. In *2016 IEEE/WIC/ACM International Conference on Web Intelligence Workshops (WIW)* (pp. 104–111). IEEE. doi:10.1109/WIW.2016.04010.1109/WIW.2016.040

Huang, W., & Stokes, J. W. (2016). MtNet : A Multi-Task Neural Network for Dynamic Malware Classification. *International Conference on Detection of Intrusions and Malware, and Vulnerability Assessment*, 399–418. doi:10.1007/978-3-319-40667-1_2010.1007/978-3-319-40667-1_20

Kingma, D. P., & Ba, J. (2014). *Adam: A method for stochastic optimization.* ArXiv Preprint ArXiv:1412.6980

Kolosnjaji, B., Zarras, A., Webster, G., & Eckert, C. (2016). Deep Learning for Classification of Malware System Call Sequences. In B. H. Kang & Q. Bai (Eds.), *Australasian Joint Conference on Artificial Intelligence* (pp. 137–149). Cham: Springer International Publishing. doi:10.1007/978-3-319-50127-7_1110.1007/978-3-319-50127-7_11

Koutnik, J., Greff, K., Gomez, F., & Schmidhuber, J. (2014). *A clockwork rnn.* ArXiv Preprint ArXiv:1402.3511

Krizhevsky, A., Sutskever, I., & Hinton, G. E. (2012). ImageNet Classification with Deep Convolutional Neural Networks. In F. Pereira, C. J. C. Burges, L. Bottou, & K. Q. Weinberger (Eds.), Advances in Neural Information Processing Systems (Vol. 25, pp. 1097–1105). Curran Associates, Inc. Retrieved from http://papers.nips.cc/paper/4824-imagenet-classification-with-deep-convolutional-neural-networks.pdf

Lang, K. J., Waibel, A. H., & Hinton, G. E. (1990). A time-delay neural network architecture for isolated word recognition. Neural Networks, 3(1), 23–43. doi:10.1016/0893-6080(90)90044-L doi:10.1016/0893-6080(90)90044-L

Le, Q. V., Jaitly, N., & Hinton, G. E. (2015). *A simple way to initialize recurrent networks of rectified linear units.* ArXiv Preprint ArXiv:1504.00941

LeCun, Y., Bengio, Y., & Hinton, G. (2015). Deep learning. Nature, 521(7553), 436–444. doi:10.1038/nature14539 PubMed doi:10.1038/nature14539 PMID:26017442

Li, J., Sun, L., Yan, Q., Li, Z., Srisa-an, W., & Ye, H. (2018). Significant Permission Identification for Machine Learning Based Android Malware Detection. IEEE Transactions on Industrial Informatics.

Martens, J. (2010). Deep learning via Hessian-free optimization. ICML, 27, 735–742.

Meng, X., Shan, Z., Liu, F., Zhao, B., Han, J., Wang, H., & Wang, J. (2017). MCSMGS: Malware Classification Model Based on Deep Learning. *2017 International Conference on Cyber-Enabled Distributed Computing and Knowledge Discovery (CyberC)*, 272–275. doi:10.1109/CyberC.2017.2110.1109/CyberC.2017.21

Nair, V., & Hinton, G. E. (2010). Rectified linear units improve restricted boltzmann machines. *Proceedings of the 27th International Conference on Machine Learning (ICML-10)*, 807–814.

Nataraj, L., Karthikeyan, S., & Manjunath, B. S. (2015). SATTVA: SpArsiTy inspired classificaTion of malware VAriants. In *Proceedings of the 3rd ACM Workshop on Information Hiding and Multimedia Security* (pp. 135-140). ACM. doi:10.1145/2756601.275661610.1145/2756601.2756616

Nataraj, L., Karthikeyan, S., Jacob, G., & Manjunath, B. S. (2011). Malware Images: Visualization and Automatic Classification. In *Proceedings of the 8th International Symposium on Visualization for Cyber Security* (p. 4:1--4:7). New York: ACM. 10.1145/2016904.2016908

Oliva, A., & Torralba, A. (2001). Modeling the Shape of the Scene: A Holistic Representation of the Spatial Envelope. International Journal of Computer Vision, 42(3), 145–175. doi:10.1023/A:1011139631724 doi:10.1023/A:1011139631724

Pascanu, R., Mikolov, T., & Bengio, Y. (2013). On the difficulty of training recurrent neural networks. *International Conference on Machine Learning*, 1310–1318.

Pascanu, R., Tour, D., Mikolov, T., & Tour, D. (2013). On the difficulty of training recurrent neural networks. *International Conference on Machine Learning*, (2), 1310–1318.

Rhode, M., Burnap, P., & Jones, K. (2017). *Early-Stage Malware Prediction Using Recurrent Neural Networks.* ArXiv Preprint ArXiv:1708.03513

Rieck, K., Holz, T., Willems, C., Düssel, P., & Laskov, P. (2008). Learning and classification of malware behavior. In D. Zamboni (Ed.), *International Conference on Detection of Intrusions and Malware, and Vulnerability Assessment* (pp. 108–125). Berlin: Springer Berlin Heidelberg. doi:10.1007/978-3-540-70542-0_610.1007/978-3-540-70542-0_6

Robinson, T., & Fallside, F. (1991). A recurrent error propagation network speech recognition system. Computer Speech & Language, 5(3), 259–274. doi:10.1016/0885-2308(91)90010-N doi:10.1016/0885-2308(91)90010-N

Robinson, T., Hochberg, M., & Renals, S. (1996). The Use of Recurrent Neural Networks in Continuous Speech Recognition BT - Automatic Speech and Speaker Recognition: Advanced Topics. Boston, MA: Springer US. 10.1007/978-1-4613-1367-0_10

Ronen, R., Radu, M., Feuerstein, C., & Yom-tov, E. (n.d.). *Microsoft Malware Classification Challenge.* Academic Press. 10.1145/2857705.2857713

Saxe, A. M., McClelland, J. L., & Ganguli, S. (2013). *Malware Analysis of Imaged Binary Samples by Convolutional Neural Network with Attention Mechanism.* Academic Press.

Schmidhuber, S. H. (1997). Long short-term memory. Neural Computation, 9(8). PubMed PMID:9377276

Sutskever, I. (2013). Training recurrent neural networks. Toronto, Canada: University of Toronto.

Symantec. (2017). Internet Security Threat Report. *Symantec.* Retrieved from Https://Www.Symantec.Com/Content/Dam/Symantec/Docs/Reports/Istr-22-2017-En.Pdf

Tobiyama, S., Yamaguchi, Y., Shimada, H., Ikuse, T., & Yagi, T. (2016). Malware Detection with Deep Neural Network Using Process Behavior. In *2016 IEEE 40th Annual Computer Software and Applications Conference (COMPSAC)* (Vol. 2, pp. 577–582). IEEE. doi:10.1109/COMPSAC.2016.15110.1109/COMPSAC.2016.151

Tsironi, E., Barros, P., Weber, C., & Wermter, S. (2017). *Neurocomputing An analysis of Convolutional Long Short-Term Memory Recurrent Neural Networks for gesture recognition.* Academic Press. 10.1016/j.neucom.2016.12.088

Williams, R. J., & Peng, J. (1990). An efficient gradient-based algorithm for on-line training of recurrent network trajectories. Neural Computation, 2(4), 490–501. doi:10.1162/neco.1990.2.4.490 doi:10.1162/neco.1990.2.4.490

Williams, R. J., & Zipser, D. (1989). A learning algorithm for continually running fully recurrent neural networks. Neural Computation, 1(2), 270–280. doi:10.1162/neco.1989.1.2.270 doi:10.1162/neco.1989.1.2.270

Yuan, Z., Lu, Y., & Xue, Y. (2016). DroidDetector. Android Malware Characterization and Detection Using Deep Learning, 21(1), 114–123.

Yuan, Z., Lyu, Y., Wang, Z., & Xue, Y. (2014). Droid-Sec: deep learning in android malware detection. SIGCOMM. doi:10.1145/2619239.2631434 doi:10.1145/2619239.2631434

Chapter 15
Anomaly Detection Using Deep Learning With Modular Networks

Manu C.
Ramaiah Institute of Technology, India

Vijaya Kumar B. P.
Ramaiah Institute of Technology, India

Naresh E.
Ramaiah Institute of Technology, India

ABSTRACT

In daily realistic activities, security is one of the main criteria among the different machines like IOT devices, networks. In these systems, anomaly detection is one of the issues. Anomaly detection based on user behavior is very essential to secure the machines from the unauthorized activities by anomaly user. Techniques used for an anomaly detection is to learn the daily realistic activities of the user, and later it proactively detects the anomalous situation and unusual activities. In the IOT-related systems, the detection of such anomalous situations can be fine-tuned with minor and major erroneous conditions to the machine learning algorithms that learn the activities of a user. In this chapter, neural networks, with multiple hidden layers to detect the different situation by creating an environment with random anomalous activities to the machine, are proposed. Using deep learning for anomaly detection would help in enhancing the accuracy and speed.

INTRODUCTION

In a Daily realistic activity so many unusual intrusions and abnormal activities has occurred at different situation. This may cause the problem while doing an important activity in day to day life like card transaction, Healthcare etc. The detection of Anomalies is very important because it may cause the problem for the activity and which may lead the activity in to different directions so the end user may not get the

DOI: 10.4018/978-1-5225-7862-8.ch015

positive result. Anomaly detection is one which can be used to identify the abnormal behavior and which do not show the expected behavior. So to detect the anomalies we further move into the Neural Networks which is efficient method by training the model by doing continuous different erroneous conditions to the network. The Neural network finally observes the learning features and we can match into the target output and actual output.

To do this initially the Dataset is very important because to train the model it is very important and from the dataset we can test in different conditions. Once the model is trained, then for Different abnormal activities the Training model that is Neural network able to find out the anomalies when different situations, video, audio etc. shown to the model. By using the neural network, we can we can find out the anomalies. Deep Learning is other one main basement in this work which efficiently learns the Features. Deep Learning is one in which is the part of the Artificial intelligence in which is capable of learning the unsupervised from the data which is not structured format that is unstructured data.

Key Issues in Deep Learning and Anomaly Detection

Deep Learning is one of the essences in the artificial intelligence. Now days the use of deep learning is wide and vast in so many fields. Along with that Anomaly detection is also an integrated part of the deep Learning. The Experimental analysis in these fields may results either the positive or negative. So to eradicate the features it's very important to make some important steps to reach the milestones in Deep Learning and Anomaly Detection. Some of the Key Issues listed below about the Deep learning and Anomaly Detection.

1. Understanding the methodology like how to choose the features which is Structural which is far being from reality.
2. How to Tune efficiently the hyper-parameter Model is one of the major cause in the field of the deep learning.
3. The Computational efficiency is another key issue in the field of Deep learning.
4. Still the Computational Efficiency leads performance on the Datasets which is large and in offline environment also.
5. Constant Memory and Time Complexity is the major serious challenge.
6. The Changes in the Data which is non-interesting and erratic metrics.
7. The Training Data which is in the format of Dirty and abundant of ground truth.

The above are the some of the major issues in the field of Deep learning and Anomaly detection.

Motivational Factors

In 21st century the technological insights playing a Major role. In this era machines are capable of learning the features and it is automated for every action and gives back the reactions. From Man to Machine there have been lot changes occurred in this technological decade. Neural network in the human being is the core heart of every action and reaction. Like the human being react and thinking capacity is also integrated to the Machines. Now the era comes, in which Machines learns the features like a Man and react as per the trained feature and which look like a human brain. Here The Deep Learning learns the integrated features in the multiple levels. Learning the multiple level distributions, training data, multiple data and Flexible models with computational efficiency shows the better models which is easily integrated to any conditions.

By considering the above motivational factor, the training model can achieve the desired outputs with respect to the inputs given. So by proper training and efficient dataset to the model can achieve the efficient computational methodologies. Deep Learning algorithms is efficient and helpful to detect the anomalies in the given dataset. The removal of anomalies from the dataset which makes the model as best model and also increase the learning capacity.

Scope of the Chapter

Now a day the anomaly detection is the major criterion which is the major problem occurring in every instance. The outliers some time cause the major drawbacks in the several areas which inherently suppress the features. That is why finding out the anomalies is taking a major place in the Artificial Intelligence unit. The Scope of this work mainly defines the outlier detection by efficiently finding out in different datasets makes the model much more efficient. To Support this Deep learning is one of best integrated features to detect the anomalies in the dataset. This work ultimately helpful to find out the anomalies by efficiently training the model and with different erroneous conditions. So by this way initially from the given dataset we train the model and after training the model if we show another dataset with anomalies. Here the Back propagation model efficiently weighs the weights to learn the features and with different erroneous conditions. Again if we input the data, the training model efficiently detects the anomalies. The Efficiency and Time Complexity is the keen features of this work.

Challenges

Challenges one of the major criteria which inherently routes into the negative impacts on the work. Some of the Challenges found in anomaly detection and Deep learning is listed below.

- Lots and Lots of Data which makes sure that the model gives the desired result.
- Requires high performance machines to compute the operations by using the deep learning.
- Training the model by using the less computational efficiency and less power.
- Incapable of multitasking features.
- Dynamically changing in the environments causes a problem in finding out the anomaly detection.
- The Major challenge in the anomaly detection is the high rate of observation which is incoming.

Objectives of the Chapter

The main objectives of this work are:

- To Train the model which is capable to detect the anomalies?
- Identify the anomalies and shows as the error output.
- With respect to Time series the model must trained efficiently.
- Achieve the Speed and accuracy.

RELATED WORK

This chapter is basic step to create the familiarity by considering the previous research work. This chapter is a cluster of the Theoretical knowledge and Methodologies which is related to the anomaly detection and deep learning.

In Yin et al. (2017), Relevance Deep learning approach is used to detect the Network intrusion. Intrusion detection is the key for the network security. Here the Restricted Boltzmann algorithm is used to train the model. Higher detection accuracy can be achieved by the deep learning which is relevance. At the end of the network intrusion detection method the depth learning shows the rate which is in the average level and along with that it's also shows the false detection rate and intrusion attack which is unknown.

The author is proposed the network level anomalies in Pattarakavin and Chongstitvatana (2016). Here outlier detection for abnormal problems. The algorithm is proposed here is estimates the by normal flows by low dimensional matrices. Extensive numerical evaluation achieves the faster convergence per iterations and performs the anomaly detection and better volume which is state of the art.

Machine learning approach is used and one of the types is used to detect the anomalies in the intrusions. So the anomalies for three methods such as the Host based IDS, Network Based IDS and along with that Hybrid IDS proposed in Zhu (2010). Initially here the model has to be trained for different intrusions and by continuously train the model and if we show a new dataset as an input, then it can be able find out the anomalies in the intrusion detection system.

The detection of anomalies in the Hard Disk manufacturing process can be automated by using the machine learning process discussed by the author in Yin et al. (2017). In Thailand the manufacture company produce the production in the continuous flow. In this paper, author proposed the machine learning to correct the error in log files and it gives the report to check the results.

Anomalies can be detected in the blood glucose level which is measured automatically by using the learning approach (Moohebbi et al., 2017). Here the author is used Hidden Markov model and along with he is used historical data for the observations. Here the author train the model detects the anomalies by daily routine.

For Type 2 Diabetics the Deep learning approach is used to base on the Type 1 Diabetics. So Insulin treatment is very essential to in order to survive the life complications. In Van, Thinh and Sach (2017), author proposed the Continuous Glucose Monitoring (CGM) signals are the basis of deep learning algorithm for T2D patient. So by using the CGM signals which would be helpful to classify the different classification. So here the Multilayer perception and Convolution neural network are used to train the model.

Now Days the security is one of the major criteria in the several industries to secure the data. Dynamically changing the network is integrated with intrusion detection method. In article by Bhuyan et al. (2014) the author presents the generative model which has a sensitive power and with a good classification and along with that author classifies the intrusions into five groups which is based on the data sources which is network related. By using the anomaly based Network intrusion detection System we can remove the anomalies with the help of Deep Learning Approach.

In the article by Anwer, Farouk, and Abdel-Hamid (2018), the patients with diabetes are continuously monitored their glucose level in blood and it is essentially to adjust the insulin level. Here the author proposed the model which predicts the changes which is imminent in the blood glucose level and warns to enable them to take the preventive measure. Here the Support Vector Regression model is used to train the data based on patient specific data. So the model performs actions which would be helpful to take the hypoglycaemic events in advance to 30 minutes.

In the article by Jidiga and Sammulal (2014), the author proposes the modular deep neural network which is heterogeneous which primarily addresses the diabetic retinopathy and abnormalities which are the five steps. Here the extract class defined by the modular approach which inherently detects the outliers by using the classical convolution network. By using the DIARETDB0 dataset which is the benchmark to approach the Extensive simulation.

Anomaly behaviour in the log data and data which is integrated with the sensor could be related to the data mining application. In the article by Malaiya et al. (2018), the different data views can be find out by and it will be the goal with respect to the detection of anomalies. Here in this paper the author is proposed in a way such that the contexts and events which are associated and one way it creates the data View. Furthermore, it comes with the 11 more different unsupervised anomalies with standard datasets.

Now a Days the attacks are evolving along with huge amount of data. So, it requires faster anomaly detection methods. In the article by Bodstrom and Hamalainen (2018), the Advanced Persistent Threat (APT) is like contains more than one ongoing attack in single network domain. For this type of attack, the authors are proposed different deep learning methods which varies with the performance efficiently reduces the APT type of attack.

In the article by Gupta (2018), KSQL is an open source engine for apache kafka and which efficiently allows to detect the abnormal pattern in real time data and using different algorithms like Decision tree classifier and Logistic regression can efficiently trace the anomaly in the huge network scenario.

In the article by Vartouni, Kasha, and Teshnehlab (2018), Intrusion detection system is a hardware where it emphasizes when the user tries to intrude on timely manner in to the system, then system automatically alerts the user about the anomaly activity.

FUNCTIONAL REQUIREMENTS FOR ANOMALY DETECTION

The Functional requirements majorly showcase the behaviour of the Functionality and it's also satisfying the input. Proposed system works with the requirements listed below.

- **Collection of Dataset:** Collection of Dataset is one of the important factors. The Different Dataset collections are helpful to train the model in the neural network by using the different algorithms.
- **Train the Model:** After collecting the data, then we have to train the model by doing different iterations. By continuously back propagate the data by varying the weight and bias factor and finally the model learns the features.
- **Training Data:** Training Data is one in which the output column is consolidated with target output and actual output. If any error occurred in the Target columns it can be again trained through back propagation algorithm by varying the weighing factor.

NON-FUNCTIONAL REQUIREMENTS FOR ANOMALY DETECTION

Non-Functional requirements comprise how the system works and along with that it comprises the prerequisites.

- **Adaptability:** The System conditions are capable to adapt to any training data set and it is shows the actual output.
- **Learnability:** The Training model learns the features from different conditions and decisions can be taken accordingly based on the training model.
- **Reliability:** The Training model has to perform correct operations as specified in the expected result and it is compared with target output.
- **Availability:** The system will be available in all conditions for all conditions with different decisions.

EXISTING SYSTEM ARCHITECTURE

This section describes the Methodologies and contributions which is the pillar for this chapter. It includes Artificial Neural networks, Back Propagation Method.

Artificial Neural Network

Artificial Neural networks are one of the fascinating trending topics in this era. With the evolution of this artificial neural network the unpredictable tasks can be conveniently can be done now. The working feature is like the human brain where neurons learn all the features when it was trained. So here machine learning is one of the integrated topics in the artificial neural networks. In some situations, the machine learning models fails to learn the features when several variables are included. So in Such situation the deep learning makes a fantasy in such situation. The Below Figure shows the architecture of the neural networks.

Input vector is a realistic function of a neuron $(y_1, \ldots, y_2)$. Here the activation function is sigmoid, which is a hyperbolic. Here f is defined as a function $f(x_j) = f\left(a_j + \sum_{i=1}^{k} w_{ij} y_j\right)$. Neuron activity representation shown in Figure 2. Corresponding to the neurons, here the Multi-Layer Perceptron Network is based on the weighted summing function.

$$x_j = \sum_{i=1}^{k} w_{ij} y_i \tag{1}$$

Single Layer Perceptron

Single layer Perceptron is one in which it contains the weights in a single layer and along with that which is integrated to the input and output along with that the bias and activation function. It is also called as the feed forward network where the information is moving only in one direction it never comes back. Figure 3 shows Single Layer Perceptron of the single model.

Figure 1. Artificial Neural Network (Dinh et al., 2017)

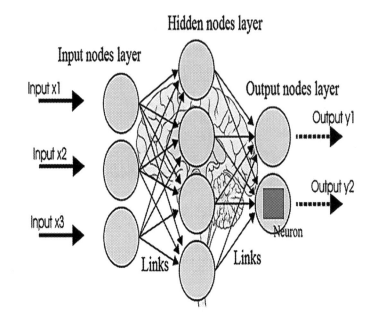

Figure 2. A single neuron in ANN (Lin et al., 2017)

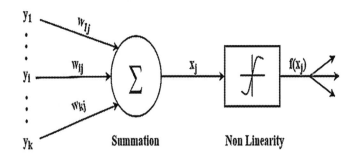

The below is the equation when single perception calculates the input signal. Where W is the weight function and x is the input function and along with that m is the summation function.

i, j and k are the different layers in the artificial neural network.

ANN Methods of Learning and Training

There are three Basic types in Neural Network Learning Methods.:

- Supervised Learning
- Unsupervised Learning
- Reinforcement Learning

Figure 3. Single layer perceptron (Chalapathy, Menon & Chawla, 2018)

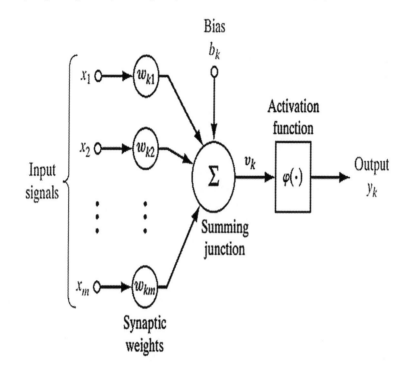

Supervised Learning

The Desired pattern or target pattern is one which is associated with every input pattern. One of the example given here is during the learning process, the corrected expected output and networks computed input efficiently determines the error. Some of the errors which makes changes the network parameters and inherently which shows the performance as improved.

Unsupervised Learning

This is another method in learning; here the network is not presented by the target output. Here, the system discovers and adapt the input patterns in structural way. The desired pattern is not present.

Reinforced Learning

In this method, computed output is predicting the available answer is correct or incorrect based on the expected answer. During the learning process the information process helps to network. This type of learning is most popular forms of learning and here the award is sequentially given for right and wrong answer.

DEEP NEURAL NETWORK

Now days, mimic of human brains is efficiently works in each and every area helps for the complex problems in the different domains. It designed basis on to recognize the complex patterns. This patterns are capable to recognize the video, audio and real world data and also it's translates into machine level language. Deep neural network is one which is composed of several layers or stacked networks which are composed like human brain. Compared to single neural network, the deep neural network consists of multi layers to process the data. Here the Deep neural network is composed of more than three layers which show the Deep learning. Figure 4 shows the diagram of deep neural network, based on previous layers output each layer inherently trains the same set of features which are distinct. As we as increase the layers, the neural network is capable to recognize the complex features by the nodes. Its aggregates and which efficiently recombines the features basis on the previous layers. Based on the different features the level of hierarchy is going to complex level by level. Inherently, as complexity and abstraction increases in the neural network, the network is capable to make the high and large dimensional data. In this type of network there are billions of parameters passed in the deep neural network.

Deep Neural Network is efficient to find out the different latent structures which include the unlabelled and unstructured data. This type of unstructured data has enormous unlabelled data in the world. In some media types like audio, video, texts and pictures which has unstructured labelled data and this type of data can't have recognized by human brains and which can't be organized the relational database. Here the deep neural network is capable to recognize and clusters the cat's photos and dog photos and human photos in different corners. In Different context when we look into the emails deep learning concepts is efficiently clusters the mails into spam mail, important mails.

Figure 4. Deep neural networks (Siddayatam et al., 2017)

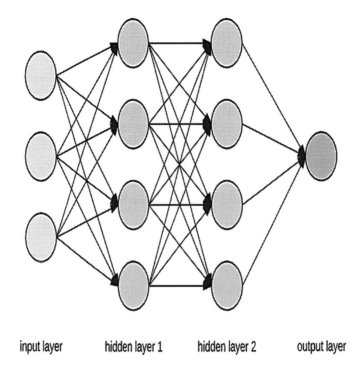

input layer   hidden layer 1   hidden layer 2   output layer

Potential Limitations that deep learning overcomes Artificial Neural Network is,

- Feed Forward is the method of Back-Propagation algorithm and it is unidirectional. The organization of feed forward is Layer wise. If multiple layers exist means that is Deep.
- Usually if it's more than two to three hidden layers is considered as Deep Neural Network. So this makes to qualify the sentence to Deep.
- Single Hidden Layer of a neural network inherently called as the "Shallow". Furthermore, in ten years the people might assume any network is less than single layers are kindergarten exercise and it is difficult on Deep neural network.

TIME SERIES USING MACHINE LEARNING AND DEEP LEARNING

A Certain set of observations at a certain interval of time called Time Series of Data. For Example, a certain set of login details at regular stipulated time can be taken as a Time Series. When Data is collected at once or anomaly, which is not considered as an actual time Series data. Figure 5 shows the time series anomaly detection.

There are two types of Time Series Data,

- **Stock Series**: It's a measure of an activity at a Particular Point of Time and which also can be taken as stock takes.
- **Flow Series**: It's a measures an activity at a Specific interval of Time. It contains effect to the intervals.

In the above figure, anomalies can be detected in the time series. There are two distinct changes and two spikes in the time series data. The level change can be detected and which can be representing by red dots and upward arrow detects the spikes.

Time Series Data applications are Such as economics, Science, environment, medicine, these are taken at a successful interval of time. In a real time, example some of the data are correlated at the specific interval of time. The time series of data can be divided into 2 categories

Figure 5. Anomaly detection in Time Series (Moustafa & Slay, 2015)

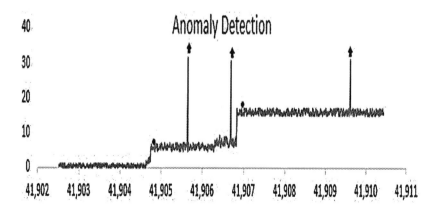

- Historical
- Validation

By using the time series data, it is possible to imagine what will happen in future and how the future will depend on current situation. Based on the historical data the model can be built to make the future prediction and it can be validated to the set of observation.

Components of Time Series Data

- Trend: In the Trend Component of the time series data, lengthy patterns affects either could be positive, negative, linear or nonlinear. If the time series does not contain any increasing or decreasing pattern, then it is called as Stationary.
- Cyclic: In this pattern there are exhibits the up and down around a time called cyclic path and along with this oscillation are depend on business cycle. The period of time is not fixed and composed of at least minimum time of months.
- Seasonal: It is fixed and known period. The Changes can be occurred at regular interval of calendar. There are two models in seasonal,
  - **Additive Model**: Trend component combined with the Seasonal Component.
  - **Multiplicative Model**: Seasonal component is multiplied with intercept one and only if the trend component is not present. Sum of intercept and trend is multiplied with the seasonal component, if time series have trend component.
- Irregular: It is also known as random component. Unpredictable components are in the time series (Alam et al., 2015); Fluctuations can be seen. Residual time series can be removed by using the trend cycle and seasonal component.

The above first figure shows the seasonal and some cyclic behaviour with the period of 6-10 years and as well as in the second figure we cannot seen the seasonality, else we can see the trend in over a 100 days. In the third figure we can see the strong seasonal and increasing trend with no cyclic behaviour cannot affordable here. In the fourth figure we can see the fluctuations can be seen in period of time, so it is irregular.

Time Series Analysis

The Performance based analysis of time series data called Time Series Analysis. Structure and Functions can be performed by understanding the analysis. A Mathematical model can be built by performing and understanding, so further monitoring, control and predictions can be performed.

To analyse the time series data there are two approaches,

- Time Domain
- Frequency Domain

Time Series analysis is mainly used for,

- Time Series Decomposition

Figure 6. Types of anomalies (Alam et al., 2015)

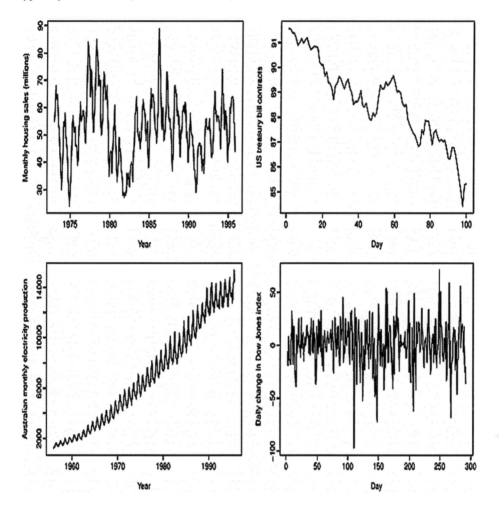

- Time Based Dependencies modelling
- Forecasting
- System Variation model and Identification.

Need of Time Series Analysis

In Machine Learning and Deep Learning, the time series is very important to build model Successful. Time Series analysis produces some observation to understand its internal structure and functions.

Time Series analysis is used for

- **Forecasting**: For Short term trends, the Prediction can be done by the previous observations.
- **Invention Analysis**: The effect performed by any event in time series data is analysed.

Different Types of Anomalies

- **Point Anomalies**: If the particular value within the dataset value is anomalous in the complete data, then it is called Point anomalies.
- **Contextual Anomalies**: For Some Specific Circumstances, the occurrence of data is anomalous then it is called as Contextual Anomalies.
- **Collective Anomalies**: With respect to the rest of the data if the data collection is anomalous then it is called collective anomalous.

Anomaly Detection in Time Series Data

- **Anomaly Detection R Package:** In the seasonality and trend time series data analysis the anomalies can be find by using the robust open source package. The Package is built on Seasonal Hybrid ESD (S-H-ESD) algorithm and E-Test. S-H-ESD algorithm can be find both local and global anomalies. Better Visualization can be view by specifying the anomalies direction.
- **Principal Component Analysis:** This Technique is useful when the expected samples are difficult obtain at particular time of situation. Its reduces the Higher Dimensional data to Lower dimensional data without losing the information. In PCA the distance metrics are used to determine the anomalies and the model is trained using the available features.

Need of Machine Learning and Deep Learning in Time Series Data

Machine Learning is more effective as we compared to other techniques like statistical. Machine Learning has two features such as Prediction and Feature Engineering. Feature Engineering is the process that with respect to the time series data which address the trend and seasonality.

Deep Learning is the process in which it combines the feature extraction and of time series and nonlinear autoregressive model for high level prediction. Without using the any human effort, we can extract the useful information automatically.

Anomaly Detection Using Machine Learning

The most effective types of Machine learning are the supervised learning and unsupervised learning. Figure 7 shows the Systematic workflow of the anomaly detection scheme.

Supervised Learning is very important because initially we have to train the data and further the data points can be classified in to anomalous and non-anomalous data points. But for Supervised learning. Prediction of data points in the series could be made by train the CART and by using the unsupervised learning.

Supervised learning algorithm is supervised neural network, Support vector machine learning, Bayesian networks, and Decision trees.

Anomaly Detection Using Deep Learning

Within the time series data to detect the anomalous data points here we considered the recurrent neural network is a type of deep learning algorithms. It consists of input layer, hidden layer and output layer.

Figure 7. Anomaly detection schemes (Dertat, 2017)

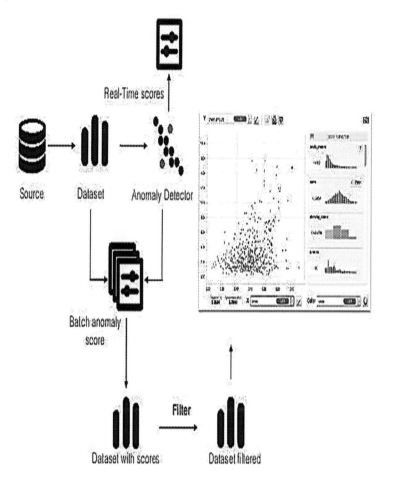

Hidden layers are responsible for the handling the internals state of the memory. They both will update when new input is fed into the network. Proposed work uses time stamps for capturing the real time data. Based on the time series, it's helpful to detect the anomalies in the network packet.

PROPOSED SYSTEM ARCHITECTURE

The Design is the most important factor for the success of the proposed system. Abstract model is the component of the high level design which efficiently describes the entire system and whereas the entire design which elaborately describes the modules which are concluded in the High Level Design. Working logic and internal details of the modules represented by the Detail Design Modules.

To develop a basic framework of the system it is necessary to describes basic system which shows the architectural design. It identifies Communication between these components and major and minor components of the system.

Figure 8 represents the proposed system of architecture; it includes some several tasks which were explained in further.

Figure 8. Proposed framework

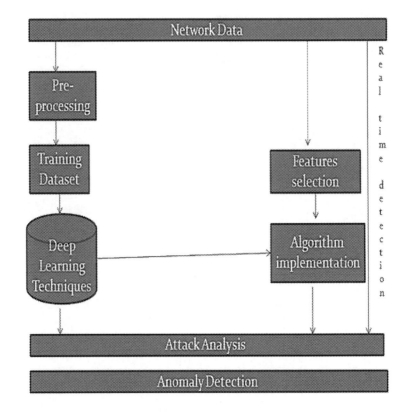

Here we have proposed the architecture of the system which is capable to find out the anomaly detection in the huge network data acquisition. After the capturing the packets from huge network data acquisition we have to pre-process the Network dataset to remove the noise and unwanted things from the dataset. In the Pre-processing stage we have spitted the Dataset into training and testing dataset. After pre-processing the dataset, we have stored the pre-processed data into HDF5 because the Mac system contains of 4GB of Ram. Train the dataset for further process to detect the anomalies in the network dataset. Apply the Deep learning techniques which are helpful to detect the anomalies for any new data which is occurred in the network data acquisition. To check the efficiency and capability of the model apply the algorithm, here we have applied the Random Forest algorithm, Extra Trees Classifier algorithm for metrics like accuracy, precision call, Hit Rate and Deep Neural Network for training the model. Further, attack analysis finds the anomaly detection in the real time.

The system architecture includes three parts such as Network data acquisition, Deep Learning Techniques, Anomaly Detection Modules, and Feature Selection Modules.

Network Data Acquisition

UNSW NB 15 Dataset has created by using the IXIA Storm tool. Here there are three servers are used such as Server 1, Server 3 are used for the Normal Traffic flow and Server 2 is used for the malware traffic packets flow. There are two routers are used such as router 1 and router 2 are used to forwards the data packets through the Internet. Firewall is also used to prevent the unauthorized activity. Beyond the limit of firewall efficiency, the Server 2 is flown the malicious packets which are categorized into 9 types of attack which can be discussed in the later section. This Network data acquisition has huge amount of data. The dataset is again classified into 4 types of dataset such as UNSW NB 15-1, UNSW NB s15-2, UNSW NB 15-3, UNSW NB 15-4 and along with that UNSW NB15- features are used to store the features which is necessary to detect the anomalies in the network traffic.

Deep Learning Techniques

Neural Network architecture is used by most deep learning methods, that's why it us called as Deep Neural networks. In Neural Networks it contains 2-3 layers, whereas when we come across deep neural network it contains Many layers. So the deep neural network is efficiently trains the data and fed the output in appropriate manner. Since we UNSW NB 15 dataset has labelled data and it's have huge amount of rows and columns, here we are using the Deep Learning Techniques to detect the anomalies in the Network packet. Here this methodology doesn't require manual feature extraction, since it has labelled data we can train the data such as training dataset is efficiently predicting the next data without any information. Deep Neural Networks learns the features from the data and it does not need any manual feature extraction data. Some of the Deep Learning techniques are used such as,

- Train the Data from the scratch
- Extract the features

The above are the some of the Deep Learning techniques which efficiently train an test the data, which can be further used to detect the anomalies in the network packets.

Feature Selection

Feature Extraction is the important step and the labelled features are prominent to detect the anomalies in the network packets. UNSW NB 15 Dataset has totally 49 Features and these features are labelled. These Features are categorized into 5 categories such as (Ozaki, 2015; Janarthanan & Zargari, 2017).

- Basic Features
- Additional Generated Feature
- Time Features
- Labelled Features
- Content Features

The Above 5 features contain 49 features which contains the labelled Name, Type and Description of each name which was labelled in the Dataset.

Anomaly Detection Modules

Anomaly detection modules are one in which is capable to detect the anomalies in the network packets. Based on the previous models operations the Anomaly detection modules analyse whether the packet contains the normal information or malicious information. This information further passed to organisation. The packet can be further labelled into the "attack or not" label or "0" for normal and "1" for attack label. By using this type of method we can detect the anomalies in the network packet in real time detection method.

Deep Neural Network Architecture of Anomaly Detection

Deep Neural Architecture for Anomaly detection is based on the Back-Propagation algorithm. The Deep Neural Network consists of M layers with 49 input neurons and the training procedures for DNN Model by using the Back-Propagation algorithm. Here we considered 49 input neurons because the feature extraction of the dataset consists of 49 Features. So, here 49 features are inherently fed as the input neurons. Here Input layer and Hidden layers consists of more than one neuron. Based on the adaptive weight the mth layer is fed as input of the $(m+1)^{th}$ layer and m^{th} layer is connected to $(m+1)^{th}$ layer (Hyndman & Athanasopoulos, 2018).

Suppose the total input to the jth neuron in 2nd hidden layer is H_j, then for 49 input neurons in the input layer is (Hyndman & Athanasopoulos, 2018)

$$T_j = \sum_{i=1}^{49}(w_{ij}^m * output_i) \tag{2}$$

In the above equation the w_{ij} represents weight of the neuron i in the input layer is connected to the neuron j of the Dense layer. Output i represents the neuron i in the input layer (Hyndman & Athanasopoulos, 2018). The sigmoid activation function is transforms the function f.

$$f(y) = \left(1 + e^{-y}\right) \tag{3}$$

There are two passes here we used, in forward pass the output of the neural network is evaluated based on the input and weight adjustment factor. In backward pass the Desired output and target output is compared and if any error again it fed back to the neural network. In equation 3 d_i^m represents desired output of mth layer in i^{th} neuron and o_i^m represents the Target output of the mth layer in i^{th} neuron

$$\theta_i^L = d_i^m - o_i^m \tag{4}$$

Figure 9 shows the architecture of the DNN for anomaly detection. Here there are number of layers are considered such as Input, Dense and Output layer. Input vector dimension such as number of input features earlier considered for training. The Dense layers is one which is linear operation where every input data is connected to the every output layer by adjusting the weight factor. Output layer efficiently labels the "attack or not" to the network packets. For the activation of the dense layers here we are using the sigmoid activation function because compared to Relu and tanh its gives the better result. For output function we are using the softmax function because the labels are categorical.

Figure 9. Deep neural network architecture

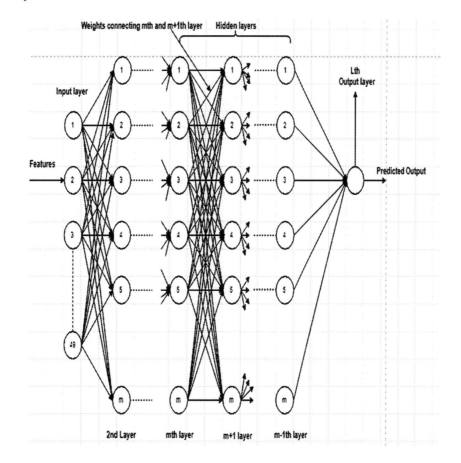

Further to enhance the experiment, we tested the real time network traffic in M S Ramaiah Institute of technology Servers. We capture the real time network traffic by using the Wireshark tool. The Below Figure 10 shows the parameters we considered for capturing Pcap files

- **Time**: Time of capturing the pcap files.
- **Source**: Source of packets
- **Destination**: Destination of Packets
- **Protocol**: Different Types of protocol such as ARP, LLMNR,NBC, TCP,UDP etc..
- **Length**: Length of the packet
- **Information**: Information of the packet.

Here after the testing this dataset we got some anomalies due to bad connection, loss of packets, Missing files in Network Packets etc. So we found some anomalies in the dataset. In future we can test it for different servers and we can analyze the servers.

The Figure 10 shows the Input output graphs of the real time network traffic in the server of M S Ramaiah Institute of Technology. The x axis shows the time in seconds and y axis shows the packets/

Figure 10. Real time network traffic

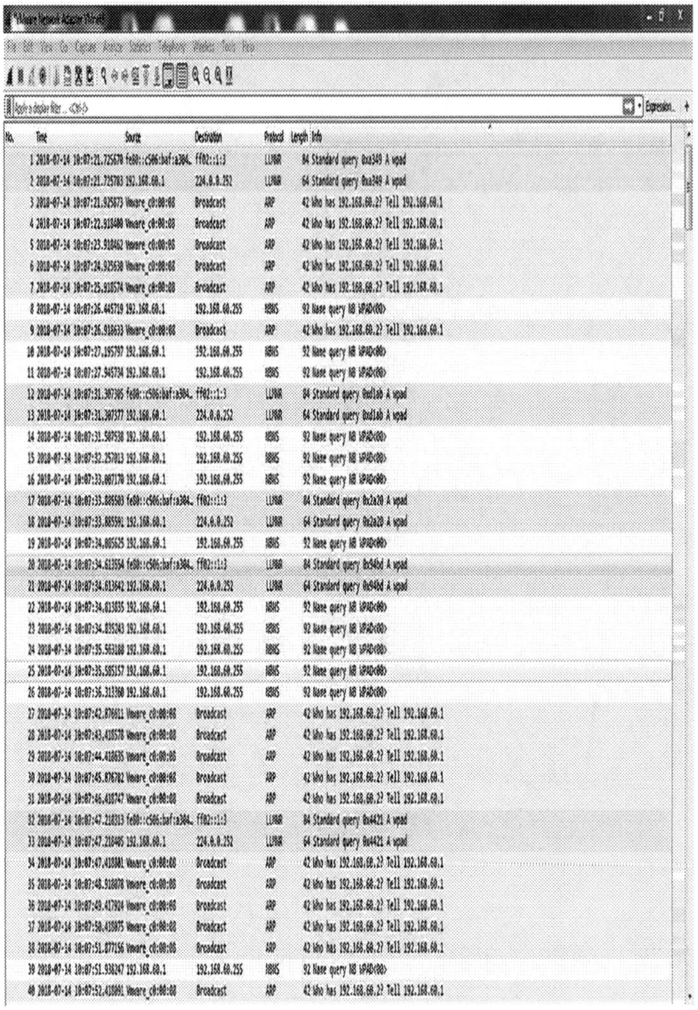

second. We can increase the packets/sec to capture the real time network traffic. By using this graph if we found any missing packets, loss of packets that could be predicted as the anomaly.

Sequence Diagram

Sequence Diagram is one in which the process and interaction between each module can be seen and it depicts the Unified Modelling Language (UML). Sequence Diagram helps to know about how sequences will run and possibility of scenarios in which they occur.

In Figure 9 Shows the sequence diagram of the anomaly detection method. Initially the network packets will travel from source point to destination point. Here the user has to captures the network packets. User has to use the TCPDump or Wireshark tool to capture the Real time network traffic. After Capturing the network packets user has to extract the packet features from the existing packets. By using feature extraction techniques user can see the various features of the packets. Features extraction is

Figure 11. IO graphs

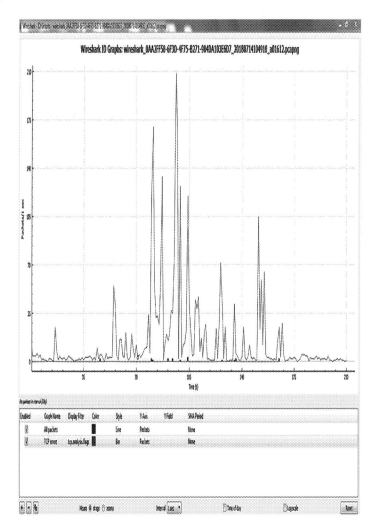

one of the important step in the anomaly detection method, because the packet features must train in the neural network. Neural Network will predict the upcoming packets or new arrival packets based on the existing features. Collect the various features such Source IP Address, Destination IP Address, Source Frame Length and Destination frame Length etc, these are the some of the feature of the network packets. After feature extraction step, user has to pre-process the data for the purpose of removal of unwanted data, noise removal in the data and slicing the data may efficiently produce the pre-processed data for further process. After user getting the pre-processed data, he has to dividing the dataset into the training and testing dataset for further process to detect the anomalies in the network packet. Deep neural network must be trained to detect the anomalies in a when any new data found in the network dataset.

After Training the dataset, next phase is to use the machine learning algorithms for the detection of anomalies in the real time network traffic dataset. Machine Learning classifier now able to classifies whether network packet is malicious or not. After classifying the packet has been labelled to "attack or

Figure 12. Sequence diagram

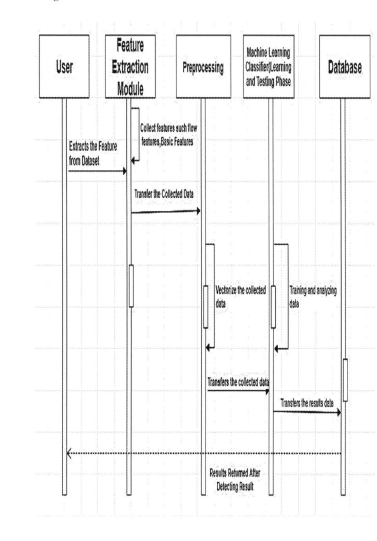

not". After analysis of the UNSW NB 15 Dataset the result will be send back to the organization or else it sends the alert or message to the user.

PROPOSED ALGORITHM

Implementation step is important after the requirement and design step. System is built and consolidated to the customer. Implementation of this work started with collection of network dataset UNSW NB 15, Data Pre-processing, Training and Testing Dataset, Applying Machine Learning algorithms and Deep Neural Network for training the dataset for prediction of new input data.

Collecting Network Data

UNSW NB 15 Dataset(University of New South Wales) consists of 4 versions of dataset such as UNSW NB 15-1, UNSW NB 15-2, UNSW NB 15-3, UNSW NB 15-4 files are in .csv format. This dataset is a hybrid of normal activities and contemporary synthetic attacks. Here the dataset is captured by Tcpdump Tool. 100 GB of data is captured by using the tcpdump tool. There are nine types of attacks in the UNSW NB 15 dataset.

- **Fuzzers**: By using the randomly generated data, fuzzer attack may suspend the network or any programs.
- **Analysis**: There are different attacks can be seen in analysis attack such as port scan, penetration of html files.
- **Backdoors**: To access computer data, this type of attack might stealthily bypass the system security mechanism.
- **Denial Service of Attack (DoS):** Here the attackers are particularly targets the server, they hack the server and suspends the resource unavailable. Suspends the host network.
- **Exploits**: The attackers known about the operating system and they mainly target the system security and exploits the vulnerability of the system.
- **Generic**: Some of the techniques may works on the SSH block cipher keys. This Block cipher keys contains the key and block size. This type of attackers is not concentrate about the block-cipher keys.
- **Reconnaissance**: Initially it gathers the information and it can simulate all strikes against the information.
- **Shell Code**: To exploits the vulnerability, the attackers use the small piece of code which can be used as payload and afterwards it might exploit the information.
- **Worms**: The idea used by the attackers here is, they replicate worms to spread over in other computers. During the security failures its efficiently spread the worms to other system.

The above are the frequent attacks used by the attack to stealthily access the information. Here there are 49 Feature are used to detect the anomalies in network intrusion detection system. Here the 49 features are listed below.

In Table 1 shows the Flow Features from 1-5 of the UNSW-NB 15 dataset which shows hosts attributes like client-to-server or server-to-client (Lin et al., 2017).

In Table 2 From 6-13 shows the Basic features which shows the attributes which represents connections of protocols (Lin et al., 2017).

Table 3 From 19-26 shows the content features of the network dataset which contains the TCP and Internet protocol and http services (Lin et al., 2017).

Table 4 From 27-28 shows the main feature that is Time Features which consists of time attributes such as packet time between start/end TCP protocol of RTT (round time trip) (Lin et al., 2017).

Table 5 From 37-47 which contains Additional Generated Features which is related to the service protocols such as HTTP, Source IP address and Destination Port Address (Lin et al., 2017).

Table 6 From 48-49 contains the Labelled Features which consists of attack categorized and label for normal and attack records (Li et al., 2017).

Table 1. Flow features

#	Name	Description
1. Flow Features		
1	Source Ip	IP address of the source
2	Source port	Port Number of the Source
3	Destination IP	Destinations IP address.
4	Destination Port	Destination port number
5	Protocol	TCP, UDP are the Protocol types

Source: Kumar & Venkatarm (2002)

Table 2. Basic features

#	Name	Description
2. Basic Features		
6	State	The Dependent Protocol and States.
7	Duration	Total Duration of Rows
8	Source Bytes	Bytes from Source bytes to Destination Bytes.
9	Destination Bytes	Bytes from Destination Bytes to Source.
10	Source Time to Live	Time to Live of Source to Destination.
11	Destination Time to Live	Time to Live of Destination to Source.
12	Source Loss	Retransmitted Packets in Source Packets.
13	Destination Loss	Retransmitted Packets in Destination Packets.
14	Services	Services like Simple mail transfer protocol and Domain name Server.
15	Source Load	Source bits per second
16	Destination Load	Destination bits per second
17	Source Packets	Count of Source Packet to Destination Packet.
18	Destination packets	Count of Destination Packet to Source Packet.

(Lin et al., 2017).

Table 3. Content features

3. Content Features		
19	Source Window	Window advertisement value of Source TCP.
20	Destination Window	Window advertisement value of Destination TCP
21	Source TCP bsn	Base Sequence Number of Source TCP.
22	Destination TCP bsn	Base Sequence Number of Destination TCP.
23	Source Mean Size	Source IP transmitted the Mean Size of the Packet.
24	Destination Mean Size	Destination IP transmitted the Mean Size of the Packet.
25	Transaction Depth	HTTP Request/Response Transaction Connection.
26	res_bdy_len	http transfers the Data and its content size..

(Lin et al., 2017)

Table 4. Time features

		4. Time Features	
27	Srcjtr	Jitter of Source.
28	Dstjtr	Jitter of Destination.
29	Source Time	Start time of Row
30	Last Time	Last Time of Row
31	Src int pkt	Inter Packet Arrival time of Source.
32	Dst intpkt	Inter Packet Arrival time of Destination.
33	Tcpr-tt	The sum of Synack and ackdat, Tcp Connection setup time.
34	Synchronized ackn	TCP Connection Setup time between SYN and SYN_ACK
35	Ackn dat	The SYN_ACK and SYN TCP Connection Setup Time.
36	is_sm_ips_ports	Assign 1 or else 0, if srcip (1) = dstip (3) and sport (2) = dsport (4)

(Lin et al., 2017)

Table 5. Additional generated features

		5. Additional Generated Features	
37	ct_ste_timetolive	Specific range of based on the each state (6) and the values of source time to live(10) and destination time to live(11).
38	ct_flows_http_methods	http services such as Get and post contained by Methods of Number of Flows.
39	ftpses_login	Assign 1 or else 0, if the session of ftp accessed by the user.
40	ct_ftp_comnd	ftp session contains number of flows.
41	ct_srvc_source	According to the last time (26) the100 rows consists of service (14) and source ip(1) of same.
42	ct_srvc_destination	According to the last time(26) the 100 rows consists of source(14) and destination ip(3) of same service.
43	ct_desn_lttm	According to the last time(26) the 100 rows consists of Destination ip(3).
44	ct_source_lttm	According to the last time(26) the100 rows consists of Source ip(1).
45	ct_source_dstnport_lttm	According to the last time(26) the 100 rows consists of source ip(1) and destination Port(4).
46	ct_dstn_sourceport_lttm	According to the last time(26) the 100 rows consists of the destination ip(3) and source port(2).
47	ct_dstn_srce_lttm	According to the last time(26) the 100 records consists of the source ip(1) and destination ip(3).

Kumar & Venkatarm (2002)

Table 6. Labelled features

		6. Labelled Features	
48	Attack category	Each attack category name
49	Label	Normal='0' and Attack record='1'

(Li et al., 2017)

Packages Used for Deep Learning Model

Since python is the user friendly language, some of the packages are very essential for building the deep learning model. For efficient Deep neural network, we have installed some of the packages we installed such as Keras, Tensorflow and Theano are essential packages to build a Deep Neural network which is effectively detects the anomalies in the network packets.

Tensorflow is one which is an open source package in the anaconda which shows the dataflow graphs by using the numerical computation. Compared to other neural network packages the tensorflow is a good package and it's a distributed computing. It's also very helpful in the multiple-GPUs.

Keras is another deep learning package which is best and better package to build the neural network for the following three reasons such as

- Keras allows to support for backend compared to Theano, here the user can switch the package based on the application dependency.
- Keras is simple and user friendly and it has good guiding principles such as modularity, minimalism.

Theano is another library led to the deep learning concepts. This library mainly used for doing the mathematical using multiple arrays. It's very fast and basically its advance to using of GPU.

Implementation Models Used for Anomaly Detection

In this implementation part here we are implementing different models such as Random Forest ensemble, Multi-Layer Perceptron and Back-Propagation algorithm to train and classifying the anomalies in the network traffic.

Random Forest Ensemble

Random Forest algorithm is one in which it classifies the object based on the input vector. It classifies the most votes based on the major votes. Random forest can be installed by using the command sklearn.ensemble.RandomForestClassifier package. Here we will get the pre-processed data and the data was clean and it will ready for training. Further, the model has to run for multiple times to train the anomaly detector model. Figure 10 shows the Random Forest workflow for classification. When using the different hyper parameters, the network is wait to run the process optimally. so that's why here we are using the validation dataset with 'k' features. Here we are dividing the dataset into three datasets such as training, testing and validation dataset. This type of approach of validation called as cross-validation. In the cross-validation approach is the training dataset is splitted into 'k' small set it's also called as the K-Folds. Finally, the model is validated with data which was remaining.

Multi-Layer Perceptron

Multilayer Perceptron is one in which we have multiple layers to train the model efficiently. Here we are used the Tensor Flow Backend and Keras models to build the efficient Multi-Layer Perceptron model. Here there are three layers constructed those are,

Figure 13. Random forest model (Narayanan, 2015)

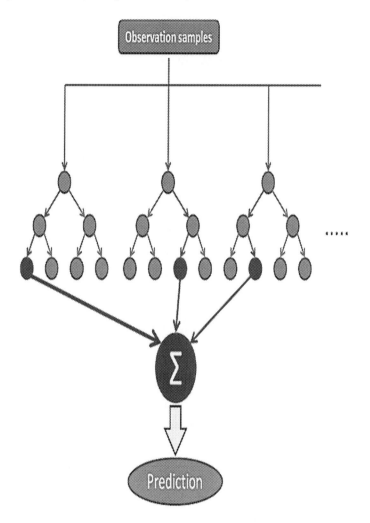

- Here the neural networks are densely connected. Rectified linear unit activator is used for the activation of layers. Most of the time it is used as general approximate.
- Here Regularization process reduces the over fitting in machine learning. Based on the interdependent feature weights it adds the loss function to the models. Dropout function is combined
- Finally, we are included Two layers in the neural network to rectify whether the packet is labelled as "attack or not".

Back-Propagation

Back-propagation is one which comes under the supervised learning algorithm, which is necessary to train the multilayer Perceptron to train the model. Figure 11 shows the Back-Propagation steps to predict the output. Here while building the neural network we have to initialize some of the important factors such as weights with different variables and values which are in the random order. By changing the parameters frequently, we can reduce the error in the neural network.

Figure 14. Back propagation model

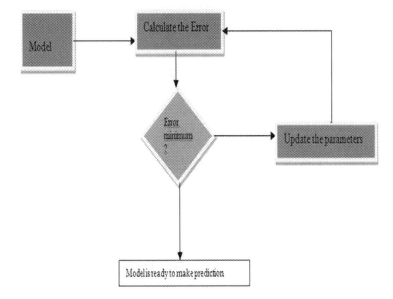

To train the model some of the steps are followed:

- **Error Calculation**: Based on the actual output we can decide how far our model is.
- **Minimization of Error**: Here we have to check the error minimization.
- **Parameters Update**: Here every time, the parameters have to update every time to minimize the error by adjusting the weight and bias.
- **Prediction Process of Model**: Feed some input to get the output, once the error become minimized.

RESULTS AND DISCUSSIONS

The Results and discussions shows or interprets the findings. This Part describes the significance of the work results which shows the new understanding of the problem. Here the result is compared with previous research problem being examined. Here we consider 4 Files of UNSW- NB 15 dataset in format of .csv. Total 552 MB of files we have taken here for this experiment. There will be a 47.3 mb training and testing data are considered for the Deep Neural Network model training. Feature extraction is one of the technique we are considered here for the extraction of the features from the UNSW-NB 15 dataset. Here we are initially choosing the 5000 samples for training and some of the basic features such as Time, Location and packet size etc. are some important features in the UNSW-NB 15 dataset.

The below table shows 9 types of categorized attacks such as analysis, backdoor, denial of service, exploits, fuzzers, generic, normal and reconnaissance. Initially we have considered 5000 samples from each categorical attack and here these training samples are trained in the deep neural network.

There were 31000 normal samples considered for classification by using the random forest algorithm and 5000 samples are considered for the neural network training. The below figures shows the feature

Algorithm 1. Back-Propagation Algorithm

```
Set Networks weights in Initialize Stage (Moustafa & Slay, 2016).
do
forEach example name ex included in training example
// forward pass
Prediction Pd = Neural-Network-output(network, example)
actual = Master-output(example)
Computation Error = (Prediction-actual) units of output
// backward pass
Enumerate {\exhibitstyle \Delta w_{h}} adjust the all weights from the hidden
layer to output layer
// backward pass continued
Enumerate {\exhibitstyle \Delta w_{h}} adjust the all weights from the input
layer to hidden layer
//error estimation not modified by input layer
amend the network weights
until criterion is satisfied stop another or classify the examples correctly
rebound the network
```

Algorithm 2. Random Forest Algorithm

```
Prerequisite: A training set T:= (x1, y1) .... (xn, yn), features F and Number
N of Trees S in Forest A (Ozaki, 2015).
RandomForest(T, F)
I <- Ø
for i ∈ 1…….. A do
T(i)<- A bootstrap sample from T
j(i)<- RandomizedTreeLearn(T, F)
J<- J U {ji}
end for
return J
end function
function RandomizedTreeLearn(T, F)
At every node:
f<- very little subset of Feature F
Divide the best feature in f
return the learned tree
end function
```

Table 7. Types of attacks

SI. No	Type of Attack	Training Samples	Total Samples
0.	Analysis	2409	2677
1.	Backdoor	2096	2329
2.	Dos	5000	16353
3.	Exploits	5000	44525
4.	Fuzzers	5000	24246
5.	Generic	5000	215481
6.	Normal	31000	2218456
7.	Reconnaissance	5000	13987
8.	Shellcode	1359	1511

importance from the feature extraction dataset. The red coloured graph shows the attacked packets from huge data network acquisition and the black graph shows the normal attacks from the data acquisition. The x label shows the Feature indices and y shows the time.

The Figure 15 and Figure 16 shows the attack analysis of all the training and total samples are taken in UNSW-NB 15 dataset. The X axis label shows the attack categories of dataset or number of attacks is affected to the service and the Y axis label shows the Samples were taken for the analysis of attacks. This graph efficiently shows the 9 type categorical attack in UNSW-NB 15 dataset.

The Above Figure 17 and Figure 18 show the Feature importance of the random forest and neural network. The X axis label shows the relative importance and Y axis shows the Time of packets arrival. Here the red plotted is labelled for attack category and black is for normal attack.

The below table shows the classification results for normal and attack categorization. Class colour red for attack and black colour for normal attack.

Figure 15. Attack analysis

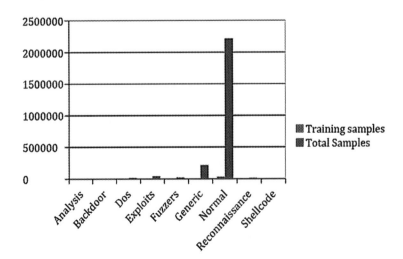

Figure 16. Metrics of analysis

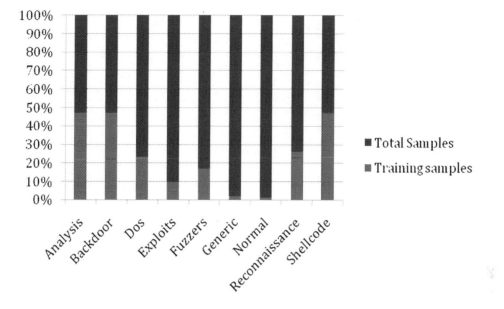

Figure 17. Feature importance of Random forest

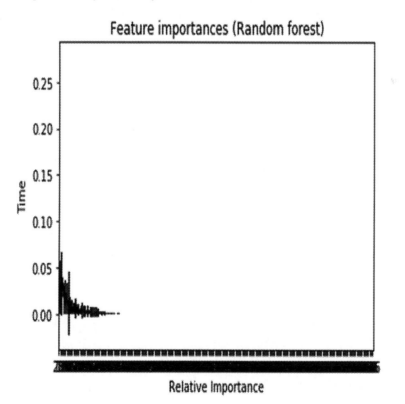

Figure 18. Feature importance of neural network

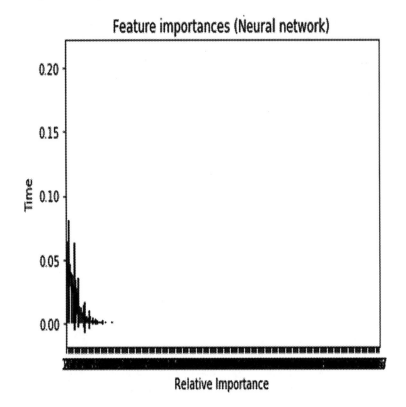

Table 8. Metrics

Class	Precision	Recall
Red	1.00	0.98
Black	0.88	1.00
Average	0.99	0.98

In Figure 19 Metrics Chart shows the results of precision and Recall are the two metrics applied which shows the efficiency of the work implementation. The X-Axis shows the attack categories such as red for attack and black for normal. Average value of this has to take for comparing the result.

COMPARISON WITH DIFFERENT TYPES OF ANOMALY DETECTION

The Classification based anomaly detection technique is one of the type of anomaly detection techniques where the classifier distinguishes the normal and abnormal classes in the feature space and along with that the Multi-Classification anomaly detection models is based on the multiple normal classes which efficiently classifies the abnormal features which doesn't have the normal score.

Figure 19. Metrics chart

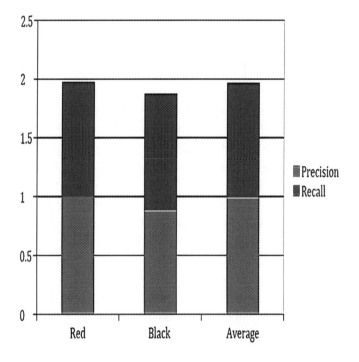

The Support Vector Machine Popularly known as SVM is based on the compressive sampling inherently discovers the anomaly behaviour in network. Bayesian Networks Based estimates for the given test instance as normal class labs and abnormal class labs for Network scenario which inherently gives higher detection rate and better computational Efficient Methods.

Compared to other methods Our Method Anomaly detection using Deep Learning Overcomes the Different Performance metrics such as Precision, recall and Time. Using a Single Self learned based model which can detect enormous anomalies in the Huge Network Scenarios. So, our method is efficient when it comes for huge network data compared to other methods.

PERFORMANCE METRICS COMPARISON

Performance Metrics is the important parameter which efficiently classifies the Performance Metric Parameter. Here we are comparing with the KDDcup99 Data set which has accuracy of 99.82 and Our Deep Learning model has a accuracy of 99.96. The Precision and recall we got here is 0.99 for attacks and 0.98 for normal respectively shows the improvement compared to other models such as decision tree and Naive Bayes classifiers has less precision and recall. The Random Forest Classifier classifies the anomaly detection with a time bound of 7 Seconds which inherently shows Good classification result.

CONCLUSION AND FUTURE SCOPE

In daily realistic activity, over 6.5 billion of user solely depends on the internet. Important information is carried out by the packets of network. Packet contains important information, so this information might destroy by unauthorized user. So to detect the anomalies in these fast flowing network packets is one of the major challenge. To resolve like this problem here we proposed the approach of Deep learning and machine learning approach. Here we splitted the network in to two categories such as "normal" and "attack" categories by using the supervised learning approach. Most of the datasets are labelled so supervised algorithms are efficiently used here. It's difficult to find out the anomalies in the huge data network acquisition, so here we proposed the Random Forest algorithm which efficiently classifies the packets in to normal packets and attacked.

Here our proposed method Random Forest Model yields the result of Accuracy 84.59%, which took time of 15 minute to train and 7 seconds to predict the anomalies in the feature importance graph. Along with that deep neural network model took a time of 45 min and 5 seconds to train and predict the output respectively shows the improvement for different datasets. The Precision and recall we got here is 0.99 for attacks and 0.98 for normal respectively shows the improvement compared to other models such as decision tree and naive bayes classifiers has less precision and recall. In this work most of the development time consumed in unbalanced data because the classifying this data has challenged task. So we found that the proposed model has got more efficient than the existing model for anomaly detection in the huge networking scenario.

Future Scope of this work is important to visualise about the outcomes based on:

- Anomaly detection can be implemented in Internet of Things (IoT) Based System.
- Anomaly detection can be implemented by using Chabot Based system which alerts the user through message.

REFERENCES

Anwer, H. M., Farouk, M., & Abdel-Hamid, A. (2018) A framework for efficient network anomaly intrusion detection with features selection. *2018 9th International Conference on Information and Communication Systems (ICICS)*.

Bernstein, M. N. (n.d.). *Random Forest algorithm*. Available from pages.cs.wisc.edu/~matrhewb/pages/notes/pdf/ensembles/RandomForests.pdf

Bhuyan, M. H., Bhattacharya, B. K., & Kalita, J. K. (2017). Network anomaly detection: Methods, systems and tools. *IEEE Communications Surveys & Tutorials, VOL., 16*(1), 2014.

Bodstrom, T., & Hamalainen, T. (2018). *State of the art literature review on network anomaly detection with deep learning*. Springer International Publishing. doi:10.1007/978-3-030-01168-0_7

Chalapathy, R., Menon, A.K. & Chawla, S. (2018). *Anomaly detection using one-neural networks*. Academic Press.

Dertat, A. (2017). Applied deep learning part 1: Artificial neural networks. *Towards Data Science.* Retrieved from: https://towardsdatascience.com/applied-deep-learning-part-1-artificial-neural-networks-d7834f67a4f6

Ding, S., & Wang, G. (2017). Research on intrusion detection technology based on deep learning. *2017 3rd IEEE International Conference on Computer and Communication (ICCC).*

Dinh, P. V., Ngo, T. N., Shone, N., MacDermott, A., & Shi, Q. (2017). Deep learning combined with de-noising data for network intrusion detection. *2017 21st Asia Pacific Symposium on Intelligent and Evolutionalry Sytems (IES).*

Gupta, R. (2018). Anomaly detection and data classification using KSQL. *International Journal of Advance Research, Ideas and Innovations in Technology, 4*(2).

Hyndman, R. J., & Athanasopoulos, G. (2018). *Forecasting: principles and practice.* Otexts.

Janarthanan, T., & Zargari, S. (2017). Feature selection in UNSW-NB15 and KDDCUP'99 datasets. *2017 IEEE 26th International Symposium on IndustrialElectronics (ISIE), 2017.*

Jidiga, G. R., & Sammulal, P. (2014) Anomaly detection using machine learning with a case study. *2014 IEEE International Conference on Advanced Communication, Control and Computing Technologies.*

Jose, S., Malathi, D., Reddy, B. & Jayaseeli, D. (2018). A survey on anomaly based host intrusion detection system. *Journal of Physics, Conference Series, 1000.*

Kumar, B. P. V., & Venkatarm, P. (2002). Prediction-based location management using multilayer neural networks. *Journal of the Indian Institute of Science*, 82, 7.

Lin, L., Zhong, S., Jia, C., & Chen, K. (2017). Insider threat detection based on deep belief network feature representation. *2017 International Conference on Green Informatics (ICGI).* 10.1109/ICGI.2017.37

Malaiya, R. K., Kwon, D., Kim, J., Suh, S. C., Kim, H., & Kim, I. (2018) An empirical evaluation of deep learning for network anomaly detection. *2018 International Conference on Computing, Networking and Communications (ICNC).* 10.1109/ICCNC.2018.8390278

Moohebbi, A., Aradottir, T. B., Johansen, A. R., Bengtsson, H., Fraccaro, M., & Morup, M. (2017). A deep learning approach to adherence detection for type 2 diabetics. *Conference Proceedings; ... Annual International Conference of the IEEE Engineering in Medicine and Biology Society. IEEE Engineering in Medicine and Biology Society. Conference.*

Moustafa, N., & Slay, J. (2015). The significant features of the UNSW-NB15 and the KDD99 data sets for network intrusion detection systems. *2015 4th International Workshop on Building Analysis Datasets and Gathering Experience Returns for Security (BADGERS).*

Moustafa, N. & Slay, J. (2016). The evaluation of Network Anomaly Detection Systems: Statsistical Analysis of the UNSW-NB15 dataset and the comparison with the KDD99 Data set. *Information Security Journal A Global Perspective, 2016.*

Narayanan, V. K., Kirpal, A., & Karampatziakis, N. (2015). Anomaly detection – Using machine learning to detect abnormalities in time series data. *Modata*. Retrieved from: https://www.mo-data.com/anomaly-detection-using-machine-learning-to-detect-abnormalities-in-time-series-data/

Ozaki, T. J. (2015). Machine learning for package users with r(5): Random forest. *Hatena Blog*. Retrieved from: https://tjo-en.hatenablog.com/entry/2015/06/04/190000

Pattarakavin, T., & Chongstitvatana, P. (2016) Detection of machine anomaly from log files in hard disk manufacturing process. *2016 International conference on Multimedia systems and Signal Processing*. 10.1109/ICMSSP.2016.022

Shafiul, Ahemd, Abir, Ul-haq, & Nikhil. (2015). *Investigations on the Influence of Cutting Fluids in Turning Composites under Variable Machining Conditions*. Academic Press. . doi:10.13140/RG.2.1.4562.0569

Siddavatam, I. A., Satish, S., Mahesh, W., & Kazi, F. (2017). An ensemble learning for anomaly identification in *SCADA System. 2017 7th International Conference on Power Systems (ICPS)*.

Van, N. T., Thinh, T. N., & Sach, L. T. (2017) An anomaly-based network intrusion detection system using deep learning. *2017 International Conference on System Science and Engineering(ICSSE)*.

Vartouni, A. M., Kasha, S. S., & Teshnehlab, M. (2018). An anomaly detection method to detect web attacks using stacked auto-encoder. *2018 6th Iranian Joint Congress on Fuzzy and Intelligent Systems (CFIS)*.

Yin, C., Zhu, Y., Fei, J., & He, X. (2017). A deep learning approach for intrusion detection using recurrent neural networks. *IEEE Access: Practical Innovations, Open Solutions, 5*, 21954–21961. doi:10.1109/ACCESS.2017.2762418

Zhu, Y. (2010). Automatic detection of anomalies in blood glucose using a machine learning approach. *Journal of Communications and Networks (Seoul), 13*(2), 125–131. doi:10.1109/JCN.2011.6157411

Glossary

Bipedal Walking Robot: A mobile robot with two legs, which primary mode of operation requires these legs to periodically acquire and break contact with the supporting surface.

Confusion Matrix: A matrix which shows the distribution of categorizations performed by the network on a labeled dataset, where the correct categorizations lie on the main diagonal.

Convolutional Neural Network: A type of artificial neural networks, which uses a set of filters with tunable (learnable) parameters to extract local features from the input data.

Eigenface: A principal components of a distribution of faces (eigenvectors). It is a covariance of matrix of the set of face images.

Fire Module: The sequence of layers that perform 1) squeezing by using conv1x1, 2) expanding into conv1x1 and conv3x3, and 3) concatenating them.

Fully Connected Layer: A layer of an artificial neural networks where each element of the layer is connected to each element of the following layer.

Keypoints: Points in an image that are interesting. They do not change when they are applied affine transformation.

Obstacle-Free Region: A region in space (on the supporting surface), which points are suitable for making contact.

SIFT Transform: Scale-invariant feature transform. It is a kind of transformation which is used to find local features such as keypoints which tolerate to operations such as rotate and scale operations.

Training: A process of tuning parameters of an artificial neural networks, based on comparing the current output of the network with the desired output; the process is often performed with gradient decent-like methods.

Compilation of References

Abadi, M., Barham, P., Chen, J., Chen, Z., Davis, A., Dean, J., . . . Kudlur, M. (2016, November). Tensorflow: a system for large-scale machine learning. In OSDI (Vol. 16, pp. 265-283). Academic Press.

Abdel-Hamid, O., Mohamed, A. R., Jiang, H., & Penn, G. (2012). Applying convolutional neural networks concepts to hybrid NN-HMM model for speech recognition. *ICASSP, IEEE Int. Conf. Acoust. Speech Signal Process. - Proc.*, 4277–4280.

Abdel-Hamid, O., Mohamed, A., Jiang, H., Deng, L., Penn, G., & Yu, D. (2014). Convolutional Neural Networks for Speech Recognition. *IEEE/ACM Transactions on Audio, Speech, and Language Processing*, *22*(10), 1533–1545.

Abouelela, M., & Benedicenti, L. (2010). Bayesian network based XP process modeling. *International Journal of Software Engineering and Its Applications*, *1*(3), 1–15. doi:10.5121/ijsea.2010.1301

Ackley David, H., Hinton Geoffrey, E., & Sejnowski Terrence, J. (1985). A Learning Algorithm for Boltzmann Machines. *Cognitive Science*, *9*(1), 147–169. doi:10.120715516709cog0901_7

Addo, P., Guegan, D., & Hassani, B. (2018). Credit Risk Analysis Using Machine and Deep Learning Models. *Risks*, *6*(2), 38. doi:10.3390/risks6020038

Adline, A., & Ramachandran, M. (2014). Predicting the software fault using the method of genetic algorithm. *International Journal of Advanced Research in Electrical, Electronics and Instrumentation Engineering, 3*(2), 390–398.

Agrawal, P., Carreira, J., & Malik, J. (2015). Learning to see by moving. In *Proceedings of the IEEE International Conference on Computer Vision* (pp. 37-45). IEEE.

Aguilar-Ruiz, J., Ramos, I., Riquelme, J. C., & Toro, M. (2001). An evolutionary approach to estimating software development projects. *Information and Software Technology*, *43*(14), 875–882. doi:10.1016/S0950-5849(01)00193-8

Ahmed, A., & Al-Shaboti, M. (2018). Implementation of Internet of Things (IoT) Based on IPv6 over Wireless Sensor Networks. *International Journal Of Sensors. Wireless Communications And Control*, *7*(2). doi:10.2174/2210327907666170911145726

Ahmed, M. A., & Al-Jamimi, H. A. (2013). Machine learning approaches for predicting software maintainability: A fuzzy-based transparent model. *IET Software, 7*(6), 317–326. doi:10.1049/iet-sen.2013.0046

Aliyev, V. (2010). *Using honeypots to study skill level of attackers based on the exploited vulnerabilities in the network*. Chalmers University of Technology.

Allen, J. B., & Rabiner, L. R. (1977). A unified approach to short-time Fourier analysis and synthesis. *Proceedings of the IEEE, 65*(11), 1558–1564. doi:10.1109/PROC.1977.10770

Alzantot, M., Balaji, B., & Srivastava, M. (2018). *Did you hear that? Adversarial Examples Against Automatic Speech Recognition*. Nips.

Amasaki, S., Takagi, Y., Mizuno, O., & Kikuno, T. (2005). Constructing a Bayesian belief network to predict final quality in embedded system development. *IEICE Transactions on Information and Systems, 88*(6), 1134–1141. doi:10.1093/ietisy/e88-d.6.1134

Amos, B., Ludwiczuk, B., & Satyanarayanan, M. (2016). *OpenFace: A general-purpose face recognition library with mobile applications (Tech. Rep.). CMU-CS-16-118*. CMU School of Computer Science.

Analytics Vidhya. (n.d.). Retrieved from: https://www.analyticsvidhya.com/blog

Anwer, H. M., Farouk, M., & Abdel-Hamid, A. (2018) A framework for efficient network anomaly intrusion detection with features selection. *2018 9th International Conference on Information and Communication Systems (ICICS).*

Arnold, T. (2017). kerasR: R Interface to the Keras Deep Learning Library. *The Journal of Open Source Software, 2*(14), 296. doi:10.21105/joss.00296

Athiwaratkun, B., & Stokes, J. W. (2017). Malware classification with LSTM and GRU language models and a character-level CNN. In *2017 IEEE International Conference on Acoustics, Speech and Signal Processing (ICASSP)* (pp. 2482–2486). IEEE. 10.1109/ICASSP.2017.7952603

Atkeson, C. G., Babu, B. P. W., Banerjee, N., Berenson, D., Bove, C. P., Cui, X., . . . Gennert, M. (2015, November). No falls, no resets: Reliable humanoid behavior in the DARPA robotics challenge. In *Humanoid Robots (Humanoids), 2015 IEEE-RAS 15th International Conference on* (pp. 623-630). IEEE.

Azam, S., & Gavrilova, M. L. (2017). Biometric Pattern Recognition from Social Media Aesthetics. *Journal of Cognitive Informatics and Natural Intelligence, 11*(3), 1–16. doi:10.4018/IJCINI.2017070101

Azar, D., & Vybihal, J. (2011). an ant colony optimization algorithm to improve software quality prediction models: Case of class stability. *Information and Software Technology, 53*(4), 388–393. doi:10.1016/j.infsof.2010.11.013

Backstrom, K., Nazari, M., Gu, I. Y., & Jakola, A. S. (2018). An efficient 3D deep convolutional network for Alzheimer's disease diagnosis using MR images. *2018 IEEE 15th International Symposium on Biomedical Imaging (ISBI 2018).* doi:10.1109/isbi.2018.8363543

Balaguer, C., Gimenez, A., & Jardón, A. (2005). Climbing robots' mobility for inspection and maintenance of 3D complex environments. *Autonomous Robots*, *18*(2), 157–169. doi:10.100710514-005-0723-0

Battenberg, E., Schmidt, E., & Bello, J. (2014). *Deep learning for music*. International Conference on Acoustics Speech and Signal Processing (ICASSP).

Bellman, R. (1958). Dynamic programming and stochastic control processes. *Information and Control*, *1*(3), 228–239. doi:10.1016/S0019-9958(58)80003-0

Bendre, M., & Thool, V. (2016). Analytics, challenges and applications in big data environment: A survey. *Journal Of Management Analytics*, *3*(3), 206–239. doi:10.1080/23270012.2016.1186578

Benedictus, M. R., Leeuwis, A. E., Binnewijzend, M. A., Kuijer, J. P. A., Scheltens, P., Barkhof, F., ... Prins, N. D. (2017). Lower cerebral blood flow is associated with faster cognitive decline in Alzheimer's disease. *European Radiology*, *27*(3), 1169–1175. doi:10.100700330-016-4450-z PMID:27334014

Bengio, Y. (2009). Learning deep architectures for AI. *Foundations and Trends in Machine Learning*, *2*(1), 1–127. doi:10.1561/2200000006

Bengio, Y., Simard, P., & Frasconi, P. (1994). Learning long-term dependencies with gradient descent is difficult. *IEEE Transactions on Neural Networks*, *5*(2), 157–166. doi:10.1109/72.279181 PMID:18267787

Bergstra, J., Breuleux, O., Bastien, F. F., Lamblin, P., Pascanu, R., Desjardins, G., ... Bengio, Y. (2010). Theano: a CPU and GPU math compiler in Python. *Proceedings of the Python for Scientific Computing Conference (SciPy)*, 1–7. Retrieved from http://www-etud.iro.umontreal.ca/~wardefar/publications/theano_scipy2010.pdf

Bernstein, M. N. (n.d.). *Random Forest algorithm*. Available from pages.cs.wisc.edu/~matrhewb/pages/notes/pdf/ensembles/RandomForests.pdf

Bhatt, M., & Prabha, S. (2015). Detection of Abnormal Blood Cells Using Image Processing Technique. *International Journal of Electrical and Electronics Engineers*, *07*, 1–6.

Bhuyan, M. H., Bhattacharya, B. K., & Kalita, J. K. (2017). Network anomaly detection: Methods, systems and tools. *IEEE Communications Surveys & Tutorials, VOL.*, *16*(1), 2014.

Bodstrom, T., & Hamalainen, T. (2018). *State of the art literature review on network anomaly detection with deep learning*. Springer International Publishing. doi:10.1007/978-3-030-01168-0_7

Borji, A., & Dundar, A. (2017). *Human-like Clustering with Deep Convolutional Neural Networks*. Academic Press.

Bosch, A., Zisserman, A., & Munoz, X. (2007, October). Image classification using random forests and ferns. In *Computer Vision, 2007. ICCV 2007. IEEE 11th International Conference on* (pp. 1-8). IEEE. 10.1109/ICCV.2007.4409066

Bouyarmane, K., Caron, S., Escande, A., & Kheddar, A. (2017). *Multi-Contact Planning and Control*. Academic Press.

Brinjikji, W., Luetmer, P. H., Comstock, B., Bresnahan, B. W., Chen, L. E., Deyo, R. A., ... Jarvik, J. G. (2015). Systematic literature review of imaging features of spinal degeneration in asymptomatic populations. *AJNR. American Journal of Neuroradiology*, *36*(4), 811–816. doi:10.3174/ajnr.A4173 PMID:25430861

Browne, M., & Ghidary, S. S. (2003). Convolutional neural networks for image processing: an application in robot vision. In *Australasian Joint Conference on Artificial Intelligence* (pp. 641-652). Springer. 10.1007/978-3-540-24581-0_55

Browniee, J. (2016, September 22). *What is Deep Learning?* Retrieved from https://machinelearning-mastery.com/what-is-deep-learning/

Buckley, R. F., Schultz, A. P., & Hedden, T. (2017). *Functional network integrity presages cognitive decline in preclinical Alzheimer's disease*. Retrieved from http://http://www.neurology.org/content/early/2017/06/07/WNL.0000000000004059.short

Calhoun, V. D., Miller, R., Pearlson, G., & Adalı, T. (2014). The Chronnectome: Time-Varying Connectivity Networks as the Next Frontier in fMRI Data Discovery. *Neuron*, *84*(2), 262–274. doi:10.1016/j.neuron.2014.10.015 PMID:25374354

Campbell, C., & Ying, Y. (2011). Learning with Support Vector Machines. *Synthesis Lectures On Artificial Intelligence And Machine Learning*, *5*(1), 1–95. doi:10.2200/S00324ED1V01Y201102AIM010

Canziani, A., Paszke, A., & Culurciello, E. (2016). *An analysis of deep neural network models for practical applications*. arXiv preprint arXiv:1605.07678

Carta, J., Cabrera, P., Matías, J., & Castellano, F. (2015). Comparison of feature selection methods using ANNs in MCP-wind speed methods. A case study. *Applied Energy*, *158*, 490–507. doi:10.1016/j.apenergy.2015.08.102

Castro Martinez, A. M., Mallidi, S. H., & Meyer, B. T. (2017). On the relevance of auditory-based Gabor features for deep learning in robust speech recognition. *Computer Speech & Language*, *45*, 21–38. doi:10.1016/j.csl.2017.02.006

Ceelie, H., Dinkelaar, R. B., & van Gelder, W. (2007). Examination of peripheral blood films using automated microscopy; evaluation of Diffmaster Octavia and Cellavision DM96. *Journal of Clinical Pathology*, *60*(1), 72–79. doi:10.1136/jcp.2005.035402 PMID:16698955

Celebi, M. E., & Smolka, B. (2016). Labeled faces in the wild: A survey. In M. Kawulok (Ed.), *Advances in face detection and facial image analysis* (pp. 189–248). Springer.

Cervantes, J. A., Rodriguez, L. F., Lopez, S., & Ramos, F. (2013). A biologically inspired computational model of moral decision making for autonomous agents. In *Proceedings of the 12th IEEE International Conference on Cognitive Informatics & Cognitive Computing (ICCI*CC'2013)* (pp. 111-117). IEEE CS Press. 10.1109/ICCI-CC.2013.6622232

Chae, J., & Quick, B. (2014). An Examination of the Relationship Between Health Information Use and Health Orientation in Korean Mothers: Focusing on the Type of Health Information. *Journal of Health Communication*, *20*(3), 275–284. doi:10.1080/10810730.2014.925016 PMID:25495418

Chakraborty, A., Harrison, B., Yang, P., Roberts, D., & St. Amant, R. (2014). Exploring key-level Analytics for Computational Modeling of typing Behavior. *Proceedings of the 2014 Symposium and Bootcamp on the Science of Security*. 10.1145/2600176.2600210

Chalapathy, R., Menon, A.K. & Chawla, S. (2018). *Anomaly detection using one-neural networks*. Academic Press.

Challa, J. S., Paul, A., Dada, Y., Nerella, V., Srivastava, P. R., & Singh, A. P. (2011). Integrated software quality evaluation: A fuzzy multi-criteria approach. *Journal of Information Process System*, *7*(3), 473–518. doi:10.3745/JIPS.2011.7.3.473

Chatzilygeroudis, K., Rama, R., Kaushik, R., Goepp, D., Vassiliades, V., & Mouret, J.-B. (n.d.). *Black-Box Data-efficient Policy Search for Robotics*. Retrieved from https://hal.inria.fr/hal-01576683

Chen, Engkvist, Wang, Olivecrona, & Blaschke. (2018). The rise of deep learning in drug discovery. Drug Discovery Today, 23(6), 1241-1250.

Cheng, Y., Wang, D., Zhou, D., & Zhang, T. (2017). A Survey of Model Compression and Acceleration for Deep Neural Networks. *IEEE Signal Processing Magazine*. Retrieved from https://arxiv.org/pdf/1710.09282.pdf

Cheng, D., & Liu, M. (2017). Classification of Alzheimer's Disease by Cascaded Convolutional Neural Networks Using PET Images. In Q. Wang, Y. Shi, H. I. Suk, & K. Suzuki (Eds.), Lecture Notes in Computer Science: Vol. 10541. *Machine Learning in Medical Imaging. MLMI 2017*. Cham: Springer. doi:10.1007/978-3-319-67389-9_13

Cheng, J.-Z., Ni, D., Chou, Y.-H., Qin, J., Tiu, C.-M., Chang, Y.-C., ... Chen, C.-M. (2016). Computer-aided diagnosis with deep learning architecture: Applications to breast lesions in US images and pulmonary nodules in CT scans. *Scientific Reports*, *6*(1), 24454. doi:10.1038rep24454 PMID:27079888

Chiriacescu, V., Soh, L.-K., & Shell, D. F. (2013). Understanding Human Learning Using a Multi-agent Simulation of the Unified Learning Model. *International Journal of Cognitive Informatics and Natural Intelligence*, *7*(4), 143–152. doi:10.4018/ijcini.2013100101

Cho, K., Van Merriënboer, B., Gulcehre, C., Bahdanau, D., Bougares, F., Schwenk, H., & Bengio, Y. (2014). *Learning phrase representations using RNN encoder-decoder for statistical machine translation*. ArXiv Preprint ArXiv:1406.1078

Choi, H., & Jin, K. H. (2018). Predicting cognitive decline with deep learning of brain metabolism and amyloid imaging. *Behavioural Brain Research*, *344*, 103–109. doi:10.1016/j.bbr.2018.02.017 PMID:29454006

Chollet, F. (2015). *Keras: Deep learning library for theano and tensorflow*. Retrieved from https://keras. io/k, 7, 8

Chollet, F. (2017). *Xception: Deep learning with depthwise separable convolutions.* arXiv preprint, 1610-02357

Chollet, F. (2017). *Deep Learning with Python.* Manning Publications.

Christopher, M. B. (2016). *Pattern Recognition and Machine Learning.* Springer-Verlag New York.

Chumachenko, K., & Technology, I. (2017). *Machine Learning for Malware Detection and Classification.* Bachelor's Thesis Information Technology.

Ciregan, D., Meier, U., & Schmidhuber, J. (2012). Multi-column deep neural networks for image classification. In *Computer Vision and Pattern Recognition (CVPR), 2012 IEEE Conference on 2012 Jun 16* (pp. 3642-3649). IEEE.

Cireşan, D., Meier, U., & Schmidhuber, J. (2012). *Multi-column deep neural networks for image classification.* arXiv preprint arXiv:1202.2745

Colombo, A., Cusano, C., & Schettini, R. (2011, November). UMB-DB: A database of partially occluded 3D faces. In *Computer Vision Workshops (ICCV Workshops), 2011 IEEE International Conference on* (pp. 2113-2119). IEEE.

Cui, Z., Xue, F., Cai, X., Cao, Y., Wang, G., & Chen, J. (2018). Detection of Malicious Code Variants Based on Deep Learning. *IEEE Transactions on Industrial Informatics, 14*(7), 3187–3196. doi:10.1109/TII.2018.2822680

Dahl, G. E., Yu, D., Deng, L., & Acero, A. (2012). Context-dependent pre-trained deep neural networks for large-vocabulary speech recognition. *IEEE Transactions on Audio, Speech, and Language Processing, 20*(1), 30–42. doi:10.1109/TASL.2011.2134090

Dai, H., & Hao, J. (2017). Mining social media data for opinion polarities about electronic cigarettes. *Tobacco Control, 26*(2), 175–180. doi:10.1136/tobaccocontrol-2015-052818 PMID:26980151

Datta, S., & Das, S. (2015). Near-Bayesian Support Vector Machines for imbalanced data classification with equal or unequal misclassification costs. *Neural Networks, 70*, 39–52. doi:10.1016/j.neunet.2015.06.005 PMID:26210983

Deep Q-network - Deep Learning with Theano. (2018). Retrieved September 23, 2018, from https://www.oreilly.com/library/view/deep-learning-with/9781786465825/ch11s04.html

DeepMind Health. Google DeepMind. (2016). Retrieved from: https://www.deepmind.com/health

Degris, T., Pilarski, P. M., & Sutton, R. S. (2012). *Model-free reinforcement learning with continuous action in practice. In American Control Conference (ACC)* (pp. 2177–2182). IEEE.

Deits, R., & Tedrake, R. (2014, November). Footstep planning on uneven terrain with mixed-integer convex optimization. In *Humanoid Robots (Humanoids), 2014 14th IEEE-RAS International Conference on* (pp. 279-286). IEEE. 10.21236/ADA609276

298

Deits, R., & Tedrake, R. (2015). Computing large convex regions of obstacle-free space through semidefinite programming. In *Algorithmic foundations of robotics XI* (pp. 109–124). Cham: Springer. doi:10.1007/978-3-319-16595-0_7

Deller, J. R. Jr, Proakis, J. G., & Hansen, J. H. (1993). *Discrete-time processing of speech signals.* New York: Macmillan.

Deng, J., Dong, W., Socher, R., Li, L. J., Li, K., & Fei-Fei, L. (2009, June). Imagenet: A large-scale hierarchical image database. In *Computer Vision and Pattern Recognition, 2009. CVPR 2009. IEEE Conference on* (pp. 248-255). IEEE. 10.1109/CVPR.2009.5206848

Deng, J., Guo, J., & Zafeiriou, S. (2018). *Arcface: Additive angular margin loss for deep face recognition.* arXiv preprint arXiv:1801.07698

Deng, L., & Yu, D. (2013). Deep Learning Methods and Applications. Foundations and Trends in Signal Processing, 7(3-4).

Deng, L. (2014). A tutorial survey of architectures, algorithms, and applications for deep learning – ERRATUM. *APSIPA Transactions On Signal And Information Processing, 3.* doi:10.1017/atsip.2014.4

Deng, L., Abdel-Hamid, O., & Yu, D. (2013). A deep convolutional neural network using heterogeneous pooling for trading acoustic invariance with phonetic confusion. *Proceedings of International Conference on Acoustics Speech and Signal Processing.* 10.1109/ICASSP.2013.6638952

Deng, L., Hinton, G. E., & Kingsbury, B. (2013) New types of deep neural network learning for speech recognition and related applications: An overview. *2013 IEEE Int. Conf. Acoust. Speech Signal Process,* 8599–8603. 10.1109/ICASSP.2013.6639344

Dertat, A. (2017). Applied deep learning part 1: Artificial neural networks. *Towards Data Science.* Retrieved from: https://towardsdatascience.com/applied-deep-learning-part-1-artificial-neural-networks-d7834f67a4f6

Despotovic, V., & Tanikic, D. (2017). Sentiment Analysis of Microblogs Using Multilayer Feed-Forward Artificial Neural Networks. *Computer Information, 36*(5), 1127–1142. doi:10.4149/cai_2017_5_1127

Dieleman, S., Schlüter, J., Raffel, C., Olson, E., Sønderby, S. K., Nouri, D., ... & De Fauw, J. (2015). *Lasagne: first release.* Academic Press.

Diez, A. (2013). *Automatic language recognition using deep neural networks* (Thesis). Universidad Autonoma de Madrid, Spain.

Ding, S., & Wang, G. (2017). Research on intrusion detection technology based on deep learning. *2017 3rd IEEE International Conference on Computer and Communication (ICCC).*

Dinh, P. V., Ngo, T. N., Shone, N., MacDermott, A., & Shi, Q. (2017). Deep learning combined with de-noising data for network intrusion detection. *2017 21st Asia Pacific Symposium on Intelligent and Evolutionalry Sytems (IES).*

Dlib. (n.d.). *Dlib C++ library.* Retrieved from http://dlib.net/

Dong, C., Loy, C. C., He, K., & Tang, X. (2014). Learning a deep convolutional network for image super-resolution. In *European Conference on Computer Vision (ECCV)* (pp. 184–199). Springer. 10.1007/978-3-319-10593-2_13

Drew, J., Hahsler, M., & Moore, T. (2017). *Polymorphic malware detection using sequence classification methods and ensembles. EURASIP Journal on Information Security.* doi:10.118613635-017-0055-6

Dundar, A., Jin, J., & Culurciello, E. (2015). *Convolutional clustering for unsupervised learning.* arXiv preprint arXiv:1511.06241

Dussart, P., Petit, L., Labeau, B., Bremand, L., Leduc, A., Moua, D., ... Baril, L. (2008). Evaluation of Two New Commercial Tests for the Diagnosis of Acute Dengue Virus Infection Using NS1 Antigen Detection in Human Serum. *PLoS Neglected Tropical Diseases*, *2*(8), e280. doi:10.1371/journal.pntd.0000280 PMID:18714359

Eliasmith, C., Stewart, T. C., Choo, X., Bekolay, T., DeWolf, T., Tang, C., & Rasmussen, D. (2012). A large-scale model of the functioning brain. *Science*, *338*(6111), 1202–1205. doi:10.1126cience.1225266 PMID:23197532

Elman, J. L. (1990). Finding structure in time. *Cognitive Science*, *14*(2), 179–211. doi:10.120715516709cog1402_1

Fallon, M. F., Marion, P., Deits, R., Whelan, T., Antone, M., McDonald, J., & Tedrake, R. (2015, November). Continuous humanoid locomotion over uneven terrain using stereo fusion. In *Humanoid Robots (Humanoids), 2015 IEEE-RAS 15th International Conference on* (pp. 881-888). IEEE. 10.1109/HUMANOIDS.2015.7363465

Fattah, S., Sung, N., Ahn, I., Ryu, M., & Yun, J. (2017). Building IoT Services for Aging in Place Using Standard-Based IoT Platforms and Heterogeneous IoT Products. *Sensors (Basel)*, *17*(10), 2311. doi:10.339017102311 PMID:29019964

Fayek, H. M., Lech, M., & Cavedon, L. (2017). Evaluating deep learning architectures for Speech Emotion Recognition. *Neural Networks*, *92*, 60–68. doi:10.1016/j.neunet.2017.02.013 PMID:28396068

Focchi, M., Del Prete, A., Havoutis, I., Featherstone, R., Caldwell, D. G., & Semini, C. (2017). High-slope terrain locomotion for torque-controlled quadruped robots. *Autonomous Robots*, *41*(1), 259–272. doi:10.100710514-016-9573-1

Fox, N. C., & Schott, J. M. (2004). Imaging cerebral atrophy: Normal ageing to Alzheimer's disease. *Lancet (London, England)*, *363*(9406), 392–394. doi:10.1016/S0140-6736(04)15441-X PMID:15074306

Funahashi, K. I. (1989). On the approximate realization of continuous mappings by neural networks. *Neural Networks*, *2*(3), 183–192. doi:10.1016/0893-6080(89)90003-8

Fu, R., Li, B., Gao, Y., & Wang, P. (2018). Visualizing and analyzing convolution neural networks with gradient information. *Neurocomputing*, *293*, 12–17. doi:10.1016/j.neucom.2018.02.080

Gábor, Z., Kalmár, Z., & Szepesvári, C. (1998). Multi-criteria Reinforcement Learning. *Proceedings of the Fifteenth International Conference on Machine Learning*, 24–27. Retrieved from https://dl.acm.org/citation.cfm?id=657298

Galloway, K., Sreenath, K., Ames, A. D., & Grizzle, J. W. (2015). Torque saturation in bipedal robotic walking through control Lyapunov function-based quadratic programs. *IEEE Access: Practical Innovations, Open Solutions*, *3*, 323–332. doi:10.1109/ACCESS.2015.2419630

Gao, X. W., & Hui, R. (2016). A deep learning based approach to classification of CT brain images. *2016 SAI Computing Conference (SAI)*. 10.1109/SAI.2016.7555958

Garcia, F. C. C., Muga, I. I., & Felix, P. (2016). *Random Forest for Malware Classification*. ArXiv Preprint ArXiv:1609.07770

Garcia, F., Cervantes, J., Lopez, A., & Alvarado, M. (2016). Fruit classification by extracting color chromaticity, shape and texture features: Towards an application for supermarkets. *IEEE Latin America Transactions*, *14*(7), 3434–3443. doi:10.1109/TLA.2016.7587652

Gavrilova, M.L & Yampolskiy, R. (n.d.). Applying biometric principles to avatar recognition. *Transactions on Computational Science, 12*, 140-158.

Gavrilova, M.L. & Azam, S. (2017). Biometric Pattern Recognition from Social Media Aesthetics. *International Journal of Cognitive Informatics and Natural Intelligence Archive, 11*(3), 1-16.

Gers, F. A., Schraudolph, N. N., & Schmidhuber, J. (2002). Learning precise timing with LSTM recurrent networks. *Journal of Machine Learning Research*, 115–143.

Gibert, D. (2016). *Convolutional Neural Networks for Malware Classification*. Academic Press.

Gibson, A., & Patterson, J. (2007). *Deep Learning*. Sebastopol, CA: O'Reilly Media.

Girshick, R. B. (2015). *Fast R-CNN*. CoRR, abs/1504.08083. Retrieved from http://arxiv.org/abs/1504.08083

Gobet, F., Gobet, F., & Lane, P.C.R. (2012). *Chunking mechanisms and learning*. Academic Press.

Gomes, C., & Mayes, A. (2014). The kinds of information that support novel associative object priming and how these differ from those that support item priming. *Memory (Hove, England)*, *23*(6), 901–927. doi:10.1080/09658211.2014.937722 PMID:25051200

Goodfellow, I.J., Bulatov, Y., Ibarz, J., Arnoud, S., & Shet, V. (2014). *Multi-digit number recognition from street view imagery using deep convolutional neural networks*. Academic Press.

Goodfellow, Mirza, Courville, & Bengio. (2013). Multi-prediction deep Boltzmann machines. *Proceedings of Neural Information Processing Systems*.

Grm, K., Štruc, V., Artiges, A., Caron, M., & Ekenel, H. K. (2017). Strengths and weaknesses of deep learning models for face recognition against image degradations. *IET Biometrics*, *7*(1), 81–89. doi:10.1049/iet-bmt.2017.0083

Gudivada, V. N., Irfan, M. T., Fathi, E., & Rao, D. L. (2016). Cognitive Analytics: Going Beyond Big Data Analytics and Machine Learning. Handbook of Statistics, 35, 169-205.

Gudivada, V., Baeza-Yates, R., & Raghavan, V. (2015). Big data: Promises and problems. *IEEE Comput., 48*(3), 20–23. doi:10.1109/MC.2015.62

Guiming, D., Xia, W., Guangyan, W., Yan, Z., & Dan, L. (2016). Speech recognition based on convolutional neural networks. *IEEE International Conference on Signal and Image Processing (ICSIP)*, 708-711. 10.1109/SIPROCESS.2016.7888355

Guo, Y., Zhang, L., Hu, Y., He, X., & Gao, J. (n.d.). *MS-Celeb-1M: a dataset and benchmark for large-scale face recognition*. Retrieved from https://arxiv.org/abs/1607.08221

Guo, P., & Lyu, M. R. (2000). Software quality prediction using mixture models with EM algorithm. *Proceedings of Quality Software in First Asia-Pacific Conference on IEEE*, 69–78.

Guo, Y., Liu, Y., Georgiou, T., & Lew, M. (2017). A review of semantic segmentation using deep neural networks. *International Journal of Multimedia Information Retrieval, 7*(2), 87–93. doi:10.100713735-017-0141-z

Gupta, D., Mittal, H.K., & Goyal, V. (2011). Comparative study of soft computing techniques for software quality model. *International Journal of Software Engineering Research Practices, 1*(1), 33–37.

Gupta, R. (2018). Anomaly detection and data classification using KSQL. *International Journal of Advance Research, Ideas and Innovations in Technology, 4*(2).

Hadad, Y. (2017). *30 amazing applications of deep learning*. Retrieved from: http://www.yaronhadad.com/deep-learning-most-amazing-applications/

Han, B. J., Choi, Y. H., & Bae, B. C. (2013). Generating malware DNA to classify the similar malwares. *Journal of the Korea Institute of Information Security and Cryptology, 23*(4), 679–694. doi:10.13089/JKIISC.2013.23.4.679

Han, S., Mao, S., & Dally, W. J. (2016). Deep compression: Compressing deep neural networks with pruning, trained quantization and Huffman coding. *International Conference on Learning Representations (ICLR)*.

Harrison, Spaeth, & Braun. (2007). *Speech Recognition: Key Word Spotting through Image Recognition*. Retrieved from http://ccrma.stanford.edu/~jos/mdft/

Hebb, D. O. (1949). *The Organization of Behavior: A Neuropsychological Theory*. New York: Wiley. Retrieved from https://deepcognition.ai/

He, K., Zhang, X., Ren, S., & Sun, J. (2015). Delving deep into rectifiers: Surpassing human-level performance on imagenet classification. In *Proceedings of the IEEE international conference on computer vision* (pp. 1026-1034). IEEE. 10.1109/ICCV.2015.123

He, K., Zhang, X., Ren, S., & Sun, J. (2016). Deep residual learning for image recognition. In *Proceedings of the IEEE conference on computer vision and pattern recognition* (pp. 770-778). IEEE.

Hemangi, B., & Nikhita, K. (2016). People counting system using raspberry pi with openCV. *International Journal for Research in Engineering Application & Management*, *2*(1).

Hershey, J. R., Chen, Z., Le Roux, J., & Watanabe, S. (2016, March). Deep clustering: Discriminative embeddings for segmentation and separation. In *Acoustics, Speech and Signal Processing (ICASSP), 2016 IEEE International Conference on* (pp. 31-35). IEEE.

He, Y., Zhang, Z., Yu, F. R., Zhao, N., Yin, H., Leung, V. C. M., & Zhang, Y. (2017). Deep-reinforcement-learning-based optimization for cache-enabled opportunistic interference alignment wireless networks. *IEEE Transactions on Vehicular Technology*, *66*(11), 10433–10445. doi:10.1109/TVT.2017.2751641

Hinton, G. (2014). Dropout : A Simple Way to Prevent Neural Networks from Overfitting. *Journal of Machine Learning Research*, *15*, 1929–1958.

Hinton, G., Deng, L., Yu, D., Dahl, G., Mohamed, A., Jaitly, N., ... Kingsbury, B. (2012). Deep neural networks for acoustic modeling in speech recognition: The shared views of four research groups. *Signal Processing*, *29*(6), 82–97. doi:10.1109/MSP.2012.2205597

Hochreiter, S., & Schmidhuber, J. (1997). Long short-term memory. *Neural Computation*, *9*(8), 1735–1780. doi:10.1162/neco.1997.9.8.1735 PMID:9377276

Hong, S., & Lee, Y. (2013). CPU Parallel Processing and GPU-accelerated Processing of UHD Video Sequence using HEVC. *Journal Of Broadcast Engineering*, *18*(6), 816–822. doi:10.5909/JBE.2013.18.6.816

Hou, S., Saas, A., Chen, L., & Ye, Y. (2016). Deep4MalDroid: A Deep Learning Framework for Android Malware Detection Based on Linux Kernel System Call Graphs. In *2016 IEEE/WIC/ACM International Conference on Web Intelligence Workshops (WIW)* (pp. 104–111). IEEE. 10.1109/WIW.2016.040

Howard, A. (2017). MobileNets: Efficient Convolutional Neural Networks for Mobile Vision Applications. *CVPR*. Retrieved from https://arxiv.org/abs/1704.04861

Huang, G., Liu, Z., Weinberger, K. Q., & van der Maaten, L. (2017, July). Densely connected convolutional networks. In *Proceedings of the IEEE conference on computer vision and pattern recognition* (Vol. 1, No. 2, p. 3). IEEE.

Huang, T., Xiong, Z., & Zhang, Z. (2011). Face recognition applications. In *Handbook of face recognition* (pp. 617–638). London: Springer London. doi:10.1007/978-0-85729-932-1_24

Huang, W., & Stokes, J. W. (2016). MtNet : A Multi-Task Neural Network for Dynamic Malware Classification. *International Conference on Detection of Intrusions and Malware, and Vulnerability Assessment*, 399–418. 10.1007/978-3-319-40667-1_20

Hu, G., Yang, Y., Yi, D., Kittler, J., Christmas, W., Li, S. Z., & Hospedales, T. (2015). When face recognition meets with deep learning: an evaluation of convolutional neural networks for face recognition. In *Proceedings of the IEEE international conference on computer vision workshops* (pp. 142-150). IEEE. 10.1109/ICCVW.2015.58

Huss, R. (2015). *Biomarkers*. Translational Regenerative Medicine. Retrieved from https://www.sciencedirect.com/science/article/pii/B9780124103962000190

Hyndman, R. J., & Athanasopoulos, G. (2018). *Forecasting: principles and practice*. Otexts.

Iandola, F. N., Han, S., Moskewicz, M. W., Ashraf, K., Dally, W. J., & Keutzer, K. (2016). *Squeezenet: Alexnet-level accuracy with 50x fewer parameters and< 0.5 mb model size*. arXiv preprint arXiv:1602.07360

Iandola, F. N., Han, S., Moskewicz, M. W., Ashraf, K., Dally, W. J., & Keutzer, K. (2016). *SqueezeNet: AlexNet-level accuracy with 50x fewer parameters and< 0.5 MB model size*. arXiv preprint arXiv:1602.07360.

Iandola, F. N., Moskewicz, M. W., Ashraf, K., Han, S., Dally, W. J., & Keutzer, K. (2016). *SqueezeNet: AlexNet-level accuracy with 50x fewer parameters and <1MB model size*. CoRR, abs/1602.07360. Retrieved from http:// arxiv.org/abs/1602.07360

Introduction to Optimization I NEOS. (2018). Retrieved September 23, 2018, from https://neos-guide.org/content/optimization-introduction

Ioffe, S., & Szegedy, C. (2015). *Batch normalization: Accelerating deep network training by reducing internal covariate shift*. arXiv preprint arXiv:1502.03167

Jaderberg, M., Mnih, V., Czarnecki, W. M., Schaul, T., Leibo, J. Z., & Silver, D. … London, D. (2016). *Reinforcement learning with unsupervised auxiliary tasks*. Retrieved from https://youtu.be/Uz-zGYrYEjA

Jain, V., & Learned-Miller, E. (2010). *Fddb: A benchmark for face detection in unconstrained settings* (Tech. Rep. No. UM-CS-2010-009). University of Massachusetts, Amherst.

Jain, A. K., Ross, A., & Prabhakar, S. (2004). An Introduction to Biometric Recognition, IEEE Trasaction. *IEEE Transactions on Circuits and Systems for Video Technology*, *14*(1), 1. doi:10.1109/TCSVT.2003.818349

Janarthanan, T., & Zargari, S. (2017). Feature selection in UNSW-NB15 and KDDCUP'99 datasets. *2017 IEEE 26th International Symposium on Industrial Electronics (ISIE), 2017*.

Jang, Y. (2015). Big Data, Business Analytics, and IoT: The Opportunities and Challenges for Business. *Journal of Information Systems*, *24*(4), 139–152. doi:10.5859/KAIS.2015.24.4.139

Jatsun, S., Savin, S., & Yatsun, A. (2016, June). Improvement of energy consumption for a lower limb exoskeleton through verticalization time optimization. In *Control and Automation (MED), 2016 24th Mediterranean Conference on* (pp. 322-326). IEEE. 10.1109/MED.2016.7535882

Jatsun, S., Savin, S., Lushnikov, B., & Yatsun, A. (2016). Algorithm for motion control of an exoskeleton during verticalization. In *ITM Web of Conferences* (Vol. 6). EDP Sciences. 10.1051/itmconf/20160601001

Jatsun, S., Savin, S., & Yatsun, A. (2016). Parameter optimization for exoskeleton control system using sobol sequences. In *ROMANSY 21-Robot Design, Dynamics and Control* (pp. 361–368). Cham: Springer. doi:10.1007/978-3-319-33714-2_40

Jatsun, S., Savin, S., & Yatsun, A. (2016, August). A Control Strategy for a Lower Limb Exoskeleton with a Toe Joint. In *International Conference on Interactive Collaborative Robotics* (pp. 1-8). Springer. 10.1007/978-3-319-43955-6_1

Jatsun, S., Savin, S., & Yatsun, A. (2016, July). Motion control algorithm for a lower limb exoskeleton based on iterative LQR and ZMP method for trajectory generation. In *International Workshop on Medical and Service Robots* (pp. 305-317). Springer.

Jatsun, S., Savin, S., & Yatsun, A. (2017, August). Walking pattern generation method for an exoskeleton moving on uneven terrain. *Proceedings of the 20th International Conference on Climbing and Walking Robots and Support Technologies for Mobile Machines (CLAWAR 2017)*. 10.1142/9789813231047_0005

Jatsun, S., Savin, S., & Yatsun, A. (2017, September). Footstep Planner Algorithm for a Lower Limb Exoskeleton Climbing Stairs. In *International Conference on Interactive Collaborative Robotics* (pp. 75-82). Springer. 10.1007/978-3-319-66471-2_9

Jatsun, S., Savin, S., Yatsun, A., & Gaponov, I. (2017). Study on a two-staged control of a lower-limb exoskeleton performing standing-up motion from a chair. In *Robot Intelligence Technology and Applications 4* (pp. 113–122). Cham: Springer. doi:10.1007/978-3-319-31293-4_10

Jha, D., & Kwon, G. (2017). Alzheimer's Disease Detection Using Sparse Autoencoder, Scale Conjugate Gradient and Softmax Output Layer with Fine Tuning. *International Journal Of Machine Learning And Computing*, *7*(1), 13–17. doi:10.18178/ijmlc.2017.7.1.612

Jia, Y., & Shelhamer, E. (2015). *Caffe model zoo*. Academic Press.

Jia, Y., Evan, S., Donahue, J., Karayev, S., Long, J., Girshick, R., & Darrell, T. (2014). *Caffe: Convolutional architecture for fast feature embedding*. arXiv preprint arXiv:1408.5093

Jidiga, G. R., & Sammulal, P. (2014) Anomaly detection using machine learning with a case study. *2014 IEEE International Conference on Advanced Communication, Control and Computing Technologies*.

Jose, S., Malathi, D., Reddy, B. & Jayaseeli, D. (2018). A survey on anomaly based host intrusion detection system. *Journal of Physics, Conference Series, 1000.*

Juneja, P., & Kashyap, R. (2016). Energy based methods for medical image segmentation. *International Journal of Computers and Applications*, *146*(6), 22–27. doi:10.5120/ijca2016910808

Juneja, P., & Kashyap, R. (2016). Optimal approach for CT image segmentation using improved energy based method. *International Journal of Control Theory and Applications*, *9*(41), 599–608.

Kajita, S., Kanehiro, F., Kaneko, K., Fujiwara, K., Yokoi, K., & Hirukawa, H. (2002). A realtime pattern generator for biped walking. In *Robotics and Automation, 2002. Proceedings. ICRA'02. IEEE International Conference on* (Vol. 1, pp. 31-37). IEEE. 10.1109/ROBOT.2002.1013335

Kajita, S., Kanehiro, F., Kaneko, K., Yokoi, K., & Hirukawa, H. (2001). The 3D Linear Inverted Pendulum Mode: A simple modeling for a biped walking pattern generation. In *Intelligent Robots and Systems, 2001. Proceedings. 2001 IEEE/RSJ International Conference on* (Vol. 1, pp. 239-246). IEEE.

Kajita, S., Kanehiro, F., Kaneko, K., Fujiwara, K., Harada, K., Yokoi, K., & Hirukawa, H. (2003, September). *Biped walking pattern generation by using preview control of zero-moment point* (Vol. 3, pp. 1620–1626). ICRA. doi:10.1109/ROBOT.2003.1241826

Kanoulas, D., Stumpf, A., Raghavan, V. S., Zhou, C., Toumpa, A., von Stryk, O., . . . Tsagarakis, N. G. (2018, February). Footstep Planning in Rough Terrain for Bipedal Robots using Curved Contact Patches. In *Robotics and Automation (ICRA), 2018 IEEE International Conference on* (pp. 108-113). IEEE.

Kapur, P. K., Khatri, S. K., & Goswami, D. N. (2008) 'A generalized dynamic integrated software reliability growth model based on neural-network approach', *Proceedings of International Conference on Reliability, Safety and Quality Engineering*, pp.831–838.

Karayilan & Kilic. (2017). Prediction of Heart Disease Using Neural Network. In *2nd International conference on Computer Science & Engineering (UBMK'17)*. Department of Computer Engineering Yildirim Beyazit University. doi:10.1109/CVPR.2015.7299117

Karpathy, A. (2016). Cs231n convolutional neural networks for visual recognition. *Neural Networks*, 1.

Karunanithi, N., Whitley, D., & Malaiya, Y. K. (1992). Using neural networks in reliability prediction. *Software, IEEE*, *9*(4), 53–59. doi:10.1109/52.143107

Kashyap, R., & Piersson, A. (2018). Big Data Challenges and Solutions in the Medical Industries. In Handbook of Research on Pattern Engineering System Development for Big Data Analytics. IGI Global. doi:10.4018/978-1-5225-3870-7.ch001

Kashyap, R., & Gautam, P. (2016). Fast level set method for segmentation of medical images. In *Proceedings of the International Conference on Informatics and Analytics (ICIA-16)*. ACM. 10.1145/2980258.2980302

Kashyap, R., & Tiwari, V. (2017). Energy-based active contour method for image segmentation. *International Journal of Electronic Healthcare*, *9*(2–3), 210–225. doi:10.1504/IJEH.2017.083165

Kashyap, R., & Tiwari, V. (2018). Active contours using global models for medical image segmentation. *International Journal of Computational Systems Engineering*, *4*(2/3), 195. doi:10.1504/IJCSYSE.2018.091404

Kemelmacher-Shlizerman, I., Seitz, S. M., Miller, D., & Brossard, E. (2016). The Megaface benchmark: 1 million faces for recognition at scale. In *Proceedings of the IEEE conference on computer vision and pattern recognition* (pp. 4873–4882). IEEE. 10.1109/CVPR.2016.527

Keretna, S., Hossny, A. H., & Creighton, D. (2013). Recognize User Identity in Twitter Social Networks via Text Mining. *IEEE International Conference on Systems, Man, and Cybernetics*, Manchester, UK. 10.1109/SMC.2013.525

Khoshgoftaar, T. M., Ganesan, K., Allen, E. B., Ross, F. D., Munikoti, R., Goel, N., & Nandi, A. (1997b). Predicting fault-prone modules with case-based reasoning. *Proceedings of Software Reliability Engineering, The Eighth International Symposium on IEEE*, 27–35. 10.1109/ISSRE.1997.630845

Khoshgoftaar, T. M., Shan, R. M., & Allen, E. B. (2000). Improving tree-based models of software quality with principal components analysis. *Proceedings of Software Engineering Reliability Engineering, ISSRE 2000 of 11th International Symposium on IEEE*, 198–209. 10.1109/ISSRE.2000.885872

Khoshgoftaar¸, T. M., & Seliya, N. (2002). Software quality classification modeling using the SPRINT decision tree algorithm. *International Journal of Artificial Intelligence Tools*, *12*(3), 207–225. doi:10.1142/S0218213003001204

Khoshgoftaar, T. M., Allen, E. B., Halstead, R., Trio, G. P., & Flass, R. (1997a). Process measures for predicting software quality. *Proceedings of High-Assurance Systems Engineering Workshop, Proceedings on IEEE*, 155–160.

Khoshgoftaar, T. M., & Seliya, N. (2002). Tree-based software quality estimation models for fault prediction. *Proceedings of Software Metrics of Eighth IEEE Symposium*, 203–214. 10.1109/METRIC.2002.1011339

Khoshgoftaar, T. M., Seliya, N., & Sundaresh, N. (2006). An empirical study of predicting software fault with case-based reasoning. *Proceedings of Software Quality Journal*, *14*(2), 85–111.

Kim, D., Jeong, Y., & Kim, S. (2017). Data-Filtering System to Avoid Total Data Distortion in IoT Networking. *Symmetry*, *9*(1), 16. doi:10.3390ym9010016

Kindermans, P-J, Schutt, K-T, Alber, M, Muller, K-R, Erhan, D., Kim, B., & Dahne, S. (2017). *Learning how to explain neural networks: PatternNet and PatternAttribution*. Academic Press.

Kingma, D. P., & Ba, J. (2014). *Adam: A method for stochastic optimization*. arXiv preprint arXiv:1412.6980

Kingma, D. P., & Ba, J. (2014). *Adam: A method for stochastic optimization*. ArXiv Preprint ArXiv:1412.6980

Kingma, D. P., & Ba, J. (2014). *Adam: A Method for Stochastic Optimization*. Retrieved from http://arxiv.org/abs/1412.6980

Klein, B., Wolf, L., & Afek, Y. (2015). A Dynamic Convolutional Layer for short range weather prediction. *2015 IEEE Conference on Computer Vision and Pattern Recognition (CVPR)*.

Koakutsu, S. (2018). Deep Learning - Current Situation and Expectation of Deep Learning and IoT. *The Journal Of The Institute Of Electrical Engineers Of Japan*, *138*(5), 270–271. doi:10.1541/ieejjournal.138.270

Kober, J., Bagnell, J. A., & Peters, J. (2013). Reinforcement learning in robotics: A survey. *The International Journal of Robotics Research, 32*(11), 1238–1274. doi:10.1177/0278364913495721

Kolosnjaji, B., Zarras, A., Webster, G., & Eckert, C. (2016). Deep Learning for Classification of Malware System Call Sequences. In B. H. Kang, & Q. Bai (Eds.), *Australasian Joint Conference on Artificial Intelligence* (pp. 137–149). Cham: Springer International Publishing. 10.1007/978-3-319-50127-7_11

Kononenko, I., & Kukar, M. (2007). *Machine learning and data mining: Introduction to principles and algorithms.* Horwood Publishing. doi:10.1533/9780857099440

Kontschieder, P., Fiterau, M., Criminisi, A., & Rota Bulo, S. (2015). Deep neural decision forests. In *Proceedings of the IEEE international conference on computer vision* (pp. 1467-1475). IEEE.

Korolev, S., Safiullin, A., Belyaev, M., & Dodonova, Y. (2017). Residual and plain convolutional neural networks for 3D brain MRI classification. *2017 IEEE 14th International Symposium on Biomedical Imaging (ISBI 2017).* doi:10.1109/isbi.2017.7950647

Kotseruba, I., & Tsotsos, J. K. (n.d.). 40 years of cognitive architectures: core cognitive abilities and practical applications. *Artificial Intelligence Review*, 1-78.

Koutnik, J., Greff, K., Gomez, F., & Schmidhuber, J. (2014). *A clockwork rnn.* ArXiv Preprint ArXiv:1402.3511

Krishnan, S. (2018). How Big Data Can Help in Treating Alzheimer's Disease. *Analytics Insight.* Available at: https://www.analyticsinsight.net/big-data-can-help-treating-alzheimers-disease/

Krizhevsky, A., Sutskever, I., & Hinton, G. E. (2012). Imagenet classification with deep convolutional neural networks. In Advances in neural information processing systems (pp. 1097-1105). Academic Press.

Krizhevsky, A., Sutskever, I., & Hinton, G. E. (2012). ImageNet classification with deep convolutional neural networks. In F. Pereira, C. J. C. Burges, L. Bottou, & K. Q. Weinberger (Eds.), *Advances in neural information processing systems 25* (pp. 1097–1105). Curran Associates, Inc. Retrieved from http://papers.nips.cc/paper/4824-imagenet-classification -with-deep-convolutional-neural-networks.pdf

Krizhevsky, A., Sutskever, I., & Hinton, G. E. (2012). ImageNet Classification with Deep Convolutional Neural Networks. In F. Pereira, C. J. C. Burges, L. Bottou, & K. Q. Weinberger (Eds.), Advances in Neural Information Processing Systems (Vol. 25, pp. 1097–1105). Curran Associates, Inc. Retrieved from http://papers.nips.cc/paper/4824-imagenet-classification-with-deep-convolutional-neural-networks.pdf

Ksiezopolski, B. (2012). QoP-ML: Quality of protection modelling language for cryptographic protocols. *Computers & Security, 31*(4), 569–596. doi:10.1016/j.cose.2012.01.006

Kuindersma, S., Permenter, F., & Tedrake, R. (2014, May). An efficiently solvable quadratic program for stabilizing dynamic locomotion. In *Robotics and Automation (ICRA), 2014 IEEE International Conference on* (pp. 2589-2594). IEEE. 10.1109/ICRA.2014.6907230

Kuindersma, S., Deits, R., Fallon, M., Valenzuela, A., Dai, H., Permenter, F., ... Tedrake, R. (2016). Optimization-based locomotion planning, estimation, and control design for the Atlas humanoid robot. *Autonomous Robots*, *40*(3), 429–455. doi:10.100710514-015-9479-3

Kumar, B. P. V., & Venkatarm, P. (2002). Prediction-based location management using multilayer neural networks. *Journal of the Indian Institute of Science*, *82*, 7.

Lachdhaf, S., Mazouzi, M., & Abid, M. (2018). Secured AODV Routing Protocol for the Detection and Prevention of Black Hole Attack in VANET. *Advanced Computing: An International Journal, 9*(1), 1-14. doi:10.5121/acij.2018.9101

Lake, B. M., Salakhutdinov, R., & Tenenbaum, J. B. (2015). Human-level concept learning through probabilistic program induction. *Science*, *350*(6266), 1332–1338. doi:10.1126cience.aab3050 PMID:26659050

Lang, K. J., Waibel, A. H., & Hinton, G. E. (1990). A time-delay neural network architecture for isolated word recognition. *Neural Networks*, *3*(1), 23–43. doi:10.1016/0893-6080(90)90044-L

Lapuschkin, S., Binder, A., Mller, K.-R., & Samek, W. (2017). *Understanding and comparing deep neural networks for age and gender classification*. Retrieved from https://arxiv.org/abs/1708.07689

LaValle, S. M. (1998). *Rapidly-exploring random trees: A new tool for path planning*. Academic Press.

LaValle, S. M., & Kuffner Jr, J. J. (2000). *Rapidly-exploring random trees: Progress and prospects*. Academic Press.

Lazuardia, L., Sanjaya, G. Y., Candradewi, I., & Holmner, A. (2013). Automatic Platelets Counter for Supporting Dengue Case Detection in Primary Health Care. *Studies in Health Technology and Informatics*, *192*. PMID:23920623

Le, Q. V., Jaitly, N., & Hinton, G. E. (2015). *A simple way to initialize recurrent networks of rectified linear units*. ArXiv Preprint ArXiv:1504.00941

LeCun, Y., Bengio, Y., & Hinton, G. (2015). Deep learning. *Nature*, *521*(7553), 436–444. doi:10.1038/nature14539 PMID:26017442

LeCun, Y., Bottou, L., Bengio, Y., & Haffner, P. (1998). Gradient-based learning applied to document recognition. *Proceedings of the IEEE*, *86*(11), 2278–2324. doi:10.1109/5.726791

Lee, I., & Lee, K. (2015). The Internet of Things (IoT): Applications, investments, and challenges for enterprises. *Business Horizons*, *58*(4), 431–440. doi:10.1016/j.bushor.2015.03.008

Lee, Y. C., Chen, J., Tseng, C. W., & Lai, S. H. (2016, September). Accurate and robust face recognition from RGB-D images with a deep learning approach. BMVC. doi:10.5244/C.30.123

LeWitt, P. A., Li, J., Lu, M., & the Parkinson Study Group-DATATOP Investigators. (2017). *Metabolomic biomarkers as strong correlates of Parkinson disease progression*. Retrieved from http://http://www.neurology.org/content/early/2017/02/08/WNL.0000000000003663.short

Li, H., Wei, T., Ren, A., Zhu, Q., & Wang, Y. (n.d.). *Deep Reinforcement Learning: Framework, Applications, and Embedded Implementations Invited Paper.* Retrieved from https://arxiv.org/pdf/1710.03792.pdf

Li, Y. (2017). *Deep Reinforcement Learning: An Overview.* Academic Press. doi:10.1007/978-3-319-56991-8_32

Liao, Y., Kodagoda, S., Wang, Y., Shi, L., & Liu, Y. (2016, May). Understand scene categories by objects: A semantic regularized scene classifier using convolutional neural networks. In *Robotics and Automation (ICRA), 2016 IEEE International Conference on* (pp. 2318-2325). IEEE.

Li, H., Ota, K., & Dong, M. (2018). Learning IoT in Edge: Deep Learning for the Internet of Things with Edge Computing. *IEEE Network, 32*(1), 96–101. doi:10.1109/MNET.2018.1700202

Li, J., Sun, L., Yan, Q., Li, Z., Srisa-an, W., & Ye, H. (2018). Significant Permission Identification for Machine Learning Based Android Malware Detection. *IEEE Transactions on Industrial Informatics.*

Lin, M., Chen, Q., & Yan, S. (2013). *Network in network.* arXiv preprint arXiv:1312.4400

Lin, M., Chen, Q., & Yan, S. (2013). *Network in network.* CoRR, abs/1312.4400. Retrieved from http://arxiv.org/abs/1312.4400

Lin, L., Zhong, S., Jia, C., & Chen, K. (2017). Insider threat detection based on deep belief network feature representation. *2017 International Conference on Green Informatics (ICGI).* 10.1109/ICGI.2017.37

Liu, J., Deng, Y., Bai, T., Wei, Z., & Huang, C. (2015). *Targeting ultimate accuracy: Face recognition via deep embedding.* arXiv preprint arXiv:1506.07310

Liua, W., Wang, Z., Liua, X., Zeng, N., Liu, Y., & Alsaad, F. E. (2017). A survey on deep neural network architectures and their applications. *Neurocomputing, 234,* 11-26.

Liu, F., Zhu, R., Zeng, D., Zhao, Q., & Liu, X. (2018, March). Disentangling features in 3D face shapes for joint face reconstruction and recognition. In *Proceedings of the IEEE Conference on Computer Vision and Pattern Recognition* (pp. 5216-5225). IEEE. 10.1109/CVPR.2018.00547

Liu, W., Wen, Y., Yu, Z., Li, M., Raj, B., & Song, L. (2017, July). Sphereface: Deep hypersphere embedding for face recognition. In *The IEEE Conference on Computer Vision and Pattern Recognition (CVPR)* (Vol. 1, p. 1). IEEE. 10.1109/CVPR.2017.713

Liu, X., & Chen, K. (2018). Teresa Wu, David Weidman, Fleming Lure, & Jing Li, Use of multi-modality imaging and artificial intelligence for diagnosis and prognosis of early stages of alzheimer's disease. *Translational Research; the Journal of Laboratory and Clinical Medicine.* doi:10.1016/j.trsl.2018.01.001

Long, X., Chen, L., Jiang, C., & Zhang, L. (2017). Prediction and classification of Alzheimer disease based on quantification of MRI deformation. *PLoS One, 12*(3), e0173372. doi:10.1371/journal.pone.0173372 PMID:28264071

Lu, D., Popuri, K., Ding, G. W., Balachandar, R., & Beg, M. F. (2018). Multimodal and Multiscale Deep Neural Networks for the Early Diagnosis of Alzheimer's Disease using structural MR and FDG-PET images. *Scientific Reports*, *8*(1). doi:10.103841598-018-22871-z PMID:29632364

MacGill, M. (2018, February 13). *Alzheimer's disease: Symptoms, stages, causes, and treatment*. Retrieved from https://www.medicalnewstoday.com/articles/159442.php

Maitra, M., Gupta, R. K., & Mukherjee, M. (2012). Detection and Counting of Red Blood Cells in Blood Cell Images using Hough Transform. *International Journal of Computers and Applications*, *53*(16).

Malaiya, R. K., Kwon, D., Kim, J., Suh, S. C., Kim, H., & Kim, I. (2018) An empirical evaluation of deep learning for network anomaly detection. *2018 International Conference on Computing, Networking and Communications (ICNC)*. 10.1109/ICCNC.2018.8390278

Martens, J. (2010). Deep learning via Hessian-free optimization. ICML, 27, 735–742.

Masi, I., Tran, A., Hassner, T., Leksut, J. T., & Medioni, G. (2016). Do We Really Need to Collect Millions of Faces for Effective Face Recognition? *European conference on computer vision*. 10.1007/978-3-319-46454-1_35

Mason, S., Righetti, L., & Schaal, S. (2014, November). Full dynamics LQR control of a humanoid robot: An experimental study on balancing and squatting. In *Humanoid Robots (Humanoids), 2014 14th IEEE-RAS International Conference on* (pp. 374-379). IEEE.

Mason, S., Rotella, N., Schaal, S., & Righetti, L. (2017). *A MPC Walking Framework With External Contact Forces*. arXiv preprint arXiv:1712.09308

Mathew, P. S., & Pillai, A. S. (2015). Big Data solutions in Healthcare: Problems and perspectives. *2015 International Conference on Innovations in Information, Embedded and Communication Systems (ICIIECS)*. 10.1109/ICIIECS.2015.7193211

Mathew, P. S., & Pillai, A. S. (2016). Big Data Challenges and Solutions in Healthcare: A Survey. In V. Snášel, A. Abraham, P. Krömer, M. Pant, & A. Muda (Eds.), *Innovations in Bio-Inspired Computing and Applications. Advances in Intelligent Systems and Computing* (Vol. 424). Cham: Springer. doi:10.1007/978-3-319-28031-8_48

Maudsley, S., Devanarayan, V., Martin, B., & Geerts, H. (2018). Intelligent and effective informatic deconvolution of "Big Data" and its future impact on the quantitative nature of neurodegenerative disease therapy. *Alzheimer's & Dementia*, *14*(7), 961–975. doi:10.1016/j.jalz.2018.01.014 PMID:29551332

Mazzei, D., Baldi, G., Montelisciani, G., & Fantoni, G. (2018). A full stack for quick prototyping of IoT solutions. *Annales des Télécommunications*, *73*(7-8), 439–449. doi:10.100712243-018-0644-5

McGue, M., & Thomas, J. (1984). Adjustment of twin data for the effects of age and sex. *Behavior Genetics*, *14*(4), 325–343. doi:10.1007/BF01080045 PMID:6542356

Meng, X., Shan, Z., Liu, F., Zhao, B., Han, J., Wang, H., & Wang, J. (2017). MCSMGS: Malware Classification Model Based on Deep Learning. *2017 International Conference on Cyber-Enabled Distributed Computing and Knowledge Discovery (CyberC)*, 272–275. 10.1109/CyberC.2017.21

Microsoft Corporation, . (2013). *Recent Advances in Deep Learning for Speech Research At Microsoft.* Author.

Miller, T. (2019). Explanation in artificial intelligence: Insights from the social sciences Author links open overlay panel. *Artificial Intelligence, 267*, 1–38. doi:10.1016/j.artint.2018.07.007

Mimura, M., Sakai, S., & Kawahara, T. (2015). Deep autoencoders augmented with phone-class feature for reverberant speech recognition. *ICASSP, IEEE Int. Conf. Acoust. Speech Signal Process. - Proc.*, 4365–4369.

Min, S., Lee, B., & Yoon, S. (2017). Deep learning in bioinformatics. *Briefings in Bioinformatics, 18*(5), 851–869. PMID:27473064

Miotto, R., Wang, F., Wang, S., Jiang, X., & Dudley, J. T. (2017). Deep learning for healthcare: Review, opportunities and challenges. *Briefings in Bioinformatics*, 1–11. PMID:28481991

Mirowski, P., Pascanu, R., Viola, F., Soyer, H., Ballard, A., Banino, A., … Hadsell, R. (2016, November 4). *Learning to Navigate in Complex Environments.* Retrieved from https://openreview.net/forum?id=SJMGPrcle

Mishkin, D., Sergievskiy, N., & Matas, J. (2017). Systematic evaluation of convolution neural network advances on the imagenet. *Computer Vision and Image Understanding, 161*, 11–19. doi:10.1016/j.cviu.2017.05.007

Mittal, H., Bhatia, P., & Goswami, P. (2008). Software quality assessment based on fuzzy logic technique. *International Journal of Soft Computing Applications, 1*(3), 105–112.

Mnih, V., Kavukcuoglu, K., Silver, D., Rusu, A. A., Veness, J., Bellemare, M. G., ... Hassabis, D. (2015). Human-level control through deep reinforcement learning. *Nature, 518*(7540), 529–533. doi:10.1038/nature14236 PMID:25719670

Mohri, M., Rostamizadeh, A. & Talwalkar, A. (n.d.). *Foundations of Machine Learning.* Academic Press.

Moohebbi, A., Aradottir, T. B., Johansen, A. R., Bengtsson, H., Fraccaro, M., & Morup, M. (2017). A deep learning approach to adherence detection for type 2 diabetics. *Conference Proceedings; ... Annual International Conference of the IEEE Engineering in Medicine and Biology Society. IEEE Engineering in Medicine and Biology Society. Conference.*

Moon, M. (2017, September 17). *AI can detect Alzheimer's 10 years before symptoms show up.* Retrieved from https://www.engadget.com/2017/09/17/ai-alzheimers-early-detection/

Moors, P., Boelens, D., Overwalle, J. V. & Wagemans, J. (2016). *Scene Integration without Awareness: No Conclusive Evidence for Processing Scene Congruency during Continuous Flash Suppression.* Academic Press.

Moustafa, N. & Slay, J. (2016). The evaluation of Network Anomaly Detection Systems: Statsistical Analysis of the UNSW-NB15 dataset and the comparison with the KDD99 Data set. *Information Security Journal A Global Perspective, 2016.*

Moustafa, N., & Slay, J. (2015). The significant features of the UNSW-NB15 and the KDD99 data sets for network intrusion detection systems. *2015 4th International Workshop on Building Analysis Datasets and Gathering Experience Returns for Security (BADGERS).*

Nair, V., & Hinton, G. E. (2010). Rectified linear units improve restricted boltzmann machines. *Proceedings of the 27th International Conference on Machine Learning (ICML-10)*, 807–814.

Narasimhan, K. R., Yala, A., & Barzilay, R. (2016). Improving Information Extraction by Acquiring External Evidence with Reinforcement Learning. *Narasimhan.* Retrieved from https://dspace.mit.edu/handle/1721.1/105337

Narayanan, V. K., Kirpal, A., & Karampatziakis, N. (2015). Anomaly detection – Using machine learning to detect abnormalities in time series data. *Modata.* Retrieved from: https://www.mo-data.com/anomaly-detection-using-machine-learning-to-detect-abnormalities-in-time-series-data/

Nataraj, L., Karthikeyan, S., Jacob, G., & Manjunath, B. S. (2011). Malware Images: Visualization and Automatic Classification. In *Proceedings of the 8th International Symposium on Visualization for Cyber Security* (p. 4:1--4:7). New York: ACM. 10.1145/2016904.2016908

Nataraj, L., Karthikeyan, S., & Manjunath, B. S. (2015). SATTVA: SpArsiTy inspired classificaTion of malware VAriants. In *Proceedings of the 3rd ACM Workshop on Information Hiding and Multimedia Security* (pp. 135-140). ACM. 10.1145/2756601.2756616

Nene, S. A., & Nayar, S. K. (1997). A simple algorithm for nearest neighbor search in high dimensions. *IEEE Transactions on Pattern Analysis and Machine Intelligence, 19*(9), 989–1003. doi:10.1109/34.615448

Ng, H. W., & Winkler, S. (2014, Oct). A data-driven approach to cleaning large face datasets. In *2014 IEEE international conference on image processing (ICIP)* (pp. 343-347). IEEE.

Ning, K., Chen, B., Sun, F., Hobel, Z., Zhao, L., Matloff, W., & Toga, A. W. (2018). Classifying Alzheimers disease with brain imaging and genetic data using a neural network framework. *Neurobiology of Aging, 68*, 151–158. doi:10.1016/j.neurobiolaging.2018.04.009 PMID:29784544

O'Meara, Schlag, & Wickler. (2018). *Applications of Deep Learning Neural Networks to Satellite Telemetry Monitoring.* SpaceOps Conference, Marseillef, France.

O'Shaughnessy, D. (1987). *Speech Communication.* Reading, MA: Addison-Wesley.

Oliva, A., & Torralba, A. (2001). Modeling the Shape of the Scene: A Holistic Representation of the Spatial Envelope. *International Journal of Computer Vision, 42*(3), 145–175. doi:10.1023/A:1011139631724

OPENCV. (n.d.). *Face detection using HAAR cascades.* Retrieved from https:// docs.opencv.org/3.4.1/ d7/d8b/tutorial_py_face detection.html

Ozaki, T. J. (2015). Machine learning for package users with r(5): Random forest. *Hatena Blog.* Retrieved from: https://tjo-en.hatenablog.com/entry/2015/06/04/190000

Palaz, D., Magimai-Doss, M., & Collobert, R. (2015). *Analysis of CNN-based speech recognition system using raw speech as input.* Retrieved from: https://ronan.collobert.com/pub/matos/2015_cnnspeech_interspeech.pdf

Panovko, G. Y., Savin, S. I., Yatsun, S. F., & Yatsun, A. S. (2016). Simulation of exoskeleton sit-to-stand movement. *Journal of Machinery Manufacture and Reliability, 45*(3), 206–210. doi:10.3103/ S1052618816030110

Parisi, S., Pirotta, M., & Restelli, M. (2016). Multi-objective Reinforcement Learning through Continuous Pareto Manifold Approximation. *Journal of Artificial Intelligence Research, 57.* Retrieved from https:// core.ac.uk/download/pdf/74313357.pdf

Parkhi, O. M., Vedaldi, A., & Zisserman, A. (2015). *Deep face recognition.* Retrieved from https://www. robots.ox.ac.uk/~vgg/publications/2015/Parkhi15/parkhi15.pdf

Parkhi, O. M., Vedaldi, A., & Zisserman, A. (2015, September). Deep face recognition. In BMVC (Vol. 1, No. 3, p. 6). Academic Press. doi:10.5244/C.29.41

Pascanu, R., Mikolov, T., & Bengio, Y. (2013). On the difficulty of training recurrent neural networks. *International Conference on Machine Learning,* 1310–1318.

Pattarakavin, T., & Chongstitvatana, P. (2016) Detection of machine anomaly from log files in hard disk manufacturing process. *2016 International conference on Multimedia systems and Signal Processing.* 10.1109/ICMSSP.2016.022

Paul, J., Baker, H. M., & Cochran, J. D. (2012). Effect of Online Social Networking on Student Academic Performance. *Computers in Human Behavior, 28*(6), 2117–2127. doi:10.1016/j.chb.2012.06.016

Payan, A., & Montana, G. (2015). *Predicting Alzheimer's disease: a neuroimaging study with 3D convolutional neural networks.* ICPRAM.

Perez, L., & Wang, J. (2017). *The effectiveness of data augmentation in image classification using deep learning.* arXiv preprint arXiv:1712.04621

Pironkov, G., Dupont, S., & Dutoit, T. (2017). Investigating the impact of the training data volume for robust speech recognition using multi-task learning. *2017 IEEE International Symposium on Signal Processing and Information Technology (ISSPIT).* 10.1109/ISSPIT.2017.8388673

Pizzi, N. J., Summers, R., & Pedrycz, W. (2002). Software quality prediction using median-adjusted class labels. *Proceedings of International Joint Conference on Neural Networks, 3,* 2405–2409.

Poornima, J., & Krishnaveni, K. (2016). Detection of Dengue Fever with Platelets Count using Image Processing Technique. *Indian Journal of Science and Technology, 9*(19), 1–7. doi:10.17485/ijst/2016/v9i19/93852

Pore, Y.N., & Kalshetty, Y.R. (2014). Review on Blood Cell Image Segmentation and Counting. *International Journal of Application or Innovation in Engineering & Management, 3*(11).

Puri, A., & Singh, H. (2014). Genetic algorithm based approach for finding faulty modules in open source software systems. *International Journal of Computer Science & Engineering Survey, 5*(3), 29–40.

Qiao, S., Liu, C., Shen, W., & Yuille, A. L. (2018). Few-shot image recognition by predicting parameters from activations. In *Proceedings of the IEEE Conference on Computer Vision and Pattern Recognition* (pp. 7229-7238). IEEE. 10.1109/CVPR.2018.00755

Rachmadi, M.F., Hernández, M.D., Agan, M.L., Perri, C.D., & Komura, T. (2018). Segmentation of white matter hyperintensities using convolutional neural networks with global spatial information in routine clinical brain MRI with none or mild vascular pathology. *Computerized Medical Imaging and Graphics, 66*, 28-43.

Radliński, L. (2011). A conceptual Bayesian net model for integrated software quality prediction. *Annales UMCS Informatica, 11*(4), 49–60.

Ranjan, R., Patel, V. M., & Chellappa, R. (2017). Hyperface: A deep multi-task learning framework for face detection, landmark localization, pose estimation, and gender recognition. *IEEE Transactions on Pattern Analysis and Machine Intelligence*. PMID:29990235

Rashid, E., Bhattacherjee, V., & Patnaik, S. (2012). The application of case-based reasoning to estimation of software development effort. *International Journal of Computer Science and Informatics, 1*(3), 29–34.

Rashid, E., Patnaik, S., & Bhattacherjee, V. (2012). Software quality estimation using machine learning: case-based reasoning technique. *International Journal of Computer Applications, 58*(14), 43–48.

Ravi, D., Wong, C., Deligianni, F., Berthelot, M., Andreu-Perez, J., Lo, B., & Yang, G.-Z. (2016).. . *Deep Learning for Health Informatics, 21*(1), 4–21.

Rayner, M. (2011). The curriculum for children with severe and profound learning difficulties at Stephen Hawking School. *Support for Learning, 26*(1), 25–32. doi:10.1111/j.1467-9604.2010.01471.x

Razzak, M. I., Naz, S., & Zaib, A. (2017). Deep Learning for Medical Image Processing: Overview, Challenges and the Future. *Lecture Notes in Computational Vision and Biomechanics Classification in BioApps*, 323-350. doi:10.1007/978-3-319-65981-7_12

Reddi, S. J., Kale, S., & Kumar, S. (2018). *On the convergence of adam and beyond*. Academic Press.

Redmon, J., & Angelova, A. (2015, May). Real-time grasp detection using convolutional neural networks. In *Robotics and Automation (ICRA), 2015 IEEE International Conference on* (pp. 1316-1322). IEEE. 10.1109/ICRA.2015.7139361

Reinforcement learning explained - O'Reilly Media. (2016). Retrieved September 23, 2018, from https://www.oreilly.com/ideas/reinforcement-learning-explained

Rhode, M., Burnap, P., & Jones, K. (2017). *Early-Stage Malware Prediction Using Recurrent Neural Networks.* ArXiv Preprint ArXiv:1708.03513

Rieck, K., Holz, T., Willems, C., Düssel, P., & Laskov, P. (2008). Learning and classification of malware behavior. In D. Zamboni (Ed.), *International Conference on Detection of Intrusions and Malware, and Vulnerability Assessment* (pp. 108–125). Berlin: Springer Berlin Heidelberg. 10.1007/978-3-540-70542-0_6

Robinson, T., & Fallside, F. (1991). A recurrent error propagation network speech recognition system. *Computer Speech & Language*, *5*(3), 259–274. doi:10.1016/0885-2308(91)90010-N

Robinson, T., Hochberg, M., & Renals, S. (1996). The Use of Recurrent Neural Networks in Continuous Speech Recognition BT - Automatic Speech and Speaker Recognition: Advanced Topics. Boston, MA: Springer US. doi:10.1007/978-1-4613-1367-0_10

Roediger, H. L. III, & Smith, M. A. (2012). The "pure-study" learning curve: The learning curve without cumulative testing. *Memory & Cognition*, *40*(7), 989–1002. doi:10.375813421-012-0213-5 PMID:22644774

Roh, Y., Kim, J., Son, J., & Kim, M. (2011). Efficient construction of histograms for multidimensional data using quad-trees. *Decision Support Systems*, *52*(1), 82–94. doi:10.1016/j.dss.2011.05.006

Ronen, R., Radu, M., Feuerstein, C., & Yom-tov, E. (n.d.). *Microsoft Malware Classification Challenge*. Academic Press. doi:10.1145/2857705.2857713

Rosales, J. H., Jaime, K., & Ramos, F. (2013). An emotional regulation model with memories for virtual agents. In *Proceedings of the 12th IEEE International Conference on Cognitive Informatics & Cognitive Computing (ICCI*CC'2013)*. IEEE. 10.1109/ICCI-CC.2013.6622253

Rosenblatt, F. (1958). The perceptron: A probabilistic model for information storage and organization in the brain. *Psychological Review*, *1958*, 65–386. PMID:13602029

Russakovsky, O., Deng, J., Su, H., Krause, J., Satheesh, S., Ma, S., ... Fei-Fei, L. (2015). ImageNet large scale visual recognition challenge. *International Journal of Computer Vision*, *115*(3), 211–252. doi:10.100711263-015-0816-y

Sabe, K., Fukuchi, M., Gutmann, J. S., Ohashi, T., Kawamoto, K., & Yoshigahara, T. (2004, April). Obstacle avoidance and path planning for humanoid robots using stereo vision. In *Robotics and Automation, 2004. Proceedings. ICRA'04. 2004 IEEE International Conference on* (Vol. 1, pp. 592-597). IEEE. 10.1109/ROBOT.2004.1307213

Sahidullah, M., & Saha, G. (2012). Design, analysis and experimental evaluation of block based transformation in MFCC computation for speaker recognition. *Speech Communication*, *54*(4), 543–565. doi:10.1016/j.specom.2011.11.004

Saon, G., & Picheny, M. (2017). Recent advances in conversational speech recognition using convolutional and recurrent neural networks. *IBM Journal of Research and Development, 61*(4/5), 1:1–1:10. doi:10.1147/JRD.2017.2701178

Savin, S. (2017, June). An algorithm for generating convex obstacle-free regions based on stereographic projection. In *Control and Communications (SIBCON), 2017 International Siberian Conference on* (pp. 1-6). IEEE. 10.1109/SIBCON.2017.7998590

Savin, S. (2018). *Neural Network-based Reaction Estimator for Walking Robots*. Academic Press.

Savin, S. (2018). *Parameter Optimization for Walking Patterns and the Geometry of In-Pipe Robots*. Academic Press.

Savin, S., & Vorochaeva, L. (2017, June). Footstep planning for a six-legged in-pipe robot moving in spatially curved pipes. In *Control and Communications (SIBCON), 2017 International Siberian Conference on* (pp. 1-6). IEEE. 10.1109/SIBCON.2017.7998581

Savin, S., Jatsun, S., & Vorochaeva, L. (2017). Trajectory generation for a walking in-pipe robot moving through spatially curved pipes. In *MATEC Web of Conferences* (Vol. 113, p. 02016). EDP Sciences. 10.1051/matecconf/201711302016

Savin, S., Jatsun, S., & Vorochaeva, L. (2017, November). Modification of Constrained LQR for Control of Walking in-pipe Robots. In Dynamics of Systems, Mechanisms and Machines (Dynamics), 2017 (pp. 1-6). IEEE. doi:10.1109/Dynamics.2017.8239502

Savin, S., & Vorochaeva, L. Y. (2017). Nested Quadratic Programming-based Controller for In-pipe Robots. *Proceedings of the International Conference On Industrial Engineering 2017.*

Savran, A., Alyüz, N., Dibeklioğlu, H., Çeliktutan, O., Gökberk, B., Sankur, B., & Akarun, L. (2008, May). Bosphorus database for 3D face analysis. In *European Workshop on Biometrics and Identity Management* (pp. 47-56). Springer. 10.1007/978-3-540-89991-4_6

Saxe, A. M., McClelland, J. L., & Ganguli, S. (2013). *Malware Analysis of Imaged Binary Samples by Convolutional Neural Network with Attention Mechanism*. Academic Press.

Schafer, R. W., & Markel, J. D. (Eds.). (1979). Speech Analysis. New York: IEEE Press.

Schmidhuber, J. (2015). Deep learning in neural networks: An overview. *Neural Networks, 61*, 85–117. doi:10.1016/j.neunet.2014.09.003 PMID:25462637

Schoentag, R. A., & Pedersen, J. T. (1979). Evaluation of an Automated Blood Smear Analyzer. *American Society of Clinical Pathologists, 71*(6), 685–694. doi:10.1093/ajcp/71.6.685 PMID:453085

Schroff, F., Kalenichenko, D., & Philbin, J. (2015). Facenet: A unified embedding for face recognition and clustering. In *Proceedings of the IEEE conference on computer vision and pattern recognition* (pp. 815-823). IEEE. 10.1109/CVPR.2015.7298682

Schuler, C. J., Christopher Burger, H., Harmeling, S., & Scholkopf, B. (2013). A machine learning approach for non-blind image deconvolution. *IEEE Explore*. Retrieved from: http://citeseerx.ist.psu.edu/viewdoc/download?doi=10.1.1.378.7602&rep=rep1&type=pdf

Senov, A. (2015). Improving Distributed Stochastic Gradient Descent Estimate via Loss Function Approximation. *IFAC-Papersonline, 48*(25), 292–297. doi:10.1016/j.ifacol.2015.11.103

Sezer, O., Dogdu, E., & Ozbayoglu, A. (2018). Context-Aware Computing, Learning, and Big Data in Internet of Things: A Survey. *IEEE Internet Of Things Journal, 5*(1), 1–27. doi:10.1109/JIOT.2017.2773600

Shafiul, Ahemd, Abir, Ul-haq, & Nikhil. (2015). *Investigations on the Influence of Cutting Fluids in Turning Composites under Variable Machining Conditions.* Academic Press. .doi:10.13140/RG.2.1.4562.0569

Shaoqing, R., Kaiming, H., Ross, G., & Jian, S. (2015). Faster R-CNN: Towards real-time object detection with region proposal networks. In *Proceedings of the 28th international conference on neural information processing systems* (pp. 91–99). Cambridge, MA: MIT Press.

Sharif, J. M., Miswan, M. F., Ngadi, M. A., Salam, M. S. H., & Jamil, M. M. B. A. (2012) Red Blood Cell Segmentation Using Masking and Watershed Algorithm: A Preliminary Study. *International Conference on Biomedical Engineering (ICoBE)*, 7, 27-28. 10.1109/ICoBE.2012.6179016

Shatnawi, A., Al-Bdour, G., Al-Qurran, R., & Al-Ayyoub, M. (n.d.). A Comparative Study of Open Source Deep Learning Frameworks. *Conference: International Conference on Information and Communication Systems.*

Shaw, R. L. (2010). Embedding reflexivity within experiential qualitative psychology. *Qualitative Research in Psychology, 7*(3), 233–243. doi:10.1080/14780880802699092

Shell, D.F., Brooks, D.W., Trainin, G., Wilson, K.M., Kauffman, D.F., & Herr, L.M. (n.d.). *The Unified Learning Model, How Motivational, Cognitive, and Neurobiological Sciences Inform Best Teaching Practices.* Academic Press.

Shen, Wu, & Suk. (2017). Deep Learning in Medical Image Analysis. *Annual Review of Biomedical Engineering, 19*, 221–248.

Siddavatam, I. A., Satish, S., Mahesh, W., & Kazi, F. (2017). An ensemble learning for anomaly identification in *SCADA System. 2017 7th International Conference on Power Systems (ICPS).*

Silver, D., Huang, A., Maddison, C. J., Guez, A., Sifre, L., Van Den Driessche, G., … Hassabis, D. (2016). *Mastering the game of Go with deep neural networks and tree search.* Academic Press. doi:10.1038/nature16961

Simonyan, K., & Zisserman, A. (2014). *Very deep convolutional networks for large-scale image recognition.* arXiv preprint arXiv:1409.1556

Simonyan, K., & Zisserman, A. (2014). *Very deep convolutional networks for large-scale image recognition.* CoRR, abs/1409.1556

Simpraga, S., Alvarez-Jimenez, R., Mansvelder, H. D., Gerven, J. M., Groeneveld, G. J., Poil, S., & Linkenkaer-Hansen, K. (2017). EEG machine learning for accurate detection of cholinergic intervention and Alzheimer's disease. *Scientific Reports, 7*(1). doi:10.103841598-017-06165-4

Sourin, A., Earnshaw, R., Gavrilova, M.L., & Sourina, O. (2016). Problems of Human-Computer Interaction in Cyberworlds. *Transactions on Computational Science, 28.*

Srivastava, N., Hinton, G., Krizhevsky, A., Sutskever, I., & Salakhutdinov, R. (2014). Dropout: A simple way to prevent neural networks from overfitting. *Journal of Machine Learning Research, 15*(1), 1929–1958.

Stanford. (n.d.). Autoencoders. *UFLDL Tutorial.* Retrieved from: http://ufldl.stanford.edu/tutorial/unsupervised/Autoencoders/

Strimbu, K., & Tavel, J. A. (2010, November). What are Biomarkers? *Current Opinion in HIV and AIDS, 5*(6), 463–466. doi:10.1097/COH.0b013e32833ed177 PMID:20978388

Su, P.-H., Gaši'c, G., Mrkši'c, N. M., Rojas-Barahona, L., Ultes, S., Vandyke, D., … Young, S. (n.d.). *On-line Active Reward Learning for Policy Optimisation in Spoken Dialogue Systems.* Retrieved from http://www.aclweb.org/anthology/P16-1230

Subbulakshmi, T. (2017). A learning-based hybrid framework for detection and defence of DDoS attacks. *International Journal of Internet Protocol Technology, 10*(1), 51. doi:10.1504/IJIPT.2017.083036

Suleiman, W., Ayusawa, K., Kanehiro, F., & Yoshida, E. (2018, March). On prioritized inverse kinematics tasks: Time-space decoupling. In *Advanced Motion Control (AMC), 2018 IEEE 15th International Workshop on* (pp. 108-113). IEEE.

Sultana, Tabassum, Sultana, Al-Ghanim, Shah, Shahid, & Mahboob. (n.d.). *A Cytogenic Monitoring Approach of Hospital Workers Occupationally Exposed to Ionizing Radiations Using Micronucleus Assay.* Academic Press.

Sultana, Tabassum, S., Sultana, T., Al-Ghanim, K. A., Shah, K., Shahid, T., & Mahboob, S. (2016). A cytogenic monitoring approach of hospital workers occultionally exposed to ionizing radiations using micronucleus assay. *African Journal of Traditional, Complementary, and Alternative Medicines, 13*(2), 185–190. doi:10.4314/ajtcam.v13i2.22

Sun, X., Wu, P., & Hoi, S. C. H. (2017). *Face detection using deep learning: An improved faster RCNN approach.* CoRR, abs/1701.08289. Retrieved from http://arxiv.org/abs/1701.08289

Sun, Y., Liang, D., Wang, X., & Tang, X. (2015). *Deepid3: Face recognition with very deep neural networks.* arXiv preprint arXiv:1502.00873.

Sutskever, I. (2013). *Training recurrent neural networks.* Toronto, Canada: University of Toronto.

Sutton, R. S. (1984). Temporal credit assignment in reinforcement learning. *Doctoral Dissertations Available from Proquest*. Retrieved from https://scholarworks.umass.edu/dissertations/AAI8410337

Symantec. (2017). Internet Security Threat Report. *Symantec*. Retrieved from Https://Www.Symantec. Com/Content/Dam/Symantec/Docs/Reports/Istr-22-2017-En.Pdf

Szegedy, C., Ioffe, S., Vanhoucke, V., & Alemi, A. A. (2017, February). Inception-v4, inception-resnet and the impact of residual connections on learning. In AAAI (Vol. 4, p. 12). Academic Press.

Szegedy, C., Liu, W., Jia, Y., Sermanet, P., Reed, S. E., Anguelov, D., . . . Rabinovich, A. (2014). *Going deeper with convolutions*. CoRR, abs/1409.4842. Retrieved from http://arxiv.org/abs/1409.4842

Szegedy, C., Liu, W., Jia, Y., Sermanet, P., Reed, S., Anguelov, D., ... Rabinovich, A. (2015). Going deeper with convolutions. In *Proceedings of the IEEE conference on computer vision and pattern recognition* (pp. 1-9). IEEE.

Taigman, Y., Yang, M., Ranzato, M. A., & Wolf, L. (2014). Deepface: Closing the gap to human-level performance in face verification. In *Proceedings of the IEEE conference on computer vision and pattern recognition* (pp. 1701-1708). IEEE. 10.1109/CVPR.2014.220

Targ, S., Almeida, D., & Lyman, K. (2016). *Resnet in Resnet: generalizing residual architectures*. arXiv preprint arXiv:1603.08029

The Keras Blog. (2016). Building autoencoders in Keras. *The Keras Blog*. Retrieved from: https://blog. keras.io/building-autoencoders-in-keras.html

Thomee, B., Shamma, D. A., Friedland, G., Elizalde, B., Ni, K., Poland, D., . . . Li, L. (2015). *The new data and new challenges in multimedia research*. CoRR, abs/1503.01817. Retrieved from http://arxiv. org/abs/1503.01817

Titanto, M., & Dirgahayu, T. (2014). Google Maps-Based Geospatial Application Framework with Custom Layers Management. *Applied Mechanics and Materials, 513-517*, 822-826. Retrieved from www.scientific.net/amm.513-517.822

Tobiyama, S., Yamaguchi, Y., Shimada, H., Ikuse, T., & Yagi, T. (2016). Malware Detection with Deep Neural Network Using Process Behavior. In *2016 IEEE 40th Annual Computer Software and Applications Conference (COMPSAC)* (Vol. 2, pp. 577–582). IEEE. 10.1109/COMPSAC.2016.151

Torrey, L., & Shavlik, J. (2009). Transfer learning. In E. Soria, J. Martin, R. Magdalena, M. Martinez, & A. Serrano (Eds.), *Handbook of research on machine learning applications*. IGI Global. Retrieved from ftp://ftp.cs.wisc.edu/machine-learning/shavlik -group/torrey.handbook09.pdf

Tsironi, E., Barros, P., Weber, C., & Wermter, S. (2017). *Neurocomputing An analysis of Convolutional Long Short-Term Memory Recurrent Neural Networks for gesture recognition*. Academic Press. doi:10.1016/j.neucom.2016.12.088

Tzanakou, E. M. (Ed.). (1999). *Supervised and unsupervised pattern recognition: feature extraction and computational intelligence*. CRC Press. doi:10.1201/9781420049770

Vala, H.J., & Baxi, A. (2013). A review on Otsu image segmentation algorithm. *International Journal of Advanced Research in Computer Engineering & Technology, 2*(2).

Van, N. T., Thinh, T. N., & Sach, L. T. (2017) An anomaly-based network intrusion detection system using deep learning. *2017 International Conference on System Science and Engineering(ICSSE)*.

Vartouni, A. M., Kasha, S. S., & Teshnehlab, M. (2018). An anomaly detection method to detect web attacks using stacked auto-encoder. *2018 6th Iranian Joint Congress on Fuzzy and Intelligent Systems (CFIS)*.

Venkatalakshmi, B., & Thilagavathi, K. (2013 May) Automatic Red Blood Cell Counting Using Hough Transform. *Proceedings of IEEE Conference on Information and Communication Technologies (ICT)*, 5. 10.1109/CICT.2013.6558103

Vijayalaxmi, A. K., Srujana, B., & Kumar, P.R. (2014). Object detection and tracking using image processing. *Global Journal of Advanced Engineering Technologies*.

Vincent, P., Larochelle, H., Bengio, Y., & Manzagol, P.-A. (n.d.). *Extracting and composing robust features with denoising autoencoders*. Retrieved from: http://www.cs.toronto.edu/~larocheh/publications/icml-2008-denoising-autoencoders.pdf

Viola, P., & Jones, M. J. (2004). Robust real-time face detection. *International Journal of Computer Vision, 57*(2), 137–154. doi:10.1023/B:VISI.0000013087.49260.fb

Vlajic, N., & Zhou, D. (2018). IoT as a Land of Opportunity for DDoS Hackers. *Computer, 51*(7), 26–34. doi:10.1109/MC.2018.3011046

Vu, H., Gomez, F., Cherelle, P., Lefeber, D., Nowé, A., & Vanderborght, B. (2018). ED-FNN: A New Deep Learning Algorithm to Detect Percentage of the Gait Cycle for Powered Prostheses. *Sensors (Basel), 18*(7), 2389. doi:10.339018072389 PMID:30041421

Vukobratovic, M., & Borovac, B. (2004). Zero-moment point—thirty five years of its life. *International Journal of Humanoid Robotics, 1*(1), 157-173.

Wagner, S. (2010). A Bayesian network approach to assess and predict software quality using activity-based quality model. *Information and Software Technology, 52*(11), 1230–1241. doi:10.1016/j.infsof.2010.03.016

Wang, H., Wang, Y., Zhou, Z., Ji, X., Li, Z., Gong, D., . . . Liu, W. (2018). *CosFace: Large margin cosine loss for deep face recognition*. arXiv preprint arXiv:1801.09414

Wang, Y., Pedrycz,W., Baciu,G., Chen, P., Wang, G., & Yao, Y., (2010). Perspectives on Cognitive Computing and Applications. *International Journal of Software Science and Computational Intelligence, 2*(4).

Wang, Y., Baciu, G., Yao, T., Kinsner, W., Chan, K., Zhang, B., ... Zhu, H. (2010). Perspectives on cognitive informatics and cognitive computing. *International Journal of Cognitive Informatics and Natural Intelligence*, *4*(1), 1–29. doi:10.4018/jcini.2010010101

Wang, Y., Widrow, B., Zadeh, L. A., Howard, N., Wood, S., Bhavsar, V. C., ... Shell, D. F. (2016). Cognitive Intelligence: Deep Learning, Thinking, and Reasoning by Brain-Inspired Systems. *International Journal of Cognitive Informatics and Natural Intelligence*, *10*(4), 1–20. doi:10.4018/IJCINI.2016100101

Watkins, C. J. C. H., & Dayan, P. (1992). Q-learning. *Machine Learning*, *8*(3–4), 279–292. doi:10.1007/BF00992698

Weber, R. (2010). Internet of Things – New security and privacy challenges. *Computer Law & Security Review*, *26*(1), 23–30. doi:10.1016/j.clsr.2009.11.008

Wen, Y., Zhang, K., Li, Z., & Qiao, Y. (2016). A discriminative feature learning approach for deep face recognition. In *European conference on computer vision* (pp. 499–515). Academic Press. 10.1007/978-3-319-46478-7_31

Williams, R. J., & Peng, J. (1990). An efficient gradient-based algorithm for on-line training of recurrent network trajectories. *Neural Computation*, *2*(4), 490–501. doi:10.1162/neco.1990.2.4.490

Williams, R. J., & Zipser, D. (1989). A learning algorithm for continually running fully recurrent neural networks. *Neural Computation*, *1*(2), 270–280. doi:10.1162/neco.1989.1.2.270

Wilson-Doenges, G., & Gurung, R. A. R. (2013). Benchmarks for scholarly investigations of teaching and learning. *Australian Journal of Psychology*, *65*(1), 63–70. doi:10.1111/ajpy.12011

Wu, X., He, R., Sun, Z., & Tan, T. (2018). A light CNN for deep face representation with noisy labels. *IEEE Transactions on Information Forensics and Security*, *13*(11), 2884–2896. doi:10.1109/TIFS.2018.2833032

Xiao, X., Zhao, S., Nguyen, D.H.H., Zhong, X., Jones, D.L., Chng, E.S., & Li, H. (2016). Speech dereverberation for enhancement and recognition using dynamic features constrained deep neural networks and feature adaptation. *EURASIP J. Adv. Signal Process.*, *2016*(1), 1–18.

Xie, J., Girshick, R., & Farhadi, A. (2016, June). Unsupervised deep embedding for clustering analysis. In *International conference on machine learning* (pp. 478-487). Academic Press.

Xing, F., Guo, P., & Lyu, M. R. (2005). A novel method for early software quality prediction based on support vector machine. *Proceedings of Software Reliability Engineering (ISSRE), 16th IEEE International Symposium on IEEE*, 10–15.

Xin, Y., Kong, L., Liu, Z., Chen, Y., Li, Y., Zhu, H., ... Wang, C. (2018). Machine Learning and Deep Learning Methods for Cybersecurity. *IEEE Access: Practical Innovations, Open Solutions*, *6*, 35365–35381. doi:10.1109/ACCESS.2018.2836950

Xu, X., Dou, P., Le, H. A., & Kakadiaris, I. A. (2017). *When 3D-Aided 2D Face Recognition Meets Deep Learning: An extended UR2D for Pose-Invariant Face Recognition.* arXiv preprint arXiv:1709.06532

Xu, M., Duan, L., Cai, J., Chia, L., Xu, C., & Tian, Q. (2004) HMM-based audio keyword generation. *5th Pacific Rim Conf. Multimed,* 566–574.

Yampolskiy, R., Cho, G., Rosenthal, R., & Gavrilova, M. L. (2012). *Experiments in Artimetrics: Avatar Face Recognition.* Academic Press.

Yang, B., Fu, X., Sidiropoulos, N. D., & Hong, M. (2016). *Towards k-means-friendly spaces: Simultaneous deep learning and clustering.* arXiv preprint arXiv:1610.04794

Yang, S., Luo, P., Loy, C. C., & Tang, X. (2016). Wider face: A face detection benchmark. In *IEEE conference on computer vision and pattern recognition.* CVPR. doi:10.1109/CVPR.2016.596

Yang, S., Tiejun, L., Maunder, R., & Hanzo, L. (2013). From Nominal to True A Posteriori Probabilities: An Exact Bayesian Theorem Based Probabilistic Data Association Approach for Iterative MIMO Detection and Decoding. *IEEE Transactions on Communications, 61*(7), 2782–2793. doi:10.1109/TCOMM.2013.053013.120427

Yao, S., Zhao, Y., Zhang, A., Hu, S., Shao, H., Zhang, C., ... Abdelzaher, T. (2018). Deep Learning for the Internet of Things. *Computer, 51*(5), 32–41. doi:10.1109/MC.2018.2381131

Yi, D., Lei, Z., Liao, S., & Li, S. Z. (2014). *Learning face representation from scratch.* CoRR, abs/1411.7923. Retrieved from http://arxiv.org/abs/1411.7923

Yin, S., Liu, C., Zhang, Z., Lin, Y., Wang, D., Tejedor, J., Zheng, T.F., & Li, Y. (2015). Noisy training for deep neural networks in speech recognition. *Eurasip J. Audio, Speech, Music Process., 2015*(1), 1–14.

Yin, C., Zhu, Y., Fei, J., & He, X. (2017). A deep learning approach for intrusion detection using recurrent neural networks. *IEEE Access: Practical Innovations, Open Solutions, 5,* 21954–21961. doi:10.1109/ACCESS.2017.2762418

Yoo, Y., Brosch, T., & Traboulsee, A. (2014). Deep learning of image features from unlabeled data for multiple sclerosis lesion segmentation. *International Workshop on Machine Learning in Medical Imaging,* 117–24. 10.1007/978-3-319-10581-9_15

Yosinski, J., Clune, J., Bengio, Y., & Lipson, H. (2014). *How transferable are features in deep neural networks?* CoRR, abs/1411.1792. Retrieved from http://arxiv.org/abs/1411.1792

Yuan, X., Khoshgoftaar, T. M., Allen, E. B., & Ganesan, K. (2000). An application of fuzzy clustering to software quality prediction. *Proceedings of Application-Specific Systems and Software Engineering Technology in 3rd IEEE Symposium on IEEE,* 85–90. 10.1109/ASSET.2000.888052

Yuan, Z., Lu, Y., & Xue, Y. (2016). DroidDetector. *Android Malware Characterization and Detection Using Deep Learning, 21*(1), 114–123.

Yuan, Z., Lyu, Y., Wang, Z., & Xue, Y. (2014). *Droid-Sec: deep learning in android malware detection.* SIGCOMM. doi:10.1145/2619239.2631434

Zawbaa, H. M., Hazman, M., Abbass, M., & Hassanien, A. E. (2014, December). Automatic fruit classification using random forest algorithm. In *Hybrid Intelligent Systems (HIS), 2014 14th International Conference on* (pp. 164-168). IEEE. 10.1109/HIS.2014.7086191

Zhang, K., Zhang, Z., Li, Z., & Qiao, Y. (2016). *Joint face detection and alignment using multi-task cascaded convolutional networks.* CoRR, abs/1604.02878. Retrieved from http://arxiv.org/abs/1604.02878

Zhang, Y., & Wu, L. (2012). Classification of fruits using computer vision and a multiclass support vector machine. *Sensors, 12*(9), 12489-12505.

Zhang, S., Yao, L., Sun, A., & Tay, Y. (2018). Deep Learning based Recommender System: A survey and New Perspectives. *ACM Computing Surveys, 1*(1).

Zhang, Y., Wang, S., Ji, G., & Phillips, P. (2014). Fruit classification using computer vision and feedforward neural network. *Journal of Food Engineering, 143*, 167–177. doi:10.1016/j.jfoodeng.2014.07.001

Zheng, Y., Pal, D. K., & Savvides, M. (2018, February). Ring loss: Convex feature normalization for face recognition. In *Proceedings of the IEEE Conference on Computer Vision and Pattern Recognition* (pp. 5089-5097). IEEE. 10.1109/CVPR.2018.00534

Zhu, Y. (2010). Automatic detection of anomalies in blood glucose using a machine learning approach. *Journal of Communications and Networks (Seoul), 13*(2), 125–131. doi:10.1109/JCN.2011.6157411

Zölzer, U. (Ed.). (2002). DAFX--Digital Audio Effects. West Sussex, UK: John Wiley and Sons, LTD. Retrieved from http://www.dafx.de/

Related References

To continue our tradition of advancing information science and technology research, we have compiled a list of recommended IGI Global readings. These references will provide additional information and guidance to further enrich your knowledge and assist you with your own research and future publications.

Aasi, P., Rusu, L., & Vieru, D. (2017). The Role of Culture in IT Governance Five Focus Areas: A Literature Review. *International Journal of IT/Business Alignment and Governance, 8*(2), 42-61. doi:10.4018/IJITBAG.2017070103

Abdrabo, A. A. (2018). Egypt's Knowledge-Based Development: Opportunities, Challenges, and Future Possibilities. In A. Alraouf (Ed.), *Knowledge-Based Urban Development in the Middle East* (pp. 80–101). Hershey, PA: IGI Global. doi:10.4018/978-1-5225-3734-2.ch005

Abu Doush, I., & Alhami, I. (2018). Evaluating the Accessibility of Computer Laboratories, Libraries, and Websites in Jordanian Universities and Colleges. *International Journal of Information Systems and Social Change, 9*(2), 44–60. doi:10.4018/IJISSC.2018040104

Adeboye, A. (2016). Perceived Use and Acceptance of Cloud Enterprise Resource Planning (ERP) Implementation in the Manufacturing Industries. *International Journal of Strategic Information Technology and Applications, 7*(3), 24–40. doi:10.4018/IJSITA.2016070102

Adegbore, A. M., Quadri, M. O., & Oyewo, O. R. (2018). A Theoretical Approach to the Adoption of Electronic Resource Management Systems (ERMS) in Nigerian University Libraries. In A. Tella & T. Kwanya (Eds.), *Handbook of Research on Managing Intellectual Property in Digital Libraries* (pp. 292–311). Hershey, PA: IGI Global. doi:10.4018/978-1-5225-3093-0.ch015

Adhikari, M., & Roy, D. (2016). Green Computing. In G. Deka, G. Siddesh, K. Srinivasa, & L. Patnaik (Eds.), *Emerging Research Surrounding Power Consumption and Performance Issues in Utility Computing* (pp. 84–108). Hershey, PA: IGI Global. doi:10.4018/978-1-4666-8853-7.ch005

Afolabi, O. A. (2018). Myths and Challenges of Building an Effective Digital Library in Developing Nations: An African Perspective. In A. Tella & T. Kwanya (Eds.), *Handbook of Research on Managing Intellectual Property in Digital Libraries* (pp. 51–79). Hershey, PA: IGI Global. doi:10.4018/978-1-5225-3093-0.ch004

Agarwal, R., Singh, A., & Sen, S. (2016). Role of Molecular Docking in Computer-Aided Drug Design and Development. In S. Dastmalchi, M. Hamzeh-Mivehroud, & B. Sokouti (Eds.), *Applied Case Studies and Solutions in Molecular Docking-Based Drug Design* (pp. 1–28). Hershey, PA: IGI Global. doi:10.4018/978-1-5225-0362-0.ch001

Ali, O., & Soar, J. (2016). Technology Innovation Adoption Theories. In L. Al-Hakim, X. Wu, A. Koronios, & Y. Shou (Eds.), *Handbook of Research on Driving Competitive Advantage through Sustainable, Lean, and Disruptive Innovation* (pp. 1–38). Hershey, PA: IGI Global. doi:10.4018/978-1-5225-0135-0.ch001

Alsharo, M. (2017). Attitudes Towards Cloud Computing Adoption in Emerging Economies. *International Journal of Cloud Applications and Computing*, 7(3), 44–58. doi:10.4018/IJCAC.2017070102

Amer, T. S., & Johnson, T. L. (2016). Information Technology Progress Indicators: Temporal Expectancy, User Preference, and the Perception of Process Duration. *International Journal of Technology and Human Interaction*, 12(4), 1–14. doi:10.4018/IJTHI.2016100101

Amer, T. S., & Johnson, T. L. (2017). Information Technology Progress Indicators: Research Employing Psychological Frameworks. In A. Mesquita (Ed.), *Research Paradigms and Contemporary Perspectives on Human-Technology Interaction* (pp. 168–186). Hershey, PA: IGI Global. doi:10.4018/978-1-5225-1868-6.ch008

Anchugam, C. V., & Thangadurai, K. (2016). Introduction to Network Security. In D. G., M. Singh, & M. Jayanthi (Eds.), Network Security Attacks and Countermeasures (pp. 1-48). Hershey, PA: IGI Global. doi:10.4018/978-1-4666-8761-5.ch001

Anchugam, C. V., & Thangadurai, K. (2016). Classification of Network Attacks and Countermeasures of Different Attacks. In D. G., M. Singh, & M. Jayanthi (Eds.), Network Security Attacks and Countermeasures (pp. 115-156). Hershey, PA: IGI Global. doi:10.4018/978-1-4666-8761-5.ch004

Anohah, E. (2016). Pedagogy and Design of Online Learning Environment in Computer Science Education for High Schools. *International Journal of Online Pedagogy and Course Design*, 6(3), 39–51. doi:10.4018/IJOPCD.2016070104

Anohah, E. (2017). Paradigm and Architecture of Computing Augmented Learning Management System for Computer Science Education. *International Journal of Online Pedagogy and Course Design*, 7(2), 60–70. doi:10.4018/IJOPCD.2017040105

Anohah, E., & Suhonen, J. (2017). Trends of Mobile Learning in Computing Education from 2006 to 2014: A Systematic Review of Research Publications. *International Journal of Mobile and Blended Learning*, 9(1), 16–33. doi:10.4018/IJMBL.2017010102

Assis-Hassid, S., Heart, T., Reychav, I., & Pliskin, J. S. (2016). Modelling Factors Affecting Patient-Doctor-Computer Communication in Primary Care. *International Journal of Reliable and Quality E-Healthcare*, 5(1), 1–17. doi:10.4018/IJRQEH.2016010101

Bailey, E. K. (2017). Applying Learning Theories to Computer Technology Supported Instruction. In M. Grassetti & S. Brookby (Eds.), *Advancing Next-Generation Teacher Education through Digital Tools and Applications* (pp. 61–81). Hershey, PA: IGI Global. doi:10.4018/978-1-5225-0965-3.ch004

Balasubramanian, K. (2016). Attacks on Online Banking and Commerce. In K. Balasubramanian, K. Mala, & M. Rajakani (Eds.), *Cryptographic Solutions for Secure Online Banking and Commerce* (pp. 1–19). Hershey, PA: IGI Global. doi:10.4018/978-1-5225-0273-9.ch001

Baldwin, S., Opoku-Agyemang, K., & Roy, D. (2016). Games People Play: A Trilateral Collaboration Researching Computer Gaming across Cultures. In K. Valentine & L. Jensen (Eds.), *Examining the Evolution of Gaming and Its Impact on Social, Cultural, and Political Perspectives* (pp. 364–376). Hershey, PA: IGI Global. doi:10.4018/978-1-5225-0261-6.ch017

Banerjee, S., Sing, T. Y., Chowdhury, A. R., & Anwar, H. (2018). Let's Go Green: Towards a Taxonomy of Green Computing Enablers for Business Sustainability. In M. Khosrow-Pour (Ed.), *Green Computing Strategies for Competitive Advantage and Business Sustainability* (pp. 89–109). Hershey, PA: IGI Global. doi:10.4018/978-1-5225-5017-4.ch005

Basham, R. (2018). Information Science and Technology in Crisis Response and Management. In M. Khosrow-Pour, D.B.A. (Ed.), Encyclopedia of Information Science and Technology, Fourth Edition (pp. 1407-1418). Hershey, PA: IGI Global. doi:10.4018/978-1-5225-2255-3.ch121

Batyashe, T., & Iyamu, T. (2018). Architectural Framework for the Implementation of Information Technology Governance in Organisations. In M. Khosrow-Pour, D.B.A. (Ed.), Encyclopedia of Information Science and Technology, Fourth Edition (pp. 810-819). Hershey, PA: IGI Global. doi:10.4018/978-1-5225-2255-3.ch070

Bekleyen, N., & Çelik, S. (2017). Attitudes of Adult EFL Learners towards Preparing for a Language Test via CALL. In D. Tafazoli & M. Romero (Eds.), *Multiculturalism and Technology-Enhanced Language Learning* (pp. 214–229). Hershey, PA: IGI Global. doi:10.4018/978-1-5225-1882-2.ch013

Bennett, A., Eglash, R., Lachney, M., & Babbitt, W. (2016). Design Agency: Diversifying Computer Science at the Intersections of Creativity and Culture. In M. Raisinghani (Ed.), *Revolutionizing Education through Web-Based Instruction* (pp. 35–56). Hershey, PA: IGI Global. doi:10.4018/978-1-4666-9932-8.ch003

Bergeron, F., Croteau, A., Uwizeyemungu, S., & Raymond, L. (2017). A Framework for Research on Information Technology Governance in SMEs. In S. De Haes & W. Van Grembergen (Eds.), *Strategic IT Governance and Alignment in Business Settings* (pp. 53–81). Hershey, PA: IGI Global. doi:10.4018/978-1-5225-0861-8.ch003

Bhatt, G. D., Wang, Z., & Rodger, J. A. (2017). Information Systems Capabilities and Their Effects on Competitive Advantages: A Study of Chinese Companies. *Information Resources Management Journal, 30*(3), 41–57. doi:10.4018/IRMJ.2017070103

Bogdanoski, M., Stoilkovski, M., & Risteski, A. (2016). Novel First Responder Digital Forensics Tool as a Support to Law Enforcement. In M. Hadji-Janev & M. Bogdanoski (Eds.), *Handbook of Research on Civil Society and National Security in the Era of Cyber Warfare* (pp. 352–376). Hershey, PA: IGI Global. doi:10.4018/978-1-4666-8793-6.ch016

Boontarig, W., Papasratorn, B., & Chutimaskul, W. (2016). The Unified Model for Acceptance and Use of Health Information on Online Social Networks: Evidence from Thailand. *International Journal of E-Health and Medical Communications, 7*(1), 31–47. doi:10.4018/IJEHMC.2016010102

Brown, S., & Yuan, X. (2016). Techniques for Retaining Computer Science Students at Historical Black Colleges and Universities. In C. Prince & R. Ford (Eds.), *Setting a New Agenda for Student Engagement and Retention in Historically Black Colleges and Universities* (pp. 251–268). Hershey, PA: IGI Global. doi:10.4018/978-1-5225-0308-8.ch014

Burcoff, A., & Shamir, L. (2017). Computer Analysis of Pablo Picasso's Artistic Style. *International Journal of Art, Culture and Design Technologies*, *6*(1), 1–18. doi:10.4018/IJACDT.2017010101

Byker, E. J. (2017). I Play I Learn: Introducing Technological Play Theory. In C. Martin & D. Polly (Eds.), *Handbook of Research on Teacher Education and Professional Development* (pp. 297–306). Hershey, PA: IGI Global. doi:10.4018/978-1-5225-1067-3.ch016

Calongne, C. M., Stricker, A. G., Truman, B., & Arenas, F. J. (2017). Cognitive Apprenticeship and Computer Science Education in Cyberspace: Reimagining the Past. In A. Stricker, C. Calongne, B. Truman, & F. Arenas (Eds.), *Integrating an Awareness of Selfhood and Society into Virtual Learning* (pp. 180–197). Hershey, PA: IGI Global. doi:10.4018/978-1-5225-2182-2.ch013

Carlton, E. L., Holsinger, J. W. Jr, & Anunobi, N. (2016). Physician Engagement with Health Information Technology: Implications for Practice and Professionalism. *International Journal of Computers in Clinical Practice*, *1*(2), 51–73. doi:10.4018/IJCCP.2016070103

Carneiro, A. D. (2017). Defending Information Networks in Cyberspace: Some Notes on Security Needs. In M. Dawson, D. Kisku, P. Gupta, J. Sing, & W. Li (Eds.), Developing Next-Generation Countermeasures for Homeland Security Threat Prevention (pp. 354-375). Hershey, PA: IGI Global. doi:10.4018/978-1-5225-0703-1.ch016

Cavalcanti, J. C. (2016). The New "ABC" of ICTs (Analytics + Big Data + Cloud Computing): A Complex Trade-Off between IT and CT Costs. In J. Martins & A. Molnar (Eds.), *Handbook of Research on Innovations in Information Retrieval, Analysis, and Management* (pp. 152–186). Hershey, PA: IGI Global. doi:10.4018/978-1-4666-8833-9.ch006

Chase, J. P., & Yan, Z. (2017). Affect in Statistics Cognition. In *Assessing and Measuring Statistics Cognition in Higher Education Online Environments: Emerging Research and Opportunities* (pp. 144–187). Hershey, PA: IGI Global. doi:10.4018/978-1-5225-2420-5.ch005

Chen, C. (2016). Effective Learning Strategies for the 21st Century: Implications for the E-Learning. In M. Anderson & C. Gavan (Eds.), *Developing Effective Educational Experiences through Learning Analytics* (pp. 143–169). Hershey, PA: IGI Global. doi:10.4018/978-1-4666-9983-0.ch006

Chen, E. T. (2016). Examining the Influence of Information Technology on Modern Health Care. In P. Manolitzas, E. Grigoroudis, N. Matsatsinis, & D. Yannacopoulos (Eds.), *Effective Methods for Modern Healthcare Service Quality and Evaluation* (pp. 110–136). Hershey, PA: IGI Global. doi:10.4018/978-1-4666-9961-8.ch006

Cimermanova, I. (2017). Computer-Assisted Learning in Slovakia. In D. Tafazoli & M. Romero (Eds.), *Multiculturalism and Technology-Enhanced Language Learning* (pp. 252–270). Hershey, PA: IGI Global. doi:10.4018/978-1-5225-1882-2.ch015

Cipolla-Ficarra, F. V., & Cipolla-Ficarra, M. (2018). Computer Animation for Ingenious Revival. In F. Cipolla-Ficarra, M. Ficarra, M. Cipolla-Ficarra, A. Quiroga, J. Alma, & J. Carré (Eds.), *Technology-Enhanced Human Interaction in Modern Society* (pp. 159–181). Hershey, PA: IGI Global. doi:10.4018/978-1-5225-3437-2.ch008

Cockrell, S., Damron, T. S., Melton, A. M., & Smith, A. D. (2018). Offshoring IT. In M. Khosrow-Pour, D.B.A. (Ed.), Encyclopedia of Information Science and Technology, Fourth Edition (pp. 5476-5489). Hershey, PA: IGI Global. doi:10.4018/978-1-5225-2255-3.ch476

Coffey, J. W. (2018). Logic and Proof in Computer Science: Categories and Limits of Proof Techniques. In J. Horne (Ed.), *Philosophical Perceptions on Logic and Order* (pp. 218–240). Hershey, PA: IGI Global. doi:10.4018/978-1-5225-2443-4.ch007

Dale, M. (2017). Re-Thinking the Challenges of Enterprise Architecture Implementation. In M. Tavana (Ed.), *Enterprise Information Systems and the Digitalization of Business Functions* (pp. 205–221). Hershey, PA: IGI Global. doi:10.4018/978-1-5225-2382-6.ch009

Das, A., Dasgupta, R., & Bagchi, A. (2016). Overview of Cellular Computing-Basic Principles and Applications. In J. Mandal, S. Mukhopadhyay, & T. Pal (Eds.), *Handbook of Research on Natural Computing for Optimization Problems* (pp. 637–662). Hershey, PA: IGI Global. doi:10.4018/978-1-5225-0058-2.ch026

De Maere, K., De Haes, S., & von Kutzschenbach, M. (2017). CIO Perspectives on Organizational Learning within the Context of IT Governance. *International Journal of IT/Business Alignment and Governance, 8*(1), 32-47. doi:10.4018/IJITBAG.2017010103

Demir, K., Çaka, C., Yaman, N. D., İslamoğlu, H., & Kuzu, A. (2018). Examining the Current Definitions of Computational Thinking. In H. Ozcinar, G. Wong, & H. Ozturk (Eds.), *Teaching Computational Thinking in Primary Education* (pp. 36–64). Hershey, PA: IGI Global. doi:10.4018/978-1-5225-3200-2.ch003

Deng, X., Hung, Y., & Lin, C. D. (2017). Design and Analysis of Computer Experiments. In S. Saha, A. Mandal, A. Narasimhamurthy, S. V, & S. Sangam (Eds.), Handbook of Research on Applied Cybernetics and Systems Science (pp. 264-279). Hershey, PA: IGI Global. doi:10.4018/978-1-5225-2498-4.ch013

Denner, J., Martinez, J., & Thiry, H. (2017). Strategies for Engaging Hispanic/Latino Youth in the US in Computer Science. In Y. Rankin & J. Thomas (Eds.), *Moving Students of Color from Consumers to Producers of Technology* (pp. 24–48). Hershey, PA: IGI Global. doi:10.4018/978-1-5225-2005-4.ch002

Devi, A. (2017). Cyber Crime and Cyber Security: A Quick Glance. In R. Kumar, P. Pattnaik, & P. Pandey (Eds.), *Detecting and Mitigating Robotic Cyber Security Risks* (pp. 160–171). Hershey, PA: IGI Global. doi:10.4018/978-1-5225-2154-9.ch011

Dores, A. R., Barbosa, F., Guerreiro, S., Almeida, I., & Carvalho, I. P. (2016). Computer-Based Neuropsychological Rehabilitation: Virtual Reality and Serious Games. In M. Cruz-Cunha, I. Miranda, R. Martinho, & R. Rijo (Eds.), *Encyclopedia of E-Health and Telemedicine* (pp. 473–485). Hershey, PA: IGI Global. doi:10.4018/978-1-4666-9978-6.ch037

Doshi, N., & Schaefer, G. (2016). Computer-Aided Analysis of Nailfold Capillaroscopy Images. In D. Fotiadis (Ed.), *Handbook of Research on Trends in the Diagnosis and Treatment of Chronic Conditions* (pp. 146–158). Hershey, PA: IGI Global. doi:10.4018/978-1-4666-8828-5.ch007

Doyle, D. J., & Fahy, P. J. (2018). Interactivity in Distance Education and Computer-Aided Learning, With Medical Education Examples. In M. Khosrow-Pour, D.B.A. (Ed.), Encyclopedia of Information Science and Technology, Fourth Edition (pp. 5829-5840). Hershey, PA: IGI Global. doi:10.4018/978-1-5225-2255-3.ch507

Elias, N. I., & Walker, T. W. (2017). Factors that Contribute to Continued Use of E-Training among Healthcare Professionals. In F. Topor (Ed.), *Handbook of Research on Individualism and Identity in the Globalized Digital Age* (pp. 403–429). Hershey, PA: IGI Global. doi:10.4018/978-1-5225-0522-8.ch018

Eloy, S., Dias, M. S., Lopes, P. F., & Vilar, E. (2016). Digital Technologies in Architecture and Engineering: Exploring an Engaged Interaction within Curricula. In D. Fonseca & E. Redondo (Eds.), *Handbook of Research on Applied E-Learning in Engineering and Architecture Education* (pp. 368–402). Hershey, PA: IGI Global. doi:10.4018/978-1-4666-8803-2.ch017

Estrela, V. V., Magalhães, H. A., & Saotome, O. (2016). Total Variation Applications in Computer Vision. In N. Kamila (Ed.), *Handbook of Research on Emerging Perspectives in Intelligent Pattern Recognition, Analysis, and Image Processing* (pp. 41–64). Hershey, PA: IGI Global. doi:10.4018/978-1-4666-8654-0.ch002

Filipovic, N., Radovic, M., Nikolic, D. D., Saveljic, I., Milosevic, Z., Exarchos, T. P., ... Parodi, O. (2016). Computer Predictive Model for Plaque Formation and Progression in the Artery. In D. Fotiadis (Ed.), *Handbook of Research on Trends in the Diagnosis and Treatment of Chronic Conditions* (pp. 279–300). Hershey, PA: IGI Global. doi:10.4018/978-1-4666-8828-5.ch013

Fisher, R. L. (2018). Computer-Assisted Indian Matrimonial Services. In M. Khosrow-Pour, D.B.A. (Ed.), Encyclopedia of Information Science and Technology, Fourth Edition (pp. 4136-4145). Hershey, PA: IGI Global. doi:10.4018/978-1-5225-2255-3.ch358

Fleenor, H. G., & Hodhod, R. (2016). Assessment of Learning and Technology: Computer Science Education. In V. Wang (Ed.), *Handbook of Research on Learning Outcomes and Opportunities in the Digital Age* (pp. 51–78). Hershey, PA: IGI Global. doi:10.4018/978-1-4666-9577-1.ch003

García-Valcárcel, A., & Mena, J. (2016). Information Technology as a Way To Support Collaborative Learning: What In-Service Teachers Think, Know and Do. *Journal of Information Technology Research*, 9(1), 1–17. doi:10.4018/JITR.2016010101

Gardner-McCune, C., & Jimenez, Y. (2017). Historical App Developers: Integrating CS into K-12 through Cross-Disciplinary Projects. In Y. Rankin & J. Thomas (Eds.), *Moving Students of Color from Consumers to Producers of Technology* (pp. 85–112). Hershey, PA: IGI Global. doi:10.4018/978-1-5225-2005-4.ch005

Garvey, G. P. (2016). Exploring Perception, Cognition, and Neural Pathways of Stereo Vision and the Split–Brain Human Computer Interface. In A. Ursyn (Ed.), *Knowledge Visualization and Visual Literacy in Science Education* (pp. 28–76). Hershey, PA: IGI Global. doi:10.4018/978-1-5225-0480-1.ch002

Ghafele, R., & Gibert, B. (2018). Open Growth: The Economic Impact of Open Source Software in the USA. In M. Khosrow-Pour (Ed.), *Optimizing Contemporary Application and Processes in Open Source Software* (pp. 164–197). Hershey, PA: IGI Global. doi:10.4018/978-1-5225-5314-4.ch007

Ghobakhloo, M., & Azar, A. (2018). Information Technology Resources, the Organizational Capability of Lean-Agile Manufacturing, and Business Performance. *Information Resources Management Journal*, *31*(2), 47–74. doi:10.4018/IRMJ.2018040103

Gianni, M., & Gotzamani, K. (2016). Integrated Management Systems and Information Management Systems: Common Threads. In P. Papajorgji, F. Pinet, A. Guimarães, & J. Papathanasiou (Eds.), *Automated Enterprise Systems for Maximizing Business Performance* (pp. 195–214). Hershey, PA: IGI Global. doi:10.4018/978-1-4666-8841-4.ch011

Gikandi, J. W. (2017). Computer-Supported Collaborative Learning and Assessment: A Strategy for Developing Online Learning Communities in Continuing Education. In J. Keengwe & G. Onchwari (Eds.), *Handbook of Research on Learner-Centered Pedagogy in Teacher Education and Professional Development* (pp. 309–333). Hershey, PA: IGI Global. doi:10.4018/978-1-5225-0892-2.ch017

Gokhale, A. A., & Machina, K. F. (2017). Development of a Scale to Measure Attitudes toward Information Technology. In L. Tomei (Ed.), *Exploring the New Era of Technology-Infused Education* (pp. 49–64). Hershey, PA: IGI Global. doi:10.4018/978-1-5225-1709-2.ch004

Grace, A., O'Donoghue, J., Mahony, C., Heffernan, T., Molony, D., & Carroll, T. (2016). Computerized Decision Support Systems for Multimorbidity Care: An Urgent Call for Research and Development. In M. Cruz-Cunha, I. Miranda, R. Martinho, & R. Rijo (Eds.), *Encyclopedia of E-Health and Telemedicine* (pp. 486–494). Hershey, PA: IGI Global. doi:10.4018/978-1-4666-9978-6.ch038

Gupta, A., & Singh, O. (2016). Computer Aided Modeling and Finite Element Analysis of Human Elbow. *International Journal of Biomedical and Clinical Engineering*, *5*(1), 31–38. doi:10.4018/IJBCE.2016010104

H., S. K. (2016). Classification of Cybercrimes and Punishments under the Information Technology Act, 2000. In S. Geetha, & A. Phamila (Eds.), *Combating Security Breaches and Criminal Activity in the Digital Sphere* (pp. 57-66). Hershey, PA: IGI Global. doi:10.4018/978-1-5225-0193-0.ch004

Hafeez-Baig, A., Gururajan, R., & Wickramasinghe, N. (2017). Readiness as a Novel Construct of Readiness Acceptance Model (RAM) for the Wireless Handheld Technology. In N. Wickramasinghe (Ed.), *Handbook of Research on Healthcare Administration and Management* (pp. 578–595). Hershey, PA: IGI Global. doi:10.4018/978-1-5225-0920-2.ch035

Hanafizadeh, P., Ghandchi, S., & Asgarimehr, M. (2017). Impact of Information Technology on Lifestyle: A Literature Review and Classification. *International Journal of Virtual Communities and Social Networking*, *9*(2), 1–23. doi:10.4018/IJVCSN.2017040101

Harlow, D. B., Dwyer, H., Hansen, A. K., Hill, C., Iveland, A., Leak, A. E., & Franklin, D. M. (2016). Computer Programming in Elementary and Middle School: Connections across Content. In M. Urban & D. Falvo (Eds.), *Improving K-12 STEM Education Outcomes through Technological Integration* (pp. 337–361). Hershey, PA: IGI Global. doi:10.4018/978-1-4666-9616-7.ch015

Haseski, H. İ., Ilic, U., & Tuğtekin, U. (2018). Computational Thinking in Educational Digital Games: An Assessment Tool Proposal. In H. Ozcinar, G. Wong, & H. Ozturk (Eds.), *Teaching Computational Thinking in Primary Education* (pp. 256–287). Hershey, PA: IGI Global. doi:10.4018/978-1-5225-3200-2.ch013

Hee, W. J., Jalleh, G., Lai, H., & Lin, C. (2017). E-Commerce and IT Projects: Evaluation and Management Issues in Australian and Taiwanese Hospitals. *International Journal of Public Health Management and Ethics*, 2(1), 69–90. doi:10.4018/IJPHME.2017010104

Hernandez, A. A. (2017). Green Information Technology Usage: Awareness and Practices of Philippine IT Professionals. *International Journal of Enterprise Information Systems*, 13(4), 90–103. doi:10.4018/IJEIS.2017100106

Hernandez, A. A., & Ona, S. E. (2016). Green IT Adoption: Lessons from the Philippines Business Process Outsourcing Industry. *International Journal of Social Ecology and Sustainable Development*, 7(1), 1–34. doi:10.4018/IJSESD.2016010101

Hernandez, M. A., Marin, E. C., Garcia-Rodriguez, J., Azorin-Lopez, J., & Cazorla, M. (2017). Automatic Learning Improves Human-Robot Interaction in Productive Environments: A Review. *International Journal of Computer Vision and Image Processing*, 7(3), 65–75. doi:10.4018/IJCVIP.2017070106

Horne-Popp, L. M., Tessone, E. B., & Welker, J. (2018). If You Build It, They Will Come: Creating a Library Statistics Dashboard for Decision-Making. In L. Costello & M. Powers (Eds.), *Developing In-House Digital Tools in Library Spaces* (pp. 177–203). Hershey, PA: IGI Global. doi:10.4018/978-1-5225-2676-6.ch009

Hossan, C. G., & Ryan, J. C. (2016). Factors Affecting e-Government Technology Adoption Behaviour in a Voluntary Environment. *International Journal of Electronic Government Research*, 12(1), 24–49. doi:10.4018/IJEGR.2016010102

Hu, H., Hu, P. J., & Al-Gahtani, S. S. (2017). User Acceptance of Computer Technology at Work in Arabian Culture: A Model Comparison Approach. In M. Khosrow-Pour (Ed.), *Handbook of Research on Technology Adoption, Social Policy, and Global Integration* (pp. 205–228). Hershey, PA: IGI Global. doi:10.4018/978-1-5225-2668-1.ch011

Huie, C. P. (2016). Perceptions of Business Intelligence Professionals about Factors Related to Business Intelligence input in Decision Making. *International Journal of Business Analytics*, 3(3), 1–24. doi:10.4018/IJBAN.2016070101

Hung, S., Huang, W., Yen, D. C., Chang, S., & Lu, C. (2016). Effect of Information Service Competence and Contextual Factors on the Effectiveness of Strategic Information Systems Planning in Hospitals. *Journal of Global Information Management*, 24(1), 14–36. doi:10.4018/JGIM.2016010102

Ifinedo, P. (2017). Using an Extended Theory of Planned Behavior to Study Nurses' Adoption of Healthcare Information Systems in Nova Scotia. *International Journal of Technology Diffusion*, 8(1), 1–17. doi:10.4018/IJTD.2017010101

Ilie, V., & Sneha, S. (2018). A Three Country Study for Understanding Physicians' Engagement With Electronic Information Resources Pre and Post System Implementation. *Journal of Global Information Management*, 26(2), 48–73. doi:10.4018/JGIM.2018040103

Inoue-Smith, Y. (2017). Perceived Ease in Using Technology Predicts Teacher Candidates' Preferences for Online Resources. *International Journal of Online Pedagogy and Course Design*, 7(3), 17–28. doi:10.4018/IJOPCD.2017070102

Islam, A. A. (2016). Development and Validation of the Technology Adoption and Gratification (TAG) Model in Higher Education: A Cross-Cultural Study Between Malaysia and China. *International Journal of Technology and Human Interaction, 12*(3), 78–105. doi:10.4018/IJTHI.2016070106

Islam, A. Y. (2017). Technology Satisfaction in an Academic Context: Moderating Effect of Gender. In A. Mesquita (Ed.), *Research Paradigms and Contemporary Perspectives on Human-Technology Interaction* (pp. 187–211). Hershey, PA: IGI Global. doi:10.4018/978-1-5225-1868-6.ch009

Jamil, G. L., & Jamil, C. C. (2017). Information and Knowledge Management Perspective Contributions for Fashion Studies: Observing Logistics and Supply Chain Management Processes. In G. Jamil, A. Soares, & C. Pessoa (Eds.), *Handbook of Research on Information Management for Effective Logistics and Supply Chains* (pp. 199–221). Hershey, PA: IGI Global. doi:10.4018/978-1-5225-0973-8.ch011

Jamil, G. L., Jamil, L. C., Vieira, A. A., & Xavier, A. J. (2016). Challenges in Modelling Healthcare Services: A Study Case of Information Architecture Perspectives. In G. Jamil, J. Poças Rascão, F. Ribeiro, & A. Malheiro da Silva (Eds.), *Handbook of Research on Information Architecture and Management in Modern Organizations* (pp. 1–23). Hershey, PA: IGI Global. doi:10.4018/978-1-4666-8637-3.ch001

Janakova, M. (2018). Big Data and Simulations for the Solution of Controversies in Small Businesses. In M. Khosrow-Pour, D.B.A. (Ed.), Encyclopedia of Information Science and Technology, Fourth Edition (pp. 6907-6915). Hershey, PA: IGI Global. doi:10.4018/978-1-5225-2255-3.ch598

Jha, D. G. (2016). Preparing for Information Technology Driven Changes. In S. Tiwari & L. Nafees (Eds.), *Innovative Management Education Pedagogies for Preparing Next-Generation Leaders* (pp. 258–274). Hershey, PA: IGI Global. doi:10.4018/978-1-4666-9691-4.ch015

Jhawar, A., & Garg, S. K. (2018). Logistics Improvement by Investment in Information Technology Using System Dynamics. In A. Azar & S. Vaidyanathan (Eds.), *Advances in System Dynamics and Control* (pp. 528–567). Hershey, PA: IGI Global. doi:10.4018/978-1-5225-4077-9.ch017

Kalelioğlu, F., Gülbahar, Y., & Doğan, D. (2018). Teaching How to Think Like a Programmer: Emerging Insights. In H. Ozcinar, G. Wong, & H. Ozturk (Eds.), *Teaching Computational Thinking in Primary Education* (pp. 18–35). Hershey, PA: IGI Global. doi:10.4018/978-1-5225-3200-2.ch002

Kamberi, S. (2017). A Girls-Only Online Virtual World Environment and its Implications for Game-Based Learning. In A. Stricker, C. Calongne, B. Truman, & F. Arenas (Eds.), *Integrating an Awareness of Selfhood and Society into Virtual Learning* (pp. 74–95). Hershey, PA: IGI Global. doi:10.4018/978-1-5225-2182-2.ch006

Kamel, S., & Rizk, N. (2017). ICT Strategy Development: From Design to Implementation – Case of Egypt. In C. Howard & K. Hargiss (Eds.), *Strategic Information Systems and Technologies in Modern Organizations* (pp. 239–257). Hershey, PA: IGI Global. doi:10.4018/978-1-5225-1680-4.ch010

Kamel, S. H. (2018). The Potential Role of the Software Industry in Supporting Economic Development. In M. Khosrow-Pour, D.B.A. (Ed.), Encyclopedia of Information Science and Technology, Fourth Edition (pp. 7259-7269). Hershey, PA: IGI Global. doi:10.4018/978-1-5225-2255-3.ch631

Karon, R. (2016). Utilisation of Health Information Systems for Service Delivery in the Namibian Environment. In T. Iyamu & A. Tatnall (Eds.), *Maximizing Healthcare Delivery and Management through Technology Integration* (pp. 169–183). Hershey, PA: IGI Global. doi:10.4018/978-1-4666-9446-0.ch011

Kawata, S. (2018). Computer-Assisted Parallel Program Generation. In M. Khosrow-Pour, D.B.A. (Ed.), Encyclopedia of Information Science and Technology, Fourth Edition (pp. 4583-4593). Hershey, PA: IGI Global. doi:10.4018/978-1-5225-2255-3.ch398

Khanam, S., Siddiqui, J., & Talib, F. (2016). A DEMATEL Approach for Prioritizing the TQM Enablers and IT Resources in the Indian ICT Industry. *International Journal of Applied Management Sciences and Engineering*, *3*(1), 11–29. doi:10.4018/IJAMSE.2016010102

Khari, M., Shrivastava, G., Gupta, S., & Gupta, R. (2017). Role of Cyber Security in Today's Scenario. In R. Kumar, P. Pattnaik, & P. Pandey (Eds.), *Detecting and Mitigating Robotic Cyber Security Risks* (pp. 177–191). Hershey, PA: IGI Global. doi:10.4018/978-1-5225-2154-9.ch013

Khouja, M., Rodriguez, I. B., Ben Halima, Y., & Moalla, S. (2018). IT Governance in Higher Education Institutions: A Systematic Literature Review. *International Journal of Human Capital and Information Technology Professionals*, *9*(2), 52–67. doi:10.4018/IJHCITP.2018040104

Kim, S., Chang, M., Choi, N., Park, J., & Kim, H. (2016). The Direct and Indirect Effects of Computer Uses on Student Success in Math. *International Journal of Cyber Behavior, Psychology and Learning*, *6*(3), 48–64. doi:10.4018/IJCBPL.2016070104

Kiourt, C., Pavlidis, G., Koutsoudis, A., & Kalles, D. (2017). Realistic Simulation of Cultural Heritage. *International Journal of Computational Methods in Heritage Science*, *1*(1), 10–40. doi:10.4018/IJCMHS.2017010102

Korikov, A., & Krivtsov, O. (2016). System of People-Computer: On the Way of Creation of Human-Oriented Interface. In V. Mkrttchian, A. Bershadsky, A. Bozhday, M. Kataev, & S. Kataev (Eds.), *Handbook of Research on Estimation and Control Techniques in E-Learning Systems* (pp. 458–470). Hershey, PA: IGI Global. doi:10.4018/978-1-4666-9489-7.ch032

Köse, U. (2017). An Augmented-Reality-Based Intelligent Mobile Application for Open Computer Education. In G. Kurubacak & H. Altinpulluk (Eds.), *Mobile Technologies and Augmented Reality in Open Education* (pp. 154–174). Hershey, PA: IGI Global. doi:10.4018/978-1-5225-2110-5.ch008

Lahmiri, S. (2018). Information Technology Outsourcing Risk Factors and Provider Selection. In M. Gupta, R. Sharman, J. Walp, & P. Mulgund (Eds.), *Information Technology Risk Management and Compliance in Modern Organizations* (pp. 214–228). Hershey, PA: IGI Global. doi:10.4018/978-1-5225-2604-9.ch008

Landriscina, F. (2017). Computer-Supported Imagination: The Interplay Between Computer and Mental Simulation in Understanding Scientific Concepts. In I. Levin & D. Tsybulsky (Eds.), *Digital Tools and Solutions for Inquiry-Based STEM Learning* (pp. 33–60). Hershey, PA: IGI Global. doi:10.4018/978-1-5225-2525-7.ch002

Lau, S. K., Winley, G. K., Leung, N. K., Tsang, N., & Lau, S. Y. (2016). An Exploratory Study of Expectation in IT Skills in a Developing Nation: Vietnam. *Journal of Global Information Management*, *24*(1), 1–13. doi:10.4018/JGIM.2016010101

Lavranos, C., Kostagiolas, P., & Papadatos, J. (2016). Information Retrieval Technologies and the "Realities" of Music Information Seeking. In I. Deliyannis, P. Kostagiolas, & C. Banou (Eds.), *Experimental Multimedia Systems for Interactivity and Strategic Innovation* (pp. 102–121). Hershey, PA: IGI Global. doi:10.4018/978-1-4666-8659-5.ch005

Lee, W. W. (2018). Ethical Computing Continues From Problem to Solution. In M. Khosrow-Pour, D.B.A. (Ed.), Encyclopedia of Information Science and Technology, Fourth Edition (pp. 4884-4897). Hershey, PA: IGI Global. doi:10.4018/978-1-5225-2255-3.ch423

Lehto, M. (2016). Cyber Security Education and Research in the Finland's Universities and Universities of Applied Sciences. *International Journal of Cyber Warfare & Terrorism, 6*(2), 15–31. doi:10.4018/IJCWT.2016040102

Lin, C., Jalleh, G., & Huang, Y. (2016). Evaluating and Managing Electronic Commerce and Outsourcing Projects in Hospitals. In A. Dwivedi (Ed.), *Reshaping Medical Practice and Care with Health Information Systems* (pp. 132–172). Hershey, PA: IGI Global. doi:10.4018/978-1-4666-9870-3.ch005

Lin, S., Chen, S., & Chuang, S. (2017). Perceived Innovation and Quick Response Codes in an Online-to-Offline E-Commerce Service Model. *International Journal of E-Adoption, 9*(2), 1–16. doi:10.4018/IJEA.2017070101

Liu, M., Wang, Y., Xu, W., & Liu, L. (2017). Automated Scoring of Chinese Engineering Students' English Essays. *International Journal of Distance Education Technologies, 15*(1), 52–68. doi:10.4018/IJDET.2017010104

Luciano, E. M., Wiedenhöft, G. C., Macadar, M. A., & Pinheiro dos Santos, F. (2016). Information Technology Governance Adoption: Understanding its Expectations Through the Lens of Organizational Citizenship. *International Journal of IT/Business Alignment and Governance, 7*(2), 22-32. doi:10.4018/IJITBAG.2016070102

Mabe, L. K., & Oladele, O. I. (2017). Application of Information Communication Technologies for Agricultural Development through Extension Services: A Review. In T. Tossy (Ed.), *Information Technology Integration for Socio-Economic Development* (pp. 52–101). Hershey, PA: IGI Global. doi:10.4018/978-1-5225-0539-6.ch003

Manogaran, G., Thota, C., & Lopez, D. (2018). Human-Computer Interaction With Big Data Analytics. In D. Lopez & M. Durai (Eds.), *HCI Challenges and Privacy Preservation in Big Data Security* (pp. 1–22). Hershey, PA: IGI Global. doi:10.4018/978-1-5225-2863-0.ch001

Margolis, J., Goode, J., & Flapan, J. (2017). A Critical Crossroads for Computer Science for All: "Identifying Talent" or "Building Talent," and What Difference Does It Make? In Y. Rankin & J. Thomas (Eds.), *Moving Students of Color from Consumers to Producers of Technology* (pp. 1–23). Hershey, PA: IGI Global. doi:10.4018/978-1-5225-2005-4.ch001

Mbale, J. (2018). Computer Centres Resource Cloud Elasticity-Scalability (CRECES): Copperbelt University Case Study. In S. Aljawarneh & M. Malhotra (Eds.), *Critical Research on Scalability and Security Issues in Virtual Cloud Environments* (pp. 48–70). Hershey, PA: IGI Global. doi:10.4018/978-1-5225-3029-9.ch003

McKee, J. (2018). The Right Information: The Key to Effective Business Planning. In *Business Architectures for Risk Assessment and Strategic Planning: Emerging Research and Opportunities* (pp. 38–52). Hershey, PA: IGI Global. doi:10.4018/978-1-5225-3392-4.ch003

Mensah, I. K., & Mi, J. (2018). Determinants of Intention to Use Local E-Government Services in Ghana: The Perspective of Local Government Workers. *International Journal of Technology Diffusion*, *9*(2), 41–60. doi:10.4018/IJTD.2018040103

Mohamed, J. H. (2018). Scientograph-Based Visualization of Computer Forensics Research Literature. In J. Jeyasekar & P. Saravanan (Eds.), *Innovations in Measuring and Evaluating Scientific Information* (pp. 148–162). Hershey, PA: IGI Global. doi:10.4018/978-1-5225-3457-0.ch010

Moore, R. L., & Johnson, N. (2017). Earning a Seat at the Table: How IT Departments Can Partner in Organizational Change and Innovation. *International Journal of Knowledge-Based Organizations*, *7*(2), 1–12. doi:10.4018/IJKBO.2017040101

Mtebe, J. S., & Kissaka, M. M. (2016). Enhancing the Quality of Computer Science Education with MOOCs in Sub-Saharan Africa. In J. Keengwe & G. Onchwari (Eds.), *Handbook of Research on Active Learning and the Flipped Classroom Model in the Digital Age* (pp. 366–377). Hershey, PA: IGI Global. doi:10.4018/978-1-4666-9680-8.ch019

Mukul, M. K., & Bhattaharyya, S. (2017). Brain-Machine Interface: Human-Computer Interaction. In E. Noughabi, B. Raahemi, A. Albadvi, & B. Far (Eds.), *Handbook of Research on Data Science for Effective Healthcare Practice and Administration* (pp. 417–443). Hershey, PA: IGI Global. doi:10.4018/978-1-5225-2515-8.ch018

Na, L. (2017). Library and Information Science Education and Graduate Programs in Academic Libraries. In L. Ruan, Q. Zhu, & Y. Ye (Eds.), *Academic Library Development and Administration in China* (pp. 218–229). Hershey, PA: IGI Global. doi:10.4018/978-1-5225-0550-1.ch013

Nabavi, A., Taghavi-Fard, M. T., Hanafizadeh, P., & Taghva, M. R. (2016). Information Technology Continuance Intention: A Systematic Literature Review. *International Journal of E-Business Research*, *12*(1), 58–95. doi:10.4018/IJEBR.2016010104

Nath, R., & Murthy, V. N. (2018). What Accounts for the Differences in Internet Diffusion Rates Around the World? In M. Khosrow-Pour, D.B.A. (Ed.), Encyclopedia of Information Science and Technology, Fourth Edition (pp. 8095-8104). Hershey, PA: IGI Global. doi:10.4018/978-1-5225-2255-3.ch705

Nedelko, Z., & Potocan, V. (2018). The Role of Emerging Information Technologies for Supporting Supply Chain Management. In M. Khosrow-Pour, D.B.A. (Ed.), Encyclopedia of Information Science and Technology, Fourth Edition (pp. 5559-5569). Hershey, PA: IGI Global. doi:10.4018/978-1-5225-2255-3.ch483

Ngafeeson, M. N. (2018). User Resistance to Health Information Technology. In M. Khosrow-Pour, D.B.A. (Ed.), Encyclopedia of Information Science and Technology, Fourth Edition (pp. 3816-3825). Hershey, PA: IGI Global. doi:10.4018/978-1-5225-2255-3.ch331

Nozari, H., Najafi, S. E., Jafari-Eskandari, M., & Aliahmadi, A. (2016). Providing a Model for Virtual Project Management with an Emphasis on IT Projects. In C. Graham (Ed.), *Strategic Management and Leadership for Systems Development in Virtual Spaces* (pp. 43–63). Hershey, PA: IGI Global. doi:10.4018/978-1-4666-9688-4.ch003

Nurdin, N., Stockdale, R., & Scheepers, H. (2016). Influence of Organizational Factors in the Sustainability of E-Government: A Case Study of Local E-Government in Indonesia. In I. Sodhi (Ed.), *Trends, Prospects, and Challenges in Asian E-Governance* (pp. 281–323). Hershey, PA: IGI Global. doi:10.4018/978-1-4666-9536-8.ch014

Odagiri, K. (2017). Introduction of Individual Technology to Constitute the Current Internet. In *Strategic Policy-Based Network Management in Contemporary Organizations* (pp. 20–96). Hershey, PA: IGI Global. doi:10.4018/978-1-68318-003-6.ch003

Okike, E. U. (2018). Computer Science and Prison Education. In I. Biao (Ed.), *Strategic Learning Ideologies in Prison Education Programs* (pp. 246–264). Hershey, PA: IGI Global. doi:10.4018/978-1-5225-2909-5.ch012

Olelewe, C. J., & Nwafor, I. P. (2017). Level of Computer Appreciation Skills Acquired for Sustainable Development by Secondary School Students in Nsukka LGA of Enugu State, Nigeria. In C. Ayo & V. Mbarika (Eds.), *Sustainable ICT Adoption and Integration for Socio-Economic Development* (pp. 214–233). Hershey, PA: IGI Global. doi:10.4018/978-1-5225-2565-3.ch010

Oliveira, M., Maçada, A. C., Curado, C., & Nodari, F. (2017). Infrastructure Profiles and Knowledge Sharing. *International Journal of Technology and Human Interaction*, *13*(3), 1–12. doi:10.4018/IJTHI.2017070101

Otarkhani, A., Shokouhyar, S., & Pour, S. S. (2017). Analyzing the Impact of Governance of Enterprise IT on Hospital Performance: Tehran's (Iran) Hospitals – A Case Study. *International Journal of Healthcare Information Systems and Informatics*, *12*(3), 1–20. doi:10.4018/IJHISI.2017070101

Otunla, A. O., & Amuda, C. O. (2018). Nigerian Undergraduate Students' Computer Competencies and Use of Information Technology Tools and Resources for Study Skills and Habits' Enhancement. In M. Khosrow-Pour, D.B.A. (Ed.), Encyclopedia of Information Science and Technology, Fourth Edition (pp. 2303-2313). Hershey, PA: IGI Global. doi:10.4018/978-1-5225-2255-3.ch200

Özçınar, H. (2018). A Brief Discussion on Incentives and Barriers to Computational Thinking Education. In H. Ozcinar, G. Wong, & H. Ozturk (Eds.), *Teaching Computational Thinking in Primary Education* (pp. 1–17). Hershey, PA: IGI Global. doi:10.4018/978-1-5225-3200-2.ch001

Pandey, J. M., Garg, S., Mishra, P., & Mishra, B. P. (2017). Computer Based Psychological Interventions: Subject to the Efficacy of Psychological Services. *International Journal of Computers in Clinical Practice*, *2*(1), 25–33. doi:10.4018/IJCCP.2017010102

Parry, V. K., & Lind, M. L. (2016). Alignment of Business Strategy and Information Technology Considering Information Technology Governance, Project Portfolio Control, and Risk Management. *International Journal of Information Technology Project Management*, *7*(4), 21–37. doi:10.4018/IJITPM.2016100102

Patro, C. (2017). Impulsion of Information Technology on Human Resource Practices. In P. Ordóñez de Pablos (Ed.), *Managerial Strategies and Solutions for Business Success in Asia* (pp. 231–254). Hershey, PA: IGI Global. doi:10.4018/978-1-5225-1886-0.ch013

Patro, C. S., & Raghunath, K. M. (2017). Information Technology Paraphernalia for Supply Chain Management Decisions. In M. Tavana (Ed.), *Enterprise Information Systems and the Digitalization of Business Functions* (pp. 294–320). Hershey, PA: IGI Global. doi:10.4018/978-1-5225-2382-6.ch014

Paul, P. K. (2016). Cloud Computing: An Agent of Promoting Interdisciplinary Sciences, Especially Information Science and I-Schools – Emerging Techno-Educational Scenario. In L. Chao (Ed.), *Handbook of Research on Cloud-Based STEM Education for Improved Learning Outcomes* (pp. 247–258). Hershey, PA: IGI Global. doi:10.4018/978-1-4666-9924-3.ch016

Paul, P. K. (2018). The Context of IST for Solid Information Retrieval and Infrastructure Building: Study of Developing Country. *International Journal of Information Retrieval Research*, *8*(1), 86–100. doi:10.4018/IJIRR.2018010106

Paul, P. K., & Chatterjee, D. (2018). iSchools Promoting "Information Science and Technology" (IST) Domain Towards Community, Business, and Society With Contemporary Worldwide Trend and Emerging Potentialities in India. In M. Khosrow-Pour, D.B.A. (Ed.), Encyclopedia of Information Science and Technology, Fourth Edition (pp. 4723-4735). Hershey, PA: IGI Global. doi:10.4018/978-1-5225-2255-3.ch410

Pessoa, C. R., & Marques, M. E. (2017). Information Technology and Communication Management in Supply Chain Management. In G. Jamil, A. Soares, & C. Pessoa (Eds.), *Handbook of Research on Information Management for Effective Logistics and Supply Chains* (pp. 23–33). Hershey, PA: IGI Global. doi:10.4018/978-1-5225-0973-8.ch002

Pineda, R. G. (2016). Where the Interaction Is Not: Reflections on the Philosophy of Human-Computer Interaction. *International Journal of Art, Culture and Design Technologies*, *5*(1), 1–12. doi:10.4018/IJACDT.2016010101

Pineda, R. G. (2018). Remediating Interaction: Towards a Philosophy of Human-Computer Relationship. In M. Khosrow-Pour (Ed.), *Enhancing Art, Culture, and Design With Technological Integration* (pp. 75–98). Hershey, PA: IGI Global. doi:10.4018/978-1-5225-5023-5.ch004

Poikela, P., & Vuojärvi, H. (2016). Learning ICT-Mediated Communication through Computer-Based Simulations. In M. Cruz-Cunha, I. Miranda, R. Martinho, & R. Rijo (Eds.), *Encyclopedia of E-Health and Telemedicine* (pp. 674–687). Hershey, PA: IGI Global. doi:10.4018/978-1-4666-9978-6.ch052

Qian, Y. (2017). Computer Simulation in Higher Education: Affordances, Opportunities, and Outcomes. In P. Vu, S. Fredrickson, & C. Moore (Eds.), *Handbook of Research on Innovative Pedagogies and Technologies for Online Learning in Higher Education* (pp. 236–262). Hershey, PA: IGI Global. doi:10.4018/978-1-5225-1851-8.ch011

Radant, O., Colomo-Palacios, R., & Stantchev, V. (2016). Factors for the Management of Scarce Human Resources and Highly Skilled Employees in IT-Departments: A Systematic Review. *Journal of Information Technology Research*, *9*(1), 65–82. doi:10.4018/JITR.2016010105

Rahman, N. (2016). Toward Achieving Environmental Sustainability in the Computer Industry. *International Journal of Green Computing*, 7(1), 37–54. doi:10.4018/IJGC.2016010103

Rahman, N. (2017). Lessons from a Successful Data Warehousing Project Management. *International Journal of Information Technology Project Management*, 8(4), 30–45. doi:10.4018/IJITPM.2017100103

Rahman, N. (2018). Environmental Sustainability in the Computer Industry for Competitive Advantage. In M. Khosrow-Pour (Ed.), *Green Computing Strategies for Competitive Advantage and Business Sustainability* (pp. 110–130). Hershey, PA: IGI Global. doi:10.4018/978-1-5225-5017-4.ch006

Rajh, A., & Pavetic, T. (2017). Computer Generated Description as the Required Digital Competence in Archival Profession. *International Journal of Digital Literacy and Digital Competence*, 8(1), 36–49. doi:10.4018/IJDLDC.2017010103

Raman, A., & Goyal, D. P. (2017). Extending IMPLEMENT Framework for Enterprise Information Systems Implementation to Information System Innovation. In M. Tavana (Ed.), *Enterprise Information Systems and the Digitalization of Business Functions* (pp. 137–177). Hershey, PA: IGI Global. doi:10.4018/978-1-5225-2382-6.ch007

Rao, Y. S., Rauta, A. K., Saini, H., & Panda, T. C. (2017). Mathematical Model for Cyber Attack in Computer Network. *International Journal of Business Data Communications and Networking*, 13(1), 58–65. doi:10.4018/IJBDCN.2017010105

Rapaport, W. J. (2018). Syntactic Semantics and the Proper Treatment of Computationalism. In M. Danesi (Ed.), *Empirical Research on Semiotics and Visual Rhetoric* (pp. 128–176). Hershey, PA: IGI Global. doi:10.4018/978-1-5225-5622-0.ch007

Raut, R., Priyadarshinee, P., & Jha, M. (2017). Understanding the Mediation Effect of Cloud Computing Adoption in Indian Organization: Integrating TAM-TOE- Risk Model. *International Journal of Service Science, Management, Engineering, and Technology*, 8(3), 40–59. doi:10.4018/IJSSMET.2017070103

Regan, E. A., & Wang, J. (2016). Realizing the Value of EHR Systems Critical Success Factors. *International Journal of Healthcare Information Systems and Informatics*, 11(3), 1–18. doi:10.4018/IJHISI.2016070101

Rezaie, S., Mirabedini, S. J., & Abtahi, A. (2018). Designing a Model for Implementation of Business Intelligence in the Banking Industry. *International Journal of Enterprise Information Systems*, 14(1), 77–103. doi:10.4018/IJEIS.2018010105

Rezende, D. A. (2016). Digital City Projects: Information and Public Services Offered by Chicago (USA) and Curitiba (Brazil). *International Journal of Knowledge Society Research*, 7(3), 16–30. doi:10.4018/IJKSR.2016070102

Rezende, D. A. (2018). Strategic Digital City Projects: Innovative Information and Public Services Offered by Chicago (USA) and Curitiba (Brazil). In M. Lytras, L. Daniela, & A. Visvizi (Eds.), *Enhancing Knowledge Discovery and Innovation in the Digital Era* (pp. 204–223). Hershey, PA: IGI Global. doi:10.4018/978-1-5225-4191-2.ch012

Riabov, V. V. (2016). Teaching Online Computer-Science Courses in LMS and Cloud Environment. *International Journal of Quality Assurance in Engineering and Technology Education*, 5(4), 12–41. doi:10.4018/IJQAETE.2016100102

Ricordel, V., Wang, J., Da Silva, M. P., & Le Callet, P. (2016). 2D and 3D Visual Attention for Computer Vision: Concepts, Measurement, and Modeling. In R. Pal (Ed.), *Innovative Research in Attention Modeling and Computer Vision Applications* (pp. 1–44). Hershey, PA: IGI Global. doi:10.4018/978-1-4666-8723-3.ch001

Rodriguez, A., Rico-Diaz, A. J., Rabuñal, J. R., & Gestal, M. (2017). Fish Tracking with Computer Vision Techniques: An Application to Vertical Slot Fishways. In M. S., & V. V. (Eds.), Multi-Core Computer Vision and Image Processing for Intelligent Applications (pp. 74-104). Hershey, PA: IGI Global. doi:10.4018/978-1-5225-0889-2.ch003

Romero, J. A. (2018). Sustainable Advantages of Business Value of Information Technology. In M. Khosrow-Pour, D.B.A. (Ed.), Encyclopedia of Information Science and Technology, Fourth Edition (pp. 923-929). Hershey, PA: IGI Global. doi:10.4018/978-1-5225-2255-3.ch079

Romero, J. A. (2018). The Always-On Business Model and Competitive Advantage. In N. Bajgoric (Ed.), *Always-On Enterprise Information Systems for Modern Organizations* (pp. 23–40). Hershey, PA: IGI Global. doi:10.4018/978-1-5225-3704-5.ch002

Rosen, Y. (2018). Computer Agent Technologies in Collaborative Learning and Assessment. In M. Khosrow-Pour, D.B.A. (Ed.), Encyclopedia of Information Science and Technology, Fourth Edition (pp. 2402-2410). Hershey, PA: IGI Global. doi:10.4018/978-1-5225-2255-3.ch209

Rosen, Y., & Mosharraf, M. (2016). Computer Agent Technologies in Collaborative Assessments. In Y. Rosen, S. Ferrara, & M. Mosharraf (Eds.), *Handbook of Research on Technology Tools for Real-World Skill Development* (pp. 319–343). Hershey, PA: IGI Global. doi:10.4018/978-1-4666-9441-5.ch012

Roy, D. (2018). Success Factors of Adoption of Mobile Applications in Rural India: Effect of Service Characteristics on Conceptual Model. In M. Khosrow-Pour (Ed.), *Green Computing Strategies for Competitive Advantage and Business Sustainability* (pp. 211–238). Hershey, PA: IGI Global. doi:10.4018/978-1-5225-5017-4.ch010

Ruffin, T. R. (2016). Health Information Technology and Change. In V. Wang (Ed.), *Handbook of Research on Advancing Health Education through Technology* (pp. 259–285). Hershey, PA: IGI Global. doi:10.4018/978-1-4666-9494-1.ch012

Ruffin, T. R. (2016). Health Information Technology and Quality Management. *International Journal of Information Communication Technologies and Human Development*, 8(4), 56–72. doi:10.4018/IJICTHD.2016100105

Ruffin, T. R., & Hawkins, D. P. (2018). Trends in Health Care Information Technology and Informatics. In M. Khosrow-Pour, D.B.A. (Ed.), Encyclopedia of Information Science and Technology, Fourth Edition (pp. 3805-3815). Hershey, PA: IGI Global. doi:10.4018/978-1-5225-2255-3.ch330

Safari, M. R., & Jiang, Q. (2018). The Theory and Practice of IT Governance Maturity and Strategies Alignment: Evidence From Banking Industry. *Journal of Global Information Management, 26*(2), 127–146. doi:10.4018/JGIM.2018040106

Sahin, H. B., & Anagun, S. S. (2018). Educational Computer Games in Math Teaching: A Learning Culture. In E. Toprak & E. Kumtepe (Eds.), *Supporting Multiculturalism in Open and Distance Learning Spaces* (pp. 249–280). Hershey, PA: IGI Global. doi:10.4018/978-1-5225-3076-3.ch013

Sanna, A., & Valpreda, F. (2017). An Assessment of the Impact of a Collaborative Didactic Approach and Students' Background in Teaching Computer Animation. *International Journal of Information and Communication Technology Education, 13*(4), 1–16. doi:10.4018/IJICTE.2017100101

Savita, K., Dominic, P., & Ramayah, T. (2016). The Drivers, Practices and Outcomes of Green Supply Chain Management: Insights from ISO14001 Manufacturing Firms in Malaysia. *International Journal of Information Systems and Supply Chain Management, 9*(2), 35–60. doi:10.4018/IJISSCM.2016040103

Scott, A., Martin, A., & McAlear, F. (2017). Enhancing Participation in Computer Science among Girls of Color: An Examination of a Preparatory AP Computer Science Intervention. In Y. Rankin & J. Thomas (Eds.), *Moving Students of Color from Consumers to Producers of Technology* (pp. 62–84). Hershey, PA: IGI Global. doi:10.4018/978-1-5225-2005-4.ch004

Shahsavandi, E., Mayah, G., & Rahbari, H. (2016). Impact of E-Government on Transparency and Corruption in Iran. In I. Sodhi (Ed.), *Trends, Prospects, and Challenges in Asian E-Governance* (pp. 75–94). Hershey, PA: IGI Global. doi:10.4018/978-1-4666-9536-8.ch004

Siddoo, V., & Wongsai, N. (2017). Factors Influencing the Adoption of ISO/IEC 29110 in Thai Government Projects: A Case Study. *International Journal of Information Technologies and Systems Approach, 10*(1), 22–44. doi:10.4018/IJITSA.2017010102

Sidorkina, I., & Rybakov, A. (2016). Computer-Aided Design as Carrier of Set Development Changes System in E-Course Engineering. In V. Mkrttchian, A. Bershadsky, A. Bozhday, M. Kataev, & S. Kataev (Eds.), *Handbook of Research on Estimation and Control Techniques in E-Learning Systems* (pp. 500–515). Hershey, PA: IGI Global. doi:10.4018/978-1-4666-9489-7.ch035

Sidorkina, I., & Rybakov, A. (2016). Creating Model of E-Course: As an Object of Computer-Aided Design. In V. Mkrttchian, A. Bershadsky, A. Bozhday, M. Kataev, & S. Kataev (Eds.), *Handbook of Research on Estimation and Control Techniques in E-Learning Systems* (pp. 286–297). Hershey, PA: IGI Global. doi:10.4018/978-1-4666-9489-7.ch019

Simões, A. (2017). Using Game Frameworks to Teach Computer Programming. In R. Alexandre Peixoto de Queirós & M. Pinto (Eds.), *Gamification-Based E-Learning Strategies for Computer Programming Education* (pp. 221–236). Hershey, PA: IGI Global. doi:10.4018/978-1-5225-1034-5.ch010

Sllame, A. M. (2017). Integrating LAB Work With Classes in Computer Network Courses. In H. Alphin Jr, R. Chan, & J. Lavine (Eds.), *The Future of Accessibility in International Higher Education* (pp. 253–275). Hershey, PA: IGI Global. doi:10.4018/978-1-5225-2560-8.ch015

Smirnov, A., Ponomarev, A., Shilov, N., Kashevnik, A., & Teslya, N. (2018). Ontology-Based Human-Computer Cloud for Decision Support: Architecture and Applications in Tourism. *International Journal of Embedded and Real-Time Communication Systems, 9*(1), 1–19. doi:10.4018/IJERTCS.2018010101

Smith-Ditizio, A. A., & Smith, A. D. (2018). Computer Fraud Challenges and Its Legal Implications. In M. Khosrow-Pour, D.B.A. (Ed.), Encyclopedia of Information Science and Technology, Fourth Edition (pp. 4837-4848). Hershey, PA: IGI Global. doi:10.4018/978-1-5225-2255-3.ch419

Sohani, S. S. (2016). Job Shadowing in Information Technology Projects: A Source of Competitive Advantage. *International Journal of Information Technology Project Management, 7*(1), 47–57. doi:10.4018/IJITPM.2016010104

Sosnin, P. (2018). Figuratively Semantic Support of Human-Computer Interactions. In *Experience-Based Human-Computer Interactions: Emerging Research and Opportunities* (pp. 244–272). Hershey, PA: IGI Global. doi:10.4018/978-1-5225-2987-3.ch008

Spinelli, R., & Benevolo, C. (2016). From Healthcare Services to E-Health Applications: A Delivery System-Based Taxonomy. In A. Dwivedi (Ed.), *Reshaping Medical Practice and Care with Health Information Systems* (pp. 205–245). Hershey, PA: IGI Global. doi:10.4018/978-1-4666-9870-3.ch007

Srinivasan, S. (2016). Overview of Clinical Trial and Pharmacovigilance Process and Areas of Application of Computer System. In P. Chakraborty & A. Nagal (Eds.), *Software Innovations in Clinical Drug Development and Safety* (pp. 1–13). Hershey, PA: IGI Global. doi:10.4018/978-1-4666-8726-4.ch001

Srisawasdi, N. (2016). Motivating Inquiry-Based Learning Through a Combination of Physical and Virtual Computer-Based Laboratory Experiments in High School Science. In M. Urban & D. Falvo (Eds.), *Improving K-12 STEM Education Outcomes through Technological Integration* (pp. 108–134). Hershey, PA: IGI Global. doi:10.4018/978-1-4666-9616-7.ch006

Stavridi, S. V., & Hamada, D. R. (2016). Children and Youth Librarians: Competencies Required in Technology-Based Environment. In J. Yap, M. Perez, M. Ayson, & G. Entico (Eds.), *Special Library Administration, Standardization and Technological Integration* (pp. 25–50). Hershey, PA: IGI Global. doi:10.4018/978-1-4666-9542-9.ch002

Sung, W., Ahn, J., Kai, S. M., Choi, A., & Black, J. B. (2016). Incorporating Touch-Based Tablets into Classroom Activities: Fostering Children's Computational Thinking through iPad Integrated Instruction. In D. Mentor (Ed.), *Handbook of Research on Mobile Learning in Contemporary Classrooms* (pp. 378–406). Hershey, PA: IGI Global. doi:10.4018/978-1-5225-0251-7.ch019

Syväjärvi, A., Leinonen, J., Kivivirta, V., & Kesti, M. (2017). The Latitude of Information Management in Local Government: Views of Local Government Managers. *International Journal of Electronic Government Research, 13*(1), 69–85. doi:10.4018/IJEGR.2017010105

Tanque, M., & Foxwell, H. J. (2018). Big Data and Cloud Computing: A Review of Supply Chain Capabilities and Challenges. In A. Prasad (Ed.), *Exploring the Convergence of Big Data and the Internet of Things* (pp. 1–28). Hershey, PA: IGI Global. doi:10.4018/978-1-5225-2947-7.ch001

Teixeira, A., Gomes, A., & Orvalho, J. G. (2017). Auditory Feedback in a Computer Game for Blind People. In T. Issa, P. Kommers, T. Issa, P. Isaías, & T. Issa (Eds.), *Smart Technology Applications in Business Environments* (pp. 134–158). Hershey, PA: IGI Global. doi:10.4018/978-1-5225-2492-2.ch007

Thompson, N., McGill, T., & Murray, D. (2018). Affect-Sensitive Computer Systems. In M. Khosrow-Pour, D.B.A. (Ed.), Encyclopedia of Information Science and Technology, Fourth Edition (pp. 4124-4135). Hershey, PA: IGI Global. doi:10.4018/978-1-5225-2255-3.ch357

Trad, A., & Kalpić, D. (2016). The E-Business Transformation Framework for E-Commerce Control and Monitoring Pattern. In I. Lee (Ed.), *Encyclopedia of E-Commerce Development, Implementation, and Management* (pp. 754–777). Hershey, PA: IGI Global. doi:10.4018/978-1-4666-9787-4.ch053

Triberti, S., Brivio, E., & Galimberti, C. (2018). On Social Presence: Theories, Methodologies, and Guidelines for the Innovative Contexts of Computer-Mediated Learning. In M. Marmon (Ed.), *Enhancing Social Presence in Online Learning Environments* (pp. 20–41). Hershey, PA: IGI Global. doi:10.4018/978-1-5225-3229-3.ch002

Tripathy, B. K. T. R., S., & Mohanty, R. K. (2018). Memetic Algorithms and Their Applications in Computer Science. In S. Dash, B. Tripathy, & A. Rahman (Eds.), Handbook of Research on Modeling, Analysis, and Application of Nature-Inspired Metaheuristic Algorithms (pp. 73-93). Hershey, PA: IGI Global. doi:10.4018/978-1-5225-2857-9.ch004

Turulja, L., & Bajgoric, N. (2017). Human Resource Management IT and Global Economy Perspective: Global Human Resource Information Systems. In M. Khosrow-Pour (Ed.), *Handbook of Research on Technology Adoption, Social Policy, and Global Integration* (pp. 377–394). Hershey, PA: IGI Global. doi:10.4018/978-1-5225-2668-1.ch018

Unwin, D. W., Sanzogni, L., & Sandhu, K. (2017). Developing and Measuring the Business Case for Health Information Technology. In K. Moahi, K. Bwalya, & P. Sebina (Eds.), *Health Information Systems and the Advancement of Medical Practice in Developing Countries* (pp. 262–290). Hershey, PA: IGI Global. doi:10.4018/978-1-5225-2262-1.ch015

Vadhanam, B. R. S., M., Sugumaran, V., V., V., & Ramalingam, V. V. (2017). Computer Vision Based Classification on Commercial Videos. In M. S., & V. V. (Eds.), Multi-Core Computer Vision and Image Processing for Intelligent Applications (pp. 105-135). Hershey, PA: IGI Global. doi:10.4018/978-1-5225-0889-2.ch004

Valverde, R., Torres, B., & Motaghi, H. (2018). A Quantum NeuroIS Data Analytics Architecture for the Usability Evaluation of Learning Management Systems. In S. Bhattacharyya (Ed.), *Quantum-Inspired Intelligent Systems for Multimedia Data Analysis* (pp. 277–299). Hershey, PA: IGI Global. doi:10.4018/978-1-5225-5219-2.ch009

Vassilis, E. (2018). Learning and Teaching Methodology: "1:1 Educational Computing. In K. Koutsopoulos, K. Doukas, & Y. Kotsanis (Eds.), *Handbook of Research on Educational Design and Cloud Computing in Modern Classroom Settings* (pp. 122–155). Hershey, PA: IGI Global. doi:10.4018/978-1-5225-3053-4.ch007

Wadhwani, A. K., Wadhwani, S., & Singh, T. (2016). Computer Aided Diagnosis System for Breast Cancer Detection. In Y. Morsi, A. Shukla, & C. Rathore (Eds.), *Optimizing Assistive Technologies for Aging Populations* (pp. 378–395). Hershey, PA: IGI Global. doi:10.4018/978-1-4666-9530-6.ch015

Wang, L., Wu, Y., & Hu, C. (2016). English Teachers' Practice and Perspectives on Using Educational Computer Games in EIL Context. *International Journal of Technology and Human Interaction, 12*(3), 33–46. doi:10.4018/IJTHI.2016070103

Watfa, M. K., Majeed, H., & Salahuddin, T. (2016). Computer Based E-Healthcare Clinical Systems: A Comprehensive Survey. *International Journal of Privacy and Health Information Management, 4*(1), 50–69. doi:10.4018/IJPHIM.2016010104

Weeger, A., & Haase, U. (2016). Taking up Three Challenges to Business-IT Alignment Research by the Use of Activity Theory. *International Journal of IT/Business Alignment and Governance, 7*(2), 1-21. doi:10.4018/IJITBAG.2016070101

Wexler, B. E. (2017). Computer-Presented and Physical Brain-Training Exercises for School Children: Improving Executive Functions and Learning. In B. Dubbels (Ed.), *Transforming Gaming and Computer Simulation Technologies across Industries* (pp. 206–224). Hershey, PA: IGI Global. doi:10.4018/978-1-5225-1817-4.ch012

Williams, D. M., Gani, M. O., Addo, I. D., Majumder, A. J., Tamma, C. P., Wang, M., ... Chu, C. (2016). Challenges in Developing Applications for Aging Populations. In Y. Morsi, A. Shukla, & C. Rathore (Eds.), *Optimizing Assistive Technologies for Aging Populations* (pp. 1–21). Hershey, PA: IGI Global. doi:10.4018/978-1-4666-9530-6.ch001

Wimble, M., Singh, H., & Phillips, B. (2018). Understanding Cross-Level Interactions of Firm-Level Information Technology and Industry Environment: A Multilevel Model of Business Value. *Information Resources Management Journal, 31*(1), 1–20. doi:10.4018/IRMJ.2018010101

Wimmer, H., Powell, L., Kilgus, L., & Force, C. (2017). Improving Course Assessment via Web-based Homework. *International Journal of Online Pedagogy and Course Design, 7*(2), 1–19. doi:10.4018/IJOPCD.2017040101

Wong, Y. L., & Siu, K. W. (2018). Assessing Computer-Aided Design Skills. In M. Khosrow-Pour, D.B.A. (Ed.), Encyclopedia of Information Science and Technology, Fourth Edition (pp. 7382-7391). Hershey, PA: IGI Global. doi:10.4018/978-1-5225-2255-3.ch642

Wongsurawat, W., & Shrestha, V. (2018). Information Technology, Globalization, and Local Conditions: Implications for Entrepreneurs in Southeast Asia. In P. Ordóñez de Pablos (Ed.), *Management Strategies and Technology Fluidity in the Asian Business Sector* (pp. 163–176). Hershey, PA: IGI Global. doi:10.4018/978-1-5225-4056-4.ch010

Yang, Y., Zhu, X., Jin, C., & Li, J. J. (2018). Reforming Classroom Education Through a QQ Group: A Pilot Experiment at a Primary School in Shanghai. In H. Spires (Ed.), *Digital Transformation and Innovation in Chinese Education* (pp. 211–231). Hershey, PA: IGI Global. doi:10.4018/978-1-5225-2924-8.ch012

Yilmaz, R., Sezgin, A., Kurnaz, S., & Arslan, Y. Z. (2018). Object-Oriented Programming in Computer Science. In M. Khosrow-Pour, D.B.A. (Ed.), Encyclopedia of Information Science and Technology, Fourth Edition (pp. 7470-7480). Hershey, PA: IGI Global. doi:10.4018/978-1-5225-2255-3.ch650

Yu, L. (2018). From Teaching Software Engineering Locally and Globally to Devising an Internationalized Computer Science Curriculum. In S. Dikli, B. Etheridge, & R. Rawls (Eds.), *Curriculum Internationalization and the Future of Education* (pp. 293–320). Hershey, PA: IGI Global. doi:10.4018/978-1-5225-2791-6.ch016

Yuhua, F. (2018). Computer Information Library Clusters. In M. Khosrow-Pour, D.B.A. (Ed.), Encyclopedia of Information Science and Technology, Fourth Edition (pp. 4399-4403). Hershey, PA: IGI Global. doi:10.4018/978-1-5225-2255-3.ch382

Zare, M. A., Taghavi Fard, M. T., & Hanafizadeh, P. (2016). The Assessment of Outsourcing IT Services using DEA Technique: A Study of Application Outsourcing in Research Centers. *International Journal of Operations Research and Information Systems*, 7(1), 45–57. doi:10.4018/IJORIS.2016010104

Zhao, J., Wang, Q., Guo, J., Gao, L., & Yang, F. (2016). An Overview on Passive Image Forensics Technology for Automatic Computer Forgery. *International Journal of Digital Crime and Forensics*, 8(4), 14–25. doi:10.4018/IJDCF.2016100102

Zimeras, S. (2016). Computer Virus Models and Analysis in M-Health IT Systems: Computer Virus Models. In A. Moumtzoglou (Ed.), *M-Health Innovations for Patient-Centered Care* (pp. 284–297). Hershey, PA: IGI Global. doi:10.4018/978-1-4666-9861-1.ch014

Zlatanovska, K. (2016). Hacking and Hacktivism as an Information Communication System Threat. In M. Hadji-Janev & M. Bogdanoski (Eds.), *Handbook of Research on Civil Society and National Security in the Era of Cyber Warfare* (pp. 68–101). Hershey, PA: IGI Global. doi:10.4018/978-1-4666-8793-6.ch004

About the Contributors

Aboul Ella Hassanien (Abo) is a Professor at Cairo University, Faculty of Computers and Information, IT Department and the Chair of Scientific Research Group in Egypt (SRGE). Abo is the chair of the International Rough Sets Society-Egypt Chapter. He received his B.Sc. with honors in 1986 and M.Sc degree in 1993, both from Ain Shams University, Faculty of Science, Pure Mathematics and Computer Science Department, Cairo, Egypt. On September 1998, he received his doctoral degree from the Department of Computer Science, Graduate School of Science & Engineering, Tokyo Institute of Technology, Japan. He works in a multidisciplinary environment involving machine intelligence, network security and cryptology, data mining, various issues in intelligent environment including monitoring pollutions, technologies for disabled people including text-to-speech for blind people, Arabic sign Language, Social networks, biomedical engineering and bioinformatics and their applications to various real-world problems. He has authored/coauthored over 360 research publications in peer-reviewed reputed journals, book chapters and conference proceedings. He has served as the program committee member of various international conferences and reviewer for various international journals. He has received the excellence younger researcher award from Kuwait University for the academic year 2003/2004. He has guest edited many special issues for international scientific journals. He has directed many funded research projects. He is the editor and co-editor for more than 30 books in the area of rough computing, computational intelligence, social networks, bioinformatics, and E-commerce. For more details http://www.egyptscience.net.

Chiranji Lal Chowdhary received his Ph.D. in information technology and engineering from VIT University; his M.Tech. in computer science and engineering from (M. S. Ramaiah Institute of Technology, Bangalore), Visvesvaraya Technological University, Belagavi; and his B.E. in computer science and engineering from MBM Engineering College, Jai Narain Vyas University, India. He is currently working as an Associate Professor in the School of Information Technology and Engineering, VIT University. He has 15 years of experience in academia and 6 months of experience in the industry. He has received research awards for publishing research papers in refereed journals from VIT University 5 times consecutively. He has guided more than 20 graduate projects and more than 20 postgraduate level projects. His publications are indexed by the Clarivate Analytics, IEEE Computer Society, SCOPUS, the ACM Digital Library, and other abstract and citation databases. He is a reviewer for many reputed journals. He is a life member of the Computer Society of India, the Indian Science Congress Association, and the Indian Society for Technical Education. He has published many papers in refereed journals and has attended international conferences. He has contributed many chapters and is currently in the process of editing books. He has written 3 books and editing 3 books with a reputed publisher. His current research included digital image processing, deep learning, pattern recognition, soft computing, and biometric systems.

* * *

Rajithkumar B. K. obtained B.E degree in Electronics and Communication Engineering from Visvesvaraya Technological University during 2012, completed M.Tech in Digital Electronics and Communication Systems at Malnad College of Engineering, Hassan. He has published 14 International Journal Papers and his area of interested are Image processing, Signal processing, Digital signal Processing, Microprocessor. Presently, working as Assistant Professor at RV College of Engineering Bengaluru in Electronics and Communication Engineering Department.

Vijaya Kumar B. P. (SMIEEE, Fellow IETE, LMISTE, SMIACSIT) Ph.D in Electrical Communication Engineering (2003), Indian Institute of Science, Banaglore, M.Tech in Computer Science and Technology, India Institute of Technology) (1993), BE in Electronics and Communication, First class with distinction, Mysore Unversity (1987),. Presently he is a Professor and Head, Information Science and Engg., Dept, M S Ramaiah Institute of Tech., Bangalore. His research interest Applying Computational Intelligence - to meet the future smart-network's requirement such as cognitive computing approaches for intelligent networks. Involved in designing an adaptable, reliable, scalable and stabilizable routing algorithms for mobile adhoc and sensor networks, and also includes mobility based issues and context-aware service strategies by using intelligent techniques, i.e., swarm & bio-inspired computing and Neural Networks to solve the optimization or/and function approx. problems in mobile networks for better services. Protocol Engineering - Conformance testing and optimal Test sequence generation form formal methods.

Uma B. V. obtained Ph.D degree from Visvesvaraya Technological University . She has published 15 International Journal Papers and his area of interested are Image processing, VLSI, Signal processing. Presently, working as Professor at RV College of Engineering Bengaluru in Electronics and Communication Engineering Department.

Adrian Bell has many years of experience lecturing on higher education undergraduate courses and is module leader for construction technology. Adrian is approachable, supportive, encouraging and passionate about surveying and construction. As a lecturer, he's been nominated for Anglia Ruskin's Made a Difference award for two consecutive years.

Parimala Boobalan working as Assistant Professor (Senior) in Vellore Institute of Technology has a experience of more than eight years in field of teaching and research. She received her PhD in the field of Data Mining. Research has been carried out in interdisciplinary settings of Data Mining, epidemiology and social network analysis. Expertise in modeling disease dynamics and mining pattern from social network. Possess comprehensive knowledge in computer programming Java and R. Published research papers in reputed journals, written book chapters and presented papers in reputed conference.

Manu C. currently pursuing MTech in software engineering at Ramaiah Institute of Technology, MSR Nagar, Bangalore, Karnataka.

Chantana Chantrapornchai obtained her Bachelor degree (Computer Science) from Thammasat University of Thailand in 1991. She graduated from Northeastern University at Boston, College of Computer Science, in 1993 and University of Notre Dame, Department of Computer Science and Engineering, in 1999, for her Master and Ph.D degrees respectively. Currently, she is an associated professor of Dept. of Computer Engineering, Faculty of Engineering, Kasetsart University, Thailand. Her research interests include: parallel computing, big data processing, semantic web, computer architecture, and fuzzy logic. She is also currently with HPCNC laboratory and a principle investigator of GPU Education program at Kasetsart University.

Shipa D. R. obtained Ph.D degree in Electronics and Communication Engineering from Visvesvaraya Technological University during 2017. She has published 07 International Journal papers and her area of interests are VLSI Design for biomedical applications, ASIC's. Presently, working as Associate Professor at RV College of Engineering, Bengaluru in Electronics and Communication Engineering Department.

Naresh E. received the M.Tech degree in software engineering from MS Ramaiah Institute of Technology, Bangalore in 2008 and pursuing Ph.D. from Jain University, Bangalore under the guidance of Dr. Vijaya Kumar B. P. Currently, he is working as an Assistant Professor in the Department of Information Science and Engineering at MSRIT, Bangalore. His research interests include Software cost and effort estimation, empirical software engineering, and software process improvement. He is a member for ACM and Indian Society for Technical Education.

Md. Mahmudul Hasan is currently serving as a PhD researcher under Anglia Ruskin IT Research Institute (ARITI) at Anglia Ruskin University, UK. He has worked as a senior lecturer in the Department of CSE at Daffodil International University, Dhaka. He has graduated from the University of Essex, UK and specialized in machine learning, games and mobile apps development in different platforms. His research interests include virtual reality amalgamation in the real world scenario and deep reinforcement learning.

Aleksei Ivakhnenko received bachelor of techniques and technologies degree in Automotion and Control and engineer degree in Mechatronics. Received PhD in 2016 after defending thesis "Quality Indicators Tolerances Synthesis in Engineering Products Design and Operation" in Southwest State University. Since 2012 works in Applied Parallel Computing LLC (APC LLC) as CUDA/OpenCL/OpenACC expert, providing outsourcing and on-site trainings on High-Performance Computing. Starting from 2016 is a deep learning team lead at APC LLC. Had given more than 60 trainings in European Universities, such as ETH Zurich, LMU Munich, MSU and Tubitak Uzay. Gives open lectures and online courses in PDMI RAS Computer Science club. Main areas of interest: Robotics, Optimization, Computer Vision, High-Performance Computing, Computer Science, Machine Learning and Deep Learning.

Rekh Ram Janghel is working as a assistant professor in Department of Information and Technology at NIT Raipur. He has trained well in machine learning, image processing, medical diagnosis systems and neural networks. He is strong in disease diagnosis and disease detection and classification. He has hands on expertise with breast cancer diagnosis system and classification techniques. He has also guided various B. Tech. and M. Tech. projects of image processing, soft computing, classification algorithms, wireless communications and medical diagnosis. He has recently worked on Deep Learning and medical diagnosis using time series data like EEG, ECG and Alzheimer's disease. He has sound knowledge of various software's such as Image Processing and soft computing tools, Android application development, Python, MySQL and wireless communications which will be helpful in this project. The soft computing model and its performance comparison were studied in his PhD thesis work belonging to the broad category of classification and detection of various diseases. The idea of expanding the study of detection and classification of rice grain diseases using different soft computing based models would provide interesting directions to solve the various agricultural problems and developmental challenges in agriculture industries for him.

Ramgopal Kashyap's areas of interest are image processing, pattern recognition, and machine learning. He has published many research papers in international journals, and conferences like Springer, Inderscience, Elsevier, ACM, and IGI-Global indexed by Science Citation Index (SCI) and Scopus (Elsevier) and many book chapters. He has Reviewed Research Papers in the Science Citation Index Expanded, Springer Journals and Editorial Board Member and conferences programme committee member of the IEEE, Springer international conferences and journals held in countries: Czech Republic, Switzerland, UAE, Australia, Hungary, Poland, Taiwan, Denmark, India, USA, UK, Austria, and Turkey. He has written many book chapters published by IGI Global, USA, Springer and Elsevier.

Vijay Kumar received the M.Tech. from Guru Jambheshwer University of Science and Technology, Hisar. He has done his Ph.D. degree in Computer Engineering with National Institute of Technology, Kurukshetra. He has been an Assistant Professor with the Department of Computer Science and Engineering, Thapar Institute of Engineering and Technology, Patiala.

Yassine Maleh is a PhD of the University Hassan 1st in Morocco, since 2013. He is IT Senior Analyst at the National Port Agency in Morocco. He is senior member of the IEEE, member of the International Association of Engineers IAENG and The Machine Intelligence Research Labs. Maleh has made contributions in the fields of information security and Privacy, Internet of Things Security, Wireless and Constrained Networks Security. His research interests include Information Security and Privacy, Internet of Things, and Networks Security. He has published over than 30 papers and 2 edited books. He has served and continues to serve on the executive and technical program committees and a reviewer of numerous international conference and journals such as IEEE Sensor Journal, International Journal of Security and Privacy, International Journal of Networks Security and International Journal of Sensor Networks and Data Communications. He serve as an Associate Editor for the International Journal of Digital Crime and Forensics (IJDCF) and the International Journal of Information Security and Privacy (IJISP).

Vanyashree Mardi pursuing her M.Tech degree in software engineering from Ramaiah Institute of Technology, Bangalore in 2018 under the guidance of prof. Naresh. E. Currently, she is working as an Assistant Professor in the Department of Information Science and Engineering at Alva's Institute of Engineering and Technology, Moodbidri, Mangaluru, Karnataka. Her research interests include Deep learning, Internet of Things (IoT), Cloud computing, BigData Analytics and software process improvement.

Bindu Menon is the Head of Department and Senior Consultant Neurologist, Apollo Hospitals. She was head of Department of Neurology at Narayana Medical College Hospitals for 6 years and started the DM Neurology course. She has a teaching experience of 14 years. After completing her MBBS and MD (Medicine) she pursued her neurology training from Bombay under Prof BS Singhal with DM and DNB (Neurology). Later she did her Post Graduate Diploma in Clinical Neurology at Queensquare Institute of Neurology and Neurosurgery, London. She has been conferred FRCP by the Royal College of Physicians Edinburgh, awarded the Member of National Academy of Medical Sciences (MNAMS) from Diplomate National Board, New Delhi. She has been principal investigator for various international and national projects in epilepsy; Indian Council of Medical Research, International Epilepsy Trust. The research has provided the first data from the country on the state of bone health in patients with epilepsy. She has over 50 publications in various international and national journals, presented 70 papers and has 14 chapters to her credit. She is on the Editorial Board of International Journal of Epilepsy and reviewer of 8 international journals. She has organized 15 conferences with 16 credit hours from the medical council. She holds various posts like Editor-Epilepsy India, President-Epilepsy association, Nellore, Webmaster-IEA 2013-15, GC member- IES 2015-17, EC member IEA - 2011-13; 2015-17. She has been a recipient of 18 international and national awards for epilepsy and stroke care which includes the prestigious International league against Epilepsy (ILAE) Leadership Program Award at Barcelona, 2017, WORLD STROKE DAY AWARD under Individual Achievement category from the World Stroke organization April 2018 at Montreal, "H. C. Bajoria oration" award, Fellow - Geriatric Society of India, honorary adjunct title of 'Distinguished Clinical Tutor', Dr Karimullah, Indian Medical Association Oration Gold Medal among others. She is a member of various national Neurology and Epilepsy association. She founded Dr. BINDU MENON FOUNDATION in August 2013. Conducts regular school and college awareness programmes since 2008 and has completed 100 till date. Every month free consultation to more than 300 patients below poverty line with medicines, blood tests is done since last 4 years. She has been instrumental in starting 3 innovative projects for the FIRST TIME IN THE COUNTRY, 1) A novel rural project "NEUROLOGY ON WHEELS" 2) Mobile Application; epilepsy app "EPILEPSY HELP" for epilepsy patients. 3) TELE AWARENESS PROGRAMME for Epilepsy and Stroke. She has adopted orphanage Pragati charity children with epilepsy. She has published several eeducational materials like books, pamphlets and comics in epilepsy.

Parvathi R. is an Associate Professor of School of Computing Science and Engineering at VIT University, Chennai since 2011. She received the Doctoral degree in the field of spatial data mining in the same year. Her teaching experience in the area of computer science includes more than two decades and her research interests include data mining, big data and computational biology.

Md Shahinur Rahman is a software engineer at Leads Corporation Limited, Bangladesh under the Department of Analytics, Innovation and Mobile apps at Artificial Intelligence team. Mr. Shahinur Rahman researching on Computer vision, Deep Learning, and Machine Learning. He has completed Bachelor degree from Daffodil International University, Bangladesh under the Department of Computer Science & Engineering. As a student, Shahinur Rahman was a Teacher Assistant and Core member of DIU NLP & Machine Lab from Jan 2017 to April 2018 at Daffodil International University.

Yogesh Kumar Rathore received M. Tech. degree in Computer Science Engineering from Chhattisgarh Swami Vivekanand Technical University, Bhilai, India in the year 2010.He has 12 Years experience of working as a Asst. Prof. (Department of Computer Science Engineering) at Raipur Institute of Technology, Raipur (C.G) India. Currently he is pursuing his Ph.D. from National Institute of Technology, Raipur. His interests include pattern recognition, image processing, Deep Learning, machine learning, and artificial intelligence.

Satya Prakash Sahu is an Assistant Professor in the Department of Information Technology, NIT Raipur. His research of interest includes artificial intelligence, machine learning, image processing, medical imaging, and soft computing. He has authored more than 13 research papers in national and international conferences and journals.

Sergei Savin has obtained a bachelor degree in Automation and Control and an engineering degree in Mechatronics at Southwest State University. He finished a postgraduate program in Dynamics and Reliability of Machines and Equipment and obtained a candidate of science degree in 2014. He holds a senior researcher position at the laboratory of Robotics and Mechatronics. His areas of interest include walking robotics, in-pipe robots, optimal control, dynamics and machine learning. His current research is focused on exoskeletons, walking in-pipe robots and anthropomorphic bipedal robots. He also currently works as a docent at the department of Mechanics, Mechatronics and Robotics where he gives lectures on Mathematical Modelling in Mechatronics and Robotics, Information System in Mechatronics and Robotics and on Information System of Mobile Robots for bachelor and master student programs. He authored more than 70 papers and is a co-author of textbooks on applied simulation methods in Robotics.

Sahil Sharma received the M.E. from Thapar University, Patiala in 2015. He is currently pursuing his PhD degree in Computer Vision with the Department of Computer Science and Engineering, Thapar Institute of Engineering and Technology, Patiala. He is also a Non Tenure lecturer with the Department of Computer Science and Engineering, Thapar Institute of Engineering and Technology, Patiala.

Index

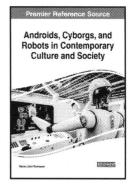

Ensure Quality Research is Introduced to the Academic Community

Become an IGI Global Reviewer for Authored Book Projects

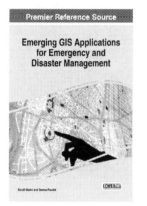

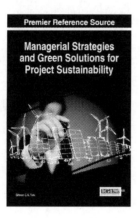

The overall success of an authored book project is dependent on quality and timely reviews.

In this competitive age of scholarly publishing, constructive and timely feedback significantly expedites the turnaround time of manuscripts from submission to acceptance, allowing the publication and discovery of forward-thinking research at a much more expeditious rate. Several IGI Global authored book projects are currently seeking highly qualified experts in the field to fill vacancies on their respective editorial review boards:

Applications may be sent to:
development@igi-global.com

Applicants must have a doctorate (or an equivalent degree) as well as publishing and reviewing experience. Reviewers are asked to write reviews in a timely, collegial, and constructive manner. All reviewers will begin their role on an ad-hoc basis for a period of one year, and upon successful completion of this term can be considered for full editorial review board status, with the potential for a subsequent promotion to Associate Editor.

If you have a colleague that may be interested in this opportunity,
we encourage you to share this information with them.

Are You Ready to Publish Your Research?

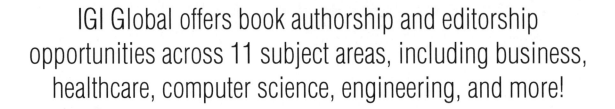

IGI Global offers book authorship and editorship opportunities across 11 subject areas, including business, healthcare, computer science, engineering, and more!

Benefits of Publishing with IGI Global:

- Free one-to-one editorial and promotional support.

- Expedited publishing timelines that can take your book from start to finish in less than one (1) year.

- Choose from a variety of formats including: Edited and Authored References, Handbooks of Research, Encyclopedias, and Research Insights.

- Utilize IGI Global's eEditorial Discovery® submission system in support of conducting the submission and blind-review process.

- IGI Global maintains a strict adherence to ethical practices due in part to our full membership to the Committee on Publication Ethics (COPE).

- Indexing potential in prestigious indices such as Scopus®, Web of Science™, PsycINFO®, and ERIC – Education Resources Information Center.

- Ability to connect your ORCID iD to your IGI Global publications.

- Earn royalties on your publication as well as receive complimentary copies and exclusive discounts.

Get Started Today by Contacting the Acquisitions Department at:

acquisition@igi-global.com

The Premier Reference for Information Science & Information Technology

Encyclopedia of
Information Science and Technology
Fourth Edition

100% Original Content
Contains 705 new, peer-reviewed articles with color figures covering over 80 categories in 11 subject areas

Diverse Contributions
More than 1,100 experts from 74 unique countries contributed their specialized knowledge

Easy Navigation
Includes two tables of content and a comprehensive index in each volume for the user's convenience

Highly-Cited
Embraces a complete list of references and additional reading sections to allow for further research

Included in:

Encyclopedia of Information Science and Technology Fourth Edition
A Comprehensive 10-Volume Set

Mehdi Khosrow-Pour, D.B.A. (Information Resources Management Association, USA)
ISBN: 978-1-5225-2255-3; © 2018; Pg: 8,104; Release Date: July 2017

For a limited time, receive the complimentary e-books for the First, Second, and Third editions with the purchase of the *Encyclopedia of Information Science and Technology, Fourth Edition* e-book.*

The **Encyclopedia of Information Science and Technology, Fourth Edition** is a 10-volume set which includes 705 original and previously unpublished research articles covering a full range of perspectives, applications, and techniques contributed by thousands of experts and researchers from around the globe. This authoritative encyclopedia is an all-encompassing, well-established reference source that is ideally designed to disseminate the most forward-thinking and diverse research findings. With critical perspectives on the impact of information science management and new technologies in modern settings, including but not limited to computer science, education, healthcare, government, engineering, business, and natural and physical sciences, it is a pivotal and relevant source of knowledge that will benefit every professional within the field of information science and technology and is an invaluable addition to every academic and corporate library.

Scan for Online Bookstore

Pricing Information

Hardcover: **$5,695**   E-Book: **$5,695**   Hardcover + E-Book: **$6,895**

Both E-Book Prices Include:
- *Encyclopedia of Information Science and Technology, First Edition E-Book*
- *Encyclopedia of Information Science and Technology, Second Edition E-Book*
- *Encyclopedia of Information Science and Technology, Third Edition E-Book*

*Purchase the Encyclopedia of Information Science and Technology, Fourth Edition e-book and receive the first, second, and third e-book editions for free. Offer is only valid with purchase of the fourth edition's e-book through the IGI Global Online Bookstore.